'The mounting concern about climate change has distracted attention from the fact that CO_2 emissions are just part of the existential problem facing humanity. We need urgently to reduce our use of ALL the resources, not just fossil fuels. This new book is the best point of departure I know for doing that. The five-fold increase of resource productivity it describes is impressive, but perfectly feasible, and it would give the world a bit more time to learn how to adapt to ecological collapse. The book has two especially important innovations. The authors deal seriously with the rebound effect, and they base their scenarios on a long-term trajectory of rising energy prices.'
Dennis Meadows, Co-author *Limits to Growth* and 2009 Japan Prize Laureate

'Is it possible to imagine a world where we can actually phase out fossil fuels before the climate phases us out? It's now feasible by reading *Factor Five*.'
Peter Newman, Professor of Sustainability, Curtin University and author of *Resilient Cities*

'[There can be] no sustainable development without a sustainable development of companies. *Factor Five* provides compelling arguments and examples that sustainable business is achievable and profitable on a large scale and that companies play a key role in creating sustainable development. *Factor Five* confirms the crucial role of increasing eco-efficiency to foster sustainable development.'
Stefan Schaltegger, Professor of Sustainability Management, Leuphana University, Germany

'The world needs radical eco-innovation to shape an opportunity out of the current crisis. This book provides excellent key examples in a systems perspective. Written by radical thinkers with a unique experience on how change can be managed, this book is a must-read for both leaders and academics.'
Professor Dr Raimund Bleischwitz, Wuppertal Institute, Co-Director 'Material Flows and Resource Management', Professor at the College of Europe, Bruges/Belgium

'Some may have ignored the message of *Factor Four* 15 years ago. We can no longer afford to ignore it, and should now embrace the strengthened message of *Factor Five*.'
Professor Bedrich Moldan, Senator, Czech Republic, Former Chairman, European Environment Agency, and former Czechoslovak Environment Minister

'We are living in the most exciting era of human history. We are in the process of expanding our perspectives from a focus on short-term economic and materialistic growth to a whole-system approach with true, long-term happiness for all at its core. We are adding the need for "sufficiency" to "efficiency" and "productivity" in our discussions on how to reduce human impacts on the Earth. Economy and ecology are not an "either/or" trade-off. We now know that both are critical in every aspect of society. We must advance science and technology based on values and vision. The "leapfrog" effect should be promoted in developing nations – not only in terms of technology but also in terms of lifestyles and societal values. Our urgent imperative is to figure out how to maximize happiness while minimizing environmental impacts. *Factor Five* provides the West and East alike with a compass to set our visions and to measure our progress.'
Junko Edahiro, Environmental Affairs Journalist, co-Chief Executive, Japan for Sustainability

'*Factor Five* is the clearest non-partisan handbook on ecological renaissance available to date. It should be read by every policy maker and practitioner irrespective of their political position on global change.'
Professor Calestous Juma, Harvard Kennedy School

'We all know what will happen if we go on producing and consuming the same way as in the 20th century. But we don't really know how to produce and consume in a planet-friendly way. This is why we need this book so urgently.'
Brice Lalonde, French Climate Ambassador, former environment minister of France

'Strong economic signals and innovative technologies make a powerful combination, and are the best hope – indeed, the only hope – of the changes needed to protect the environment. Building on the robust foundation of *Factor Four*, Ernst von Weizsäcker and his colleagues write an inspiring manifesto for change to reduce resource use while minimizing the impact on living conditions. If their recipe is sometimes over-optimistic, that is a good fault. The environment needs some optimistic friends these days.'
Frances Cairncross, Exeter College, Oxford, and author of *Costing the Earth*

'Climate change represents the biggest challenge our generation has experienced. *Factor Five* shows us through sustainable business practices we can achieve positive environmental and economic outcomes. They are not mutually exclusive concepts – sustainability is just good business.'
Dan Atkins, Managing Director, Shaper Group

'Even if the climate were not changing, the need for the transition from fossil fuels to renewable, regenerative systems would be just as urgent. This is a

recipe book for a far more economically rational world, as well as a more sustainable one.'
Professor Janis Birkeland, Queensland University of Technology (QUT), and author of *Positive Development*

'Every lawyer and lobbyist who is asked to defend "Business-as-Usual" should read *Factor Five*. This manual for re-engineering the future holds out both hope and profit in equal parts – if only we can get the political framework right, and align the lobbies with the interests of humanity.'
Tom Spencer, Former Member of the European Parliament, Founder and Executive Director of the European Centre for Public Affairs, and Vice Chairman, Institute for Environmental Security

'Today, the world is faced by many challenges which all derive from the unsustainable ways in which we use our resources. Despite the most severe global economic crisis, resource prices have not returned to the low price levels of the 1990s, demonstrating that we have to reduce our "resource obesity" as an economy and come to sustainable levels of resource consumption. A factor five improvement in resource efficiency is not only necessary, it is imperative for economies and companies to survive in a new resource and atmosphere-constrained world. This book not only clearly makes this point, but also shows that it is possible with what we know today. This key message makes this book essential reading.'
Professor Ernst Worrell, Utrecht University, lead author, IPCC Working Group III, Fourth Assessment Report (2004–2007)

'*Factor Five* is about how to achieve the resource productivity gains that are necessary for the world to avoid a future with declining human well-being. It provides a clear way forward. In the past, the pursuit of efficiency gains has sometimes led to loss of resilience, resulting in unexpected and unwanted outcomes (like salinized irrigation systems). I applaud the *Factor Five* initiative, and urge it to embrace the equally important goal of maintaining resilience in the face of the looming global shocks confronting the world.'
Dr Brian Walker, CSIRO Research Fellow, Resilience Alliance Program Director and Chair of Board

'Surely the ingenuity and creativity of human civilization can rise above economic activity saddled with collateral damage? The opportunity to build new markets, new industries and new jobs while rebuilding ecosystem resilience is an exciting challenge. Are we up to the task of our future? Well, only if we act speedily. Read *Factor Five* and rejoice that there are still options. Then ask what role you can play to make sure the global effort arrives in time and at sufficient scale.'
Fiona Wain, Chief Executive Officer, Environment Business Australia

'*Factor Five* links together the two pillars of future planetary sustainability: (1) implementation of "five-times" as productive technologies and systems across resource intensive industries and (2) adoption of new political frameworks and understandings for promoting rapid, ethical and just transition away from a prosperity that creates unacceptable environmental damage. We now have the tools! Do we have the courage?'
Professor Mary E. Clark, author of *Contemporary Biology, Ariadne's Thread* and *In Search of Human Nature*

'*Factor Five* is an essential reference which shows companies who were inspired to action by *An Inconvenient Truth* how to radically reduce CO_2 emissions AND reduce costs. It is one of the first books to feature the world's best practice sectoral case studies and then explain how they have achieved such large CO_2 reductions cost effectively. It will help all CEOs identify significant cost saving opportunities and strategies to reduce risks in a carbon constrained future. We must all be committed to achieving significant greenhouse gas reductions – and *Factor Five* shows us how!'
Molly Harriss Olson, Founder National Business Leaders' Forum on Sustainable Development and Phillip Toyne, Director EcoFutures

'There is a paucity of publications that holistically address the needs seen in pursuing the goal of sustainable development in a realistic way. *Factor Five* is thus a welcome addition to the body of knowledge and literature available today, since it shows both policy makers and society as a whole the various solutions and policy options that are available. All we need to do now is to implement them.'
Professor Walter Leal Filho, Hamburg University of Applied Sciences (HAW Hamburg)

'*Factor Five* is an important contribution to a growing corpus of work regarding energy and resource efficiency – work that is critical if the world is to meet the looming challenges of greenhouse gas emissions, sensible resource use, marketplace success and global equity. *Factor Five* is especially appealing because it asks the right questions about what we do, why we do it and, most importantly, how we do it. The authors have not only delved into the major resource-consuming systems we humans create, but also rigorously explore how they can be improved – by at least five times or more.'
Cameron M. Burns, senior editor and journalist, Rocky Mountain Institute

'Every day and all around us, you can see the Earth's resources being wasted by us and our style of consumption, as if there is no tomorrow. Doing more with less has been around in many cultures for thousands of years, but not ours today, as you and I mostly don't do it at all. We all need to practise in our everyday work, business and home choices the immediate consideration and behaviours of using less in ways that allow both more and retention of a

quality of life. If this new book, *Factor Five*, can provide us with inspiration from practical and meaningful examples then we better get on with it now, and start acting on its tips. Bring Factor Five into your consumption choices at home and at work, with your colleagues and friends and stop wasting our planet by 80 per cent as if life on Earth didn't count. Make Factor Five your first choice, not your last.'
Greg Bruce, Executive Manager – Integrated Sustainability, City of Townsville

'The Climate Exchange concept has proved that once GHG reductions programmes build momentum there is no limit to the innovation and creativity that can be harnessed within companies. And of course innovation will be a critical part of the solution. *Factor Five* shows the potential for major resource intensive sectors to significantly reduce greenhouse gas emissions in a cost-effective manner. Whether through emissions trading or other market-based mechanisms, our experience at the Chicago Climate Exchange and the European Climate Exchange has made it clear that companies at the forefront of confronting the challenge will be leaders in their sectors.'
Richard L. Sandor, Executive Chairman of Climate Exchange plc. (CLE.L), an AIM-listed company which owns the Chicago Climate Exchange, Chicago Climate Futures Exchange and the European Climate Exchange

'In an ever more crowded and production-oriented world, the need to reduce the global ecological footprint, and hence provide the "space" for ecosystem services to support a healthy biosphere, is paramount. *Factor Five*, through its exploration of the interwoven roles of technology, regulatory and economic tools and socio-political frameworks in achieving greater resource use efficiency, provides the basis for transition to a lower footprint future. This is an important book not least because it provides clear directions for achieving a more secure and sustainable planetary future.'
Dr Ronnie Harding, Institute of Environmental Studies, University of New South Wales, Australia

'The authors articulate the technical and legislative solutions needed to drive massive resource efficiency and realign consumption patterns with natural renewal rates by taking a whole systems approach. It is obvious that our challenges have as much, if not more, to do with leadership and political will than with technical difficulties. *Factor Five* provides case studies that challenge the status quo and will inspire every engineer, architect and technician to strive for greater resource efficiency and address rapidly encroaching global constraints. At the same time, it provides a vision and road map for legislative solutions and a platform for elected officials to be purposeful leaders – exactly what we need right now to solve the most pressing problems human civilization has faced. A must read!'
Archie Kasnet, Partner, Aedi Group

'Throughout my experience as a young scientist across several countries, I have learned that working solely in environmentalism is not enough to tackle the problem of climate change; the integration of politics, science and the global economy are necessary to provide solutions. *Factor Five* embodies these principles and provides a clear path forward to realize the lowest hanging fruits in resource efficiency.'
Mary Louise Gifford, Energy and Resources Group, UC Berkeley, USA

'As natural resources become scarcer and we begin to price water and carbon, resource productivity becomes a critical driver for future growth. This book will be an essential tool for all those who wish to understand and seize the opportunities of this future world.'
James Bradfield Moody, Executive Director, Development, CSIRO, and past member and co-founder of The Natural Edge Project

'A deeply researched report on the increasing worldwide potentials of energy and water productivity. The authors are renowned experts in this vital field and show in this book where the greatest improvements are to be found. Essential reading!'
Hazel Henderson, author of *Ethical Markets: Growing the Green Economy*, and President of Ethical Markets Media (USA and Brazil)

'We've seen some change since *Factor Four* was published 12 years ago, but more is possible, and much more is needed. There are still those in the building, construction, steel and cement sectors who argue that four- to five-fold efficiency gains are not possible, and policy makers who don't understand what is needed to drive that change. *Factor Five* is a timely reminder of just what is possible, and a clarion call to policy makers that we need a new sense of direction and political decisions on framing conditions to realize that change.'
Maria Atkinson, Global Head of Sustainability, Lend Lease Corporation

'In the wake of a global financial crisis, climate change, water scarcity and energy security, the question of "Resource Efficiency" for many professional engineers and their clients is no longer "why?", but rather "how?" *Factor Five* is the perfect companion for decision makers and solutions providers who are seeking the answers to that important question.'
Darren Bilsborough, Director of Sustainability, Parsons Brinckerhoff, and Adjunct Professor of Sustainability, Curtin University

'For too long, politicians and industry, amongst others, have prioritized economic growth and regarded it as the key measure of success. Even when we became aware of the ecological impacts of that growth, we were reluctant to revise our thinking because of the perceived cost. Climate change now leaves us with little choice. All sectors have to face up to the fact that our future is indeed

bleak if we do not mitigate greenhouse gas emissions dramatically and rapidly. We need to adopt a 'whole systems approach' to production, regulation and consumption. *Factor Five* sets out an agenda for achieving this and gives us hope that it may be achievable.'
Professor Juliet Roper, Associate Dean of Sustainability, Waikato University Management School and President of the Asia Pacific Academy of Business in Society (APABIS)

'Nobel Laureate Albert Szent-Gyorgyi (1893–1986) once said that "Discovery consists of seeing what everybody has seen and [then] thinking what nobody has thought." – and so it was with *Factor Four*. Genuine ideas staring us in the face until brought to light by people looking at it a little differently. The application of the ideas in *Factor Five* will enhance one's design work, but the process and approach you will learn from reading it, can only enrich one's work and transform our society.'
Philip Bangerter, Global Director – Sustainability, Hatch Engineering

'There is an emerging consensus that it is time to stop talking about climate change and do something about it. The authors of *Factor Five* have scoured the world for leading efforts and, by way of clearly written case studies, the book explores each of the resource intensive sectors of the economy with a view to increasing productivity by a factor of five. This ambitious yet practical book is an important contribution to engineering, design and policy making for the new millennium.'
Dr Stephen Horton – Urban Research Program, Griffith University

'A five-fold increase of energy and resource productivity opens exciting opportunities for industry while helping to mitigate global warming and other environmental threats. Eco-efficiency is a key component of an industrial strategy towards sustainable development.'
Dr Stephan Schmidheiny, Chairman, Anova, and founding chairman of the World Business Council for Sustainable Development

Quotes from the Sponsors

'The world faces numerous complex "diabolical" policy and technical challenges that are unprecedented in human history. How do we maintain prosperity, feed and power a growing population, and ensure healthy natural ecosystems in a carbon constrained, climate challenged future? The challenge can only be addressed by a comprehensive, integrated response at global, national and local scales. This publication makes a significant contribution in responding to the global change imperative and should be required reading for politicians, industry leaders and ordinary citizens alike.'
Dr Andrew Johnson, Group Executive – Environment, CSIRO

'Griffith University has long had a focus on the environment and sustainable development, and this work from some of our early career academics is another welcome contribution to the field. Facilitating the capacity for people to lead productive and fulfilling lives is a key role of the higher education sector and in the coming years we will see increasing emphasis on the importance of sustainability in that equation. Innovations in energy, water and materials use will need to be accelerated and progressively incorporated into university education. Griffith University co-hosts The Natural Edge Project and is a proud sponsor of this work which we think will make a significant contribution to addressing these needs.'
Professor Ned Pankhurst, Deputy Vice Chancellor (Research), Griffith University

'The Aachen Foundation Kathy Beys is proud to have supported the development of this book, to bring to the world's attention the significant opportunities associated with resource productivity, balanced with many years of policy and operational understanding. The Foundation has been focused on progressing the 'Factor X' resource productivity agenda for more than 10 years, and we look forward to seeing the work in *Factor Five* become a reality over the coming decades.'
B. Stephan Baldin, Aachen Foundation Kathy Beys

'The two big challenges facing our generation are our population explosion (physical growth) and climate change (managing our natural resources). Leadership, vision and partnership are essential ingredients in meeting these challenges, and many governments around the world are now providing such leadership, particularly the US and UK governments, and also the Premier of Queensland who has called for a Climate Change Council of which I am honoured to be a part. But government cannot meet these challenges without creative partnerships with industry and the community. *Factor Five* is a crucial imperative, and hence the reason why Conics Ltd agreed to be a major sponsor in its development. Governments and industries around the world can find in the following pages a wealth of opportunity not only to significantly increase resource productivity but to reduce environmental pressures. I commend the team behind the book and look forward to seeing its lessons expanded and implemented across the globe.

Jim McKnoulty, Chairman, Conics Ltd

For too long, the deep, crucial issues of resource use efficiency and decoupling of production from material and energy throughput have lacked a coherent framework and synthesis. *Factor Five* provide this in a superbly timely fashion, setting out positive pathways for policy and practice – the book is a cause for optimism and action.

Professor Stephen Dovers, Fenner School of Environment and Society, Australian National University

Factor Five

Factor Five

Transforming the Global Economy through 80%
Improvements in Resource Productivity

A Report to the Club of Rome

*Ernst von Weizsäcker, Karlson 'Charlie' Hargroves, Michael
H. Smith, Cheryl Desha and Peter Stasinopoulos*

publishing for a sustainable future

The Natural Edge
P R O J E C T

London • Sterling, VA

First published by Earthscan in the UK and USA in 2009

ISBN: 978-1-84407-591-1

Typeset by MapSet Ltd, Gateshead, UK
Cover design by Andrew Corbett

For a full list of publications please contact:

Earthscan
Dunstan House
14a St Cross St
London, EC1N 8XA, UK
Tel: +44 (0)20 7841 1930
Fax: +44 (0)20 7242 1474
Email: earthinfo@earthscan.co.uk
Web: www.earthscan.co.uk

22883 Quicksilver Drive, Sterling, VA 20166-2012, USA

Earthscan publishes in association with the International Institute for
Environment and Development

A catalogue record for this book is available from the British Library

Library of Congress Cataloging-in-Publication Data

Factor five : transforming the global economy through 80% improvements in
resource productivity / Ernst von Weizsacker ... [et al.].
      p. cm.
Includes bibliographical references and index.
ISBN 978-1-84407-591-1 (hardback)
   1. Industrial productivity. 2. Technological innovations. 3. Environmental
protection. 4. Climatic changes. I. Weizsäcker, Ernst U. von (Ernst Ulrich),
1939-
T58.8.F33 2009
338'.06—dc22

                                                        2009026246

For further publications by The Natural Edge Project
see www.naturaledgeproject.net.

At Earthscan we strive to minimize our environmental impacts and carbon
footprint through reducing waste, recycling and offsetting our CO_2 emissions,
including those created through publication of this book. For more details of our
environmental policy, see www.earthscan.co.uk.

This book was printed in Malta by Gutenberg Press.
The paper used is FSC certified and the
inks are vegetable based.

Mixed Sources
Product group from well-managed
forests, and other controlled sources
www.fsc.org Cert no. TT-CoC-002424
© 1996 Forest Stewardship Council

FSC

The paper used for this book is FSC-certified and
totally chlorine-free. FSC (the Forest Stewardship
Council) is an international network to promote
responsible management of the world's forests.

Contents

Part II Making it Happen

Ernst von Weizsäcker

About the Authors

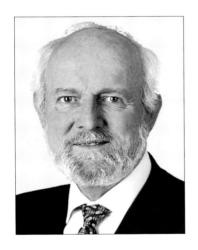

Ernst von Weizsäcker is Co-Chair of the International Panel for Sustainable Resource Management, set up by the United Nations Environment Programme. From 2006 to 2008, he served as Dean of the Bren School of Environmental Science and Management, University of California, Santa Barbara. He was a Member (SPD) of the German Parliament (Bundestag) from 1998 to 2005 and served as Chairman of the Environment Committee. Before entering politics, he was the Founding President of the Wuppertal Institute for Climate, Environment and Energy, from 1991 to 2000, during which time he wrote *Factor Four*, together with Amory Lovins and Hunter Lovins. From 1984 to 1991, Ernst was Director of the Institute for European Environmental Policy, an international think-tank with offices in Bonn, London, Paris and Brussels. From 1981 to 1984 he was Director of the Policy Division of the United Nations Centre for Science and Technology for Development in New York, and previous to this he served as Founding President of the University of Kassel, Germany (1975–1980). From 1972 to 1975 he was a full professor of biology at the University of Essen, Germany. Ernst's education includes a physics Masters, obtained from Hamburg University, and a PhD in zoology from Freiburg University. He is a member of the Club of Rome, Member of the European Academy of Arts and Science, and of the World Academy of Art and Science, Honorary Professor of the Technical University of Valparaiso, Chile. His publications include *Ecological Tax Reform* (1992), *Earth Politics* (1994), *Factor Four* (1997) and *Limits to Privatization*, with Oran Young and Matthias Finger (2005). He has an honorary degree from Soka University, Japan, and has received several international awards, including the Premio de Natura (Italy), the Takeda Award (Japan), the WWF Gold Medal and, most recently, the prestigious German Environment Prize.

Karlson 'Charlie' Hargroves is a co-founder and the Executive Director of The Natural Edge Project (TNEP), a sustainable development research collaboration based in Australia, TNEP is a collaboration between Griffith University and the Australian National University, after being incubated within the Institution of Engineers Australia. TNEP's mission is to contribute to and succinctly communicate leading research, case studies, tools, policy and strategies for achieving sustainable development across government, business and civil society. Working with the TNEP team since its foundation in 2002 Charlie has worked on a number of books, published by Earthscan, including co-authoring and co-editing *The Natural Advantage of Nations* (2005), and co-authoring *Whole System Design* (2008), *Factor Five* (2009), *Cents and Sustainability* (2010), *Energy Transformed* (2010) and *Engineering Education for Sustainable Development* (2010). Charlie graduated in 2000 from the University of Adelaide, holding a Bachelor of Civil and Structural Engineering, and is currently completing a PhD on 'Resource productivity policies and practices' under the supervision of Professor Peter Newman. In 2004, Charlie spent 12 months on secondment as the CEO of start-up consulting firm Natural Capitalism Inc. based in Colorado, under the supervision of Hunter Lovins, and currently represents the team as an associate member of the Club of Rome. Charlie has delivered over 30 international keynote addresses and with the TNEP team has facilitated a number of workshops, charrettes and training sessions, and is currently based at Griffith University as a research fellow.

Michael Smith is a co-founder and the Research Director of The Natural Edge Project. Working with the TNEP team since its foundation in 2002 Michael has led research into a range of practical applications of sustainable development with international partners such as the Chicago Climate Exchange and the World Federation of Engineering Organisations, and Australian partners such as the Institution of Engineers Australia, Plastics and Chemicals Industry Association, and the Australian Paper, Timber Products and Paper Council. Michael is also a co-author and co-editor of *The Natural*

Advantage of Nations (2005), and a co-author of *Whole System Design* (2008), *Factor Five* (2009), *Cents and Sustainability* (2010) and *Energy Transformed* (2010). Michael is a graduate of the University of Melbourne, holding a Bachelor of Science with a double major in Chemistry and Mathematics with honours and has submitted his PhD thesis under Professor Steve Dovers and Professor Michael Collins at The Australian National University (ANU). While undertaking his studies Michael was awarded the ANU Environment Achievement award in 2001 for a range of efforts, including assisting to catalyse the Australian Campuses Towards Sustainability Network. Michael is currently based at the ANU Fenner School of Environment and Society as a research fellow.

Cheryl Desha is the Education Director of The Natural Edge Project and a lecturer at Griffith University. Working with the TNEP team since 2003 Cheryl has contributed to a wide range of education and training for sustainable development initiatives, including professional capacity building and university curriculum renewal. She is a co-author of *The Natural Advantage of Nations* (2005), *Whole System Design* (2008), *Factor Five* (2009), *Energy Transformed* (2010) and the lead author on *Engineering Education for Sustainable Development* (2010). Cheryl is a graduate of Griffith University, holding a Bachelor of Environmental Engineering with first class honours and receiving a University Medal and Environmental Engineering Medal. She is currently completing a PhD in education for sustainable development under Professor David Thiel at Griffith University. Prior to joining TNEP in 2003, Cheryl worked for an international consulting engineering firm for four years. In 2005, she was selected as the Institution of Engineers Australia 'Young Professional Engineer of the Year', and in 2008 was selected as one of 1000 Australians to attend the Prime Minister's 2020 Summit. Cheryl is based at Griffith University as a lecturer in the School of Engineering.

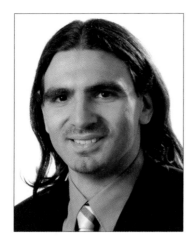

Peter Stasinopoulos is the Technical Director of The Natural Edge Project. Peter began as a research assistant with TNEP and rapidly increased his contribution, becoming the lead co-author of *Whole System Design* (2008), followed by being a co-author of *Factor Five* (2009) and *Energy Transformed* (2010). Peter is a graduate of the University of Adelaide, holding a Bachelor of Mechatronic Engineering with first class honours and a Bachelor of Mathematical and Computer Science, and has submitted his Masters thesis in Whole System Design under Associate Professor Kazem Abhary and Professor Lee Luong at the University of South Australia. Peter is currently completing a PhD in Systems Design under Dr Paul Compston, Dr Barry Newell and Dr Haley Jones at The Australian National University.

Acknowledgements

The authors would like to thank the following individuals and groups for making the development of this publication possible.

Firstly, a special thank you must go to the authors' families. Ernst von Weizsäcker would like to thank his wife Christine for enduring another round of book-writing and coming up with often surprising comments, and his son Jakob von Weizsäcker and daughter Paula Bleckmann, who, when challenged, were also full of good ideas. Charlie would like to thank his wife, Stacey, for her patient and loving support and for bringing joy into his life. Mike would like to thank his wife Sarah Chapman for her love, support and for sharing a lifelong passion for design and environmental sustainability. Cheryl would like to thank her family for their love and support of her commitment to sustainable engineering. Peter would like to thank his fiancée Jacquelina, and his family and friends for their love and support. The authors would also like to thank Fatima Pinto for her tireless efforts in managing The Natural Edge Project (TNEP) office, Candia Bruce from 'Working On It' for her amazing support for our team, and of course Harry 'Bunny' Desha for his positive influence on team spirit.

The authors would like to express their gratitude to both Amory B. Lovins and L. Hunter Lovins, as co-authors of the original work *Factor Four*, for providing us with their blessing to undertake this sequel, and allowing us to make ample use of their earlier thoughts and subsequent work. Since developing *Factor Four* both Amory and Hunter have been actively expanding the solution space for sustainable development, and have produced a range of works that have strongly underpinned this work. Amory Lovins, co-founder, Chairman, and Chief Scientist of Rocky Mountain Institute (RMI), has led the development of a range of outstanding publications, including co-authoring 29 books, based on a wealth of practical and research experience from almost four decades of practice. These include *Natural Capitalism*, *Winning the Oil Endgame* and *Small is Profitable* – along with hundreds of papers and articles, including extensive work on automotive design, particularly of cars and trucks, that underpins much of Chapter 5 of this book. Hunter Lovins leads the team at Natural Capitalism Solutions (NCS), after co-founding RMI and working there for over 20 years, and is widely regarded as one of the best sustainability thinkers and communicators in the world. Hunter has co-authored nine books, including *Natural Capitalism*, and consulted for scores of industries and governments worldwide. Hunter is also a founding Professor of Business at Presidio School of Management, one of the first accredited programmes offering an MBA in Sustainable Management.

This book is of course not the only work that has built on from and extended the influential work in *Factor Four*, and further to the work of the original co-authors a number of leaders in the field have been working for many years to advance the sustainable development and resource productivity agendas, and have both informed and assured the development of *Factor Five*. We wish to acknowledge and thank the following for their outstanding efforts: Paul Anastas, Ray Anderson, Geoff Andrews, Dan Atkins, Alan AtKisson, Janine Benyus, Raimund Bleischwitz, Michael Braungart, Lester Brown, Val Brown, Greg Bruce, Gro Brundtland, Rachel Carson, Stephen Chu, Stephen Dovers, Dexter Dunphy, Wolfgang Feist, Klaus Fichter, Tim Flannery, Thomas Friedman, Brendan Gleeson, Peter Gleick, Al Gore, Leo Jensen, Eberhard Jochem, Eng Loc Lee, Ian Lowe, Bill McDonough, Jim McNeill, Dennis Meadows, Donella Meadows, Peter Newman, Molly Olsen, David Orr, Alan Pears, Rajendra Pachauri, Jonathan Porritt, Robert Purves, Jeffery Sachs, Friedrich Schmidt-Bleek, Walter Stahel Nicholas Stern, Björn Stigson, Philip Sutton, David Suzuki, Klaus Töpfer, Louise Vickory, Che Wall, Barbara Ward, Paul Weaver, James Woolsey, Ernst Worrell and Cathy Zoi. It is not within the scope of this book to outline all of their individual efforts. Also we need to note that there are in addition to this list, numerous other R&D bodies, universities, NGOs, companies and organizations across the world that have helped to promote and take forward the ideas of *Factor Four*, such as green building councils, sustainable business groups and conservation foundations to name a few.

The authors would also like to thank Wolfgang Feist for his contribution to Chapter 2, and Klaus Fichter, Roland Geyer, Dexter Dunphy and Susan Benn for their contributions to the online bonus case studies. Thanks also goes to Greg Bratman, Angie Reeves and Andrew Went for their enthusiastic assistance with the research to develop the book, and particularly to Greg Bratman for both contributing to the research and supporting Ernst von Weizsäcker throughout the process. Students of Ernst von Weizsäcker and Faculty at the Bren School for Environmental Science and Management, University of California, Santa Barbara, greatly helped in furthering the discussion on resource productivity throughout the last three years; notably the valuable inputs from Professor Roland Geyer and PhD student Vered Doctori-Blass. Ernst would like to further acknowledge the many fruitful discussions of the issues related to decoupling wealth from resource consumption, in the context of the UNEP International Panel for Sustainable Resource Management, notably with Professor Mark Swilling of the University of Stellenbosch, South Africa, and Professor Marina Fischer-Kowalski, University of Klagenfurt, Austria.

The work was copyedited by TNEP professional editor Stacey Hargroves, based at Griffith University, who the authors thank for her patience and invaluable attention to detail.

Work on original graphics and enhancements to existing graphics in prepa-ration for both the colour and greyscale versions has been carried out by the gifted graphic designer Roger Dennis and the TNEP Technical Director Peter Stasinopoulos. Ernst von Weizsäcker personally contributed the additional costs related to the colour printing of the hard cover volume in English.

The authors would also like to thank the sponsors of the book:

- The Aachen Foundation Kathy Beys, focused on promoting the concepts and practices of resource productivity for the benefit of all, in particular Stephan Baldin.
- Griffith University, for both providing a grant towards the development of the book, in particular the Deputy Vice Chancellor (Research) Professor Lesley Johnson, and providing the team from TNEP with in-kind adminis-trative hosting, in particular Pro-Vice Chancellor for Science, Engineering, Environment and Technology (SEET), Professor Ned Pankhurst, SEET Dean (Research) Professor Gillian Bushell and the Director of the Urban Research Program, Professor Brendan Gleeson.
- Australia's Commonwealth Scientific and Industrial Research Organisation (CSIRO), in particular the Group Executive for Environment, Dr Andrew Johnson.
- Conics Ltd, an Australian development services consultant focusing on sustainable urban growth and infrastructure projects, in particular long-time TNEP supporters and mentors, Chairman Jim McKnoulty and Partner and Senior Planner Cameron Hoffmann.
- Australian National University, for providing in-kind hosting for members of TNEP, in particular the Director of the Fenner School of Environment and Society, Professor Stephen Dovers, the Executive Director of the ANU Climate Change Institute, Professor Will Steffen, and the Associate Dean (Undergraduate) for the ANU Faculty of Engineering and Information Technology, Dr Paul Compston.

We would also like to thank Earthscan for their dedicated efforts in developing the English version, and in particular Jonathan Sinclair-Wilson, Rob West, Michael Fell and Claire Lamont. We would also like to thank the publishers of the translations, and in particular Thomas Tilcher of Droemer Knaur (German translation) and Clare Sun of Shanghai Century Publishing Co. (Chinese Mandarin translation), and we look forward to the opportunity to develop further translations of the work.

Finally, the team from The Natural Edge Project would like to thank Ernst von Weizsäcker for his commitment to this project and for his mentoring of our team. Working with Ernst has been an amazing experience, one that will continue to influence our work for many years to come.

List of Acronyms and Abbreviations

3CEE	Three Country Energy Efficiency Project
ACF	Australian Conservation Foundation
ACTU	Australian Council of Trade Unions
AISI	American Iron and Steel Institute
ANU	Australian National University
APU	auxiliary power unit
ASHRAE	The American Society of Heating, Refrigerating and Air-Conditioning Engineers
BAU	business-as-usual
BedZED	Beddington Zero Energy Development
BIPV	building-integrated photovoltaic
BOF	basic oxygen furnace
BOMA	Building Owners and Managers Association
BREEAM	Building Research Establishment Environmental Assessment Method
CAFE	Corporate Average Fuel Economy
CCI	Clinton Climate Initiative
CCS	carbon capture and storage
CDM	Clean Development Mechanism
CEPHES	Cost Efficient Passive Houses as European Standards
CER	certified emission reductions
CFC	chlorofluorocarbon
CFI	Carbon Financial Instrument
CFL	compact fluorescent
CH2	Council House II
CIMIS	California Irrigation Management Information System
CNG	compact natural gas
CPI	consumer price index
CSAA	California State Automobile Association
CSIRO	Commonwealth Scientific and Industrial Research Organisation
CSO	civil society organization

CSR	corporate social responsibility
DEFRA	Department of Environment, Food and Rural Affairs
DERA	Diesel Emission Reduction Act
DFID	Department for International Development
DJSI	Dow Jones Sustainability Index
DRI	direct reduced iron
DWD	Drinking Water Directive
EAF	electric arc furnace
ECBC	Energy Conservation Building Code
ECX	European Climate Exchange
EDF	Environmental Defense Fund
EEB	Energy Efficient Buildings
EMS	environmental management system
EPI	energy performance index/indicator
ETR	ecological tax reform
ETS	emissions trading scheme
FAO	Food and Agricultural Organization
FIT	feed-in-tariff
GPS	global positioning system
GRI	Global Reporting Initiative
GJ/t	gigajoules per ton
Gt	gigaton
HBI	hot briquetted iron
HCCI	homogeneous charge compression ignition
HCFC	hydrochlorofluorocarbon
HDI	Human Development Index
HDR	hot dry rock
HDU	hybrid drive unit
HEV	hybrid electric vehicle
HHV	hybrid hydraulic vehicle
HRV	heat recovery ventilation
HVAC	heating, ventilation and air-conditioning
ICE	internal combustion engine
ICLEI	International Council of Local Environmental Initiatives
IEA	International Energy Agency
IET	International Emissions Trading
IFAD	International Fund for Agricultural Development
IISI	International Iron and Steel Institute
ILO	International Labour Organization
IMO	International Maritime Organization
IPCC	Intergovernmental Panel on Climate Change
ISEW	Index for Sustainable Economic Welfare
JI	Joint Implementation (projects)
km/l	kilometres per litre
kPa	kilopascal

kWh/t	kilowatt-hours per ton
LATS	Landfill Allowance Trading Scheme
LBNL	Lawrence Berkeley National Laboratory
LCD	liquid crystal display
LED	light emitting diode
LEED	Leadership in Energy & Environmental Design
Li-ion	lithium-ion
LNG	liquefied natural gas
MEPS	mandatory energy performance standards
ML/d	million litres per day
mpg	miles per gallon
Mt	million tons
NCS	Natural Capitalism Solutions
NEPA	National Environmental Policy Act
NiMH	nickel-metal-hydride
NGO	non-governmental organization
NREL	National Renewable Energy Laboratories
OECD	Organisation for Economic Co-operation and Development
PCIA	Partnership for Clean Indoor Air
PHEV	plug-in hybrid electric vehicle
PHPP	Passive House Planning Package
pph	persons per hour
ppm	parts per million
PV	photovoltaic
RMI	Rocky Mountain Institute
rpm	revolutions per minute
SCM	supplementary cementitious material
SEET	Science, Engineering, Environment and Technology
SUV	sports utility vehicle
TJ	terajoule
tkm	ton-kilometre
TNEP	The Natural Edge Project
TOD	transit-oriented design
UNCHE	United Nations Conference on the Human Environment
UNDP	United Nations Development Programme
UNEP	United Nations Environment Programme
UNESCO	United Nations Educational, Scientific and Cultural Organization
USAID	United States Agency for International Development
US EPA	US Environmental Protection Agency
VOC	volatile organic compound
WBCSD	World Business Council for Sustainable Development
WHO	World Health Organization
WTO	World Trade Organization

Introduction
Factor Five: The Global Imperative

Ernst von Weizsäcker

At the crossroads

The human race is poised at a time before great change. At no time in history have we been faced with a greater challenge. We have been so successful in developing our knowledge and skills that we have created untold wealth and material prosperity – prosperity that could only be dreamed of 100 years ago. The world's innovators at the time could barely glimpse the world they were contributing to build, let alone the impacts that this new world might have on the environment. The electrical and digital revolutions accelerated this progress to the point that now the human race covers much of the habitable land on the planet and harnesses resources from all its four corners. In the 21st century, we stand at a crossroads, where the size of the impacts from our global community is now rivalling the size of our home's ability to cope.

Responding to growing concerns of this in earlier days, environmental policy was enacted and was focused on saving the environment for our grand-children to enjoy parks, animals and coral reefs, and to secure healthy air and water. However, today it is about rescuing the environment and preserving it as the basis of life as we know it. As our communities have grown and developed, so too has the pressure on the environment; pressure for ongoing supply of resources such as oil, food, water and metals, and pressure to assimilate growing amounts of waste, pollution and greenhouse gases. The 21st century will mark the time when the impact of its human inhabitants will have the potential to destroy its ability to support us. If the world we live in was three, or three hundred, times larger we would not be writing this book. The truth that the world is now rapidly coming to grips with is that we are damaging our planet to the point that it may not be able to maintain the conditions we have come to take for granted.

The 21st century will see monumental change. Either the human race will use its knowledge and skills and change the way it interacts with the environment, or the environment will change the way it interacts with its inhabitants. In the first case we would use the sophisticated understanding in areas such as physics, chemistry, engineering, biology, commerce, business and governance that we have accumulated in the last 1000 years to bring to bear on the challenge of dramatically reducing our pressure on the environment. The second case, however, is the opposite scenario. It will involve the decline of the planet's ecosystems until they reach thresholds where recovery is not possible. Following this we have no idea what happens next. If the average temperature of our planet's surface increases by 4–6 degrees Celsius (°C) we will see staggering changes to our environment, rapidly rising sea level, withering crops, diminishing water reserves, drought, cyclones, floods. Allowing this to happen will be the failure of our species, and those that survive will have a deadly legacy. In this book we support the many recent calls from leading governments to achieve 80 per cent reductions in environmental pressures and provide a reasonable and realistic approach to reaching this target by 2050, leading to and requiring already profound innovations across industries, across communities and across cultures.

The results of the 2006 *Stern Review* of the economics of climate change[1] provide a glimpse of what is coming upon us regarding global warming. Business-as-usual (BAU) – that is, a continuation of growth trends from the past without any serious decoupling of growth from grenhouse gas emissions – will lead to doubling annual emissions compared with the amounts from 2000. If we are able to stabilize greenhouse gas concentrations at 450 parts per million (ppm), we would have to reduce annual emissions by 50 per cent at least, which is a factor of 5 less than the BAU scenario. Even this extremely ambitious trajectory will not prevent some additional global warming in the range from 1 to 3.8°C. Coming to grips with this situation may require more capacity than our communities possess. Responding to the challenges now faced may require more understanding than our professions possess. And admitting that change is needed, and needed fast, may require more humility and courage than our typical national leaders possess; legally speaking, they are accountable to their respective national constituencies, not to the Earth.

The purpose of this book is not to repeat the litany of problems that face us. This has been thoroughly and rigorously presented in a number of recent works by UNEP, OECD, the IPCC[2] and individual authors such as Lester Brown,[3] Al Gore[4] and David Suzuki.[5] Nor is the purpose of this book to depict economic growth as the inevitable reason for destruction, as has been the motto of Edward J. Mishan,[6] and much of the *Limits to Growth*[7] debate of the 1970s. Nor is it our purpose to decry capitalism as the ultimate evil, as has become fashionable in our days after the deep dive the world economy took since the second half of 2008. But we surely join critics of capitalism to a certain extent – as some features of deregulated financial markets have been disastrous and demand careful re-regulation. What's more, in the context of the ecological state of the world, there is a need for regulation to prevent capital from investing in destructive industries and instead encouraging investment in value-creating activities conserving natural treasures.

The purpose of this book is to inspire hope. It is not good enough simply to present a highly theoretical picture of how technology could save the world. Instead we want to present practical pictures of whole systems of technologies, infrastructures, legal rules, education and cultural habits interacting to produce economic progress while conserving a healthy environment. Virtually all the strategies outlined in this book can be applied now by nations, companies and households to achieve Factor Five. This 'whole system approach' will also help overcome the *rebound effect* of additional consumption gobbling up all technological efficiency gains that were meant to save resources and conserve the environment.

To fill this message with real world substance, we present numerous examples of resource productivity improvements from the most relevant sectors, showing that the said Factor Five, or 80 per cent, reduction of environmental impacts per unit of economic output, is available. This multifaceted universe of opportunities represents the core body of our book.

While we strongly advocate for significant improvements in resource productivity, we add, however, that there will also need to be consideration of aspects related to *sufficiency* (discussed in Chapter 11). We shall need some rules of constraint or insights into other forms of satisfaction than the maximization of monetary throughput, or GDP. Relating to capitalism and regulation, we repeat and support my understanding from some 20 years ago that 'communism collapsed because it was not allowing prices to tell the economic truth, and that capitalism may also collapse if it does not allow prices to tell the ecological truth'. Markets are superb at steering an efficient allocation of resources and stimulating innovation, but they don't provide public order and law, moral standards, basic education and infrastructures, and markets are miserably inefficient, often even counterproductive, when it comes to protecting the commons and steering innovation into a long-term sustainable direction. Human societies, and the environment, will need a healthy balance between public and private goods, or between the state and the markets, as suggested in Chapter 10. The mindset dominating much of the world during the past couple of decades of weakening and ridiculing the state, was gravely mistaken. We do need strong states and engaged citizens working together to create good legal and moral frames for the markets. Moreover, citizens, nation states and the international communities of states and of citizens are expected permanently to act on those markets, as consumers, innovators, workers and guardians against destruction, and for technological and civilizational progress in harmony with the conditions of nature.

Whether we want it or not, we are in the midst of highly political issues when getting serious about protecting and restoring the basis of life on Earth.

Balancing economic aspirations with ecological imperatives

Balancing private with public goods means to a large extent balancing economic aspirations with ecological imperatives, and during early human history there has been no visible evidence of such balancing. The environment seemed endless, for all practical purposes, and was often seen as hostile. Human civilization developed by taming wild parts of nature and harnessing the powers of nature to extract some of the natural treasures and resources. Economic survival and the increase of welfare seemed like the natural mission and mandate for humanity, with impacts on the environment remaining a negligible affair. Even during early industrialization, until as late as the 1960s, environmental impacts of economic activities looked mostly like local and peripheral concerns – a steel mill, a chemical plant, a textile dye factory here and there. A small power plant to supply the energy needed for factories caused local air and water pollution and local health problems, but the environment as such, outside the cities, was not seen as affected. It was not until the 1960s, when human population was approaching four billion people that 'the environment' became a major political issue.

Overcoming some initial resistance on the part of industry, democratic states such as Japan, the US and Canada, and the West European states initiated and adopted pollution control legislation, with muscles to enforce the law – and it worked. The cleaning of industry made rapid progress. Banning a few particularly unhealthy substances, filtering exhaust gases and purifying waste waters, and finally redesigning some processes were the means of decoupling industrial outputs from polluting nuisances. After a mere 25 years, the foam hills on rivers had disappeared and the industrial agglomerations, such as the Ruhr in Germany, Osaka in Japan, or Pittsburgh in the US got cleaner than they had been for a hundred years. This success story surprised many sceptics who had seen the cause of the problem as economic growth as such. The lesson from pollution control seemed even to reverse such earlier fears: it was the rich, and further growing, democratically organized countries, or regions inside countries, that were the most effective in cleaning their environment, leaving the dirt to the poor and to the non-democratic societies. A very attractive new paradigm emerged – the Kuznets curve of pollution, shown in Figure 1, whereby countries having the economic maturity and financial means to deal with pollution control would engage in this agenda and move towards a wonderful harmony of 'rich and clean'.

During the 1980s, this convenient paradigm began to dominate the debate about the mutual relation between economic aspirations and ecological imperatives. It became perfectly respectable even for environmentalists to say: 'let the economy grow and take care of environmental concerns later'. Understandably, this attitude became the standard frame of mind of the leaders and representatives of developing countries in all international environmental negotiations.

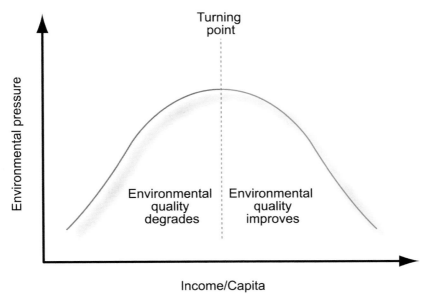

Note: The historic development is typically from left to right, meaning that countries start poor and clean, then they industrialize to be come rich and polluted, until they are so rich that the can afford strict pollution control so that they end up rich and clean.
Source: Based on Grossman and Krueger (1991)[8]

Figure 1 *Stylized Kuznets environmental curve*

And the rich countries of the North had little to put against this view, as well as having no intention to contradict anyway.

Alas, the Kuznets curve paradigm does not work for the global environmental problems of our days. Pollution control is actually a very restricted part of environmental reality. Impacts such as climate change, resource shortages and biodiversity losses follow a completely different logic from pollution control. In reality, it is the 'rich and clean' countries that are the biggest cause of such impacts. Carbon footprints so far relentlessly grow with increasing prosperity. The situation gets much worse for the rich if historical carbon emissions are also counted. The per capita cumulated carbon dioxide load from the US is about 1000 metric tons, in China it is about 60 metric tons, in India 25, in Germany nearly 800.[9] Figures get still somewhat worse for the rich countries if worldwide supply chains are considered as well. Many countries have outsourced the energy- and carbon-intensive segments of the supply chain to countries like China, which thereby got ever larger carbon footprints in the service of others.

In any case, the strong correlation between carbon footprints and GDP led many people in the US as well as in the developing countries to believe that reducing CO_2 emissions was tantamount to reducing economic welfare and was therefore politically unacceptable. The most convenient way of dealing

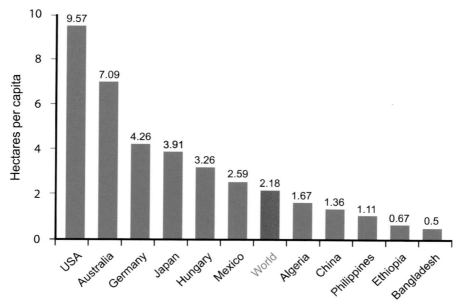

Source: Courtesy of Mathis Wackernagel, Global Footprint Network

Figure 2 *Ecological footprints of different nations*

with that situation was, of course, denying that there was any scientific proof of global warming or of human causes for additional warming. Fortunately, that's the past, at least as regards the attitude of the US government. But the challenge remains to find a new and healthy balance between economic aspirations and ecological imperatives. Addressing global warming is the most prominent aspect in our days of ecological imperatives. But biodiversity protection is no smaller challenge. Biodiversity losses result mostly from land-use changes, and these usually occur in the service of more production, that is, more economic growth. The most commonly used measure for land use in the service of consumption is 'ecological footprints', which estimates the land required for specific goods or services, or for the standard of living of average citizens of different countries. US (or European) footprints include land areas abroad that are needed for goods and services consumed at home. Bananas from Ecuador, copper from Chile, palm oil from Malaysia and the life-cycle footprints caused by computer manufacturing in China, all count towards the European footprints to the extent that Europeans consume bananas, copper, palm oil or computers. It is therefore not surprising that ecological footprints tend to be biggest for the rich, as can be read from Figure 2.

On our invitation, Mathis Wackernagel and Kristin Kane explain further:

> *Humanity's Ecological Footprints have grown too large.*
> *According to research by the Global Footprint Network, since*

the late 1980s humanity's Footprint has exceeded the world's estimated biocapacity. The Ecological Footprint is a measure of the biologically productive area (or biocapacity) a human population requires to produce the resources it consumes, and absorb its wastes, using prevailing technology. Populations with a Footprint larger than the regenerative capacity of their region run ecological deficits. If humanity uses more ecological services than what nature can replenish, humanity is in global overshoot.

To know our demand on the biosphere, as well as how much of the biosphere's biocapacity is within our region, we need to measure our use of nature. We need resource accounts that keep track of how much nature we have, and how much we use. Ecological accounting operates like financial accounting: it tracks income (the ecological services nature provides) and expenditures (human use of these ecological services). As with financial assets, it is possible to spend more than is being regenerated. But this is possible only for a limited period of time. Continued ecological deficit spending leads to environmental bankruptcy, eroded economies, decreased quality of life and societal instability.

We obtain our resources from forests, cropland, fisheries and grazing land, and other ecosystems. Additionally, ecosystems absorb and assimilate the wastes we produce as a result of our resource consumption. The Ecological Footprint adds up these ecosystem services in terms of the biologically productive areas needed to provide the services. In other words, Ecological Footprint analysis builds on a mass flow balance, and each flow is translated into the ecologically productive areas necessary to support these flows. The largest and most dramatically growing component in the footprints is the 'Carbon Footprint'. This is the land needed to absorb the excess carbon dioxide from burning fossil fuel. Since it is such a large component of the overall Footprint, the Carbon Footprint is getting currently most attention. However, reducing the Carbon Footprint at the cost of increasing other Footprint components, as in the case of many first-generation bio-fuels, may lead to a net loss, not a gain.

Global Footprint Network's latest estimates conclude that humanity's demand in 2005 exceeded the regenerative capacity of the planet by about 30 per cent. This means, humanity is in ecological overshoot. Per person, the biosphere offers about two global hectares of biologically productive space. Global hectares are hectares with world average productivity, relating to the productive quarter of the world's surface – the rest is deserts, ice fields and deep oceans. The average US Footprint is roughly ten global hectares per person, the average Indian Footprint is *nearing one global hectare per person. In other words, it would take about five planet Earths if all humanity adopted American lifestyles, or about half the Earth's capacity if all lived like the average Indians.*

A global green new deal

The second half of 2008 marked the beginning of the biggest economic downturn in 60 years. The economic crisis, which is on everybody's mind, is likely to be felt for another couple of years, at least. Millions have lost their jobs already, and many more are in danger of losing them.

Many countries reacted by launching massive packages of economic stimuli. Fortunately for the environment and for the long-term durability of measures, most countries allowed for a considerable environmental emphasis within the packages. HSBC, the London-based international bank, has done a survey of those 'green' components. On average, more than 10 per cent of the money appears to be committed to environmentally friendly activities. In South Korea, that share is above 80 per cent. Figure 3 shows the result of the survey. Doubts as to the legitimacy of the expenditure are allowed – if HSBC's criteria for 'green' were strict enough – but it is clear that some countries, notably South Korea, China, France, Germany and the US, tried to use the packages for moving the economy in the direction of a healthy environment.

HSBC has undertaken a thorough analysis of the stimulus packages of 17 nations in order to learn what types of public and private green investments produce the highest economic multipliers.[10] It found that most investments in a low-carbon economy led to strong economic multipliers, with the highest of those multipliers being building for energy efficiency, renewable energy technologies, low-carbon vehicles, rail transport and finally 'smart' grid and 'smart' meters. It is worth noting that South Korea's stimulus package, and most other nations' stimulus packages focus on sectors of the economy that are presented in Part I of this book – namely green buildings, ultra-efficient green cars/trains and bikes, green infrastructure and recycling. Thus Part I is designed

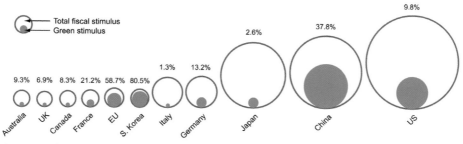

Source: Based on data from HSBC. Picture courtesy of German Institute for Development (DIE)

Figure 3 *Eco-friendly components of fiscal stimuli 2008/2009*

to assist nations like South Korea ensure they achieve the maximum resource productivity improvements from their investments. For example, South Korea's stimulus package includes the following:

- *Housing*: US$6 billion for (a) the construction of one million green homes, (b) energy efficiency upgrades for one million homes, (c) energy conservation improvements in villages and schools and (d) the installation of light emitting diode (LED) lighting in public facilities. Chapter 2 provides a detailed overview of how to improve energy productivity in this sector and how to design green homes.
- *Forestry*: US$1.7 billion for (a) forestry management, including tree planting to increase carbon sink capacity and (b) the construction of new facilities that use wood as biomass energy. The online companion to Chapter 3 overviews advances in the pulp and paper industry along with Chapter 4 which investigates the agricultural opportunities for energy generation.
- *Water*: US$11.1 billion for river restoration and water resource management. Chapter 4 features an in-depth analysis of how to achieve Factor Five improvements in resource productivity in the agricultural sector which will help South Korea and other nations enable more water to be returned to rivers to restore environmental flows and river ecosystems. The remaining chapters in Part I all show how to achieve Factor Five water efficiency improvements and thus demonstrate also how cities can reduce their water usage as well. Improving water efficiency in irrigation, residential and commercial buildings, and industry also reduces the amount of energy needed to pump the water or heat it. Part I shows that there is a strong energy/water nexus across all major sectors of the economy.
- *Cars*: US$1.8 billion towards the development of fuel-efficient vehicles, such as electric and hybrid cars, by automakers Hyundai and Kia. Resource efficiency opportunities for this sector are covered in the opening section of Chapter 5.
- *Trains and bikes*: US$7 billion for (a) the expansion of electrified rail tracks, (b) the construction of new high-speed rail links and (c) the construction of more than 4000km of bicycle paths. South Korea and other nations can learn from best-practice case studies of what other nations are doing in this area in Chapter 5.
- *Recycling*: US$670 million for resource recycling, including the construction of electricity plants that run on the methane emissions generated from rubbish. Recycling to achieve greater materials efficiency is a critical strategy to enable many energy-intensive industries to also achieve Factor Five energy productivity gains. The in-depth sector studies in Part I look at ways to increase recycling levels and use more recycled materials as feedstocks in those sectors to simultaneously achieve large energy and material resource productivities. Part I also shows that there is a strong energy/materials productivity nexus in most sectors.

The South Korean government believes that such investments will drive economic growth and help position South Korean companies at the forefront of the next wave of innovation – the green economy. South Korea is also aiming to become the home of the world's first 'smart national grid', which uses information and communication technology to maximize electricity transmission efficiency. However, on the whole, such stimulus packages by definition will be temporary measures, and their environmental components are likely to be considerably smaller than 1 per cent of the GDP. What can be done to create a more lasting environmental effect? One proposal tries to answer this question, namely to call all the new public debts 'climate debts' and to enter political commitments of repaying the debts by raising energy taxes or auctioning carbon emission permits. This proposal was first published by Jakob von Weizsäcker.[11] His expectation is that such commitment would serve as a long-lasting signal of making climate-endangering energy consumption economically less attractive.

We are arguing in this book that the world will have to move on to a green economy anyway, irrespective of the momentary financial crisis. We therefore fully support the idea articulated by UNEP's Executive Director, Achim Steiner, of a 'Global Green New Deal'. Obviously, the idea alliterates Franklin D. Roosevelt's New Deal of the early 1930s which helped pull the US out of the deep depression that unfolded after Wall Street's collapse of October 1929. The idea of a Green New Deal is to spend public money to create jobs for the public good of a sustainable environment. And the Global Green New Deal is meant to coordinate the most important economies of the world to give the Green New Deal sufficient impetus and volume. National commitments of the kind shown in Figure 3 are still much too timid, with the notable exception of South Korea. We assume that the world has too little confidence so far in the opportunities lying in a new green technological revolution. We obviously hope that this book will help create strong additional confidence in this regard.

There is widespread confidence that eventually the financial crisis will come to an end. Some key ingredients are there for a new economic upswing. Demand is almost unlimited, notably in the developing countries, but even in the rich and seemingly saturated countries, demand is still on the rise: for education, health, personal care and entertainment. Labour, capital and technologies are also there to satisfy such new demand. Reassuring signs come also from politics. The G20 Summit in London in April 2009 showed a new sense of partnership among the most economically significant countries of the world. Some first steps were made to re-regulate financial markets, which had gone wild. And the erroneous dreams of perfectly self-stabilizing markets and of a weak state have come to an end.

What seems to be missing is a clear sense of direction. It was there in earlier centuries when prosperity growth with little regard to the environment was the guiding philosophy nearly everywhere. There were technological break-throughs from time to time, spurring growth and creating a sense of excitement. Those breakthroughs included the steam engine, railways, electricity, cars, chemical technologies, radio and TV, and, most recently, IT, biotechnology and nanotechnology. Also the globalization of industrial supply chains can be seen as a breakthrough, notably in terms of keeping consumer prices down. However, there are signs of fatigue with this kind of progress as it hits its natural limits. For the world economy to find its way back to healthy and robust development, a new and reliable sense of direction will be needed. Providing this new sense of direction is the basic motive both of the Global Green New Deal and of our book. We suggest that we are at the dawn of a new long-term cycle, a new 'Kondratiev Cycle', or wave of innovation.

Kondratiev Cycles[12]

During a time of recession, commentators often speak about, and hope for, the 'next upswing'. Usually it is the short kind of business cycles people have in their minds. But there are also long-term cycles, every 30–50 years, which can be attributed to major technological innovations, such as the ones mentioned above. Although standard economic literature does not necessarily accept the idea of long-term cycles, they have been a useful way of describing, characterizing and perhaps even explaining historical periods that are associated with technology-driven major economic upswings. The best-known early scholar to describe such long-term cycles was the great Russian economist Nikolai D. Kontratiev (1892–1938).[13] His pivotal book was called *The Major Economic Cycles* and was published in 1925.[14] Kondratiev himself had no strong emphasis on technological change, but Joseph Schumpeter, the famous Austrian and later American economist, saw business cycles and long-term cycles as associated with major technological innovations. It was Schumpeter himself who suggested honouring Kondratiev (killed in 1938 by Stalin's 'Purge' firing squads), by calling the long cycles 'Kondratiev Cycles'. Paulo Rodriguez Pereira gives a crisp account of the long cycle discussion, with some emphasis on what it means for developing countries.[15] Referring to Joseph Schumpeter, Christopher Freeman and Carlota Perez, Pereira says that Kondratiev cycles are not an exclusive economic phenomenon but result from a reorientation of industrial organization and management, based on 'technologies that underlie the existing economic cycle. Kondratiev cycles are thus associated with major technical changes'.[16] From this observation, he also derives the need for developing countries to strengthen their technological capacities.

In line with such a 'Schumpeter–Freeman–Perez' paradigm of waves, Pereira describes the five familiar historical cycles as:

1. the early mechanization cycle since the 1770s;
2. the steam power and railway cycle since the 1830s;
3. the electrical and heavy engineering cycle since the 1880s;
4. the Fordist and mass production cycle since the 1930s (although he could have given an earlier start for that one);

5   the information and communication cycle since the 1980s (he could have added biotechnology to the description).[17]

Our point is that, according to historical evidence since Kondratiev's pivotal work, the magic of technological innovations tends to fade after some 20 to 30 years of its beginning. So it may not be too surprising that even the most exciting recent wave of innovations in information technology, biotechnologies and, somewhat more recently, nanotechnologies, is no longer strong enough to support worldwide economic growth.

The new cycle will be green

Fading excitement with certain technologies would not yet make for a massive – and sudden – economic downturn. The arrogance and failures of much of the financial sector was the obvious cause of the present crisis. But if we want the economy to gain strength again, an exciting new wave of technologies might be the biggest hope for the world. A couple of years before the present crisis, Paul Hawken, Amory Lovins and Hunter Lovins, in *Natural Capitalism*, also summarizing the theory of long-term cycles, came up with the suggestion of a new industrial revolution unfolding, with energy and resource efficiency at its core.[18] Building on from this pivotal work, Charlie Hargroves and Michael Smith from The Natural Edge Project, and co-authors of this book, suggested in their 2005 book, *The Natural Advantage of Nations*, that the emerging wave of green technologies could be seen as the beginning of a new Kondratiev Cycle, as shown in Figure 4, and noting that the time frame for such waves is quickening.

As we have observed before, some greening of technologies and the economy is already under way. We do suggest that the process of greening, being the logical answer to the environmental constraints, will generate the new and reliable sense of direction that could pull us out of the recession. For this to happen, some additional momentum will be highly desirable. If the conviction spreads that the greening trend is inevitable and can take the shape of a full-size Kondratiev Cycle, we are confident that the desired momentum will come. Investors then have clarity about where to put their bets.

Reflecting on the ingredients for a big new cycle, we seem to discover three that can be identified in each of the earlier Kondratiev cycles.

1   One ingredient, as we said, seems to be the loss of magnetism of the technologies that characterized the former cycle. Such was the case with the railroads around 1900. The discoveries and innovations of electricity, the internal combustion engine and chemical technologies created a lot more excitement at the time than a further expansion of the railway network would have done. Thomas Edison, Gottlieb Daimler and Henry Ford, and European chemical innovators and entrepreneurs became the heroes of a new wave of growth and innovation. The next wave, characterized by petrochemicals, aviation and early electronics, was generated

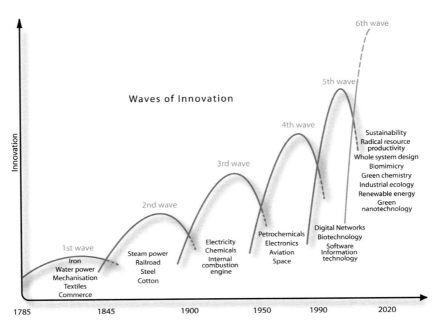

Source: Courtesy of The Natural Edge Project[19]

Figure 4 *Waves of innovation*

almost entirely in the US – but later also fertilized the Old World, including the Soviet Union. It was triggered, in part, by the fading excitement with classical electrical and chemical engineering.

2   Another ingredient for a new wave is strong demand for new products and services. It should be noted, however, that much of the demand may be sleeping in the early phase of the new wave. Perhaps the best example for that has been information technology. Mainframe computers did not look like they would be useful to everybody. Electric typewriters, copiers and printers were widely used but did not spell excitement. TVs became widespread as well, but nobody associated them with computer screens or data processing. The miniaturization of electronics to save weight for spaceships and aeroplanes remained an 'outlandish' affair. However, when computers, typewriters, TV screens and miniature electronics merged into the desktop computer technology, a whole new universe of applications and demand was awakened. Endless waves of software development, breathtaking advances in further miniaturization and finally the development of the Internet and of search machines made IT a seemingly non-ending success story, constantly creating its own additional demand. Also, earlier technological waves met with moderate demand at the beginning, but more demand germinated and blossomed as supplies got ever more affordable. This was surely the case for textiles, railroads, strong machinery, automobiles, chemical plastics, fertilizers and machinery for the

farm, pharmaceuticals and diagnostics, electric appliances, air travel and industrial robots. And mass manufacture, explicitly mentioned by Rodriguez Pereira for the fourth Kondratiev cycle, clearly made goods more affordable and thereby stimulated demand that was unimaginable at the beginning of the cycle.

3   The third ingredient for a new big wave is perhaps the most visible: the invention and development of exciting new technologies – the steam engine, the internal combustion engine, chemical plastics, aircraft, the TV, uranium fission, penicillin, the laser, home computers, and centralized data storage and search engines – were all celebrated as scientific inventions or technological breakthroughs. But hundreds of other inventions were also made without having big economic impacts.

So we suggest that much of the dynamics leading to a Kondratiev cycle comes from a combination of the three major ingredients: fading excitement with old technologies, rising demand for and affordable supplies of the new goods and services, and indeed some exciting new technologies. At any rate, we feel that all three ingredients are there for the launching of a very major new wave of innovation, the Green Kondratiev cycle, or the 6th Wave of Innovation. In this case we suggest that the strongest pull factor is demand. A world population almost twice the size of the time of the last big cycle wants food, shelter and huge amounts of additional goods and services, and all under conditions of decreasing or stagnating supplies of energy, water, land and minerals. The greenhouse effect greatly exacerbates the problem by further reducing energy and farming options. Some fatigue can be observed also with the old technologies, notably inasmuch as they are seen as destructive to the environment. Even IT and biotechnology are experiencing some signs of saturation. IBM, one of the most successful companies in the modern high-tech world, sold their computer manufacturing to China. And Silicon Valley in California, the cradle of the IT revolution, is shifting its attention to green technologies. Biotechnology companies try to prove their usefulness by offering drought-resistant crops or energy-saving microbes for washing and cleaning. Nanotechnologies came into lots of controversies and legal questions[20] and are in need of proving their usefulness for resource-saving technologies as well. What is more, and this is the core of our book, is the availability of a wide range of fascinating new technologies promising to be roughly five times more resource efficient than those still dominating industry, households and the service sector. So we do not hesitate to call for and promote a new Green Kondratiev cycle.

This vision is actually closely related to Thomas Friedman's line of thinking in his brilliant 2008 bestseller *Hot, Flat and Crowded*.[21] His book has the subtitle: *Why We Need a Green Revolution and How It Can Renew America*. Quite so. The greening of production and consumption has become a powerful method of renewing a country's fabric. What holds for the US, should be even more suggestive for countries like China or India, less richly endowed with natural resources but with much higher economic growth rates and much larger populations. These two giants stand symbolic for the 'crowded' world of soon to be seven billion people living on a small planet that is still losing forests, fertile land, fish stock, minerals, water stores and fossil energy resources at an alarming rate.

From labour productivity to resource productivity

Greening the economy is perhaps a popular way of characterizing the innovations we expect to happen in the course of the Green Kondratiev. But we suggest going one philosophical step further. We observe, as economic historians are likely to agree, that the first 200 years of modern age economic development had the 'increase of labour productivity' as the one unifying motto. Labour productivity rose at a pace of roughly 1 per cent per year during the 19th century until the middle of the 20th century. From then on, owing to the accelerated global spread of technologies, progress increased by about 2–3 per cent per year. Overall, labour productivity has increased twentyfold over those last 200 years. Figure 5 shows a time window of some 120 years marking the impressive acceleration after World War II.

Today, labour is not in short supply. Otherwise the International Labour Organization (ILO) would not speak of a shortfall of 800 million jobs to create a situation of near full employment. On the other hand, as we have indicated before, energy and other natural resources are in short supply, and the scarcity is getting worse every decade. This situation calls for a reversal of the emphasis on

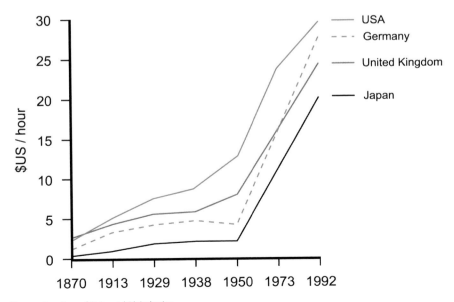

Source: Courtesy of Raimund Bleischwitz

Figure 5 *The development of labour productivity over 120 years*

technological progress. Resource productivity should become the main feature of technological progress in our days. Countries making the scarce production factors more productive should enjoy major economic advantages over those ignoring the new scarcities. This is another way of emphasizing the need for a new technological cycle and a new orientation for the world economy, for national economies, and for individual firms. To relate this to the long cycle considerations, the Green Kondratiev should become the first cycle during which resource productivity grows faster than labour productivity. In developing countries, the increase of labour productivity will, of course, remain a high priority because they want to catch up with industrialized countries. But they should avoid doing so at the expense of resource productivity. Many studies show that such a focus will help to boost the economy and create jobs, while reducing environmental pressures. As The Natural Edge Project explain in their upcoming publication *Cents and Sustainability*, investments in resource productivity transform and stimulate the economy in three main ways:[22]

1   First, investments in resource productivity, such as building energy efficiency, have a higher economic multiplier than general expenditure, as resource efficiency investments provide a tangible financial return on investment as well as usually providing additional productivity improvements. A recent 2007 study by McKinsey & Company[23] has found that, through investing in energy efficiency, global emissions could be reduced by 20–30 per cent by 2020 without harming business profitability or economic growth at all. Thus once the return on investment is achieved, usually within 1–2 years, business, government departments and households have lower annual costs and thus more money to spend elsewhere. If they then choose to invest this money in additional cost-effective resource efficiency opportunities, still more funds are generated over time, which can be reinvested, further stimulating economic activity.

2   Secondly, investments in improving resource efficiency and recycling have a higher economic welfare outcome than general expenditure on many goods and services because they reduce demand for energy, water and virgin resources and thus delay (and even in some cases prevent) the need to spend billions on new energy and water supply infrastructure and new extractive industries. Resource efficiency investments and demand management has been shown to help nations avoid infrastructure investment so that infrastructure funding can be targeted to where it is most needed. This is an important consideration since there are already insufficient funds to spend on all the potential and desirable infrastructure projects. Take the electricity sector in Australia. Experts say if current demand for electricity continues to rise with the current trend, A$30 billion will need to be spent on new electricity supply infrastructure. By contrast, in California, energy efficiency, greener building codes and demand management have led to a flattening over the last 20 years of previously rising electricity demand.[24] California through its strong climate change policies has achieved signifi-

cant reductions in electricity consumption per capita compared to the rest of the US – an estimated net saving of US$1000 per family. Sweden, the UK and the Netherlands have all achieved flattening of previously rising electricity demand through policies that encourage energy efficiency.[25] Thus, tens of billions of dollars can be saved by avoiding unnecessary infrastructure investments, and thus freeing up capital to instead be invested in additional eco-efficiency initiatives, recycling plants and local distributed renewable supply options for energy and water.

3   Thirdly, jobs are created locally by green initiatives. This results in more of a city's or town's energy, water and materials dollars being spent in a way that supports local jobs and the local economy. Also these new local 'green' jobs have a direct effect of attracting more people to the city or town who then contribute to that local economy. California's energy-efficiency policies created nearly 1.5 million jobs from 1977 to 2007.[26] Germany claims to have 1.2 million green jobs already, and another 500,000 on the drawing board. The UK has announced a target of one million green jobs.[27] US President Obama has promised to create five million green jobs. In Australia, as mentioned above, the Australian Council of Trade Unions (ACTU) and Australian Conservation Foundation (ACF) says almost one million jobs could be created in the next 20 years if the Federal Government promotes green industries.[28] Their 2008 report showed that, with the right policy settings, six market sectors in the Australian economy (renewable energy, energy efficiency, sustainable water systems, green buildings, biomaterials and recycling and waste), currently valued at US$15.5 billion and employing 112,000 people, could grow to a value of A$243 billion and 847,000 jobs by 2030.[29]

Kick it off, quickly but smoothly

The next question is how the new Kondratiev can be kicked off. Do we have to wait for the whole world to be persuaded towards the new paradigm? Can single countries or companies go it alone or do they need a broadly accepted business environment for resource productivity and the rest? We suggest that pioneers can go ahead prudently with little if any risk to their economic performance. Philips has decided to concentrate on LED for example, and Toyota went ahead, together with Honda to introduce the hybrid car and was very successful domestically and abroad. Véolia Environment pioneered 'city mining', the extraction of valuable metals from old waste dumps. Japan during the period from 1974 to 1980 went ahead with the phasing out of energy intensive manufacturing such as aluminium smelting from bauxite, and celebrated fabulous successes in other branches such as electronics and optics. Germany became the leader in renewable energies through a law of generous feed-in tariffs.

However, in the absence of certain framework conditions such as rising petrol prices, high electricity prices in Japan, high scrap metal prices from 2003 to 2007 and global warming concerns, it is less clear if such pioneers could have been successful. This is slightly different from the pioneers of the IT revolution who did not really need favourable framing conditions to make their technological advances a commercial success. This indicates that for the Green Kondratiev cycle to really take off, some political decisions on framing conditions would be most welcome. As a matter of fact, we devote the entire second part of this book to the politics, economics and psychology of framing conditions for a massive launch of the exciting new efficiency and renewable energy technologies that are available right now. We describe them in the following Part I of this book. The transition into the Green Kondratiev cycle may actually be less dramatic than one might fear. The systems approach taken in this book essentially means redesigning the systems of industry, transport, buildings or agriculture, which were found to be destructive to the climate and the environment. The process of redesigning, as radical as it may be in terms of a new philosophy, can be a gradual and smooth one, encouraged by prudently designed and predictably changing framing conditions. We don't need to lose much physical or financial capital that is invested in our industrialized world. We only have to avoid investing fresh money into outdated and destructive operations and technologies.

For the smooth transition, we certainly need an educated workforce, educated consumers and a new generation of researchers, engineers, marketing people, investors and politicians. Achieving a Factor Five transition is as much a technical challenge as it is a social one. Renewing education systems and curricula, fostering sustainable behaviour, developing policy and mechanisms to allow commerce and economic development, will all be crucial components. This book will focus on the range of options available for achieving significant design improvements, in Part I, and will then provide commentary as to how governments can best support their economy and offer structure and direction to underpin a prosperous transition, in Part II. Before starting the in-depth sector studies in Part I, Chapter 1 of this book addresses a significant barrier to the uptake of Factor Five resource productivity opportunities, namely the historic failure of designers, engineers, architects and technicians to take a whole-system approach to the identification and implementation of resource productivity opportunities.

Notes

1   Stern (2007).
2   UNEP = United Nations Environment Programme, OECD = Organisation for Economic Co-operation and Development; IPCC = Intergovernmental Panel on Climate Change.
3   Brown, L. (2008).
4   Gore (2006).
5   Suzuki and Gordon (1991); Suzuki et al (2007).
6   Mishan (1967).
7   Meadows et al (1972).

8   Grossman and Krueger (1991).
9   World Resources Institute (undated) 'Earth Trends Portal: Cumulative CO_2 emissions 1900–2004', World Resources Institute, WRI.
10   Robins et al (2009).
11   von Weizsäcker (2009).
12   This subchapter and the next two summarize deeper discussions on technologies and long-term cycles presented by Hargroves and Smith (2005) Chp 1, Chp 6 and Chp 13.
13   Jacob an Gelderen and Samuel de Wolff are the two Dutch economists who proposed long-term cycles as early as 1913, but their work, written in Dutch, remained unknown to N. Kondratiev, J. Schumpeter and others and was translated into English only recently.
14   Kondratiev (1925) *The Major Economic Cycles* (Russian), Translated and published in English as Kondratiev (1984). See also Kondratiev et al (1998).
15   Pereira (1994).
16   Pereira (1994) p2.
17   Pereira (1994) pp4–6.
18   Hawken et al (1999).
19   Hargroves and Smith (2005) pp39–42.
20   Bennett-Woods (2008).
21   Friedman (2008).
22   Smith and Hargroves (2010).
23   McKinsey & Company (2007).
24   Shirley (2006).
25   Smith and Hargroves (2009) This article includes excerpts from the forthcoming publication on how to decouple economic growth from environmental pressures to underpin a new era of 'green' growth – Smith and Hargroves (2010).
26   Roland-Holst (2008).
27   ACTU/ACF (2008).
28   ACTU/ACF (2008).
29   ACTU/ACF (2008).

Part I
A Whole System Approach to Factor Five

The Natural Edge Project

Preface to the Sector Studies

The Natural Edge Project

The coming decades will see the most pressing and widespread imperative for change that our species has ever experienced. Since the early times, much of our history has been a story of survival – a story that tells of a vulnerable but clever species that rose to the top of its planet's food chain, and achieved, for some, staggering levels of affluence and luxury – a story however that is already taking a turn for the worse, and may again call for us to fight for our very own survival. The awful consequence of the rapid industrialization of much of the world is that it has relied on significant levels of pollution, environmental damage and resource consumption, the impact of which is now rivalling the planet's ability to accommodate it. The next chapter of civilization's history will be dictated by the manner in which we respond to the realization that as a global community we need to significantly and rapidly reduce our pressure on the environment, and in particular our generation of greenhouse gas emissions – a challenge made particularly difficult by the 2008 global financial crisis.

The realization that underpins the message of this book is that over the coming decades we need to implement a range of solutions across the world in a way that enables the global economy to grow out of the current economic crisis, while creating a strong and sustainable economic platform for the future. The reality is that even though the financial crisis is severe, concerted government action can help business and the financial markets recover in a matter of a few years. However, climate change is long term, and if not addressed will lead to devastating impacts on the environment and on the global economy. To put this into perspective, consider that the global financial crisis has been estimated to result in the world economy reducing by around 7 per cent in the year 2009, resulting in a net GDP growth of minus 1.3 per cent – the global economy's worst performance in more than 60 years.[1] This is indeed a significant impact; however, after reviewing the economics of climate change, Sir Nicholas Stern came to the conclusion that if action is not taken, the economic impacts associated with climate change would reduce the global GDP by between 5 and 20 per cent each year.[2] In effect this would not only repeat the devastation of the 2008 financial crisis every year, but the crisis would worsen as environmental feedbacks compound. Allowing this to happen would be catastrophic and would surely crash the global economy. On the other hand Stern estimates that a concerted effort to stabilize greenhouse gas emissions at an acceptable level would require a mere 1 per cent of global GDP per year, a small price to pay to secure our common future.

Most experts now agree that the most cost effective and quickest way to reduce greenhouse gas emissions is through a focus on rapidly improving resource productivity and switching to more sensible methods of production; however, such a focus will require a whole-of-society approach. Governments will need to revise related policies, business and industry will need to carefully reassess operations, the professions will need to rapidly renew their curriculum and practice,[3] research organizations will need to further clarify and solidify the issues and opportunities, citizens will need to revise purchase choices, and so on. In 1997 a book called *Factor Four* was written to assist in such changes. In a collaboration between the Founder and then President of the Wuppertal Institute for Climate, Environment and Energy in Germany, Professor Ernst von Weizsäcker, and the Founders and Principals of Rocky Mountain Institute in the United States, Amory Lovins and Hunter Lovins, the book presented evidence for the first time to show that significant reductions in the consumption of energy and water, and hence reductions in environmental pressures, could be profitably achieved across our societies. The book quickly became an international bestseller and was translated into 12 languages, and to this day is widely recognized as one of the most influential books in the field of sustainable development. As groundbreaking as the message of *Factor Four* was in 1997, more than a decade later, as the world realizes the severity of the 'climate crisis', its message has now become critical – a message this book seeks to update.

> *The time for delay is over. The time for denial is over. We all believe what the scientists have been saying on climate change for many years now. I think what is exciting about the conversation is that it is not only a problem but it is also an opportunity. As we have started to develop a framework for our economic recovery plan ... we have an opportunity now to create jobs all across this country in all 50 states to repower America, to redesign how we use energy and think about how we can increase energy efficiency to make our economy stronger, make us more safe, reduce our dependence on foreign oil and make us competitive for decades to come – even as we save the planet. We are not going to miss this opportunity.*
>
> President Elect Barack Obama, December 2008[4]

Although it would be easy to think that our efforts can't make a difference, since *Factor Four* was published numerous teams of innovative thinkers, designers, policy makers and practitioners around the world have been diligently working to create truly outstanding solutions, that when brought together will contribute to a sustainable world. The purpose of this sequel to *Factor Four* is to profile and explain the significance of such efforts in a simple to understand but rigorous and thorough way. Developed in two distinct parts, the first part presents a whole system approach to achieving up to 80 per cent resource productivity improvements across the major energy- and water-intensive industries (namely buildings, industry, agriculture and transportation). The second part then presents reflections from many years of experience and expertise by Ernst von Weizsäcker in preparing governments and industry for a rapid transition to such improvements. The second part of the book covers topics including the effectiveness of regulation, economic instruments and taxation reform, overcoming the rebound effect, balancing private and public goods, and the relevance of a focus on sufficiency in a civilized modern world.

However, before we present this important material we take a moment to explain how our team came to collaborate with Professor von Weizsäcker on this important publication. Ironically the journey began with *Factor Four*, as this was the book that brought our group of young engineers and scientists together to form The Natural Edge Project (TNEP), back in 2002. At a time when we were becoming dismayed by the world's unsustainable development path and felt like there was little we could do to change the situation, *Factor Four* showed our team that much of what we understood about our professions was set to be revolutionized. Following this realization, our team asked, 'how can we contribute?', and we realized that the first step was to learn all we could about the field and then focus our efforts on truly making a contribution.

Reading books like *Natural Capitalism* and *Cradle to Cradle*, it became clear to us that these changes, as part of the so-called 'next Industrial Revolution', would require a scale and pace of creativity and innovation even greater than responding to the creation of electricity, keeping up with the space race or even the revolution of the digital age. Like so many young engineers and scientists concerned about the future, we were aware that there was growing activity in innovating sustainable solutions, but until we read these books (which did not appear in our undergraduate curriculum at the time) we had no idea that such opportunities existed throughout the whole economy, and when combined could actually make a significant difference. Effectively, reading the work of these leaders transformed our growing fears and anxieties about the future into a strong focused drive to contribute to changing it, leading to the formation of TNEP. Once on this path our sense of hope and excitement grew as we contemplated a future that saw the societies of the world truly harnessing 300 years of industrialization to create a low-impact existence that could sustain life as we know it.

Our first project was a three-year process, working with many co-authors, mentors and advisers, to develop our first book, *The Natural Advantage of Nations*,[5] published in 2005 as a response by the next generation to *Natural Capitalism*.[6] Working on this book allowed us to focus on catching up with the field of sustainable development, to study the work of the leaders, and to meet with them to discuss their ideas and experience. We were astounded by the openness and willingness to help, which all of the experts we approached offered – such as meeting Amory Lovins at an event in Canberra that led to us staying at Rocky Mountain Institute for three weeks and significantly rewriting parts of the book, or spending many hours listening intently to Hunter Lovins fill the many gaps in our understanding over a coffee or a bourbon, or having Bill McDonough phone us after hearing about our book to take the time to talk to us to ensure that we properly understood his work, or having Molly Olsen ensure our active involvement in the National Business Leaders Forum on Sustainable Development each year. Experiences like this, and others after finishing this first book – including touring with Janine Benyus or Hunter Lovins in Australia, or sitting in Jim McNeill's lounge room and discussing the best way to respond to *Our Common Future*[7] – allowed us to take what we read and then explore it in conversation with its creators, and ensure that our work is guided by their latest insights and wisdom gained from a lifelong commitment to sustainable development.

These experiences have changed our lives. For instance, on one particular visit to Snowmass in 2003, while standing in Amory Lovins' kitchen we asked him what a team of young engineers and scientists could do to make a difference to our profession. He responded simply that we should contribute to the 'non-violent overthrow of bad engineering', and he impressed on our team the importance of working with the engineering community to help share and mainstream the insights from *Factor Four* and *Natural Capitalism*. This inspired us to focus our efforts on assisting designers and led to the development of our 2008 book, *Whole System Design: An Integrated Approach to Sustainable Engineering*.[8] After completing this book, and eager to move on to another project to support engineers and designers, Charlie had the good fortune to meet Ernst von Weizsäcker at a conference in China and hear him talk of his experiences since *Factor Four*, and after a few beers and some authentic Chinese food, the idea to develop a sequel, *Factor Five*, was born.

Now, some two and a half years after this conversation, and as we write this our last paragraph of our contribution to *Factor Five* before sending it to the publisher, we feel honoured to have been part of developing this book, and having had the privilege of working with Ernst von Weizsäcker, a true champion with a tireless commitment to our common future. We have taken the responsibility to assist in the development of this book very seriously and hope that the Sector Studies provide others with a similar level of assurance and inspiration that *Factor Four* provided us, and we look forward to future collaborations.

Charlie Hargroves, Michael Smith, Cheryl Desha and Peter Stasinopoulos
The Natural Edge Project

Notes

1   IMF (2009).
2   Stern (2007) p10.
3   See the forthcoming book on this subject, Desha and Hargroves (2010).
4   Martin (2008).
5   Hargroves and Smith (2005).
6   Hawken et al (1999).
7   Leading to the development of Smith and Hargroves (2010).
8   Stasinopoulos et al (2008).

1
A Framework for Factor Five

The Natural Edge Project

Building on from *Factor Four*

In 1997, the book *Factor Four* brought together 50 case studies from around the world that demonstrated the potential to profitably achieve significant improvements in resource productivity. This concept transformed how many economists, policy makers, engineers, entrepreneurs and business leaders thought about innovation, environmental protection and wealth creation. The book was among a small number of books that inspired the formation of The Natural Edge Project (TNEP), as it not only assured us that significant innovation in resource productivity, and hence reductions in environmental pressures, was available, but it also made engineering and design exciting, even in the face of a looming global environmental catastrophe. The book, translated into 12 languages, effectively demonstrated to the world the value to business and government of moving on from environmental protection and pollution control, to a focus on resource productivity and pollution prevention. Specifically, the case studies in *Factor Four* included:

- 20 energy productivity case studies covering cars, buildings, super-windows, appliances, super-refrigerators, lighting, office equipment and computers, food with low freight miles, fans/pumps and motor systems, and air-conditioning;
- 15 materials productivity case studies such as durable products, electronic books/catalogues, reducing material flows in industry, retrofitting rather than demolishing buildings, and various options for recycling;
- 5 water productivity case studies such as subsurface drip irrigation, water efficiency in manufacturing, residential water efficiency and reducing water usage in cotton production;

- 10 transportation case studies such as car design, railways, light-rail, bus rapid-transit systems, videoconferencing and email to avoid travel, and car sharing.

Part 1 of this new book, *Factor Five*, builds on from these insights to demonstrate that after 15 years there is now real potential to cost-effectively achieve 80 per cent, or fivefold, improvements in resource productivity across most of the major sectors of the economy – that is buildings, industry, agriculture and transport (and further presents a number of supporting online Sector Studies, in the pulp and paper, information, and food and hospitality sectors). This new publication is not designed to replace but to complement the original work and we recommend that readers first read *Factor Four*.[1] Thus, taken together, these two books show how at least 75–80 per cent resource productivity improvements can be made throughout most sectors of the economy. *Factor Five* deliberately focuses on the sectors that are responsible for most of the global energy, water and materials usage, and greenhouse gas emissions. Part I provides a guide to inform efforts to technically achieve significant resource productivity improvements cost effectively. Part II then outlines many years of experience by Ernst von Weizsäcker in 'Making it Happen', and covers topics such as the effectiveness of regulations related to the environment, the use of economic instruments, dealing with the rebound dilemma, and presents his position on long-term ecological tax reform, in light of the need to balance private and public goods. The book is then concluded by Ernst commenting on the concept of '*sufficiency*' and how this will play a role in the future of our global society.

Even though it sounds obvious, the first place to start is in asking the right questions before beginning a design, rather than assuming the answers from the last time, as this has been shown to lead to significant resource productivity improvements, cost reductions, and superior performance and outcomes. This process is often undertaken as part of a facilitated scoping or design charrette or workshop that involves the design and project teams. The process often starts with raising the question of '*what is the required service or product, and how else can this same service or product be provided with less environmental impact?*' Asking such a question typically leads to different or new design options being selected that can dramatically change the outcome of the design but still provide the same service. As the Sector Studies in this book show, there are now a range of profitable options for meeting society's needs and providing products and services that have a significantly reduced environmental impact than previous solutions. As Head of Engineering Practice for the Institution of Engineers Australia, Martin Dwyer explained when reflecting on the work in the book *Whole System Design*, 'Systems thinking and asking the right questions opens up far more design options and solutions than we first think. And some of those solutions bring the breakthrough improvements that go far beyond the incremental'.[2]

For instance, when considering the need to meet with clients and partners, a number of companies now use videoconferencing to reduce the use of air travel; or when considering how to light a building, more and more designers are using natural light, light shelves and advanced lamps to reduce the use of energy-intensive lights; or when considering the need for cooking equipment, a number of restaurants are now installing super-insulated equipment to reduce the generation of heat that air-conditioners are generally employed to overcome. On a larger scale, when considering how to provide the building industry with cement, innovative companies are now making geopolymers to replace the energy-intensive Portland cement. Furthermore, power utilities are now investigating options to meet growing demand with energy efficiency measures in a way that provides real financial rewards to both the utility and the customer. By asking the right questions at the start of the design process, or in the beginning stages of a retrofit design, the nature of the essential design outcomes can be clarified along with the required energy and resource inputs. This will then allow the consideration of alternative ways of achieving the required outcomes, or even ways to reduce the need for it. For example, a car manufacturer may ask what service its product provides – essentially the answer is *mobility*, but it also enables the creation of significant amounts of greenhouse gas and other pollution. Hence the company can ask itself, 'is there another way to provide mobility and reduce the environmental pressure?' As Chapter 5 will outline, this can be done through both the redesign of cars and in reducing the need to use them. For example, by increasing the use of public transport options or by shifting freight carriage to lower-impact modes – with both options requiring vehicles to be designed and maintained – a potential new market is created for the forward-thinking car companies of today (much like the steam railway engine companies that shifted into making cars in the mid 20th century).

The basic premise is that fundamentally people do not want barrels of oil or cars, kilowatt-hours or coal-fired power stations, electrons or incandescent light bulbs, or steel tins and aluminium cans. Rather, people are interested in the services that these products provide, such as mobility, energy, lighting and a container in which to store food and drink. Rather than continuing the previous mindset for the delivery of such services, a holistic approach to design opens the door to considering a new and expanding range of exciting options. Hence, if designed appropriately, the same energy, lighting and container services can be provided by renewable energy, energy-efficient light globes and natural light, and cans made from recycled metals, many of which can be recycled endlessly. In each case the consumer would be unaware of the change behind the scenes as the service they require is delivered; however, the resulting reductions in energy demand, greenhouse gas emissions and pressures on the environment could be significant. Along with such changes behind the scenes to the design of products and services, consumers can of course make choices to reduce resource consumption and the associated environmental pressures. For example, ask yourself how else can you get to work other than using your car? For instance, if getting to work by train was faster, cheaper and more reliable, would you take the train? We suggest that most would say 'yes', but most would also say that the current form of public transport available to them was neither faster nor more reliable than taking their car. However, if the system is designed appropriately, as it is in a number of cities,[3] public transport can provide a very competitive alternative, as well as significantly reducing the energy consumption, and greenhouse gas emissions per passenger.

The Sector Studies chosen for Part I of this book feature sectors of the economy that focus on fundamental human needs, namely: the need for shelter and places to work and play (design of buildings and the manufacture of steel and cement); the need for food and water (agricultural practices and operations); and mobility/trade of goods and services (transportation). At a fundamental level, many of these services can be made significantly more resource productive, reducing their resource consumption and associated environmental impacts – as well as their use being able to be reduced and substituted by lower-impact options, and even eliminated through lifestyle choices and a focus on sufficiency, as expanded in Chapter 11. Humankind has been researching, innovating and experimenting with better ways to meet these needs for thousands of years. Yet, as each of the Sector Studies will show, it is still possible to achieve Factor Five, or 80 per cent, resource productivity improvements, starting with asking the *right questions*.

Each of the Sector Studies seeks to cover a number of critical questions relevant to most sectors, including the following '*right questions*':

- Is the current method of delivering the product or service the only way to do so? (*Often the first thought when answering this question is 'yes'; however, further investigation in most sectors leads to a range of alternatives – from system upgrades, such as energy-efficient motors in an industrial application, to completely new processes, such as shifting to a process to predominantly use scrap metal rather than processing primary resources to make steel.*)
- If it is the only way, what are the major areas of energy, water and materials usage? What options are available to reduce the need for such inputs? What alternatives are available to provide these inputs that have lower environmental pressures? (*The search for such alternative options and inputs can be driven by a requirement to reduce environmental impacts, but also as part of a strategy to improve competitive advantage by reducing input costs, which are inevitably set to increase in the future as availability and impact are factored in.*)
- If it is not the only way, what alternatives can be used to profitably deliver the product or service with less resource intensity and environmental pressure? (*For instance, in Chapter 3 we show that geopolymers can be used to create cement with at least 80 per cent less energy intensity, while eliminating the significant process emissions of greenhouse gases associated with Portland cement.*)

Once the initial questions as to the best way to meet the design requirement have been answered the conceived system needs to be benchmarked against best practice in order to understand the potential for performance. For instance, if a state-of-the-art subsurface deprivation drip irrigation system (as presented in Chapter 4) has been selected (rather than the typical flood irrigation system) the designers need to study applications of such designs in order to understand the potential of the system and to investigate the operating parameters. However, in many cases the new design concept will be part of an emerging wave of innovation as explained in the Introduction and hence there may be little precedent to provide a benchmark. Further, even if there are established examples of the new design, such processes and methodologies are unlikely to be incorporated into university or professional development courses. In this case modelling based on the theoretical performance, and calibrated by the current best practice, can be used to guide the expectations of the design. As the International Energy Agency (IEA) reported in 2006:

> *The energy intensity of most industrial processes is at least 50% higher than the theoretical minimum determined by the laws of thermodynamics. Many processes have very low energy efficiency and average energy use is much higher than the best available technology would permit.*[4]

Although designing projects that are outside the realm of the well-established solutions is challenging, it can offer significant rewards, especially as the requirement to reduce environmental pressures is only set to increase in the future. Leading Australian whole system designer, Adjunct Professor Alan Pears, states that:

> *I have used benchmarking and modelling as part of a whole system design approach to improve resource efficiency of products and industrial processes often by a Factor of 2 or better. An exciting consequence of applying a whole system design approach is the drastically reduced need for end-of-pipe treatment, both in the local area and potentially in the wider air, soil and waterways.*

It is also important to consider ways to increase the flexibility of the design outcome to help improve the utility of the design at the end of its life.[5] Opportunities include: designing buildings so that when they are dismantled materials can be re-used; designing manufactured products and transportation vehicles to maximize recyclability; and designing systems that can be used with a variety of renewable energy options. For instance, Chapter 5 shows that it is possible to significantly improve the fuel efficiency of cars, which then opens up new renewable energy and fuel options. General Motors' new plug-in hybrid concept car, the *Voltec*, is designed so that the car can run on petrol, bio-fuels or hydrogen, ensuring that the car design can take advantage of whichever fuel mixtures dominate the market in the future.

A whole system approach to resource productivity

Before presenting the in-depth Sector Studies it is important that we address a critical barrier to the achievement of Factor Five improvements in resource productivity – namely the fact that the designers, engineers, architects and technicians of today are not versed in taking a whole system approach to design. Astute readers of *Factor Four* would have realized that for many of the case studies outlined, the large resource efficiency gains were actually achieved because the whole system was considered in the design. However, even so, many energy, water and materials efficiency projects have only dealt with specific elements, say of a heating, ventilation and air-conditioning (HVAC) system in a building, an industrial sub-process, or a particular part of a vehicle or product, rather than considering the wider system. In many ways this is why such projects have failed to capture the full resource productivity opportunities, and hence given a false appreciation of their potential. This is due to the fact that in the past many of the savings captured from efficiency initiatives have been smaller than what would have been theoretically possible if the team of designers had worked together to consider the whole system. Such a process was actually quite common among Victorian engineers in the 19th century, when engineers and designers were trained across multiple disciplines and could more easily take an integrated approach. According to Rocky Mountain Institute, which through the work of Amory Lovins is reviving the art of whole system design, 'Whole-systems thinking is a process through which the interconnections between systems are actively considered, and solutions are sought that address multiple problems at the same time.'[6]

In the influential book, *Natural Capitalism*, Lovins and his colleagues explain that although many of today's solutions are designed to produce an optimized design, they actually produce sub-optimal solutions for three main reasons: 1) components are optimized in isolation from other components; 2) optimization typically considers single rather than multiple benefits; and 3) the optimal sequence of design steps is not usually considered.[7] *Natural Capitalism* continued to say that:[8]

> At the heart of this chapter, and, for that matter, the entire book, is the thesis that 90–95 per cent reductions in material and energy are possible in developed nations without diminishing the quantity or quality of the services that people want. Sometimes such a large saving can come from a single conceptual or technological leap… More often, however, it comes from systematically combining a series of successive savings. Often the savings come in different parts of the value chain that stretches from the extraction of a raw resource, through every intermediate step of

processing and transportation, to the final delivery of the service (and even beyond to the ultimate recovery of leftover energy and materials). The secret to achieving large savings in such a chain of successive steps is to multiply the savings together, capturing the magic of compounding arithmetic. For example, if a process has ten steps, and you can save 20 per cent in each step without interfering with the others, then you will be left using only 11 per cent of what you started with – an 89 per cent saving overall.

Building on from this and other leading work, the 2008 book, *Whole System Design: An Integrated Approach to Sustainable Engineering*,[9] by our team from The Natural Edge Project (and dedicated in part to the work of Amory Lovins), outlined a series of elements of a whole system design approach intended to assist in achieving significant improvements in resource productivity. The whole system design elements combine and present many years of experience and expertise from leaders such as Amory Lovins, Alan Pears, Ernst von Weizsäcker, Bill McDonough, Michael Braungart, Ben Blanchard, Michael Porter, John Todd and Janis Birkeland, to present a series of critical considerations for the design process, namely:

- Ask the right questions to ensure the need or service is met.
- Benchmark against the optimal system.
- Design and optimize the whole system.
- Account for all measurable impacts.
- Design and optimize subsystems in the right sequence.
- Design and optimize subsystems to achieve compounding resource savings.
- Review the system for potential improvements.
- Model the system.
- Track technology innovation.
- Design to create future options.

The book then compares such considerations to that of the standard design approach before presenting five detailed worked examples that demonstrate how a traditional design is undertaken, and then compares this to a whole system design – a format suggested by Amory Lovins. The purpose of *Factor Five*, however, is not to present a design process or methodology (as in *Whole System Design*) but rather, as with *Factor Four*, to provide designers who are seeking to undertake such a process with a clear and rigorous demonstration of the potential to significantly improve resource productivity across all the major energy- and water-intensive sectors (Part I). And to then provide policy makers, business leaders and decision makers with an understanding of the role of government in supporting such designs (Part II). The actual form of the design process is up to the design team, but careful consideration of the above elements is likely to achieve greater resource productivity savings. However, considering and successfully applying such elements to either the design of a specific product or process (such as the design of the process for producing steel) or to an overall project (such as a building or cement plant), is a subjective, iterative and complex process.

The reality that the engineering and design professions now face is that even with significant advances being made by designers across the world, the development of the academic field of whole system design, and sustainable engineering more broadly, is in its early stages. Contributions such as those outlined in *Whole System Design* are a start, demonstrating the significant potential of this methodology to help identify and achieve large resource productivity improvements, but significant progress needs to be made in the field before it is the norm, and this presents a problem. Our amazing Earth can't wait for many years of trial and error, research and debate, publications and papers, before we take steps to reduce environmental pressures on a meaningful scale. Hence we need to learn from what is being done in all four corners of the world and rapidly bring this knowledge together as a base for significant resource productivity improvements in the coming decades. As explained in *Whole System Design*:

> *Innovations in materials science, such as insulation, lighting, super-windows, and distributed energy options, are creating new ways to re-optimise the design of buildings. Innovation is so rapid that six months is now a long time in the world of technology. For example, consider the average refrigerator, for which most of the energy losses relate to heat transfer. The latest innovations in materials science in Europe have created a new insulation material that will allow refrigerators to consume 50 per cent less energy. Other examples include innovations in composite fibres that make it possible to design substantially lighter cars, and innovations in light metals, which can now be used in all forms of transportation, from aircraft to trains to cars, and allow resource efficiency improvements throughout the whole system.*[10]

This is particularly important because, as *Natural Capitalism* points out, 'by the time the design for most human artefacts are completed but before they have actually been built, about 80–90 per cent of their life-cycle economic and ecological costs have already been made inevitable'.[11] And as the design life of new infrastructure, buildings, vehicles and appliances can be decades long, decisions made by designers today can dictate much of humanity's environmental pressure for both this and the next generation – which is unfortunately the window of time in which significant progress in reducing environmental pressures must be achieved. However, bringing such a breadth of information together is only possible through the selection of an organizing framework, and thus in the development of the Sector Studies we have chosen to structure the material around the '*Industrial Mitigation Matrix*', as presented in the IPCC 4th Assessment.[12] From the mitigation matrix we have selected eight key strategies:[13]

1   energy efficiency;
2   fuel switching;
3   heat and power recovery;
4   renewable energy;
5   feedstock change;
6   product change;
7   materials efficiency;
8   reducing non-CO_2 greenhouse gases.

As preparation before moving into the Sector Studies we briefly discuss each of the strategies above to provide the context and background to support their use as a structure for the studies. In short, Strategy 1 is focused on reducing the requirement for energy through a range of means, with Strategies 2 to and 5 exploring options for alternatives to carbon-intensive forms of energy. For instance: *fuel switching* refers to transitioning operations away from fossil fuels to other forms of fuel; *heat and power recovery* allows energy expended onsite to create waste heat to be captured to offset input energy requirements; *renewable energy* options are then used to meet the reduced demand; and *feedstock change* is focused on changing the inputs to various processes, particularly through the use of recycled materials, to reduce resource intensity. Strategy 6 then focuses on options to change the product, goods or services, to reduce resource intensity. Strategy 7 is applied mostly to water throughout the Sector Studies; however, a range of other materials productivity opportunities are presented. Strategy 8 looks to reduce non-CO_2 greenhouse gas emissions, some of which have staggeringly larger global warming potentials and atmospheric lifetimes than CO_2, with rapidly growing emissions levels.

As the studies will show, depending on the particular sector different strategies will be of differing importance and will yield differing levels of improvements in resource productivity. However, the message from each sector is that it is an innovative combination of a range of strategies applied to the whole system at the early stages of design or retrofit that yields the 80 per cent improvements touted to be possible in this book. Hence rather than a stepwise roadmap to the various options for improving resource productivity, the Sector Studies provide an exciting and creative menu of options to be explored, integrated and tailored to each design or planning outcome.

1   Energy efficiency

Energy efficiency opportunities are a significant focus of this book because they are the quickest, easiest and most cost-effective way to start to improve energy productivity and reduce greenhouse gas emissions. As *Factor Four* pointed out, 'In the mid 1970s, the engineering–economics debate centred on whether cost effective energy savings = 10–30 per cent. In the mid 1980s, the range of the debate had shifted to 50–80 per cent. In the 1990s, some of the best practitioners were achieving 90–99 per cent in some situations'.[14] Hence, energy efficiency has already achieved remarkable results – with the 'US Alliance to

Save Energy' further estimating that the US economy would be at least 50 per cent more energy intensive today without the efficiency gains that business and households have made since the early 1970s. A *Time Magazine* article sums it up well stating that, 'This energy saving since 1973, is more than the energy the US gets from oil, twice what the US gets from coal or natural gas and six times what the US get from nuclear plants'.[15]

This book brings together new evidence to show that despite these improvements in energy efficiency, significant opportunities for further improvements remain. For instance, the American Council for an Energy-Efficient Economy argues that energy efficiency could add US$100 billion to the US economy, at a cost of US$30 billion.[16] Furthermore, sustainable design expert Amory Lovins argues that today's best techniques could save the US half of its oil and gas and three-quarters of its electricity.[17] This would allow the US to all but halt imports of oil, deliver consumers and businesses lower utility bills, and significantly reduce the nation's greenhouse gas emissions. A 2008 McKinsey study found that a global effort to boost efficiency with existing technologies could have 'spectacular results', eliminating more than 50 per cent of world energy demand by 2020. McKinsey's results from across all major sectors shows that the economics of investing in energy productivity provides an excellent return on investment, 'With an average internal rate of return of 17 percent, such investments would generate energy savings ramping up to $900 billion annually by 2020'.[18]

In the following Sector Studies we provide evidence to support designers, planners, policy makers and citizens to assist efforts to ensure that significant improvements in energy efficiency can be achieved across the major sectors. These Sector Studies are relevant for all OECD countries, but are even more relevant and critical for developing countries, as the McKinsey Global Institute explains:[19]

> *By choosing more energy-efficient cars and appliances, improving insulation in buildings, and selecting lower-energy-consuming lighting and production technologies, developing countries could cut their annual energy demand growth by more than half from 3.4 to 1.4 percent over the next 12 years... boosting energy productivity could reduce fuel imports, lower the expense of building new energy-supply infrastructure, lessen their vulnerabilities to future energy shocks, and lock in lower energy demand for generations to come. Using solely existing technologies that pay for themselves in future energy savings, consumers and businesses in developing countries could secure savings of an estimated $600 billion a year by 2020... Because of their positive returns, energy-efficiency investments are the cheapest way to meet growing energy needs.*

Hence this book focuses on a systemic approach to reducing the demand for energy in an effort not only to create less pollution, but also to reduce the demand that needs to be met, and hence improve the viability of new energy generation options (however, a detailed presentation of such options is not within the scope of this book). Such a focus on the end-users, be it buildings, industry, agriculture, food production and retail or transportation, can yield much larger reductions in resource consumption and pollution than first thought. As Amory Lovins explains, designers can create a 'cascade of resource savings' all the way back to the power plant, dam or original source of materials:

> *An engineer looks at an industrial pipe system and sees a series of compounding energy losses: the motor that drives the pump wastes a certain amount of electricity converting it to torque, the pump and coupling have their own inefficiencies, and the pipe, valves, and fittings all have inherent frictions. So the engineer sizes the motor to overcome all these losses and deliver the required flow. But by starting downstream – at the pipe instead of the pump – turns these losses into compounding savings. Make the pipe more efficient … and you reduce the cumulative energy requirements of every step upstream. You can then work back upstream, making each part smaller, simpler, and cheaper, saving not only energy but also capital costs. And every unit of friction saved in the pipe saves about nine units of fuel and pollution at the power station.*
>
> Amory Lovins, Rocky Mountain Institute, 1997[20]

2 Fuel switching

According to the Intergovernmental Panel on Climate Change (IPCC), 'While some industrial processes require specific fuels … many industries use fuel for steam generation and/or process heat, with the choice of fuel being determined by cost, fuel availability and environmental regulations'.[21] Hence the flexibility exists to explore a range of options to use alternative sources of fuel in order to generate steam and heat onsite, such as combusting natural gas, biomass and waste materials. Such efforts are separate to those focused on capturing waste heat onsite, as outlined in Strategy 3, or on renewable sources of energy, as outlined in Strategy 4. By delivering fuels onsite to generate heat and steam a focus on fuel switching can significantly reduce the generation of greenhouse gases from fossil fuel-based central power stations, both by reducing the actual demand and reducing the transmission losses associated with meeting the demand through a large distribution system of 'poles and wires'. Also, when considering the use of petroleum for transport-related activities, switching transportation fuels from petrol to appropriate bio-fuels, or electric options, has the potential to achieve significant reductions in transport-related emissions – for instance, a Canadian company now claims to be producing second generation bio-fuels that achieve Factor Five to 10 reductions in greenhouse gas emissions.[22]

As Chapter 3 will show, industries such as steel and cement are utilizing waste materials, such as landfill methane,[23] tyres, plastics, used oils and solvents, and sewage sludge as alternative combustion fuels. Although many of these may be originally derived from fossil fuels, the IPCC 4th Assessment Report highlights the fact that diverting them from their original destination of landfill or the incinerator (without energy recovery) results in an overall reduction in greenhouse gas emissions. The IPCC specifically highlights the steel industry as having capitalized on the availability of waste plastics to provide an alternative source of both fuel and a feedstock for the steel-making process.[24] By pre-treating plastic waste and burning it in coke ovens and blast furnaces,[25] the steel industry has been able to reduce emissions associated with the incineration and landfilling of those wastes, along with reducing their own demand for fossil fuels. The report points out that research has shown that the use of this technology in Japan has seen a reduction in the steel industry's net emissions by $0.6MtCO_2e/yr$.[26]

Also, various energy-intensive industries produce low-grade fuels as a by-product of the production process, such as in the manufacture of paper products. The pulp and paper sector is starting to utilize various processes and technologies to improve conversion efficiency of biomass by-products for power generation. For instance, the spent liquor produced from delignifying wood chips (called black liquor) is normally burned in a large recovery boiler to recover the chemicals used in the delignification process. However, as the online Sector Study on the 'Pulp and Paper Sector' explains, technologies such as 'gasification' allow not only the efficient use of black liquor, but also of other biomass fuels such as bark and felling rests to generate a synthesis gas that after cleaning is combusted with a high conversion efficiency (see www.factorfiveonline.info).

3 Heat and power recovery

It may be surprising to many to read that for every unit of energy used by consumers, it is estimated that two units are lost or wasted, mostly as heat, without delivering any usable service. According to the 2000 UNDP World Energy Assessment this is due to substantial losses in two main areas, firstly, in generating the energy and making it available to consumers (up to 26 per cent), and, secondly, losses in end-use processes and appliances (up to 37 per cent), mostly as low- and medium-temperature heat.[27] Considering that the 2005 world primary energy demand in all forms was almost 11.5 billion tons of oil equivalent, according to the International Energy Agency (IEA),[28] the loss of 63 per cent of this energy then equates to significant losses both in the availability of the resources used to create energy, and in the costs associated, not to mention the unnecessary greenhouse gas emissions created. Hence when considering options to reduce the global demand for energy, relieving the pressure it now places on the environment and reducing the demand for finite resources, these two areas must form a key part of the strategy, particularly as efforts in both areas can be complementary. For instance, a focus on the recovery of heat loss by capturing waste process heat – such as from exhaust gases from cement kilns and steel furnaces, by recovering the heat from refrigeration or cooking equipment in bakeries, restaurants and supermarkets, or through the process of cooling milk on diary farms – can produce electricity and heat for use onsite. Hence this not only reduces energy lost as heat, but also reduces the demand from the electricity grid, and thus reduces the associated losses in generating and distributing energy.

Currently, in much of the world, energy, in the form of electricity, is created in centralized power plants and is then distributed through an extensive network of 'poles and wires'. In such a system, large steam turbines, gas turbines or internal combustion engines are used to drive electrical generators to produce electricity, which is then distributed perhaps hundreds of kilometres to consumers. This process of electricity generation has a fuel conversion efficiency of 25–45 per cent[29] (*meaning as much as 75 per cent of the energy in the fuel can be lost when converted into electricity by the process*), while long-distance transmission and distribution is about 91 per cent efficient (*meaning that up to 9 per cent of the energy produced is then lost along the way*).[30] Hence before the electricity gets to the user much of the energy contained in the original fuel has been lost, with this being one of the main arguments for both end-use energy efficiency and decentralized, and preferably renewable, energy generation. Also, most industrial applications have a need for heat, and currently the majority of heat demand is met using boilers, where electricity is consumed or fossil fuels are combusted to heat water to produce steam. Boilers can be found on just about every industrial site (there is almost always a process that needs heat), and in many buildings in colder climates. On an average industrial site, boilers can account for 20–60 per cent of energy costs.[31] Boilers have fuel conversion efficiencies of 70–80 per cent or more[32] when correctly operated and maintained, while their steam distribution channels can have widely varied efficiencies, but at most are about 90 per cent.

An alternative to centrally generated electricity being delivered through extensive grid networks to provide industry with power, and the use of separate onsite boilers to provide heat, is the now well-known option of a 'combined heat and power' system, also known as 'co-generation' or simply 'co-gen'. It is not within the scope of this book to provide a detailed overview of co-gen systems (refer to TNEP's Energy Transformed program[33]); however, the following explanation provides a basis to support the application of heat and power recovery options in the various Sector Studies. Typically, in a co-gen system, both electricity and heat (hot air, hot water or steam) are generated at or near the point of use, usually with a gas turbine, and incorporating waste heat, from either the co-gen process itself or from other sources such as onsite process exhaust gases, being captured and re-used, and can result in significant overall fuel savings compared to centralized systems and separate boilers, as shown in Figure 1.1 below. Capturing and using the waste heat through co-generation significantly lifts the overall fuel conversion efficiency compared to separate electricity and heat generation.[34]

In the co-gen system, electricity is generated using either conventional turbine or engine technologies that are typically fuelled by natural gas or diesel (or increasingly by biomass by-products such as in the pulp and paper industry), or emerging low-carbon options such as micro-turbines,[35] fuel cells[36] and a range of renewable options. These processes are then coupled with a heat recovery process, such as a heat exchanger where heat is recovered typically through the creation of steam by using hot process exhaust gases or liquids from equipment cooling processes. A typical example of such a combination, referred to as a 'combined cycle configuration', involves using a gas turbine to produce power, then using the output gases to produce steam in a boiler, and finally using the steam in a steam turbine to produce more power. An example of an innovative emerging combination involves using a high-temperature fuel cell, fuelled by hydrogen-rich fuels, to produce electricity,[37] then using the hot output gases (that contain unspent fuel) for combustion in a gas turbine, with a recuperator used to further recover the heat in the turbine output gas, which is then channelled back into the fuel cell and turbine.[38] There are several types of fuel cells, each with their unique performance features, with solid-oxide or molten-carbonate fuel cells being the most suitable for co-generation applications due to their high temperature output. While the capital costs of fuel cells are still high, it is expected that cost will drop due to improved fabrication techniques, mass production and, in the case of the proton-exchange-membrane option, reduced catalysts loads.[39] Fuel cell co-generation systems are already being used in applications across a variety of sectors, including in

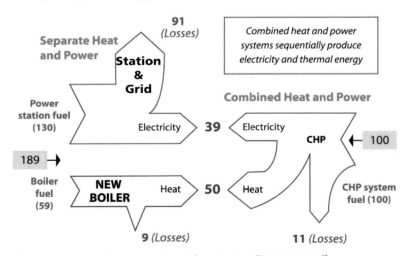

Source: Based on estimates by the American Council for an Energy-Efficient Economy[40]

Figure 1.1 *Combined heat and power systems*

residential buildings, hospitals, hotels, office buildings, breweries, refineries, shopping malls and car showrooms.[41] Additional (typically smaller-scale) heat recovery options also include: recovering heat through the use of absorption chillers that cool hot fluids and gases by piping them through a tank of refrigerant, which is often water vapour in a vacuum that readily absorbs heat; or by using desiccant dehumidifiers that remove heat from air prior to its cooling in air-conditioners – with both options viable for heating or cooling, or electricity generation in commercial buildings, manufacturing operations and a range of other applications.

Co-generation systems are ideal for industrial sites, as both electricity and heat are often in constant and relatively regular demand, which minimizes the ramping up and down of the system. Consequently, the majority of the potential for co-gen applications – of which total current electricity capacity accounts for just over 8 per cent of global demand – are found in the energy-intensive industry sectors like steel, aluminium, cement, paper and printing, chemicals, food and petroleum refining.[42] Denmark leads the world in co-gen adoption, meeting 52 per cent of its electricity needs in 2003 and supplying heat mainly to district heating systems. Across the globe, the US leads in total co-gen capacity installed, with 85GW in 2003, representing less than 10 per cent of total demand.[43] Most future growth will be in large systems (20MW or larger) in the industries that already rely on combined heat and power. However, small systems (4MW or less) represent a largely untapped market.[44] Making strong progress elsewhere, Germany sourced almost 13 per cent of its electricity from co-generation in 2005, with the government projecting that this share could reach 57 per cent.[45]

As with most technologies, energy efficiency improvements in co-generation systems are achievable in most applications by increasing the fuel conversion efficiency of the electricity generation part of the system to its cost-effective limit – particularly as, in the vast majority of practical applications, electricity demand, rather than heat demand, largely determines the system's capacity and operation requirements. Furthermore, options such as using a supplementary boiler to make up for a shortfall in heat supply is about twice as efficient as using a supplementary electricity generation system to make up for a shortfall in electricity supply.

4 Renewable energy

Companies and organizations around the world are finding that by implementing strategies such as the three above, they can significantly reduce the amount of electricity they need to source from the grid, and hence the option to meet this demand with renewable sources becomes more affordable. This has seen thousands of companies, organizations and households committing to becoming net climate neutral by reducing their energy usage (Strategies 1–3) and then purchasing renewable energy or carbon offsets to achieve the coveted neutral status. This, along with significant commitments from governments around the world, has seen renewable energy become the fastest growing source of energy in the world. It is not within the scope of this book to cover the various forms of renewable energy and show how they can feasibly supply both peak and base load power; for a summary of such arguments see the TNEP Energy Transformed program.[46]

Decentralized renewable energy sources of electricity – such as renewables (including solar, wind, wave, tidal, geothermal and hydro), or co-generation (the combined production of electricity and heat as outlined above) – surpassed nuclear power in global generating capacity back in 2002, and represent rapidly growing lucrative markets. Another factor driving increased sales in renewable energy is the reduction of costs over the last 30 years. As the sector grows, its economy of scale and increasing levels of experience has helped to bring down the manufacturing costs of different renewable energy technologies, as shown in Figure 1.2.

Renewable distributed energy now accounts for a quarter of the installed capacity of California, a third of Sweden's energy, half of Norway's and three-quarters of Iceland's, and since 2003 Denmark has generated 20 per cent of its electricity from wind power. A range of significant studies suggests strongly that there is no technological impediment to shifting to at least 80 per cent renewable energy.[48] It is widely acknowledged that renewable energy is very effective at contributing electricity to the grid to meet peak electricity load demand, as renewable energy sources like co-generation, wind and solar produce the greatest amount of energy around the peak load times of the day. However, many still have serious concerns over whether renewable energy can supply base load electricity – that is, the electricity needed around the clock,

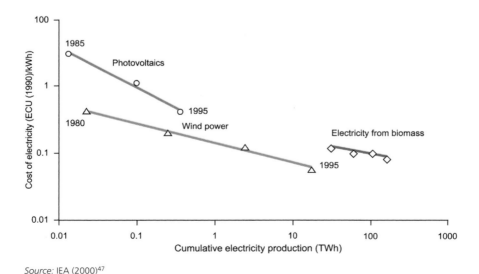

Source: IEA (2000)[47]

Figure 1.2 *IEA learning curve showing how innovation, economies of scale and experience lowers costs over time*

especially by heavy industry and for essential overnight services such as street lighting and hospitals. Concerns exist because it is believed that solar and wind are too intermittent to provide such power and are vulnerable to whether or not the sun shines or the wind blows.

However, renewable energy flows from wind and solar are much less intermittent than many assume, and turbines and panels can be located around the country and connected via the grid to avoid local low winds or cloudy conditions. Furthermore, advances in energy storage technologies are allowing solar photovoltaic (PV) and concentrated solar thermal systems to provide base load electricity. Studies show that if there are sufficiently geographically diverse sources of solar, wind, tidal and wave energy then this smooths out the intermittency, so that these renewable energy sources can effectively provide base load electricity. Graham Sinden from the Environmental Change Institute at Oxford University has investigated the potential contribution from several different renewable electricity sources in the UK.[49] Using data spanning many years on wind levels, sunshine, waves and tides at multiple sites, Sinden concludes that the major proportion of UK electricity could be generated from renewable energy sources, with wind from dispersed sites being the biggest source. As Sinden says:

> *By mixing between sites and mixing technologies, you can markedly reduce the variability of electricity supplied by renewables. And if you plan the right mix, renewable and intermittent technologies can even be made to match real-time electricity demand patterns. This reduces the need for backup, and makes renewables a serious alternative to conventional power sources.*[50]

Additionally, many forms of renewable energy are not dependent on day-to-day weather variations and hence can provide electricity just as reliably as coal or nuclear – such as hydro, tidal and biomass.[51]

Geothermal energy is another promising energy source and, even though it is not renewable, it is abundant and can be harnessed with minimal environmental impacts for hundreds, if not thousands, of years. Geothermal power supplies base load power with the same load profiles as coal and nuclear, and is being used by more and more countries. In 2001 the electric energy produced from geothermal resources represented 75 per cent of Iceland's total electricity generated, 27 per cent in the Philippines, 12.4 per cent in Kenya, 11.4 per cent in Costa Rica, and 4.3 per cent in El Salvador.[52] Research by Dr P. N. Chopra while previously at ANU (and other respected research bodies) shows that Australia has one of the largest hot dry rock (HDR) geothermal reserves in the world, which could provide electricity to meet all of Australia's needs for thousands of years. Figure 1.3 shows the estimated temperature at a depth of 5km across Australia. HDR geothermal energy relies on existing technologies and engineering processes such as drilling and hydraulic fracturing – techniques established by the oil and gas industry.[53]

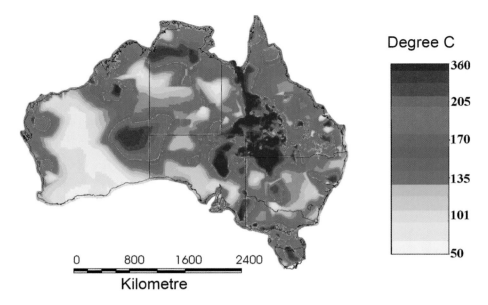

Degree C

360

205

170

135

101

50

0   800   1600   2400
Kilometre

Source: Dr P. N. Chopra, Dept of Earth and Marine Sciences, Australian National University

Figure 1.3 *Australia's geothermal resources*

5 Feedstock change (materials/energy nexus)

In assessing the IPCC '*Industry Mitigation Matrix*' for its potential to be used as a structure for the Sector Studies, we found that there was the potential for overlap between the issues and options covered here in Strategy 5 'feedstock change' and Strategy 7 'materials efficiency'. We decided for the purpose of the Sector Studies to focus the feedstock change parts mainly on materials recycling to demonstrate the benefits to energy and water intensity by both offsetting the use of virgin resources, and altering the production process.[54] For instance, in Chapter 3, we show that the use of scrap steel as a feedstock, referred to as secondary steel production, can lead to 60–70 per cent lower energy consumption if used in a particular type of steel-making process,[55] as shown by WorldSteel in Figure 1.4.

Using recycled feedstock in the production of a range of other metals and materials also yields large energy savings, with estimates including: aluminium (95 per cent),[58] copper (70[59]–85[60] per cent), lead (60[61]–80[62] per cent), zinc (60[63]–75[64] per cent), magnesium (95 per cent[65]), paper (64 per cent[66]), plastics (80[67]–88[68] per cent) and glass (68 per cent[69]). The main reason for such reductions in energy intensity arises from avoiding the energy required in the extraction and processing of raw materials and their transportation to production facilities when compared to the collection and processing of scrap and waste products. However, for some of these materials, the use of recycled materials also enables the production process itself to use less energy. For

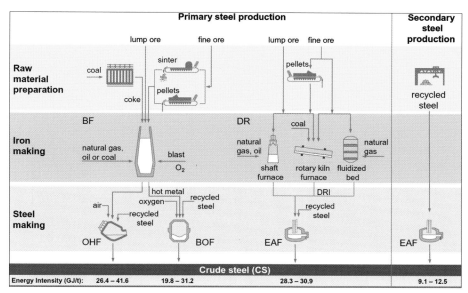

Source: WorldSteel[57]

Figure 1.4 *Energy intensity of various steel-making processes:*
(1) BOF process (58 per cent of global operations[56]);
(2) EAF/DRI process (7 per cent); and (3) EAF process (27 per cent)

example, while the formation of aluminium from alumina requires temperatures in the order of 900°C, scrap aluminium re-melts at around 660°C[70] – hence reducing the required temperature by just under a third. This, together with the fact that aluminium cans are easily separated from municipal trash, means that, according to the International Aluminium Institute, recycled aluminium now constitutes 33 per cent of world supply and is forecast to rise to 40 per cent by 2025.[71] In theory, many materials can be recycled endlessly, such as metals and glass; however, some have limitations, such as paper products only being able to be cycled around five times – although this still delivers a Factor Five materials improvement. Hence using recycled materials to replace raw material feedstock can lead to large energy and materials savings along with considerable cost reductions. However, there is significant room for improvement in recycling rates in various countries – for instance, while Germany and Finland have 80–90 per cent glass recycling rates, the US rates are just below 30 per cent,[72] and while nine members of the European Union have reached 80 per cent plastic recycling levels, at least half of the member countries still recover less than 30 per cent of the plastic they use.[73] A range of government actions is now increasing these levels, particularly in electrical equipment, with the Japanese government requiring that air-conditioners, tube television sets, refrigerators and washing machines are recycled and, as of December 2008, adding liquid-crystal/plasma television sets and clothing dryers to the list.

Other than cycling the actual atoms of a material such as steel or glass from scrap to product to scrap, waste products can also be substituted for raw inputs in a number of processes, such as the use of fly ash in the cement industry (Chapter 3). In the case of Portland cement production, a range of cementitious materials can be added to the mix to reduce the overall energy intensity of the process, such as blast furnace slag, fly ash from coal-fired power stations, or natural clays (all referred to as pozzolans).[74] However, their use is limited by their effect on the properties of the cement and currently constitutes as low as 7 per cent of Portland cement.[75] Alternative cements, such as geopolymers, presented in Chapter 3, not only significantly reduce the energy intensity of cement-making,[76] but also incorporate higher levels of these additives[77] – hence assisting in dealing with a major waste issue from fly ash and slag production.[78]

Recycled feedstock can also save water as the online Sector Study of the 'pulp and paper sector' shows, demonstrating that improvements in the production of paper results in water savings of up to 50 per cent.[79] Hence in many cases using recycled materials as feedstock enables energy, materials and water productivity improvements simultaneously, while also reducing pollution. For example, recycling glass reduces energy usage by 70 per cent and water usage by 50 per cent, and also reduces the related air pollution by 20 per cent and water pollution by 50 per cent.[80]

Furthermore, opportunities for feedstock recycling are not just limited to the actual resources, such as paper, steel or glass, but can be captured at the component level, referred to as 'remanufacturing'. As the online Sector Study on the 'information and communications sector' shows, whole products, including complex products with many parts, can be remanufactured or recycled into as-new products. This is demonstrated specifically in the section of the online Sector Study where Su Benn and Dexter Dunphy highlight the leading progress of Fuji Xerox, which began recycling its products in 1990, and then progressed to being able to remanufacture them some three years later.[81] The company's aim is to maximize remanufacturing and minimize the need for recycling – a strategy that enables the high value of end-of-life products to be retained. Fuji Xerox's best practice Eco-Manufacturing Centre in Australia is where most of the company's remanufacturing takes place. Key among the Centre's technological advances and newly developed workforce culture are its relationships with its supply chain and waste management networks for minimizing emissions and eliminating waste, and its relationships with its client networks for the supply and return of used parts. The online case study shows how the Centre now meets 80 per cent of Fuji Xerox Australia's spare parts requirements,[82] saving the company A$11.3 million over the cost of purchasing alternative parts in 2007–2008 and preventing hundreds of thousands of parts being sent to landfill each year. The company aims to increase the portion of products remanufactured, from its already impressive current level of 76 per cent, through design for disassembly. Fuji Xerox's integrated recycling centre in Thailand is where most of the company's end-of-life recycling of products in the Asia Pacific takes place. Together, the Australian and Thai Centres remanufacture or recycle 99 per cent of products in the Asia Pacific region.[83] Fuji Xerox plans to establish the Australian Centre as a regional centre and roll out its principles globally.

Finally, the online Sector Study on the 'food and hospitality sector' shows that food processors and retailers, such as bakeries, restaurants and supermarkets, can also reduce energy use by sourcing organic ingredients from sustainably managed farms, preferably locally. Organically farmed ingredients generally have a lower embodied energy than conventionally farmed ingredients because the use of energy-intensive artificial fertilizers and chemicals is avoided. In 2002, the Food and Agricultural Organization (FAO) found that, 'Organic agriculture performs better than conventional agriculture on a per hectare scale, both with respect to direct energy consumption (fuel and oil) and indirect consumption (synthetic fertilizers and pesticides), with high efficiency of energy use'.[84] Bakeries, restaurants and supermarket chains can also source local ingredients and thus reduce the food miles involved in transporting food from the '*paddock to the plate*'.

6 Product change

In most cases, activities and strategies to increase resource productivity are focused on well-established processes and seek to enhance the process with new technologies, improved practices and state-of-the-art management and monitoring. However, in a few cases the best way to reduce the resource consumption of a product is to completely change its form. The standout example, as highlighted in the IPCC 4th Assessment, is that of geopolymer cement. As we will show in Chapter 3, geopolymer cements based on aluminosilicate (rather than the calcium-silicate used in Portland cement) provide the same or better service, are cost effective, and use over 80 per cent less energy to create.[85] Hence this new product delivers a competitive low-carbon alternative to the standard product, and is gaining interest – as Australian-based geopolymer company Zeobond is finding.

It is now widely recognized that the energy and water used by products over their lifetime is usually significantly greater than the energy and water used to manufacture the product – hence not only does the process to create the products need to be improved, so too does the energy and water intensity of the product's operation over its useful life. Leading manufacturers of most products are now re-examining their product lines to try to achieve radically more resource-efficient products. In May 2005, General Electric announced 'Eco-magination' a major new business project to make all of GE's products more energy efficient. Eco-magination is expected to double revenues from more energy-efficient products to approximately US\$20 billion by 2010. This initiative will see GE double its research and development in eco-friendly products to US\$1.5 billion by 2010 and improve energy efficiency by 30 per cent by 2012. In May 2006, the company reported revenues of US\$10.1

billion from its energy-efficient and environmentally advanced products and services, up from US$6.2 billion in 2004, with orders nearly doubling to US$17 billion.

Japan was one of the first governments to help its national corporations gain increased global market share through phasing in higher energy efficiency standards. Japanese Energy Conservation Laws enacted in 1979 set demanding energy efficiency standards for refrigerators, air-conditioners and automobiles, stimulating product improvements that strengthened the international position of Japanese firms in these markets.[86] This shows how leadership by governments on energy efficiency in the manufacture of products can influence the direction of manufacturing all over the world, and suggests that those nations who lead in smart regulation of the energy efficiency of products and appliances will help position their firms well for rapidly growing global markets. Indeed, one of the first acts of President Obama was to increase the minimum fuel standard for all US vehicles by 2016. More recently we have even seen countries phasing out, by law, inefficient products such as incandescent lighting,[87] particularly Australia, California and New Jersey in the US, and the EU, who have now all passed laws to phase out inefficient lighting.[88]

7 Improving material efficiency (energy/water nexus)

As pointed out previously, there is potential for overlap between the issues and options covered in Strategy 5 'feedstock change' and Strategy 7 'materials efficiency'. Hence under materials efficiency we have focused mainly on demonstrating the opportunities for significant improvements in the efficiency and productivity of the use of water. We have done this for three main reasons:

1   To be in line with *Factor Four* as it included water efficiency opportunities in its section on materials efficiency.
2   To demonstrate that a focus on water efficiency can both reduce demand for dwindling water supplies, and also deliver significant energy demand reductions. For example, reducing the amount of water that needs to be heated in the home or business, also reduces the amount of water that the utilities need to store, treat and distribute to customers, and hence energy demand reductions can be achieved, as highlighted in the IPCC 2008 report on *Climate Change and Water*.[89]
3   To demonstrate the viability of a focus on the energy/water productivity nexus in the hope of inspiring these exciting new solutions to be incorporated into the next IPCC Mitigation Working Group report in 2012.

Most of the Sector Studies demonstrate examples of an energy/water nexus and provide evidence to support further exploration in this new area of innovation; for example:

*   *Residential buildings*: Chapter 2 shows that reducing the consumption of hot water in the home not only reduces the amount of energy used to heat water, but also reduces the energy used by water utilities to provide water

to the home. Heating water through the traditional electric storage hot water system is responsible for a significant proportion of energy consumption in residential homes around the world – representing 9 per cent in the EU-15 in 2004,[90] 11 per cent in the US in 2005[91] and 27 per cent in China in 2000.[92] Hence as the provision of hot water is energy intensive, there is a strong nexus between water and energy savings in the residential sector.[93]

- *Commercial buildings*: Chapter 2 shows that many commercial and public buildings, and in particular supermarkets and data centres, require large water-intensive cooling systems. Most of these systems are based on the use of cooling towers that remove heat from the building, essentially by evaporating water. There are estimated to be over one million cooling towers in operation globally on the top of commercial buildings,[94] and they can account for up to 40 per cent of a building's water use. Thus activities that seek to reduce the energy used for the air-conditioning of a building (through a variety of measures presented in the Sector Studies), also delivers direct reductions in the consumption of water. In addition, as Chapter 2 will show, new hybrid dry air/water cooling systems exist, which do not use water cooling towers. These hybrid systems use around 80 per cent less water while still being almost as energy efficient as water-cooled systems with cooling towers.[95]

- *Industry*: Chapter 3 shows that reconsidering a range of current industrial processes to improve energy productivity (namely in the steel, cement, and pulp and paper industries), can also lead to a reduction in water consumption. Chapter 3 features studies by Liedtke and Merton[96] which show that 'electric arc steel furnaces (EAF) use … 70 per cent less energy and one-eighth of the water … compared with traditional basic-oxygen blast furnace (BOF) steel plants.'[97] Also, it shows that shifting from 'wet' to 'dry' Portland cement-making processes not only improves energy productivity but reduces water usage. Finally, the online Sector Study on the 'pulp and paper sector' shows how the sector can both save energy and reduce water consumption through recycling paper. For example, as well as requiring less energy to process virgin pulp, recycling newspaper for instance, according to Planet Ark, 'uses approximately 20% less water'.[98]

- *Agriculture*: There is a strong energy/water nexus in the agricultural sector as the sector uses the majority of society's water, and irrigation practices can be energy intensive. Hence Chapter 4 first outlines a number of opportunities for direct energy productivity improvements available on the farm, and then focuses the majority of the study on reducing water consumption. The study cautions that even though forms of irrigation such as drip irrigation reduce water consumption significantly, shifting away from 'trench and flood' irrigation to 'pipe and pump'-based forms involves more energy usage. Hence it is important to look holistically at ways to improve the water productivity in agriculture through complementary methods, such as: appropriate selection of crop species and livestock choices that are suited to the local climatic and geological conditions; optimizing the effect of irrigation through irrigation scheduling and advanced irrigation methods; rainwater harvesting; the treatment and use of urban stormwater and wastewater in peri-urban agriculture; and utilizing renewable energy sources to power irrigation pumps.

- *Dairy industry*: Following on from the focus in Chapter 4 on agriculture, and in order to demonstrate the relevance of Factor Five to a range of typical operations, the online Sector Study on the 'food and hospitality sector' presents a 'paddock to plate' journey beginning with dairy farms. Dairy farms are heavy consumers of water.[99] Hence the online Sector Study includes a study that features a number of novel approaches, such as the option of dewatering milk on the dairy farm to produce milk solid products for market, and retaining the water for use on the farm. This is a viable option as firstly milk from cows is made of up of 95 per cent water, and secondly the milk processing industry mostly uses milk solids – in Australia only 20 per cent of the milk originally produced from dairies ends up on the shelves of supermarkets as milk.[100] This also helps farms reduce energy usage by significantly reducing the volume of milk they need to store, by law, at 4°C until it is transferred to a dairy processor, and reduces the transport energy by reducing the volume, hence a strong energy/water nexus.

- *Supermarkets*: Moving through the 'paddock to plate' journey, the online Sector Study then presents supermarkets. Modern supermarkets have much of the same water demands as typical retail outlets, such as sanitary fixtures, amenities and landscape irrigation, but they also use large quantities of water – up to half of their total consumption[101] – to cool the condenser units for the supermarket's extensive refrigeration systems.[102] Also, large supermarkets tend to use cooling towers and thus also consume water as part of their cooling systems. Hence again there is a strong energy/water nexus for this sector because the opportunity exists to simultaneously reduce a significant amount of energy and water usage from reducing both the amount of refrigeration and space cooling required.

- *Restaurants and fast food outlets*: As the last stop on the 'paddock to plate' journey, the online Sector Study presents the energy/water nexus opportunities in the restaurant sector, showing for instance that the choice of cooking equipment can halve energy and water usage. Also, the choice to serve customers filtered water from the tap instead of bottled water results in 2000 times less energy being used per bottle.[103] Making these changes can both save restaurants significant costs while also making a difference globally.[104]

To conclude, in the following Sector Studies under IPCC Strategy 5 'feedstock change' and IPCC Strategy 7 'materials efficiency' we show that there are significant energy/materials and energy/water nexus opportunities in many sectors of the economy. These nexus opportunities are important because they do not simply reduce energy costs but also deliver profitable reductions in water consumption, materials consumption, waste production, and wastewater treatment costs, thus yielding multiple cost benefits. As such these nexus opportunities are set to form an important part of strategies to improve energy productivity, and thus each Sector Study provides an overview of such opportunities.

8 Reducing non-CO_2 greenhouse gases

Carbon dioxide (CO_2) is only one of a number of significant greenhouse gases identified by the IPCC and recognized by the Kyoto Protocol. The main six greenhouse gases (other than water vapour) are carbon dioxide (CO_2), methane (CH_4), nitrous oxide (N_2O), hydrofluorocarbons (HFC), perfluoro-carbons (PFC) and sulphur hexafluoride (SF_6). The last three types of gases mentioned are all man-made, meaning that they didn't exist in the environment before industrialization. All six greenhouse gases are proposed to be included in the EU Emissions Trading Scheme and the proposed scheme for other countries like Australia. This is significant for business because the non-CO_2 greenhouse gases have significantly higher global warming potentials and atmospheric lifetimes than CO_2 (See Table 1.1).[105]

As Table 1.1 shows, non-CO_2 greenhouse gases constituted 25 per cent of global greenhouse gas emissions in 2004, hence any emissions reduction strategy needs to pay serious attention to these gases. However, to date the non-CO_2 greenhouse gases have not received the attention they deserve. This was well illustrated by the fact that it was only in June 2008 that scientists for the first time warned that there is a significant risk of increased global warming from the use of nitrogen trifluoride (NF_3) in flat screen TVs.[106] Almost half of the televisions sold around the globe so far in 2008 have been plasma or LCD TVs. But this could be coming at a huge environmental cost. This gas, NF_3, is estimated to have a global warming potential 17,000 times more powerful than carbon dioxide, but NF_3 was not included in the Kyoto protocol in 1997 as it was only produced in tiny amounts at that time. Levels of this gas in the atmosphere have not been measured, but scientists are calling for such measurements to take place and for this gas to be included in any future emissions-cutting agreement. Fortunately, some companies are finding alternatives to NF_3. Linde Electronics, a gas and chemical company, has created a process that allows pure fluorine to be used in place of NF_3, and Toshiba–Matsushita Display and LG have converted much of their manufacturing operations to fluorine instead of NF_3. This example highlights the need for decision makers and designers to better understand and proactively reduce the use and emissions of non-CO_2 greenhouse gases.

Often industry strategies to reduce non-CO_2 greenhouse gas emissions also improve energy productivity. For instance, many industries use commercial refrigeration. Historically, most commercial refrigeration used refrigerants that had very high global warming potentials. Replacing these refrigerants with alternatives that have far lower global warming potentials, also achieves energy savings. As the IPCC's 4th Assessment stated:

Table 1.1 *Kyoto Protocol recognized greenhouse gases*

Symbol	Name	Common sources	Atmospheric lifetime (years)[*]	Global warming potential	Global emissions in 2004[**]
CO_2	Carbon dioxide	Fossil fuel combustion (61%), forest clearing, organic decay, and peat thaw (14%).	50–200	1	75%
CH_4	Methane	Landfills, production and distribution of natural gas and petroleum, fermentation from the digestive system of livestock, rice cultivation, fossil fuel combustion, etc.	12	21×	15%
N_2O	Nitrous oxide	Fossil fuel combustion, fertilizers, nylon production, manure, etc.	150	310×	7.6%
HFCs	Hydrofluoro-carbons	Refrigeration gases, aluminium smelting, semiconductor manufacturing, etc.	264	Up to 11,700×	2.4%
PFCs	Perfluorocarbons	Aluminium production, semiconductor industry, etc.	10,000	Up to 9200×	
SF_6	Sulphur hexafluoride	Electrical transmission and distribution systems, circuit breakers, magnesium production, etc.	3200	Up to 23,900×	

Note: [*] Standard Industry Classification
Source: Energy Information Administration (1998); IPCC (2001)[107] ([**] Percentages from IPCC (2007)[108])

Alternative system design involves for example, applying direct systems using alternative refrigerants, better containment, distributed systems, indirect systems or cascade systems. It was found that up to 60% lower greenhouse gas emissions values can be obtained by using alternative refrigerants.[109]

A snapshot of the Sector Studies

The buildings sector

The first in-depth Sector Study, presented in Chapter 2, focuses on how to achieve a fivefold resource productivity improvement (energy and water) in the residential and commercial building sector. The building sector is presented first because it is responsible for close to 40 per cent of global greenhouse gas emissions, 12 per cent of global water use, and involves significant material flows.[110] Also, an investigation into Factor Five in the building sector will inform the following Sector Studies, both online and in the book, that involve the use of buildings and facilities, allowing the Sector Studies to focus on specific aspects of the particular sector rather than cover building-related advances again. *Factor Four* was one of the first books to argue that 75 per cent or better improvements in energy productivity could be made in building design, and 12 years later, the IPCC 4th Assessment's Mitigation Working Group findings concurred.[111] This Sector Study integrates exciting innovations in appliances, office equipment, water heaters, HVAC units and refrigeration systems to show how Factor Five improvements can be achieved in the building sector. This Sector Study builds on from the original book, *Factor Four*, bringing together new evidence from around the world to support the argument that significantly more energy- and water-efficient buildings can be built cost effectively,[112] using examples such as:

- the work of Bill Browning and Joseph Romm, in 1998, in reviewing four building retrofits and four new buildings in the US to investigate the economic returns of energy productivity improvements;
- the work of the Germany-based Passive House Institute, led by Dr Wolfgang Feist, who has pioneered the design of ultra-efficient buildings to achieve Factor Five improvements;
- the 2009 work of the US National Renewable Energy Laboratories (NREL) in their review of the potential to achieve net carbon neutral commercial buildings through a combination of energy efficiency and utilizing solar PV panels.

Hence these and a range of other findings inform the Sector Study, and show that through a whole system approach to the design or retrofitting of buildings, energy productivity can be increased by Factor Five. Each of the Sector Studies presented in this book emphasize the fact that it is essential that sustainable design options are considered at the very onset of a new or retrofit project. In order to deliver an integrated design the designers need to be able to develop their own scope of work in concert with other designers and the overall project vision, hence design charrettes are often used. The method of a siloed and reductionist scope-specific approach, used in much of project design today, does not accommodate integrated design solutions and prevents significant opportunities from being realized. Furthermore, infrastructure lasts from 30 to 100 years once it is designed and it is very costly to change its performance in the future when requirements, for say reducing energy consumption, become more stringent or costly.

To conclude, investing in Factor Five improvements in the buildings sector is essential to reducing a significant component of global greenhouse gas emissions while also boosting productivity and economic activity. Hence this is why, in Chapter 2, we first consider these exciting Factor Five opportunities for the building sector.

The heavy industry sector

Following the buildings sector we focus in Chapter 3 on answering the question of how to achieve at least 80 per cent resource productivity improvements in heavy industries. This sector is chosen next because, according to the

IPCC, by 2004 industry's share of global primary energy use was 37 per cent.[113] Since there are many potential sectors to focus on, and we do not have space to cover them all,[114] we have chosen to include in this book two of the most energy- and water-intensive industries, namely the steel and cement industries, and then have developed online Sector Studies on the pulp and paper industry, and the IT and communications sector, available on the book's online companion at **www.factorfiveonline.info**. These sectors collectively use close to half of all energy used by industry, and produce significant material flows globally. Also, they are chosen because these industries are currently growing rapidly in developing and emerging economies as their products underpin much of the world's growth. Since 1970, the global annual production of steel and cement has grown swiftly, with the steel industry increasing production by 84 per cent,[115] and the cement industry by 271 per cent.[116] Hence, as countries like China and India rapidly develop it is imperative that the innovation and ingenuity presented in this chapter, and the online studies, are used in the design of new plants and the retrofitting of existing plants, to avoid the unwanted greenhouse gas emissions and resource consumption levels that the current methods are set to deliver.

The sectors covered in this chapter are designed to build on from and complement those presented in *Factor Four*, by providing a greater level of detail, and incorporating advances since the time of publication. *Factor Four* showed for instance, that significant advances could be made if industry used the latest innovations, such as utilizing electric arc furnaces in the steel industry. In this chapter we will update this case study to show that up to 92 per cent (greater than Factor 10) energy productivity improvements can be made in the steel industry by: switching to state-of-the-art electric arc furnace systems that process recycled steel; adopting leading practices such as net shape casting; and implementing options such as energy monitoring, management systems for energy recovery and distribution between processes, and preventative maintenance. We will then outline how the cement industry can become significantly more energy productive, and even eliminate greenhouse gas emissions, through the use of geopolymers that are now well proven in practice. We then, in an online Sector Study, outline how the pulp and paper industry not only has the potential to achieve 80 per cent, Factor Five, reductions in energy consumption, but that it could then become a net positive electricity generator from renewable low-carbon energy sources. We also outline in an online Sector Study, with the help of Klaus Fichter, how to achieve Factor Five in digital processing by data centres, now the fastest growing user of electricity in the world.[117]

Readers will find that many of the options presented are also relevant to a range of other sectors and involve advances to a number of commonly used technologies and processes to deliver significant savings, as was the case in *Factor Four*.

The agricultural sector

So far the Sector Studies have been dominated with energy-intensive industry sectors like the buildings, steel and cement industries, and have demonstrated how energy consumption, and hence greenhouse gas emissions, can be reduced by 80 per cent. In Chapter 4 we turn our attention to the agricultural sector, and while we first cover a range of options to improve energy productivity, the main focus is on reducing water consumption, as the sector represents an average of 70 per cent of global water withdrawals. This chapter then underpins the online Sector Study on 'the food and hospitality sector', and allows for the majority of the online study to focus on energy productivity improvements, assuming that the water-saving practices in Chapter 4 are applied to the range of agricultural practices that support the sector. The agricultural sector is critical to enabling food security, providing employment and reducing poverty, and contributes significantly to the GDP of many countries. However, the sector is one of the most vulnerable to climate change, leading to reduced agricultural yields in OECD countries, particularly southern Europe, the US and Australia, according to the *Stern Review*.[118] The situation becomes more complicated by the fact that even without the effects of climate change, significant reductions in water consumption will be needed, as in West Asia, the Indo-Gangetic Plain in South Asia, the North China Plain and the High Plains in North America freshwater extraction rates exceed natural water replenishment rates.

Hence, as with the energy-intensive industries around the world, climate change and resource availability will mean that the agricultural sector is going to be operating under very different conditions in the coming decades – conditions that for the sector will see a growing imperative to reduce energy consumption, combined with reduced availability of water, increased cost of water, and growing uncertainty around climate and weather conditions. These changing conditions will call for a substantial re-evaluation of farming and agricultural practices and this chapter shows how Factor Five improvements to energy and water productivity can be achieved using proven methods and technologies. This is especially important as, in the case of energy, reducing consumption through the range of options presented in this chapter allows for a range of onsite renewable energy options to become viable and provides a lucrative side business for farmers. However, as stated, the main focus of this chapter is water, and to demonstrate that the agricultural sector can achieve Factor Five improvements in water productivity. This is achieved by building on from the case study of 'subsurface drip irrigation' presented in *Factor Four*, and using a whole system approach to implement a number of complementary water productivity strategies.[119] Chapter 4 will also show how the following six strategies, applied holistically, can yield Factor Five water productivity improvements with the lowest net energy usage:

1 appropriate selection of crop species;
2 efficient irrigation technologies;
3 irrigation scheduling;

4   advanced irrigation management;
5   rainwater harvesting;
6   treating and re-using urban wastewater for peri-urban agriculture.

The food and hospitality sector (Online Sector Study)

Before ingredients like wheat, corn, rice, meat and vegetables even make it to the bakery, restaurant or processing facility they have already consumed significant amounts of energy and water. Chapter 4 outlines ways to dramatically reduce this consumption on the farm, and in the online Sector Study on the 'food and hospitality sector' we follow a trail from 'paddock to plate' and demonstrate how significant reductions in energy and water consumption can be achieved. As it is impossible to cover every sub-sector in the food and hospitality industry, in this chapter we follow a progression from the farm (focusing on dairy farms), to food processors (focusing on bakeries), then to supermarkets, restaurants and finally fast food outlets, a supply chain that in the US for instance is responsible for 20 per cent of all fossil fuels used in the country.[120] These sectors have been chosen because they currently have high and growing levels of energy and water consumption; for example:

- *Dairy farms*: Within the farming sector, dairy farms are a relatively large user of both energy and water, using up to 25 per cent of allocated surface irrigation water in Australia.[121] According to Australian energy efficiency expert Geoff Andrews there is the, 'potential for the least efficient dairy farms to achieve up to 80 per cent energy productivity improvements for their direct energy use on site.'[122] Furthermore, according to Australian farming energy expert Glenn MacMillan:

  > For starters a dairy farm has the ability to source all of its energy needs from its waste streams. This is possible through conversion of waste manure from cows, waste woody biomass, wind, and sunlight into energy... With today's technologies this is feasible which allows a move away from reliance on a central electricity grid'.[123]

  This part of the Sector Study will first explore these exciting energy opportunities, and then highlight how the water-saving strategies in Chapter 4 can be applied to dairy farms.

- *Bakeries*: Baking bread is one of the oldest industries, yet today, still most bakeries are highly energy and water inefficient. But as a number of leading bakeries are now finding, there is a range of cost-effective opportunities to significantly improve this performance. This will not only lead to reduced utility bills, but reduce heat lost into the kitchen, an important factor as bakeries struggle to attract and retain staff due to the hot working conditions. As Australian energy efficiency expert Alan Pears reflects, 'Many bakeries are actually paying to overheat their staff as well as baking their bread'.[124] Hence, in this part of the Sector Study we focus mainly on ways to improve energy productivity and reduce heat loss, and show how this is being done in leading bakeries, while also briefly pointing out opportunities to save water.

- *Supermarkets*: Supermarkets are most likely the poorest energy-performing buildings and operations in the economy. From paying little attention to building design to reduce energy consumption, including lighting (as presented in Chapter 2), to leaving large refrigerated containers and freezers open all day for ease of access by customers and then having to heat the space for customer comfort. Hence a large proportion of the overall energy consumption, some 52 per cent,[125] is then used to keep open refrigerators and freezers cooled, while the cool air is adding significant load to the building's space heating requirements. This part of the Sector Study will show the numerous ways in which supermarkets can significantly reduce cooling and heating loads while still remaining customer friendly. Options such as fitting refrigerated display cabinets with doors or covers can reduce their energy consumption by an estimated 68 per cent, while preserving food more effectively and providing a host of other benefits.[126] Furthermore, some 16 per cent of the total energy demand comes from lighting,[127] which can easily be reduced through better building design and the use of ultra-efficient lighting, which also emits far less heat. Once refrigeration, lighting and space heating have been optimized, supermarkets are especially well suited to capture onsite energy generation options to provide their energy needs. A number of supermarket chains are now experimenting with harnessing the large roof space for solar energy, selecting locations within parking lots for wind micro-turbines (such as the UK supermarket chain, Tesco, that is set to power 20 of its stores with wind power[128]), and fuel cells (such as US organic supermarket chain, Whole Foods Market, set to power an entire store using combined cycle co-generation using fuel cells and heat recovery[129]).
- *Restaurants and fast food outlets*: The direct and indirect environmental impacts from restaurants and their supply chains are more significant than you would first think. According to a Canadian study, people's expenditure in restaurants is one of the largest indirect ways that we cause greenhouse gas emissions outside our home.[130] US citizens spend roughly half their food budget at restaurants,[131] and most restaurants directly use at least 15 times the energy of a typical household per person.[132] Few appreciate that globally there are now over eight million restaurants and 300,000 hotels, many of which have restaurants.[133] Hence this Sector Study finishes by focusing on the numerous ways to significantly improve the resource productivity of restaurants and fast food outlets. It features four leading restaurants that have implemented resource efficiency, green purchasing, onsite waste and water recycling, and renewable energy initiatives. All four restaurants are highly profitable and successful businesses, illustrating yet again that pursuing advanced resource productivity helps rather than harms financial performance.

The transportation sector

Transportation is chosen as the final Sector Study as it accounts for 22 per cent of global energy use,[134] and 23 per cent of world energy-related CO_2 emissions.[135] Also the rate of growth of energy usage and greenhouse gas emissions in this sector is among the highest of all the energy end-user sectors, and although advances in energy productivity have been made, these advances, particularly in cars and aeroplanes,[136] are not keeping pace with the exponential growth of these modes. This Sector Study considers a range of methods, including vehicle design, alternative modes and personal behaviour, to show how Factor Five improvements can be achieved in both passenger and freight transport – the majority of transportation. The chapter focuses on three main strategies, namely:

- *Strategy One*: the improved design of the major passenger and freight transportation vehicles (including cars, trucks, rail, shipping and aeroplanes);
- *Strategy Two*: a significant shift to lower energy-consuming modes of transportation for both passenger and freight transport (such as shifting from long-haul trucking to rail or coastal shipping);
- *Strategy Three*: a shift in transportation fuels over time to source higher percentages of energy for transportation from renewable energy sources (including electricity and alternative combustion fuels).

Chapter 5 focuses mainly on the first two strategies for both passenger and freight transport to show how Factor Five improvements in energy productivity can be achieved over the coming decades, bringing together a wealth of research to complement the pioneering work of Rocky Mountain Institute in this area.[137]

Such a dramatic reduction in energy requirements then allows a range of low-carbon and renewable energy options to power vehicles to become viable. Furthermore, demand on fossil fuels can be reduced through modal shifts in passenger transport and freight to rail, as rail can be powered by renewably generated low- or no-carbon electricity. There are now studies that demonstrate that through innovative design it is technically possible for transport to source all of its energy from renewables by 2050.[138] A focus on the three strategies mentioned above will create multiple benefits for any nation undertaking them. These additional benefits are important to note because they further justify investment in such strategies, including:

- reducing urban air pollution;
- reducing congestion costs;
- improving staff health and performance;
- reducing transportation costs;
- stimulating the economy.

Finally, a major area of concern for many countries is the level of dependence its transportation systems have on oil, especially as experts expect world oil production to peak within the coming decades[139] – with production peaking now in over 60 countries.[140] The IEA predicts that, once the global economy comes out of recession, oil prices will steadily rise to achieve new records, rebounding to more than US$100 a barrel initially, and exceeding US$200 a barrel by 2030, stating that, 'While market imbalances could temporarily cause prices to fall back, it is becoming increasingly apparent that the era of cheap oil is over.'[141] Currently, transportation systems are remarkably dependent on oil, making the world economy vulnerable to recession during extended periods of high oil prices. Since 1965 there have been five peaks of world oil price, all of which were followed by economic recessions of varying degree. The first two oil price hikes led to the two worst recessions in 1973 and 1980. Oil price increases led to a double hit to the economy by causing both rising inflation and also reducing consumer spending. Inflation rose not simply because of rising oil prices but because most economies are so dependent on oil that a rise in oil prices leads to increasing prices of numerous consumer items. The peaking of world oil production and corresponding higher oil prices could affect efforts to improve energy productivity and reduce greenhouse gas emissions from transportation positively or negatively:

- The negative risk is that since economies are so dependent on oil, many nations may feel that they have to turn rapidly to 'proven technologies', such as coal conversion oil and oil shales production, before geo-sequestration technologies are commercial, leading to higher greenhouse gas emissions.[142]
- The positive effect of peaking of world oil production is that ongoing and rising oil prices will convince business and government and citizens to invest seriously in better urban design and planning, public transport and cycling, rail, shipping and broadband infrastructure,[143] as explained in the Sector Study.

In the development of the transport sector study, we demonstrate how, assuming the second effect, transport systems can cost effectively and rapidly reduce oil dependency and greenhouse gas emissions, and achieve Factor Five energy productivity improvements.

Notes

1   von Weizsäcker et al (1997).
2   Stasinopoulos et al (2008).
3   See Newman and Kenworthy (1999).
4   International Energy Agency (IEA) (2006d).
5   Stasinopoulos et al (2008).
6   Rocky Mountain Institute, Wilson et al (1998).
7   Hawken et al (1999) Chp 6.
8   Hawken et al (1999).

9   Stasinopoulos et al (2008).

10   Stasinopoulos et al (2008).

11   Hawken et al (1999) Chp 6.

12   IPCC (2007) Chp 7, p454, Table 7.5.

13   The IPCC also lists carbon capture and sequestration as strategy 9, but given that this is not commercially available we do not focus on it in this book.

14   von Weizsäcker et al (1997) pxxvii.

15   Grunwald (2008) citing Lovins (2004).

16   American Council for an Energy-Efficient Economy (2004).

17   Lovins (2004).

18   McKinsey Global Institute (2007).

19   McKinsey Global Institute (2008).

20   Lovins (2005). See extended bibliography at www.rmi.org, accessed 23 January 2008.

21   IPCC (2007) p458.

22   Iogen (undated) 'Lowers GHGs, Increases Energy Security, Helps Build Rural Economies', www.iogen.ca/key_messages/overview/m3_reduce_ghg.html, accessed 8 April 2009.

23   US EPA (2005) 'Landfill Methane Outreach Program (LMOP)', www.epa.gov/lmop, accessed 31 May 2008.

24   Ziebek and Stanek (2001) cited in IPCC (2007) p458.

25   Okuwaki (2004) cited in IPCC (2007) p458.

26   Okazaki et al (2004) cited in IPCC (2007).

27   UNDP/WEC/UNDESA (2000) p175.

28   International Energy Agency (IEA) (2007b) p74.

29   Onsite SYCOM Energy Corporation (1999) p4; Educogen (2001) p8; Gans et al (2007) p1; Sustainability Victoria (2006) 'Fact-Sheets: Cogeneration', www.seav.sustainability.vic.gov.au/manufacturing/sustainable_manufacturing/resource.asp?action=show_resource&resourcetype=2&resourceid=23, accessed 17 April 2008; United Nations Environment Programme (undated) 'Energy Technology Fact Sheet: Cogeneration', www.uneptie.org/energy/information/publications/factsheets/pdf/cogeneration.pdf, accessed 17 April 2008.

30   Lovins (2005).

31   Australian Greenhouse Office (2005c).

32   Elliott and Spurr (1999) p1; Hooper, F. A. and Gillette, R. D. (undated) 'How Efficient is Your Steam Distribution System?', www.swopnet.com/engr/stm/steam_dist_eff.html, accessed 4 June 2009.

33   For a detailed summary see Lecture 3.3 of Smith et al (2007).

34   Onsite SYCOM Energy Corporation (1999) p4; Educogen (2001) p8; Gans et al (2007) p1; Sustainability Victoria (2006) 'Fact Sheets: Cogeneration', www.seav.sustainability.vic.gov.au/manufacturing/sustainable_manufacturing/resource.asp?action=show_resource&resourcetype=2&resourceid=23, accessed 17 April 2008; United Nations Environment Programme (undated) 'Energy Technology Fact Sheet: Cogeneration', www.uneptie.org/energy/information/publications/factsheets/pdf/cogeneration.pdf, accessed 17 April 2007.

35   Onsite SYCOM Energy Corporation (1999) p5; Educogen (2001) p47; Martin et al (2000) cited in Worrell et al (2004) p46; United Nations Environment Programme (undated) 'Energy Technology Fact Sheet: Cogeneration', www.cogen.org/Downloadables/Publications/Fact_Sheet_CHP.pdf, accessed 17 April 2008.

36   Onsite SYCOM Energy Corporation (1999) p5; Educogen (2001) p47; California Energy Commission (2003); Martin et al (2000) cited in Worrell et al (2004) p46; United Nations Environment Programme (undated) 'Energy Technology Fact Sheet: Cogeneration', www.cogen.org/Downloadables/Publications/ Fact_Sheet_CHP.pdf, accessed 17 April 2008.

37   Onsite SYCOM Energy Corporation (1999) pp23–27.

38   Onsite SYCOM Energy Corporation (1999) pp14–16, 18–19, 27.

39   Martin et al (2000) cited in Worrell et al (2004) p46.

40   Elliott and Spurr (1999).

41   Lidderdale et al (2006).

42   Chiu (2009).

43   ibid.

44   Onsite SYCOM Energy Corporation (2000) p34.

45   Chiu (2009).

46   Smith et al (2007) Lectures 7.2 and 7.3.

47   International Energy Agency (IEA) (2000) p21.

48   Groscurth et al (1998); Kruska et al (2003); Lovins et al (2004); Mathiesen et al (2008).

49   Sinden (2005).

50   Tickell (2005).

51   International Energy Agency (IEA) (2002).

52   Dickson and Fanelli (2004).

53   Smith et al (2007) Lecture 7.3.

54   British Metals Recycling Association (BMRA) (undated) 'What is Metals Recycling?', www.recyclemetals.org/whatis.php, accessed 23 August 2008; Bureau of International Recycling (BIR) (undated) 'About Recycling', www.bir.org/aboutrecycling/index.asp, accessed 23 August 2008; Eurometrec (undated) 'Position Papers', www.eurometrec.org/, accessed 23 August 2008.

55   De Beer et al (1998).

56   World Steel Association (2008) 'Fact Sheet: Steel and Energy', www.worldsteel.org/pictures/programfiles/Fact%20sheet_Energy.pdf, accessed 20 March 2009.

57   OECD (2003a).

58   British Metals Recycling Association (BMRA) (undated) 'What is Metals Recycling?', www.recyclemetals.org/whatis.php, accessed 23 August 2008; Bureau of International Recycling (BIR) (undated) 'About Recycling', www.bir.org/aboutrecycling/index.asp, accessed 23 August 2008; Eurometrec (undated) 'Position Papers', www.eurometrec.org/, accessed 23 August 2008.

59   Eurometrec (undated) 'Position Papers', www.eurometrec.org/, accessed 23 August 2008.

60   British Metals Recycling Association (BMRA) (undated) 'What is Metals Recycling?', www.recyclemetals.org/whatis.php, accessed 23 August 2008; Bureau of International Recycling (BIR) (undated) 'About Recycling', www.bir.org/aboutrecycling/index.asp, accessed 23 August 2008.

61   British Metals Recycling Association (BMRA) (undated) 'What is Metals Recycling?', www.recyclemetals.org/whatis.php, accessed 23 August 2008.

62   Eurometrec (undated) 'Position Papers', www.eurometrec.org/, accessed 23 August 2008.

63   British Metals Recycling Association (BMRA) (undated) 'What is Metals Recycling?', www.recyclemetals.org/whatis.php, accessed 23 August 2008.

64 Eurometrec (undated) 'Position Papers', www.eurometrec.org/, accessed 23 August 2008.

65 Ditze and Scharf (2008) p7.

66 Bureau of International Recycling (BIR) (undated) 'About Recycling', www.bir.org/aboutrecycling/index.asp, accessed 23 August 2008.

67 ibid.

68 Recoup (2004) 'Recycling Plastic Bottles – The Energy Equation', www.recoup.org/shop/product_documents/33.pdf, accessed 9 June 2009.

69 Ohio Department of Natural Resources (undated) 'Recycling in Ohio: Glass Recycling', www.dnr.state.oh.us/tabid/17878/Default.aspx, accessed 9 June 2009.

70 British Metals Recycling Association (BMRA) (undated) 'What is Metals Recycling?', www.recyclemetals.org/whatis.php, accessed 23 August 2008.

71 IAI (2006); Martcheck (2006).

72 UNEP/GRID-Arendal (2004).

73 European Association of Plastics Recycling and Recovery Organisations (2008).

74 Josa et al (2004).

75 IPCC (2007) see 'Industry', pp1313–1320.

76 Duxson et al (2007).

77 Duxson (2008).

78 Davidovits (2002).

79 Available online at www.factorfiveonline.info.

80 Ohio Government's Division of Recycling and Litter Prevention (undated) 'Recycling in Ohio: Glass Recycling', www.dnr.state.oh.us/tabid/17878/Default.aspx, accessed 9 June 2009.

81 Fuji Xerox Australia (2008) p27.

82 Fuji Xerox Australia (undated) 'Eco Manufacturing: FXA now exports remanufactured parts and components to the Asia Pacific region', www.fujixerox.com.au/about/eco_manufacturing.jsp, accessed 4 April 2009.

83 Fuji Xerox Australia (2008) p27.

84 Scialabba and Hattam (eds) (2002).

85 Net Balance Foundation (2007).

86 Hargroves and Smith (2005).

87 Department of Environment and Water Resources (2007) 'World first! Australia slashes greenhouse gases from inefficient lighting', DEWR Media Release, Australia.

88 *The Associated Press* (2007).

89 Bates et al (2008).

90 International Energy Agency (IEA) (2003); Waide et al (2004) cited in Bertoldi and Atanasiu (2007).

91 EIA (2006) cited in IPCC (2007).

92 Zhou (2007) cited in IPCC (2007).

93 Kenway et al (2008).

94 Harfst (2008).

95 Australian Institute of Refrigeration, Air-Conditioning and Heating (AIRAH) (2003).

96 Liedtke and Merten (1994).

97 ibid.

98 Planet Ark (undated) 'Drought Buster Recycling Tips', http://recyclingweek.planetark.org/recycling-info/tips.cfm, accessed 5 June 2009.

99 Australian Dairy Farmers (2004).

100 Dairy Australia (2007).
101 Alliance for Water Efficiency (2009) 'Supermarket Introduction',
     www.allianceforwaterefficiency.org/Supermarket_Introduction.aspx, accessed
     6 May 2009.
102 ibid.
103 Gleick and Cooley (2009).
104 The International Hotel and Restaurant Association (undated) 'IH&RA Board of
     Directors 2009', www.ih-ra.com/about/leadership/, accessed 22 April 2009.
105 The only exception is methane, which has a global warming potential of 21 times
     CO_2 but an atmospheric lifetime of only ten years compared to 50–200 years for
     CO_2. However, due to CO pollution from cars the average atmospheric lifetime
     of CH_4 has now risen to 12 years.
106 Prather and Hsu (2008).
107 Energy Information Administration (EIA) (1998); IPCC (2001).
108 IPCC (2007) p4.
109 IPCC (2007) see 'Residential and commercial buildings'.
110 OECD (2003b).
111 IPCC (2007).
112 Griffith et al (2007).
113 IPCC (2007) see 'Industry'.
114 For additional sectors see Smith et al (2007).
115 USGS (2005).
116 IPCC (2007) see 'Industry'.
117 McKinsey & Company (2008).
118 IPCC (2007).
119 Gleick (2008).
120 Food and Water Watch (2007).
121 Australian Dairy Farmers (2004).
122 Genesis Now (undated) 'Dairy Energy', www.genesisnow.com.au/html/dairy.htm,
     accessed 16 February 2009.
123 MacMillan (2009).
124 Pears (2008).
125 Australia Food and Grocery Council (2003).
126 Faramarzi et al (2002).
127 Australia Food and Grocery Council (2003).
128 Tesco (2008).
129 Whole Foods Market (2008).
130 Statistics Canada (2008) 'Greenhouse gas emissions – A focus on Canadian
     households', www.statcan.gc.ca/pub/16-002-x/2008004/article/10749-eng.htm,
     accessed 22 April 2009.
131 *Business Wire* (2006).
132 ESource (1999).
133 The International Hotel and Restaurant Association (undated) 'Leadership:
     IH&RA Board of Directors 2009', www.ih-ra.com/about/leadership/, accessed
     22 April 2009.
134 InterAcademy Council (2007) see 2.5 'Transportation Energy Efficiency'.
135 IPCC (2007) see 'Transport and its Infrastructure'.
136 Davidson (2005).
137 Lovins et al (2004) Executive Summary.
138 Lovins et al (2004); Mathiesen et al (2008).
139 Hirsch (2005).

140 Peaking of oil refers to the point when production in any oil well, field or region begins to decline. Typically, this point is reached when between one-third and one-half of the oil in a reserve has been extracted. The decline is the inevitable result of the loss of pressure in the oil reserve and despite the advanced drilling and extraction techniques now in use, it is irreversible once passed.
141 International Energy Agency (IEA) (2008).
142 Hirsch et al (2005).
143 Lovins et al (2004) Executive Summary.

2

The Buildings Sector

The Natural Edge Project

The buildings sector is responsible for close to 40 per cent of global greenhouse gas emissions;[1] hence achieving significant improvements in energy productivity in this sector is a critical component of enabling nations to achieve long-term goals for greenhouse gas stabilization. Also, buildings are responsible for 12 per cent of global water use,[2] hence this chapter, focused mainly on energy, also presents strategies to reduce water requirements in buildings by at least 80 per cent. Water productivity strategies do not simply help reduce demand for potable water, but also yield significant energy savings through the reduced requirement to service a building with potable water.[3]

1 The residential buildings sector

The potential for Factor Five improvements in residential homes resource productivity

An integrated approach to reducing energy consumption

In 1997, the book *Factor Four* presented a number of best practice case studies of the time, such as the Rocky Mountain Institute Headquarters and residential buildings in Davis, California, to show that through design changes and utilizing the latest technologies significant improvements in resource productivity could be achieved in the residential sector. At the time this was a bold claim; ten years on, however, in 2007 the Intergovernmental Panel on Climate Change (IPCC) 4th Assessment's Mitigation Working Group's report had a chapter on residential and commercial buildings which confirmed that not just a Factor 4 improvement could be achieved, but in fact Factor Five improvements in energy productivity can be achieved through a whole systems approach.[4]

Hence we have deliberately chosen to provide appropriate and relevant quotes from this latest IPCC report in this chapter to demonstrate to what extent the arguments made over ten years ago by *Factor Four* are now mainstream. For instance, the main message of *Factor Four*, concerning buildings, was that large energy productivity gains could be made by taking a whole-of-system approach to identifying and implementing energy productivity opportunities. The need for a systems approach also underpins the IPCC's latest chapter on this sector. According to the IPCC:

> *Energy efficiency strategies focused on individual energy-using devices or design features are often limited to incremental improvements. Examining the building as an entire system can lead to entirely different design solutions. This can result in new buildings that use much less energy but are no more expensive than conventional buildings. The systems approach in turn requires an integrated design process, in which the building performance is optimized through an iterative process that involves all members of the design team from the beginning.*[5]

Achieving Factor Five improvements in the residential building sector is important because it will make a significant difference to reducing greenhouse gas emissions, as according to the International Energy Agency residential buildings consume 27.5 per cent of the world's electricity, some 4.3 million GWh (4300 billion kWh),[6] with this consumption covering a range of end-uses such as heating and cooling, heating water, appliances and equipment, indoor lighting and refrigeration. The relative consumption in each of these areas varies from country to country as can be seen in Figure 2.1.

Considering this, and taking an integrated approach suggested by the IPCC, this chapter will focus on the following five areas, systematically assess-

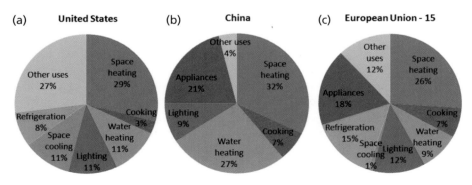

Source: Based on data from (a) EIA (2006),[7] (b) Zhou (2007),[8] and (c) IEA (2003)[9] and Waide et al (2004)[10]

Figure 2.1 *Breakdown of residential sector energy use in the United States in 2005, in China in 2000, and in the EU-15 in 2004*

ing their relative energy demands and investigating a range of possible methods for reducing this demand, namely:

1   space heating and cooling;
2   hot water systems;
3   appliances;
4   indoor lighting;
5   refrigeration.

Progress to reduce energy consumption across these end-uses will become an area of increased activity as governments around the world begin to require improved energy performance from homes as part of national greenhouse reduction strategies. For example, the UK government set the target in late 2008 that all homes built in the UK after 2016 will be 'zero-carbon' homes, as part of its commitment to reduce greenhouse gas emissions by 80 per cent by 2050. As Housing Minister Margaret Beckett stated in a press release in 2008.

> *Climate change is one of the biggest challenges facing the world, and introducing zero carbon homes is an important part of our plans to tackle this… I am absolutely committed to our 2016 target, and this demanding goal is already spurring action here and abroad.*[11]

Such a bold move by the government has created significant interest in developments that already meet these criteria, with the Beddington Zero Energy Development (also known as BedZED[12]) one of the early standouts. According to George Monbiot, in his recent book *Heat*, 'BedZED uses just 10 per cent of the energy that ordinary buildings of the same size would need for heating'.[13]

When considering energy consumption in the home, one may ask, if we can source our energy from renewable sources, then why do we need to be efficient? Among the many reasons is simply 'economics'. In this chapter we have chosen to focus on reducing energy consumption based on the fact that in order to cost-effectively transition the energy sector away from fossil fuel-based energy generation and towards renewable decentralized options, the demand for energy needs to be significantly reduced. Once the demand is reduced, potentially by as much as 60–80 per cent, the task to meet this demand using renewable options will be much more feasible in the short term, and thus will assist in delivering the significant reductions in greenhouse gas emissions required globally. Evidence from around the world presented in the following Sector Study confirms that significant reductions in residential energy requirements can be achieved, and further, that the designs do not need to be 'stark' or 'space aged' and can look very 'normal', as many leading examples now show, such as in Figure 2.2.

These and a growing number of residential developments are now employing a number of energy-saving methods which, when combined, give them

Notes: (a) The Folsom home is the product of a collaboration between BP Solar, OCR Solar & Roofing, R.J. Walter Homes and the Sacramento Municipal Utility District.[14] It is the first Leadership in Energy & Environmental Design (LEED) Platinum home on the west coast of the US, exceeding the LEED requirements and achieving an 83 per cent energy demand reduction.
(b) The Paterson home is the first single family residence on the east coast of the US to earn LEED Platinum.
(c) Eco-apartments in China.
Source: Courtesy of (a) the Sacramento Municipal Utility District (Photo by Judy Lew-Loose), (b) BASF Corporation, and (c) The Shanghai Research Institute of Building Sciences

Figure 2.2 *(a) Home of the Future, Folsom, Sacramento, (b) The BASF Near-Zero Energy Home in Paterson, and (c) Eco-apartments in Shanghai, China*

Factor Five or more improvements in energy consumption. As part of this chapter we will outline various methods to reduce energy consumption, within each of the five major areas – space heating and cooling, domestic hot water, appliances, lighting and refrigeration. However, as it is the integration of these methods that achieves the Factor Five or more improvement in household energy consumption, before doing so Dr Wolfgang Feist will explain the impressive 'Passivhaus' as an example of best practice in residential building energy design.

Best Practice case study – The 'Passivhaus'

This case study was contributed on invitation from Ernst von Weizsäcker by Dr Wolfgang Feist, Passive House Institute, and edited by The Natural Edge Project.

The leading practice in residential home energy performance is the 'Passivhaus'. According to the Passive House Institute, 'A Passive House is a

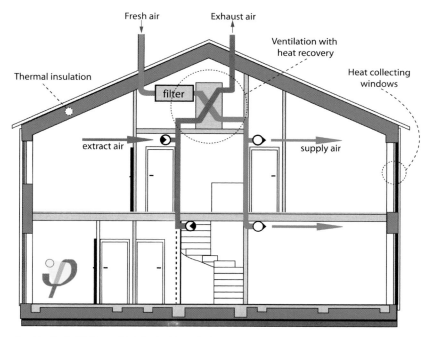

Source: Provided by Dr Wolfgang Feist, Passive House Institute

Figure 2.3 *Cross-section through a typical German or Austrian Passive House*

building in which a comfortable interior climate can be maintained without active heating and cooling systems.' Accreditation as a 'Passive House' by the Institution is subject to three main criteria:

1 Annual heat and cooling requirement of less than 15kWh/m^2/year, without alternative heating options.
2 Very low building envelope air gaps, tested to less than 0.6ACH at 50 pascal pressure, measured by the blower door test – meaning that with the building de-pressurized to 50Pa below atmospheric pressure by a blower door, the building must not leak more air than 0.6 times the house volume per hour.
3 Primary energy consumption is less than 120kWh/m^2/year, including heat, hot water and household electricity.

This is achieved by a combination of a range of options, including passive solar design, using super-insulation, using advanced window technology using heat recovery ventilation (HRV) and using efficient systems for generating the heat. The resulting designs deliver homes that achieve significant reductions in energy requirements compared to the standard design, predominantly from reduced requirements for space heating (and space cooling in warmer climates) along with reductions in domestic hot water, and household electricity for appliances, lighting and refrigeration.

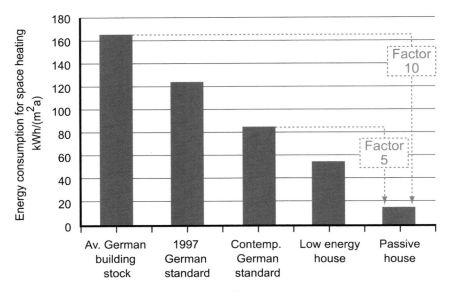

Source: Provided by Dr Wolfgang Feist, Passive House Institute

Figure 2.4 *Comparison of energy requirements in Passive Houses – less then 15kWh/m²/year – to average existing and ordinary new buildings*

The Passive House is the paradigm for the principles of *Factor Five*, and results in ultra-efficient buildings that require less than one-tenth of the energy demanded for space heating in average buildings, while keeping comfort at a very high level. According to the Passive House Institute, Passive House designs have achieved significant reduction in heating requirements in Germany with a Factor Five improvement over contemporary German standards, and a Factor 10 improvement over the average German building stock, as shown in Figure 2.4.

To be able to meet the criteria for a Passive House a number of design tools need to be employed, and the Passive House Institute has developed the 'Passive House Planning Package' (PHPP) to assist design. Using the PHPP, the Cost Efficient Passive Houses as European Standards initiative (CEPHES)[15] calculated the potential reductions in space heating demand using 'Passive House' methods for over 100 dwellings in 11 sub-projects across Germany, Austria and Switzerland. The results showed significant opportunities to reduce the heating demand in the order of 70–90 per cent across the dwellings. These results were verified through the measured performance of the buildings, and Figure 2.5 below shows the actual performance of the constructed dwellings compared with the demand from conventional new buildings, with similar geometry and built in accordance with locally applicable law.

Passive Houses achieve such significant reductions in the requirements for space heating using a number of methods, including:

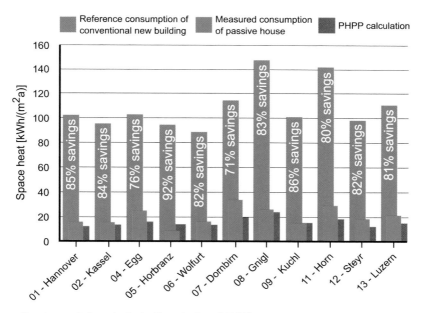

Source: Based on results from the Passive House Institute (2003)[17]

Figure 2.5 *Space heat consumption level comparisons between Passive Houses and standard buildings for over 100 dwellings in 11 sub-projects across Germany, Austria and Switzerland*[17]

- *Making use of passive solar design*: Where possible, buildings are compact in shape to reduce their surface area, with the greatest windows oriented towards the south (in the northern hemisphere) to maximize passive solar gain.
- *Super-insulation*: Passivhaus buildings employ super-insulation to significantly reduce the heat transfer through walls, roofs and floors. A wide range of insulation materials and construction details can be used to provide the required low U-values, typically 0.10–0.15W/m²K in central Europe, and 0.05–0.1W/m²K in northern and eastern Europe. Special attention is given to reduce thermal bridges to almost zero.
- *Advanced window technology*: Central European Passive House windows are manufactured with exceptionally low U-values, typically 0.7–0.85W/m²K for the entire window including the frame. These normally combine triple-pane insulated glazings, a 'warm edge' glass spacer and specially developed insulated window frames. Some 50 small and medium enterprises in Austria, Germany, Switzerland, the Czech Republic and Belgium started to produce these windows, which realize a positive energy balance even during cold and cloudy central European winters.
- *Minimal air gaps*: The standard requires the building to achieve very low levels of air gaps, much lower than are achieved in conventional construc-

tion. Air barriers, careful sealing of construction joints, and sealing of all service penetrations are used to achieve this. Reducing the gaps in the building envelope minimizes the amount of warm (or cool) air that can pass through the structure, enabling the mechanical ventilation system to effectively recover the heat, to be used to warm incoming fresh air, before discharging.

- *Heat recovery ventilation*: Mechanical HRV systems, with a heat recovery rate of at least 75 per cent and high-efficiency motors, are employed to maintain air quality, and to recover sufficient heat. Since the building is essentially airtight, the rate of air change can be optimized and carefully controlled at about $0.4h^{-1}$ (air-changes per hour) to ensure appropriate indoor air quality. The air-heating element can be heated by a small heat pump, by solar thermal energy, or simply by a natural gas or even small oil burner.
- *Efficient systems for generating heat*: In addition to the heat exchanger, often a micro-heat pump extracts heat from the exhaust air and heats the ventilation air and the domestic hot water. In addition to using passive solar gain, Passive House buildings make extensive use of their intrinsic heat from internal sources – such as waste heat from lighting, white goods (major appliances) and other electrical devices (but not dedicated heaters) – as well as body heat from the people and animals inside the building. Together with the comprehensive energy conservation measures taken this means that a conventional central heating system is not necessary, although the design is allowed to use whatever system a user wants, as long as it meets the overall performance requirements.

When *Factor Four* was published, there were just a few demonstration buildings which had been completed according to the 'Passive House Standard'. That changed during the last 12 years – until by 2008 more than 12,000 Passive Houses have been realized (see Figure 2.6 below for indicative results). Based on this success the political support for further expansion of the Passive House requirements is growing as demonstrated by the EU Energy Commissioner, Andris Piebalgs, stating in 2006 that, 'As indicated in the Plan, the Commission will propose action to ensure that in the longer term our buildings become "near zero emitting" – called also "passive houses".'[18] In 2007, the state government of Vorarlberg (Austria) was the first to take action with all new council houses being required to be built to the Passive House Standard.

Since the first 'Passive House' was built at Darmstadt Kranichstein in 1990[20] the techniques have been applied to a range of new buildings, varying from old-fashioned brick walls to prefabricated concrete buildings and light-weight timber construction – all with high levels of insulation, use of super-windows, and HRV in common. The first office buildings using Passive House Standard were built in 1998, the first school buildings and production building following in 2001. Now there are nurseries, kindergartens, a super-market and even an alpine refuge using Passive House technology.

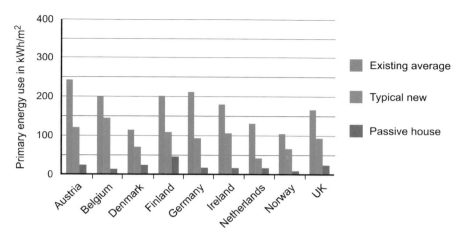

Source: Based on results from Promotion of European Passive Houses (2006)[19]

Figure 2.6 *Yearly primary space heating energy uses per dwelling, comparing 'existing average', 'typical new' and 'passive'*

The Smith House, located in Urbana Illinois and shown in Figure 2.8, was the first house in the US assessed by the Passive House Institute in Germany (undertaken by Wolfgang Feist), as being built to the Passive House Standard, in 2002. Its designer and owner, architect Katrin Klingenberg describes the 1200 square foot house as a 'simple shed-roofed house insulated on all six sides to at least R-56'.[21] Klingenberg reflected to the authors that, 'looking back the thing that surprised us the most was that it did not cost much more than typical construction, at least not as much as the first German Passive Houses'. Four years later, in 2006, the Waldsee BioHaus, constructed in Minnesota and shown below, was then the first house in the US to be officially certified by the Passive House Institute. The house requires a mere 11 per cent of the energy

Source: Provided by Dr Wolfgang Feist, Passive House Institute

Figure 2.7 *(a) A 'Passive' school near Munich, and (b) A 'Passive' kindergarten near Dresden*

required for a home built to the Minnesota Code – a Factor 10 improvement. The house was built in partnership between Waldsee, Concordia Language Villages, and Deutsche Bundesstiftung Umwelt (DBU).

According to the designer of the Waldsee BioHaus, Stephan Tanner:

> *Specific attention was paid to insulating throughout the slab floor to the ground, exterior walls to the roof including windows and doors. A new insulation technology, Vacuum Insulation Panels, were used on the upper floor for the exterior walls with aluminum cladding. A flat roof form was selected for this design with an extensive green roof ... establishing a heat buffer ... [the] design ... is optimal for an effective use of daylight and solar gain in the winter... [The building uses] a ground to air heat exchange system for the fresh air intake and a high efficiency heat recovery system. Heating requirements are met using ground source heat pump and passive solar gain. The high volume hot water needs are met with a solar hot water system.*[22]

Further to the application to new buildings Passive House methods have more recently been applied to existing buildings – with energy savings of 75 per cent to over 90 per cent. Renovated buildings usually have an existing heat distribution system and there is no reason not to use the very same system after renovation. With the renovation the heat requirement is reduced, then the system temperatures can also be reduced. Therefore, high-efficiency boilers and heat pumps can then be used. Good thermal insulation and high-efficiency mechanical equipment go hand in hand.

Source: (a) US Passive House Institute, and (b) Concordia Language Village

Figure 2.8 *(a) The Smith House, Illinois, USA, and (b) Waldsee BioHaus, Minnesota, USA*

Source: Provided by Dr Wolfgang Feist, Passive House Institute

Figure 2.9 *(a) Apartment building before and*
(b) after Passive House refurbishment

A whole systems approach to Factor Five in residential buildings

IPCC Strategy One: Energy efficiency opportunities

Space heating and cooling

Overview: Space heating and cooling is responsible for a significant proportion of energy consumption in residential homes around the world, representing 27 per cent in the European Union 15 (EU-15) in 2004,[23] 31 per cent in China in 2000[24] and 40 per cent in the US in 2005.[25] Requirements for space heating and cooling can be reduced by at least 30 per cent through a range of cost-effective options, including: passive solar design; improved insulation of the building envelope; double-glazed windows; and minimized air leaks in the home, particularly through the roof and around doors. As Alan Pears explains:

> *Analysis of the typical 150 square metre house with just ceiling insulation shows a design heating capacity requirement of 18.4kW. Changing the house to double glazing, R2 wall insulation, R3 ceiling insulation, concrete slab-on-ground with edge insulation, and an air-change rate of 0.5 air-changes per hour, reduced the design heating capacity requirement to 5.7kW [an improvement of 70 per cent].[26]*

Solutions: Achieving significant reductions in space heating and cooling involves the implementation of a range of complementary actions, such as:[27]

- *Passive cooling*: In regions of the world where morning temperatures during summer are less than 17°C it is possible to significantly cool a residential building simply by opening the windows and doors to let the fresh cool morning air push out and replace the hot air in the house. This process is valuable as it allows the cool morning air to also cool the thermal mass of the building. Sensors can detect when the air outside is

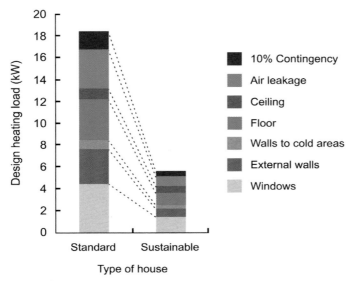

Source: Courtesy of Alan Pears

Figure 2.10 *Breakdown of design heating loads for standard versus energy-efficient housing*

suitably cooler than the air inside, whereupon windows (usually louvres) can be automatically opened to allow the cool air into the building.

- *Block air leaks*: To ensure that the early morning cool air stays in the build-ing, and the heat of the day is kept out, the building envelope needs to have minimal air leaks. Some leaks are less obvious, for example an unsealed ceiling exhaust fan can increase cooling load by several kilowatts on a hot windy day. According to the IPCC:

  Cost-effective measures that can be undertaken without a major renovation of residential buildings include: sealing points of air leakage around baseboards, electrical outlets and fixtures, plumbing, the clothes dryer vent, door joists and window joists; weather stripping of windows and doors; and adding insulation in attics, to walls or wall cavities. Bell and Lowe believe that a reduction of 50 per cent could be achieved at modest cost using well-proven (early 1980s) technologies, with a further 30–40 per cent reduction through additional measures.[28]

- *Improve insulation and thermal efficiency of the building envelope*: Once the building is appropriately sealed the goal is to reduce the amount of heat entering the building through the roof, walls and structure. By improving the insulation of the building envelope and installing double-glazed windows/winter windows, external shading of windows, and improved curtains with pelmets, significant reductions in heat transfer can be achieved. According to the IPCC:

> *The thermal performance of windows has improved greatly through the use of multiple glazing layers, low-conductivity gases between glazing layers, low emissivity coatings on one or more glazing surfaces, and use of framing materials with very low conductivity. Glazing that reflects or absorbs a large fraction of the incident solar radiation reduces solar heat gain by up to 75 per cent.*[29]

- *Upgrade air-conditioning ductwork*: Once the building is passively cooled (if possible), and air leakage has been reduced, as well as incoming heat or cold, the next area to focus on is the performance of the air-conditioning system, and particularly the ductwork for central systems. Ducting is often poorly insulated and as it is often installed in non-air-conditioned spaces (roofs, walls etc.) much of the cool or heat can be lost before it enters the living spaces of the building, especially if the ducting leaks or has a poor aerodynamic configuration.[30] According to the IPCC, '... leaks in ducts can increase heating and cooling energy requirements by 20–40 per cent.'[31]

- *Reduce the space that needs to be air-conditioned*: By focusing only on the various areas of the house that need cooling, that is, the rooms that are used the most, the load can be reduced.

- *Use the most efficient air-conditioners (if needed)*: In the tropics, or sub-tropical regions the items above are not sufficient to negate the need for air-conditioning of some sort. Alan Pears writes that:

  > *Obviously, use of evaporative cooling instead of refrigerative cooling can make a big difference to electricity demand in climates where wet bulb temperatures are not too high. But if refrigerative cooling is used, a number of factors can impact on efficiency such as the equipment efficiency, and cycling and other losses ... it seems feasible to air-condition a thermally-efficient bedroom at night using the same amount of electricity as is now used by a ceiling fan.*[32]

*Case study: The Fraunhofer Institute for Solar Energy Solar House –
Cold Climate Housing*[33]

The city of Freiburg, Germany, is one of the leading examples of a city council taking a progressive stance on reducing energy consumption through its energy-efficient housing standard, which has resulted in reductions of up to 80 per cent in energy use for space heating. Enacted in 1992, the council's energy-efficient housing standard requires energy consumption for heating purposes in households to be limited to $65kWh/m^2$ for all construction under the council's jurisdiction (including construction on land bought from the council and in projects funded by the council). This is approximately a 70 per cent improvement on typical older European homes of $220kWh/m^2$ per annum. According to the Clinton Climate Initiative:

The entire Vauban and Rieselfeld districts have been constructed to this 65k Wh/m² standard, comprising a population of 18,000 people. Around 150 units have been constructed to 'passive house' (15k Wh/m²) or 'plus energy' (houses producing energy surpluses) standards, saving around 2100 tonnes of CO_2 each year. Additional energy for passive houses is required for only a few weeks each year – a wood chip biomass combined heat and power plant provides this energy... Low-energy housing costs around 7 per cent more to build than traditional housing, yet energy consumption falls by up to 80 per cent... Construction costs for multi-unit buildings are lower. Costs associated with energy efficient construction are initially added directly to the purchase price, but the public has accepted these additional costs, in the anticipation of reduced running costs.[34]

An example of this is the Fraunhofer Institute Solar House, constructed to demonstrate that by focusing on reducing the energy requirement of a home, including applying the elements listed above, all of the energy needed could be supplied by the solar energy falling on the roof and walls. The house, located in Freiburg, is not connected to the grid and incorporates passive heating, cooling and ventilation, onsite energy generation and day-lighting. According to Wigginton and Harris:

Sixty-five percent of the southern facade incorporates transparent insulation, which helps to provide sufficient thermal insulation while still allowing light into the building to provide solar gain. The transparent insulation traps enough heat in the house to last for eight hours after the sun sets. The solar gain is collected by heavyweight walls, which produce a heat surplus on all but about 15 days per year. Supplementary heating comes from a variety of sources, including: a ground heat exchanger; air-to-air heat recovery from the kitchen and bathrooms; and flameless, hydrogen gas, diffusion burners, whose only combustion by-product is water.[35]

Appliances
Overview: Household appliances are responsible for a major proportion of energy consumption in residential homes around the world, representing 21 per cent in China in 2000,[36] 25 per cent in the EU-15 in 2004[37] and 27 per cent in the US in 2005.[38] The consumption of appliances can be reduced by more than 50 per cent, by implementing best available technologies. Home entertainment equipment (including TVs, DVD players, home computers and gaming consoles) is a major growth area in residential energy use. Other additional load comes from more members of the family or household owning and using computers at home for work or school homework, and

mobile phone rechargers. It is important to identify and use the most efficient appliances to reduce domestic electricity demand because this enables much of this demand to be met by small cost-effective solar photovoltaic systems, with the minimal size of battery storage. As Amory Lovins et al from the Rocky Mountain Institute (RMI) wrote in 2002, 'lights and appliances to reduce average household electrical load from somewhat more than 1kW to ~0.1kW permits a small, cheap photovoltaic array with modest storage to suffice.'[39]

Solutions: According to the IPCC:

> *The most efficient appliances require a factor of two to five less energy than the least efficient appliances available today ... for example, in the USA, the best horizontal-axis clothes-washing machines use less than half the energy of the best vertical-axis machines, while refrigerator/freezer units meeting the current US standard require about 25 per cent of the energy used by refrigerator/freezers sold in the USA in the late 1970s (about 1800kWh/yr) and about 50 per cent of energy used in the late 1980s.*[40]

The IPCC further cites research that suggests that, despite the fact that the use of home appliances in developing countries represents a small amount of the overall demand,

> *the rapid increase in their saturation in many dynamically developing countries such as China, especially in urban areas, demonstrates the expected rise in importance of appliances in the developing world as economies grow.*[41]

For instance it is estimated that in 1985 only 7 per cent of homes in China had refrigerators, and 17 per cent of homes had TVs, but by 2005 these figures had risen to 75 per cent and 86 per cent respectively.[42]

There is much that can be done to reduce the demand of appliances such as TV screens and home computers, including:

- *Plasma TVs*: Liquid crystal display (LCD) TVs are now widely available, and are much more efficient than plasma TV screens, at least halving the electricity used. Light emitting diode (LED) TVs have recently entered the market and use around 80 per cent less energy than plasma screen TVs.[43]
- *Computers*: Home computer usage has increased dramatically in recent years, with each desktop computer using 100–120 watts while operating.[44] As *Factor Four* showed, laptop computers have been designed in novel ways to reduce energy usage by at least 75 per cent,[45] now using on average around 20 watts.[46] Also, LCD computer monitors use a quarter to

a half as much as conventional monitors, hence using LCD monitors alone will reduce overall computer energy use by 30–45 per cent.[47] Finally, combining these innovations with appropriate active and passive standby modes enables a computer's energy usage to be reduced by close to Factor Five, compared to desktop computers.[48]

Also, more energy-efficient versions of traditional domestic appliances which further reduce energy usage in the home are now entering the market. A survey of the latest energy-efficient domestic appliances is beyond the scope of this one book. So instead, we next consider a few examples to illustrate how design improvements can enable significant energy efficiency savings in this area.

- *Kettles*: Kettles use far more energy than one would assume. The UK Department of Environment, Food and Rural Affairs (DEFRA) has quantified this with the following statement: 'If everyone boiled only the water they needed to make a cup of tea instead of "filling" the kettle every time, we could save enough electricity to run practically all the street lighting in the UK.'[49] The latest designs of kettles make three changes that can reduce the energy used by kettles around 80 per cent, namely:

  1 Only boil the amount of water needed – a number of kettles are now on the market that enable you to specify with the press of a button how many cups of water you want boiled. Trials show that this design change alone saves 31 per cent of energy compared to standard kettle usage.[50]

  2 Better insulation – keep the water hotter longer by insulating the kettle and thus reducing the energy required for reboils. The options available for insulating the kettle include using a vacuum (similar to those used in thermos flasks), expanded foam or an air gap.

  3 Include a temperature gauge – therefore reducing the number of re-boils. This shows the user that the water is still sufficiently hot to make a beverage without having to reboil.

- *Toaster*: Toasters lose heat through the top of the toaster that is traditionally open. Providing an automated lid which shuts while the toast is being toasted alone reduces energy use by approximately 34 per cent, and Morphy Richards has launched a new affordable toaster using this design change.[51]

- *Ovens*: Rocky Mountain Institute has shown that significant energy efficiency gains can be made by choosing more wisely the types of ovens we use, finding that:

  > *Conventional ovens or ranges are inherently inefficient because in order to heat up food, they must first heat up about 35 pounds of steel and a large amount of air. Tests indicate that only about 6 per cent of the energy output of a typical oven is actually absorbed by the food. When it comes to ovens, your best bet for saving energy is to use it only when cooking large dishes or batches, and to opt instead for a smaller appliance, such as a*

toaster oven or microwave, whenever possible… microwave ovens use up to two-thirds less electricity than conventional electric ovens. Microwaves heat food directly by exciting water and fat molecules in the food. They don't waste energy heating air and metal, and they don't generate surplus heat that burdens your air conditioner.[52]

Further to selecting appliances that require less energy to operate, choosing appliances that use minimal energy in active and passive standby mode, and which are easy to turn off, is also vitally important. According to the Lawrence Berkeley National Laboratories, 'An individual product draws relatively little standby power, but a typical American home has forty products constantly drawing power. Together these amount to almost 10 per cent of residential electricity use.'[53] According to George Monbiot, 'Move Associates have developed a smart meter which not only displays the breakdown of household energy usage but also contains an off switch, as you go out, you can turn off the entire house, except for gadgets you have already selected to stay on permanently.'[54]

For further information on appliance energy efficiency opportunities please refer to Rocky Mountain Institutes' Home Energy Briefing Series.[55]

Domestic hot water

Overview: Heating water is also responsible for a significant proportion of energy consumption in residential homes around the world, representing 9 per cent in the EU-15 in 2004,[56] 11 per cent in the US in 2005[57] and 27 per cent in China in 2000.[58] Energy requirements for water heating can be reduced by at least 90 per cent, through a range of cost-effective options, including: reducing consumption of hot water; improving thermal properties of hot water systems; recovering lost heat; and selecting low energy consumption hot water systems, such as solar thermal or heat pumps. According to the IPCC, 'The integrated effect of all of these measures can frequently reach a 90 per cent saving.'[59]

Solutions: The most cost-effective way to reduce the amount of energy used for domestic hot water is by first investing in water-saving fixtures and appliances, such as water-efficient shower heads and washing machines, to reduce the amount of hot water needed. Then secondly to identify a low energy consumption option for heating water. Electric storage systems are the highest energy consumers and are being phased out by government regulation in many countries. However, electric storage systems powered by a solar thermal system or a heat pump can significantly reduce this consumption. Shifting to gas storage systems allows for smaller tanks as they have faster heat recovery times, although, as Pears cautions, transitioning to a gas hot water heater is generally accompanied by a 15 per cent increase in hot water usage.[60] Shifting to on-demand systems further reduces consumption, as approximately 30 per cent of the electricity used to heat water in storage systems is lost through losses in the pipes and the tanks,[61] hence an instantaneous gas hot water system would be expected to be up to 30 per cent more efficient.

Main methods for reducing the energy required for water heating include;

- *Insulate hot water storage tanks and pipes*: Much of the energy consumed by storage-based hot water systems is used to heat water to overcome the lost heat through the walls of the tank and the pipework. According to RMI:

    Unless your water heater tank is already insulated to at least R-24, adding an insulating jacket to your water heater is one of the most cost effective do-it-yourself energy saving projects. The jacket should reduce heat loss through the walls of the tank by 25–45 per cent, saving about 4–9 per cent of water heating costs... Insulate hot water pipes wherever they are accessible, especially within three feet of the water heater. The split foam rubber type is effective and easy to use; be sure to choose the right size so it closes fully around the pipe, put it on crack downward and tape the seams with acrylic tape.[62]

- *Control the use of the system*: Ensuring that the systems are not heating water when the water is not required, that is, during the early hours of the morning, during work hours and over vacation periods. According to RMI:

    You can save an additional 5–12 per cent of water heating energy by turning water heaters off for certain periods. You can control your own water heater with a timer that automatically turns the heater off for preset periods.[63]

- *Ensure appropriate water temperature settings*: Temperature settings for hot water systems vary across various models and government require-ments. Typically a system will be set to a range of 50–75°C. When considering the temperature to set a hot water system there is a range of variables, including: tolerable shower temperature (approximately 40–45°C); scald prevention, as 60°C or higher can cause third degree burns; and minimizing bacteria contamination, as temperatures under 50°C may increase the risk of Legionnaires' disease. Hence water tempera-ture is best set in consideration of local government requirements.

- *Correctly sized water heaters*: Current domestic water heating systems are oversized for most homes and units in OECD countries. This means that the volume of water, which has to be heated, is much larger than what is needed, leading to significant waste of energy. The response of the industry, to date, has been the invention of the instantaneous hot water heater with electronic ignition, which is an improvement. With the instantaneous gas hot water heater, the water no longer needs to be maintained at a hot temperature all the time. But for at least 50 per cent of the market these are a long way from being optimized to the right size. Modelling, by Alan Pears, shows that for a household of one to two people (with the OECD estimating that in member countries single person households/units represent 20–30 per cent of the total, and two person households/units represent 10–20 per cent),[64] with people having a sequence of showers, with AAA shower heads, a well-insulated 30 litre hot water heater has a large enough capacity to meet their daily shower needs.[65] This is significantly smaller than the standard smallest domestic water systems which hold 135–250 litres. Pears shows that such a highly efficient unit with a well-insulated 30 litre storage tank, using a moderately large burner and electronic ignition can achieve significantly higher efficiencies than either the 4-star instantaneous hot water heater systems or the smallest standard 135 litre systems. As shown in Figure 2.11, this improved efficiency is considerable, right down to the very low usage levels, without the standby losses of a large water heater. Taking the Australian domestic hot water sector as an example, currently it is assumed that a base level of 200 litres is required for showers by the average Australian household. Pears' analysis of Australian demographics shows that a 200 litre domestic hot water system is now only needed per day by 15 per cent of all households in Australia. The domestic hot water industry in Australia has optimized gas hot water heaters for only a small percentage of the market. Thus there is potential to

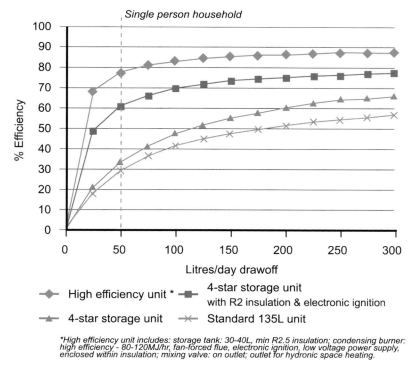

Source: Courtesy of Alan Pears

Figure 2.11 *Comparison of task efficiencies of standard, 4-star rated and high-efficiency hot water systems*

achieve even higher energy savings than predicted by the IPCC if these insights were used to redesign and properly size hot water systems.

Lighting

Overview: Household lighting is responsible for a growing proportion of energy consumption in residential homes around the world, representing 9 per cent in China in 2000,[66] 11 per cent in the US in 2005[67] and 12 per cent in the EU-15 in 2004.[68] The consumption of energy from lighting can be reduced by up to 90 per cent, by implementing a range of cost-effective options, including replacing incandescent light bulbs with low-energy options, such as compact fluorescent lamps (CFLs), halogen lamps with dimmer switches, and LEDs, and reducing the need for artificial lighting through building design and day-lighting. According to the IPCC:

> *Lighting energy use can be reduced by 75–90 per cent (Factor 4–10) compared to conventional practice through (i) use of day-lighting with occupancy and daylight sensors to dim and switch off electric lighting; (ii) use of the most efficient lighting devices available; and (iii) use of such measures as ambient/task lighting. Advances in lamps have been accompanied by improvements in occupancy sensors and reductions in cost.*[69]

Solutions: Combining passive solar design to maximize day-lighting together with more efficient lighting, steps (i) and (ii), is usually enough to achieve Factor Five. Traditional incandescent lights are remarkably inefficient, only turning 5–10 per cent of the energy they consume into light and thus wasting 90–95 per cent of electricity as heat.[70] More efficient forms of residential light-ing are available, such as compact fluorescent and LED lighting that provide a 75 and 90 per cent improvement respectively. Lester Brown reflects on this in the 2008 update of his book, *Plan B*, stating that:

> *Replacing the inefficient incandescent light bulbs that are still widely used today with new CFLs can reduce electricity use by three fourths ... though a CFL may cost twice as much as an incandescent, it lasts 10 times as long. Shifting to CFLs in homes, to the most advanced linear fluorescents in office buildings, commercial outlets and factories, and to LEDs in traffic lights would cut the world share of electricity used for lighting from 19 per cent to 7 per cent. This would save enough electricity to avoid building 705 coal-fired power plants. By way of comparison, today there are 2,370 coal-fired plants in the world.*[71]

Refrigeration

Overview: Household refrigerators are responsible for approximately 12 per cent of energy consumption in residential homes in the developed world, representing 8 per cent in the US in 2005,[72] and 15 per cent in the EU-15 in 2004.[73] The consumption of energy from refrigerators has been significantly reduced since the 1970s and can be further reduced by up to 50 per cent. According to Lester Brown:

> *A refrigerator in Europe uses roughly half as much electricity as one in the United States, for example, but the most efficient refrigerators on the market today use only one fourth as much electricity as the average refrigerator in Europe – a huge opportunity for improvement.*[74]

An effective refrigerator is in essence a well-insulated box with a cooling mechanism, with the technology rapidly improving over the last few decades. For example, by 1972, the average US model sold used 3.36kWh/y. By 1987, when California bought efficiency standards, the average model used 1.87kWh/y.[75] Since 1983, Sun Frost have been making refrigerators that only use 0.19kWh/y, a Factor 16 improvement on the average US refrigerator from 1972.[76] In the US, advances in technology have cut average refrigerator energy use by over 60 per cent in the past 20 years.[77] Energy efficiency improvements in the everyday domestic refrigerator in Australia, as a result of energy labelling and mandatory energy performance standards (MEPS), mean they now use roughly 70 per cent less energy than the refrigerators of 1980 as shown in Figure 2.12.

One might assume that after such a significant improvement there would be little potential left for further reductions in energy consumption. But at least another 50 per cent improvement is possible through designing refrigerators with better insulation and door seals, more efficient compressors, fans and internal lighting (with the latter reducing heat generation in the unit).

Solutions: The most efficient fridges on the market today achieve their results by using better insulation and door seals, more efficient compressors and fans with variable speed drives, and LED internal lighting (with the latter reducing heat generation in the unit). Two standout examples are Arçelik's ultra-efficient domestic refrigerator, being manufactured in Turkey, and the Sun Frost refrigerator, made in America.

1 *Arçelik refrigerator*: In 2008, Turkish consumer goods company Arçelik was recognized by the EU Commission for producing the most energy-efficient refrigerator to date.[79] The Arçelik refrigerator has achieved impressive energy efficiency results by using very efficient compressors, and effective insulation, seals and controls.[80] The Arçelik refrigerator has a variable speed compressor, as it is better to vary the compressor's speed to enable it to run at a lower rate with lower output than to stop and start the fridge. This 'stop–start' approach results in the compressor then having to run at a higher rate, resulting in higher energy usage overall.[81] Thus,

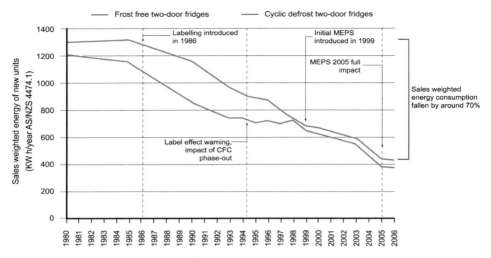

Source: Based on Harrington and Holt (2002)[78]

Figure 2.12 *Energy efficiency trends in the family size refrigerator from 1980 to 2005 in Australia*

Arçelik have applied many of the suggested strategies outlined in the original publication, *Factor Four*, to improve the performance of their fridges.[82]

2   *Sun Frost refrigerator*: Another standout example of this progress, which was featured in *Factor Four*, and still is one of the best-performing fridges, is the Sun Frost fridge. The Sun Frost fridge reduces energy requirements by up to 80 per cent and has a life expectancy of over 24 years, compared to the average 15 years for a conventional unit, incorporating aspects including, including:

- *A top-mounted cooling system*: According to the manufacturers, this configuration reduces energy consumption due to the fact that heat generated by the compressor and condenser rises above and away from the unit, rather than up through the unit, as in standard refrigerators.
- *Improved insulation*: The walls of the refrigerator contain 2.5 to 4.5 inches of polyurethane foam, and the manufactures point out that, 'Unlike many other refrigerators, the insulation in the walls of the SUN FROST refrigerator is not degraded by thermal bridges (metal supports between the inner and outer walls)'.
- *Separated air flow*: The refrigerator is designed so there is no air circulation between the refrigerator and freezer sections, in an attempt to reduce the loss of coolth in one section when the door to the other is opened.
- *Cooler summer kitchen*: The manufacturers point out that the SUN FROST produces much less heat than the typical refrigerator and that:
  During the summer, a typical refrigerator adds as much heat to your kitchen as a 1000-watt heater running five hours

per day! The energy needed by your air conditioner to remove this excess heat will be about half the energy consumed by your refrigerator, increasing the cost of running it by an additional 50 percent.

Factor Four showed that even the Sun Frost fridge could be further improved through the following steps:[83]

- using even better insulation, compressors and seals (with improved materials);
- reducing the need for and frequency of defrosting;
- improving the design of the condenser coil.

Factor Four discussed all these strategies in great detail. Take insulation, for instance. There are a number of types of insulating material that can insulate 2–12 times better per unit thickness than the best plastic foam which is currently the main insulation used in refrigerators. Thus there is already available insulation that is good enough to enable the everyday refrigerator to stay cool while automatically being turned on and off to save energy. As Weizsäcker et al wrote in *Factor Four*:

> *Perhaps the most intriguing of these new insulation materials is simply two sheets of stainless steel, edge-welded a few millimetres apart (separated by little glass balls), with a hard vacuum inside and with the inside coated with a special film to block heat-robbing infrared rays. A cardboard-thin layer of such 'compact vacuum' insulation can stop heat flow as well as 7cm of mineral wool. It costs more, but it can also super-insulate the refrigerator while making its walls much thinner.*[84]

The Arçelik refrigerator, featured above, can also be made still more efficient. Currently, the Arçelik refrigerator, like most refrigerators, uses only one compressor to cool both the freezer and the main food storage area. According to Alan Pears, there is a large temperature difference between them and the larger the temperature difference, the more inefficient a compressor works. This problem could be solved if instead two compressors were used with variable speed drives.[85]

IPCC Strategy Seven: Materials efficiency – water

Residential water use accounts for close to 8 per cent of global water extraction, although within some regions such as Europe, this can be as high as 13 per cent.[86] The amount of water used in the home, and how that water is used, varies from country to country. OECD countries tend to use as much as ten times per capita more water for residential needs as developing countries.[87] It is estimated that the average person in developed countries uses 500–800 litres per day (300m^3 per year), compared to 60–150 litres per day (20m^3 per year) in developing countries.[88] Hence the focus of this part is on achieving Factor Five improvements in water productivity in the residential sector of OECD and rapidly emerging economies. The main areas of residential water usage for such households are, on average, from largest to smallest use – the bathroom (showers and toilets), laundry, kitchen and garden.[89] The following material focuses on water efficiency improvements, water tanks and greywater systems (that alone achieve up to 65 per cent demand reductions for mains water),[90] and water-sensitive gardens, and dual reticulation, that together then enable 80 per cent, or Factor Five, water productivity improvements to be achieved.

Water productivity strategies do not simply help reduce demand for fresh potable water, but also yield significant energy savings, as this reduces the amount of energy that is needed to purify and then pump potable water from central water storages, such as dams and tanks. Reducing hot water usage in particular provides significant benefits in that it reduces both energy and water bills, and reduces water demand, and hence energy requirements for water utilities.[91] Hence as the provision of water is energy intensive, there is a strong nexus between water and energy savings in the residential sector.

Water efficiency measures

Overview: Water efficiency measures are the most cost-effective way to reduce water consumption in the home. Table 2.1 shows that the use of efficient shower heads, water-efficient appliances, dual-flush toilets and low-flow aerators for taps, can improve the water productivity for an average home by over 60 per cent.[92]

A 2008 study of urban water usage showed that using water-efficient shower heads cut energy required to heat water by around 50 per cent.[93] Further, the study showed that replacing an old washing machine with a new efficient front-loading model would cut energy use by more than half, and save 10,000 litres of water annually, assuming 250 washes a year.

Use of rainwater and onsite greywater

Overview: Currently, relatively little of the water that falls on urban areas as rain is used, and in the case of coastal cities much of this rainfall simply flows into stormwater drains and out to sea.[94] Rainwater tanks can capture water to be used for watering gardens, flushing toilets, washing clothes or in showers. Greywater is wastewater from non-toilet fixtures such as showers, basins and taps which does not contain human excreta (water that contains excreta is known as blackwater).[95] Most governments permit greywater re-use outdoors as well as for toilet flushing and laundry after appropriate treatment.[96] Large rainwater tanks and greywater recycling systems can reduce demand for potable water significantly.[97]

An example of the potential for water savings from greywater re-use is shown by the Mawson Lakes Estate Development in South Australia. This 3500-home residential estate was designed so that 80 per cent of used greywater is recycled for toilets and gardening.[98] Some households are going

Table 2.1 *Daily water consumption for standard domestic appliances in Australia*

Water use	Using standard appliances (L/person/day)	Using efficient appliances (L/person/day)
Toilet	50	33
Bath and shower	50	19
Hand basin tap	10	1
Kitchen	10	3
Tap	*7*	*1*
Dishwasher	*3*	*2*
Laundry	30	11
Tap	*5*	*1*
Washing machine	*25*	*10*
Total	**190**[99]	**64**

Source: NSW Health Department (2001)[100]; Ecological Homes (2002)[101]

even further and paying for larger domestic water tanks and onsite water treatment systems so that there are homes completely water self sufficient. Another well-known example in Australia is the work of Michael Mobbs and Helen Armstrong, having retrofitted an old terrace house in one of the most densely populated suburbs in Sydney to be almost entirely water self-sufficient. Through onsite collection of rainwater, as well as onsite wastewater treatment, Mobbs and Armstrong have reduced their already relatively low consumption of mains water to virtually zero. This house does not have a particularly large roof but nevertheless it can still capture enough water in the 8500 litre tank, located beneath the back deck, to meet the potable water needs of the family of four.[102] It is also possible to achieve self-sufficiency for a residential estate. Currumbin Ecovillage is the first Australian self sufficient residential estate development (off both the mains water and sewerage systems) which captures, treats and recycles water onsite to meet all its needs in a near closed loop water cycle. Water efficiency measures are employed, as well as landscaping techniques such as swales and retention ponds. Over 80 per cent of the water used by households is recycled.

Using recycled water through dual reticulation
Overview: Residential estates can be designed with dual reticulation systems which enable recycled water to be used for toilets and gardening. Dual reticulation is the use of two water supplies – recycled water and drinking water. An example in Australia is the Aurora Estate.[103] It is an 8500-person development, led by the Victorian Government and Yarra Valley Water, that is incorporating dual reticulation along with the strategies outlined above. Pimpana-Coomera Scheme in the Gold Coast area is another impressive application of duel reticulation, this time to 150,000 people. Building on from the Aurora Estate, this development,

incorporates new materials, technologies, standards and practices to reduce the size and capital and maintenance costs of water collection and distributions systems. The scheme will provide overall an 80 per cent reduction in demand for potable water with capital costs only 10 per cent above conventional approaches and lower life cycle costs if headwork costs are incorporated.[104]

Water-sensitive garden design

Overview: Up to 60 per cent of household water is used outdoors on gardens.[105] The landscape of the garden can be redesigned to be made up of plants that need significantly less water than the average household garden in OECD countries. Planting drought-tolerant species, mulching around plants to reduce evaporation, and installing drip irrigation systems can all lead to significant savings.

Factor Five in homes in developing countries

We now turn the focus of this Sector Study to developing countries. Given that water usage in the home is relatively small, and that the items above will be quite relevant,[106] we focus here on ways to enable developing countries to reduce energy consumption by Factor Five within the home. As non-OECD countries represent approximately 35 per cent of the energy demand for this sector globally,[107] reducing this demand must play a key role in global efforts, if the world is to achieve a Factor Five improvement, along with reducing a number of related health concerns, particularly from indoor air pollution.

According to the 1999 World Development Report, approximately 1.8 billion people lack access to electricity, and in order to provide indoor and night-time lighting must burn fuels such as kerosene, paraffin, wood or diesel. Even though fuel-based lighting options provide just 1 per cent of lighting globally,[108] their health and environmental burden is disproportionately greater. Such practices contribute to the major health hazards posed by indoor air pollution in developing countries, and generate 20 per cent of lighting-related CO_2 emissions,[109] the main source of greenhouse gas emissions in developing countries,[110] while consuming 3 per cent of the global oil supply.[111] According to the World Bank, about 780 million women and children inhale kerosene fumes, which include many harmful particulates, and is equivalent to the smoke from two packets of cigarettes per day. Consequently, two-thirds of adult females with lung cancer are non-smokers and the average lifespan in the regions is just 42 years.[112]

However, as many of these locations will continue to be unable to access electricity from national grid systems it is vital that any new options for lighting and cooking are cost-effectively powered onsite. Driven by the growing demand in the developed world, progress in the efficiency, efficacy and longevity of new forms of electric lighting (such as LEDs and CFLs) mean that by using them the electricity demand can be significantly less. Hence, small-scale onsite renewable energy options can cost-effectively deliver lighting to undertake common household tasks.[113]

> *An emerging opportunity for reducing the global costs and green-house gas emissions associated with this highly inefficient form of lighting energy use is to replace fuel-based lamps with white solid-state (LED) lighting which can be affordably solar-powered. Doing so would allow those without access to electricity in the developing world to affordably leapfrog over the prevailing incandescent and fluorescent lighting technologies in use today throughout the electrified world.*
>
> Evan Mills, US Lawrence Berkeley Labs, 2005[114]

According to Mills, new technologies for lighting can be 1000 times more efficient than kerosene lamps, and by using solar panels this technology shift can replace millions of tons of kerosene consumed per year and significantly improve the quality of life of millions of people. Globally US$48 billion/year is spent on kerosene for lighting;[115] thus, this combined with aid and micro-credit schemes should allow a cost-effective transition away from kerosene. Life-cycle costing analysis shows that many rural families can pay back the investment in a solar-LED system within 1–2 years, hence only requiring basic micro-credit services.[116] Such a micro-credit service can work with residents paying a deposit on their new lighting system, and then redirecting their regular kerosene costs towards paying off their investment, or like a leasing arrangement, whereby residents pay a regular fee for the use of the lighting system. In either case, once the cost of the lighting system has been recovered, payments cease, the residents own their lighting system and the saved money can be invested into needs such as income-generating assets, improving diet, medical care and education. Hence, cumulative savings from kerosene replacement by LED systems (even with systems priced at approximately US$100) effectively boost family income. The long life of LEDs, and low power requirements result in extremely low ongoing maintenance costs (rarely exceeding a few dollars a year), and once the system is installed, the LED-powered lamps should last for 20–40 years. Realizing this potential a number of NGOs have formed to support this transition, notably the Lighting Up the World Foundation,[117] which is assisting poor households in developing countries to shift to LEDs powered by solar and rechargeable batteries. Lighting Up the World was started in 2000, when LED technology had progressed sufficiently for a single 0.1 watt white LED to provided adequate light for reading in the dark. The Foundation has since worked with poor people and micro-credit banks to supply more than 100,000 people in 14,000 homes spanning 42 countries with solar-powered LED. Other locally focused projects, such as the Barefoot Solar Engineering Institute in India,[118] and micro-credit initiated programmes, such as the Grameen Bank Shakti Solar Energy Program in

Bangladesh, are looking at ways to empower previously illiterate workers, mostly female, to become 'solar engineers'. For instance, at the Barefoot Engineering College illiterate women have been trained to make circuits for solar lighting, and also to install and maintain hand pumps, water tanks, solar cooking heaters and pipelines. Take the now well-documented example of Gulab Devi, aged 45, a quintessential rural woman from Rajasthan. Previously illiterate, and a mother of four, she is now a successful pioneer in the Barefoot Solar Engineering Project. Gulab is the sole bread-winner for her four children and her ailing husband. Not only is she running her household comfortably with her salary from this work, she is also one of the most respected members of her community.[119]

Such female 'barefoot solar engineers', who previously would have been seen as illiterate poverty-stricken women, are now so respected by the communities in north-east India they are being asked to represent the region in government. Maurice Dewulf, deputy senior resident representative, United Nations Development Programme (UNDP), comments, 'The project has demonstrated how solar energy provides a solution not just for cooking and lighting, but also for education, agriculture, health, and income generation.' Supported by the Indian Ministry of Non-Conventional Energy Sources, the European Commission and the UNDP, the Barefoot Solar Engineering Project draws on the world's leading technologies to allow communities across the developing world to experience a new quality of life. For example, the solar lanterns programme allows schools to operate at night in areas that require children to work during the day for their families to survive. Inspired by its success, the Indian government and overseas aid has enabled over half a million such solar lanterns to now be in use throughout India.

The cooking stove is another major energy-using appliance in developing countries. According to the International Energy Agency (IEA), 'Two-and-a-half billion people in developing countries depend on biomass – wood, dung, charcoal and agricultural residues – to meet their cooking energy needs.'[120] According to the World Health Organization (WHO), this results in the premature deaths of an estimated 1.6 million people each year from breathing elevated levels of indoor smoke, resulting in indoor air pollution being the fourth leading cause of death in poor developing countries.[121] The WHO has estimated that indoor smoke from solid fuel causes about one-third of lower respiratory infections, and about one-fifth of chronic obstructive pulmonary disease. In addition, in early 2008, scientists discovered that black carbon, a form of particulate air pollution produced from biomass burning and cooking, has a global warming effect in the atmosphere three to four times greater than previous estimates, and could prove to be a significant contributor to global warming.[122] Black carbon particles only remain airborne for weeks compared to CO_2, which remains in the atmosphere for more than a century;[123] however, as Ramanathan and Carmichael write, 'Black carbon in soot is an efficient absorbing agent of solar irradiation that ... can form atmospheric brown clouds in mixture with other aerosols.'[124] Between 25 and 35 per cent of black carbon in the global atmosphere comes from China and India, emitted from the burning of wood and cow dung in household cooking and through the use of coal to heat homes.

Options available to reduce domestic cooking energy needs include: improved efficiency of biomass stoves; non-electric options such as solar cookers; and improved biomass stoves, which can save from 10 to 50 per cent of biomass consumption for the same cooking service, at the same time reducing indoor air pollution by up to one-half.[125] The Partnership for Clean Indoor Air (PCIA), which involves over 160 partners worldwide, is assisting efforts to address the problem by funding projects in Asia, Africa and Latin America to identify and demonstrate effective approaches for increasing the use of clean, reliable, affordable, efficient and safe home cooking and heating practices that reduce people's exposure to indoor air pollution. For example, the PCIA are promoting the design of more efficient wood-burning cooking stoves. These efficient stoves achieve roughly a 50 per cent improvement and dramatically reduce indoor air pollution. Additional efforts are being made to promote the use of solar thermal cookers that have been improved to achieve greater than 80 per cent efficiencies cost effectively. As Lester Brown states:

> *These inexpensive cookers, made from cardboard and aluminum foil and costing $10 each, cook slowly, much like a crockpot. They require less than two hours of sunshine to cook a complete meal. They can also be used to pasteurize water, thus saving lives.*[126]

Solar cookers do not simply eliminate indoor air pollution and reduce dependency on scarce wood or biomass supplies needed for cooking, they also reduce the risks for those collecting fuel, predominantly woman, of being targeted for violent abuse as they forage further and further into forest areas. A solar cooking project involving Solar Cookers International and partners, which has distributed tens of thousands of solar cookers – costing US$30 each – to women in the refugee camps in Chad and Darfur, has transformed the lives of women there.

Responding to the need to assist poor families to access clean and cost-effective forms of lighting and cooking, the Grameem Bank, founded by Nobel peace laureate Muhammad Yunus, has created a non-profit subsidiary, Grameen Shakti, which expands on the bank's original micro-credit financing model to enable poor people to purchase electricity and cooking systems that are powered by renewable energy, along with asking every customer to plant five trees on their property.

The two main options for renewable energy are:

- The solar home system, which incorporates a solar panel, a battery, a charge controller, a fluorescent tube, an electronic ballast, an installation kit and connecting devices. The system capacity ranges from 10 to 75 watts and has a life of 25 years. Customers can chose to pay a 10–25 per cent deposit and then 24 to 42 monthly instalments at a flat service charge of 4–6 per cent. According to the programme, the total cost of the most popular size, a 50-watt system, is US$400 and it can power four to six low-energy lamps, a radio, a TV and mobile phone charging.

- The biogas plant for cooking uses poultry and cow waste to produce gas while the remaining slurry can be used in organic fertilizers. The plant capacity ranges from 1.6m^3 to 70m^3 of biogas production. The total cost ranges from about US$215 for an individual household to $1400 for a cluster of houses.

These initiatives help to generate surplus carbon credits that may be used to offset emissions in developed countries. This opportunity has already been recognized by the World Bank in the form of a carbon-offsetting deal for the company's solar panel systems. Grameen Shakti was created in 1997, when it serviced 228 homes. As of 2008, the company had serviced over 135,000 homes, its current rate was 5000 additional homes per month, and has led to three million trees being planted by customers. Grameen Shakti's target is to have one million solar-powered lighting systems and one million biogas plants by 2015 through enlisting local entrepreneurs who will market, install, repair and maintain the systems on behalf of the company.[127]

2 The office and commercial buildings sector

The potential for Factor Five improvements in office and commercial buildings resource productivity

This Sector Study complements and updates the discussion on energy productivity in office/commercial buildings presented in *Factor Four*, supported by real world case studies like the ING Bank Headquarters in the Netherlands. Since *Factor Four* was written, the growth of the green building industry globally has been enormous, and this Sector Study, learning from such efforts, provides a discussion of how to achieve Factor Five improvements in both energy and water productivity in the commercial building sector, mainly in office buildings. We recognize that it is also important to address the energy intensity of materials used in this sector. Rather than cover these here, this book investigates in depth how to achieve Factor Five resource productivity improvements in cement and steel production in Chapter 3.

The main focus of this Sector Study is on energy productivity because, according to the IEA, commercial buildings consume 23.6 per cent of the world's electricity. In OECD countries like the US, commercial buildings are responsible for 18 per cent of the energy usage, and contribute 18 per cent of greenhouse gas emissions.[128] The commercial office building sector is also a significant user of water. For example, office water use can account for 10 per cent of capital city water consumption. According to the Australian Department of Environment, Water Resources, Heritage and the Arts, 'A moderate sized building of 10,000m^2 typically consumes over 20,000 litres per day or more than seven million litres per year – enough to supply 40 average homes.'[129] Just as with residential buildings, there is a strong nexus of mutually reinforcing energy- and water-saving productivity opportunities in the commercial building sector.

An integrated approach to reducing energy consumption

> The steps in the most basic IDP [Integrated Design Process] for a commercial building include (i) selecting a high performance envelope and highly efficient equipment, properly sized; (ii) incorporating a building energy management system that optimises the equipment operation and human behaviour, and (iii) fully commissioning and maintaining the equipment.[130]
>
> These steps alone can usually achieve energy savings in the order of 35–50% for a new commercial building, compared to standard practice, while utilization of more advanced or less conventional approaches has often achieved savings in the order of 50–80%.[131]
>
> IPCC, 4th Assessment Report, 2007[132]

According to the IEA, commercial buildings consume some 3700 billion kWh of energy,[133] with this consumption covering a range of end-uses such as: heating, ventilation and air-conditioning (HVAC), indoor lighting, outdoor lighting, office equipment, servers and data centres. The relative consumption in each of these areas varies from country to country as can be seen in Figure 2.13.

As with residential buildings, progress across this range of areas will become an area of increased activity as governments around the world begin to require significant energy performance improvements from commercial buildings. With utilities struggling to meet the escalating requirements of new high-demand buildings tapping into existing energy networks with finite and strained capacity, the stress on urban infrastructure is evident in increasing 'brownout' and 'blackout' events where electricity supply is reduced or stopped. In addressing this stress there is an immediate opportunity for growth in commercial development – in both new and existing buildings – to have very low demands on the existing electricity grids, perhaps even becoming net energy providers. We begin by discussing the existing situation and efforts to date in encouraging significant energy efficiency improvements, as recommended by the IPCC. We then consider opportunities for both new buildings and retrofits, focusing on a number of elements that can contribute to Factor Five reductions in electricity demand.

As this chapter will show, there are existing buildings and studies from around the world showing that 50–80 per cent energy productivity improvements can be affordably achieved. Numerous rating schemes have emerged over the last decade to address this issue of assessing and recognizing the

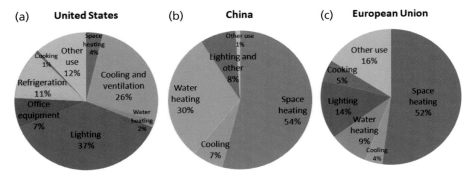

Source: Based on data from (a) EIA (2003),[134] (b) Zhou et al (2008)[135] and (c) Janssen (2004)[136]

Figure 2.13 *Breakdown of commercial building sector energy use in the US in 2005 (electricity), in China in 2000 (total energy) and in the EU-15 in 2004 (electricity)*

improved performance of 'green buildings' with regard to energy, water and materials consumption and greenhouse gas emissions, in addition to aspects such as occupant comfort and productivity. As the industry matures, each of the leading schemes internationally continue to use differing methods to measure the environmental impact of buildings and there has been a growing demand for consistency and comparability between the tools, particularly in how they account for carbon emissions. In 2009, the US, UK and Australian Green Building Councils formed an alliance to develop common metrics to measure emissions of CO_2 equivalents from new homes and buildings, across Building Research Establishment Environmental Assessment Method (BREEAM) (UK), LEED (US) and Green Star (Australia).[137] Within this part we refer all comparisons to LEED for consistency.

The Sector Study begins by reflecting on a number of important international collaborations and national endeavours that, since the publication of *Factor Four*, have made progress in achieving significant productivity improvements for commercial buildings, including:

- In 2001, Engineers Australia, the peak professional body for engineers in Australia, created a Sustainable Energy Building and Construction Taskforce to examine opportunities for the built environment sector. The taskforce report concluded that, 'energy neutral commercial building stock should be the goal which industry and government should be now moving.'[138] They demonstrated that, in 2001, energy efficiency savings of 60 per cent could be achieved in retrofitted buildings and at least 70 per cent in new buildings, based on experience from Australia and around the world. They highlighted that as far back as 1996, Pacific Gas and Electric undertook a project with the California State Automobile Association (CSAA) to determine the cost-effective technical potential for energy-efficient commercial/office building design. The project demonstrated overall energy savings (lighting, heating, cooling and office equipment) of 70 per cent below the strict California Title 24 Code for energy efficiency in buildings.[139]

- The Three Country Energy Efficiency Project (3CEE) was jointly initiated in 2001 by the World Bank, the UNEP's Risoe Centre on Energy, Climate and Sustainable Development, and partners in Brazil, China and India to promote energy efficiency projects in these three countries by easing typical investment requirements of financial institutions. Energy specialist and 3CEE leader Robert Taylor states, 'Improving energy efficiency for existing buildings and other infrastructure could cut current energy consumption by 25 per cent or more in India, China and Brazil, amounting to millions of tons in reduced greenhouse gas emissions and hundreds of millions of dollars in energy savings.'[140] As President of the UN Foundation Timothy Wirth reflects, 'Energy efficiency in these three countries is a win–win strategy. It is one of the cleanest, cheapest and fastest ways to reduce carbon emissions.'[141]

- The World Business Council for Sustainable Development (WBCSD) is a strong proponent of energy efficiency in commercial buildings, and in 2004–2007 it undertook an Energy Efficient Buildings (EEB) project which focused on assessing the environmental impacts of buildings and developing means to achieve zero net energy use for residential and commercial buildings.[142] The project covered six countries or regions that are together responsible for two-thirds of world energy demand, namely: Brazil, China, Europe, India, Japan and the US. It brought together leading companies in the building industry to bridge isolated specialist 'silos' in order to develop a cross-industry view of energy efficiency and to identify the approaches that can be used to transform energy performance. The final reports highlight opportunities to promote green building know-how and technologies as the WBCSD pushes for zero net energy construction worldwide.[143]

- The US National Renewable Energy Laboratories (NREL) is America's primary laboratory for renewable energy and energy efficiency research and development. In 2007 it published a report suggesting that by 2025 in the US, the majority of commercial buildings could achieve large energy productivity gains and also become self-sufficient by using renewable energy on their roofs,[144] referred to as 'net zero energy buildings'. The NREL's 2007 report on the research concluded that a net zero energy (or net zero carbon) goal for office and commercial buildings – that is, greater than Factor Five – is largely achievable:

  Energy efficiency improvements that use the best available technologies and practices and integrated, whole-building design approaches can, on average, reduce consumption by 43%. Reducing consumption through energy efficiency is important in the net zero energy building context because it requires much less photovoltaic solar panels to reach net-zero energy... If [energy

> *efficiency strategies] projected future technology and PV systems were applied to all buildings by 2025 ... new buildings in the commercial sector could, on average, consume 86% less than current stock.*[145]

- Around the world there are numerous examples within Europe, Australia and America of professional and government collaborations creating energy efficiency programmes that encourage the commercial sector to improve their buildings' energy performance. A notable example with significant global application is the Building Owners and Managers Association (BOMA) and the Clinton Climate Initiative (CCI) on the development of an energy performance contracting model, which allows building owners and operators to execute sophisticated energy efficiency retrofits to existing buildings. BOMA and CCI, in collaboration with real estate and energy service companies, identified barriers to energy efficiency investment in the commercial real estate sector and developed a standardized, user-friendly contracting model that allows building owners and operators to successfully execute larger, more sophisticated retrofits and bring greater operational improvements to investment real estate.[146] BOMA and CCI anticipate that the new model and relationships formed during the initiative will reduce the time it takes to complete these types of retrofits from 18–36 months to 12 months or less.
- The UN-supported Global Reporting Initiative (GRI) has been developed over the last two decades as a 'non-profit, multi-stakeholder governed institution' collaborating to provide sustainability reporting guidelines which were first published in 2000. The latest guidelines ('GRI G3') were released in 2006. Responding to the particular needs of various sectors, GRI is in the process of developing a number of 'Sector Supplements' which complement these guidelines, including a 'construction and real estate' Sector Supplement which was initiated in 2008 with a key focus on energy efficiency of building design.[147] A GRI survey of 17 companies globally on the theme of most importance to developers identified 'Increased energy efficient design, e.g. designing buildings to achieve maximum efficiency leading to reduced energy consumption once the buildings are occupied'.[148]

In addition to such international organizational collaborations, government leadership and guidance is an essential component of a significant transition to energy efficiency in the built environment. As WBCSD president Bjorn Stigson reflects, 'In order to achieve a step change in energy efficiency in buildings, there is a need for strongly supportive policies and regulatory frameworks. Governments and local authorities need to develop sound policies.'[149] Such leadership is being shown in the two largest and fastest growing economies in the world – that of China and India – which already rank among the world's top energy consumers with energy growth rates near 10 per cent per year.[150]

- In China, the Vice-Minister of Commerce, Mr Jiang Zengwei, reflects that retail enterprises are big energy consumers in a country where energy consumption accounts for 40 per cent of operating cost in department stores and retail chains.[151] To address this significant load the Ministry of Commerce, since 2007, has been promoting an energy conservation campaign among developers and retailers, aiming to reduce their energy costs by 20 per cent by 2010. However, there is still much to be done, with energy consumption per unit of GDP (referred to as 'energy intensity') for 2006 and 2007 falling only 1.79 and 3.66 per cent respectively, and falling only 3.46 per cent over the first three quarters of 2008, which is just below the annual goal of 4 per cent required to meet the 20 per cent reduction from 2006 to 2010.[152]
- In India, the Bureau of Energy Efficiency[153] estimates that the period 2006–2010 has been and will continue to be dominated by a growth in office buildings, which will increase by nearly 5.1 million m^2 (55 million ft^2) per year country-wide to keep pace with growing demand. Just under half (1.9 million m^2, or 20 million ft^2) of this growth is in New Delhi, Mumbai and Bangalore alone. Retail is a significant contributor to this growth, with the 15 largest cities in India housing approximately 7.3 million m^2 (79 million ft^2) of shopping centre space.[154] Most Indian commercial buildings have an energy performance index (EPI) of 200–400kWh/m^2/year in comparison to less than 150kWh/m^2/year in similar buildings in North America and Europe. Energy-conscious building design, however, has been shown to reduce a building's EPI to 100–150kWh/m^2/year, although, in India, the development of such buildings is currently left up to the discretion of the more environmentally sensitive corporate businesses. In order to address the rapid expansion of electricity use in the commercial sector, the Indian government has developed the Energy Conservation Building Code (ECBC) for all five climatic zones in the country, covering: 1) the building envelope (walls, roofs, windows); 2) lighting (indoor and outdoor); 3) heating ventilation and air-conditioning (HVAC) system; 4) solar hot water heating; and 5) electrical systems. Beginning in 2007 as a voluntary initiative and with a strong government focus on its own buildings, ECBC is intended to eventually become mandatory for all buildings with a connected load of 500kW or more. It is anticipated that implementation of the ECBC will reduce energy consumption by 25–40 per cent.[155]

As developers and investors explore business opportunities in 'green' commercial buildings, particularly in light of the 2008 economic crisis, a number of historic regulatory, market and institutional perceptions related to the economics and practicalities of achieving green buildings are being revaluated.[156]

For example, a recent study by researchers at Maastricht University, the Netherlands, and University of California Berkeley, has investigated in detail the economic benefits from commercial buildings achieving LEED or similar certification. The investigation covered more than 10,000 buildings (comparing 893 buildings rated under 'Energy Star' or 'LEED' in the US compared with 7488 control non-rated buildings) finding that certified buildings

> *command rental rates that are roughly three per cent higher per square foot than otherwise identical buildings... Selling prices of green buildings are higher by about 16 per cent. At prevailing capitalization rates ... conversion of the average non-green office building sold in 2004–2007 to a green building would add $5.7 million in market value.*[157]

In relation to energy performance the investigation found that:

> *an increase of ten per cent in the site energy utilization efficiency of a green building is associated with a 50 basis points increase in effective rent [equating to 4 per cent if achieving a Factor Five increase], and an increase in value of about two per cent [equating to 16 per cent for Factor Five].*

This study builds on more than a decade of growing awareness about such opportunities, including the less tangible benefits of employee productivity, as presented in Romm and Browning's 1998 report, *Greening the Building and the Bottom Line: Increasing Productivity Through Energy-Efficient Design*.[158]

In their report, Romm and Browning reviewed four green building retrofits and four new green building constructions in the US, and found that they demonstrated very attractive economic returns, not only through savings in electricity and other energy sources, but also far more significantly through sustained savings in employee-related costs, such as improved productivity, improved work quality and reduced absenteeism.[159] The energy-efficient measures used – such as efficient lighting, heating and cooling – were certainly cost effective when accounting only for energy savings but were, as the authors describe, 'indispensable' when also accounting for the employee-related savings. The report concluded that savings arise in buildings where the quality of employee workspaces are improved, through improved visual acuity and thermal comfort, and that such improvements can be achieved concurrently with large energy savings. In 2003, the Californian government commissioned a study that analysed the economics of 33 LEED-certified buildings in the state. The study clearly demonstrated that sustainable building can be a cost-effective investment, concluding that although certification raised construction costs by US$44 per m² ($4 per ft²), the buildings actually earned a profit over the first 20 years because operating costs, as well as employee absenteeism and turnover, were lower and productivity was higher than in non-certified buildings. The standard and silver certified sustainable buildings earned a profit of $544 per m² ($49 per ft²), and the gold and platinum certified buildings earned $744 per m² ($67 per ft²).[160]

Given the demonstrated need for, and benefit of, significant improvements in commercial building performance, we will now consider examples from around the world to show *how* Factor Five improvements in energy productivity can be made through an integrated approach to commercial building design in developing and developed countries. As with residential buildings, once energy demand is reduced in commercial buildings the task to meet this demand using renewable options can then become a feasible and affordable consideration.

Three main areas typically assessed in commercial buildings for energy demands and options for reduction are:

1   heating, ventilation and air-conditioning (HVAC) systems;
2   indoor lighting;
3   office equipment.

Achieving Factor Five improvements in typical commercial buildings

Achieving improved design outcomes for commercial buildings may greatly assist nations to reduce their energy demand and greenhouse gas emissions. Commercial buildings rely on energy (and thereby create greenhouse gas emissions) in two key areas:

1   the energy required to create the building (e.g. the building materials, and transport of materials), and to then destroy it at the end of its life;
2   the energy required for the building to operate over its lifetime.

Approximately 8–10 per cent of a standard commercial building's greenhouse gas emissions are attributed to the embodied energy of the building's materials, while the remaining 90–92 per cent is attributed to the running energy needs of the building over its lifetime.[161] Efficiency expert Joseph Romm explains why a strategic design approach is essential for achieving optimized design solutions in this context:

> *Although up-front building and design costs may represent only a fraction of the building's life-cycle costs, when just 1 per cent of a project's up-front costs are spent, up to 70 per cent of its life-cycle costs may already be committed. When 7 per cent of project costs are spent, up to 85 per cent of life-cycle costs have been committed.*[162]

As shown in Figure 2.14, when considering both new construction and retrofit projects, it is essential that opportunities for energy-efficient design solutions are considered at the very onset of a project, so the design team members can develop their own scope of work, in coordination with other design team members and the overall project vision. Because buildings last for 50–100 years or longer, it is often assumed that increasing energy efficiency in the

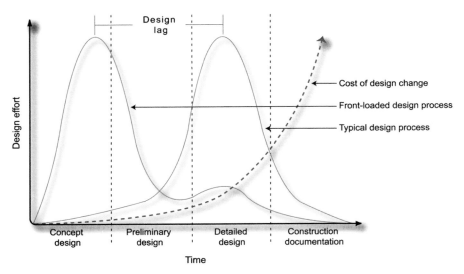

Source: TNEP, as published in Stephens et al (2007)[163]

Figure 2.14 *Front-loaded design as a benefit of a whole system design approach*

building sector is a long-term process. But that is not the case. An energy retro-fit of an older inefficient building can cut energy use by 20–50 per cent. The next step is to shift entirely to carbon-free electricity, either generated onsite or purchased, to heat, cool and light the building – and then we will have a zero-carbon building.

The following text provides examples of whole system design strategies for reducing energy demand in commercial buildings, both in new construction and in retrofitting existing building stock. We then present a whole system assessment of the potential for significant reductions in energy demand in commercial buildings.

Best practice case studies – New construction

There are numerous 'green buildings' being planned and under construction around the world, but far fewer examples of buildings that achieve in the order of Factor Five improvements. Here we consider three significant commercial buildings with regard to their Factor Five components – a private office build-ing in China, a retail outlet in Canada and a government office building in Australia. We then summarize key design attributes for a number of other new commercial building examples.

Pearl River Tower – China

The Chinese government recently set the goal of reducing the nation's carbon emissions by 10 per cent by 2010. As the city of Guangzhou experiences some

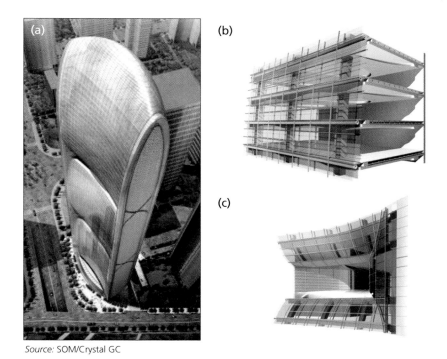

Source: SOM/Crystal GC

Figure 2.15 *The Pearl River Tower in Guangzhou, in the province of Guangdong, China*

of the worst air pollution in the world, the city and its province, Guangdong (southern China), are a major focus in this initiative. The Pearl River Tower skyscraper in Guangzhou is due for completion in late 2010, and is planned to incorporate the latest sustainable technology to create the world's most energy-efficient high-rise structure.[164]

According to designers Skidmore, Owings and Merrill (SOM) the 310 metre tall, 214,100m² (2.3 million ft²) tower will be the most energy-efficient super-tall tower ever built, and perhaps the world's first 'zero-energy' skyscraper, consuming nearly 60 per cent less energy than a traditional building of similar size, and sourcing its energy needs from renewable sources.[165] The building uses cutting-edge technologies including radiant slabs, geothermal heat sinks and integrated photovoltaic panels, with significant energy efficiency opportunities harnessed through synergies between the various technologies.[166] Located in a hot and humid subtropical environment, Pearl River Tower integrates a number of highly innovative features, including:[167]

- The design of the 'zero-energy' tower was developed through a careful understanding of solar and wind patterns around the site, optimizing the solar path and using the sun to the building's advantage. The building also minimizes the interference of wind forces and uses them to relieve the structural burdens imposed by high-wind pressures.

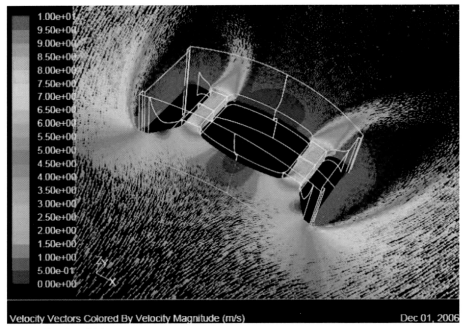

Velocity Vectors Colored By Velocity Magnitude (m/s)   Dec 01, 2006

Source: SOM/Crystal GC

Figure 2.16 *The Pearl River Tower in Guangzhou, wind velocity tests*

- Pearl River's sculpted body includes two vertical-axis integrated wind turbines which harness prevailing winds from the south and the north with minor efficiency loss, to generate energy for the building's HVAC systems.
- The office tower is chilled by a combination of displacement ventilation, radiant panel cooling and chilled beams and incorporates optimized air and water delivery systems and optimized building management systems. The chilled beams and radiant cooling system delivers sensible cooling directly to the space by incorporating chilled water piping that cools the room by natural convection and radiation heat transfer.
- Exhaust air is routed through the cavity of the double-layer curtain-wall, heating up as it travels upward to the mechanical floor, and the ventilation and dehumidification system uses this hot, dry air from the double-wall as an energy source.
- A photovoltaic system is integrated into the building's external shading system and glass outer skin.
- Energy consumption is reduced by maximizing natural day-lighting, reducing solar gain in air-conditioned spaces, and by utilizing solar gain for providing the building's hot water supply.
- The design incorporates a dynamic high-performance building envelope, where solar collectors integrated into the facades transform the sun's energy to usable AC current.

- An internally ventilated high-performance double skin facade with automated blinds is used for the northern and southern orientation, and a triple-glazed facade with external shades and automated blinds within the glazing cavity is used for the east and west elevations.

Wal-Mart discount department stores

Wal-Mart is an American corporation which operates approximately 7800 discount department stores in 15 countries worldwide (trading under names such as Asda in the UK and Seiyu in Japan), employing more than two million staff. In 2008 it was the world's largest public corporation by revenue for the fifth time in six years and the largest grocery retailer in the US with an estimated 20 per cent of the retail grocery and consumables business.[168] In 2005, Wal-Mart announced it would implement several measures to improve energy efficiency, including spending US$500 million a year to: increase fuel efficiency in its truck fleet by 25 per cent over three years and double it within ten; reduce greenhouse gas emissions by 20 per cent in seven years; reduce energy use at stores by 30 per cent; and cut solid waste from US stores by 25 per cent in three years.[169] The first experimental store was opened in McKinney, Texas to study opportunities such as fuelling the heating in the store with used cooking and motor oil. Two other experimental stores in Aurora, Colorado, and Las Vegas, Nevada, have installed solar panels, wind turbines, boilers that run on bio-fuel, and water-cooled refrigerators, and have planted water-efficient gardens. The first Canadian environmental demonstration store in Burlington, Ontario, features a first-of-its-kind application of geothermal technology in a large-scale Canadian retail operation and energy-conserving lighting innovations.[170] The new Burlington super-centre is expected to use an estimated 60 per cent less energy than the company's typical super-centre store. According to David Cheesewright, Wal-Mart Canada's president and CEO, 'There's a tremendous opportunity to reduce our construction and operating costs and to pass those savings on to our customers, who are looking for lower prices now more than ever.' Design features of the store include:

- A white roof membrane deflects sunlight by an estimated 85 per cent to reduce heat gain in summer and subsequent demand. This is supported by increased insulation in the roof which reduces heat and cooling loss.
- Geothermal heating and cooling are facilitated by 15km of piping buried under the parking lot. The in-floor radiant heating and cooling system circulates water to transfer heat and coolth, instead of using air vents, thus requiring less electricity.
- An environmentally preferable CO_2 refrigeration system allows the heat from the refrigeration system is captured and re-used to store heat.
- 100 per cent renewable power is augmented through purchasing power from sources like wind and low-impact water power.

- A daylight harvesting system uses skylights to refract daylight throughout the store. Light sensors monitor the amount of natural light available and raise, dim or turn off lighting as needed.
- Energy-saving motion-activated LED lights are used in the refrigerator and freezer cases, as well as low-wattage parking lot lights and LED external signs to reduce energy use.

Council House II – Australia[171]

Council House II (CH2) is one the world's leading green buildings, and is one of the earliest 'Six Star' buildings under the Green Building Council of Australia's rating system (similar to a LEED platinum rating).[172] It has since received numerous commendations for its innovative and functional design process, including extensive design charrettes with the design team early in the process. According to the City of Melbourne, the building cost A\$51 million (approximately US\$39 million), including A\$11.3 million (22 per cent), for sustainability features. Considering the A\$1.45 million annual savings from such features, Council is expecting a payback period on the sustainability features of less than ten years, and then ongoing savings.[173] The business case for the building included a requirement that the investment fund money could only be used if the project demonstrated a minimum financial yield of 8.5 per cent. The business case included a conservative estimation of improved staff productivity benefits of 4.8 per cent per year over 20 years for the financing calculations, which when capitalized into the building costs allowed the project to spend an extra A\$25 million on innovations. An independent productivity survey undertaken in 2008 found the financial yield to be much higher for CH2 than the minimum required – coming in at 10.8 per cent (A\$2.4 million per year, or \$270 per m^2 for the 9000m^2 of floor space, which is almost as much as the rent for the space).[174]

The building consumes 82 per cent less energy than the first Council building, has reduced gas consumption by 87 per cent, produces only 13 per cent of the emissions, and reduces demand on the water mains supply by 72 per cent. According to Council there has also been nearly 5 per cent improvement in staff effectiveness as a result of the healthier building (clean fresh air and non-toxic finishes).

Key features of Council House II include the following:[175]

- Roof-mounted wind turbines on top of vertical air stacks purge air from the building during the night and also generate electricity.
- The air-conditioning system comprises chilled beam ceiling panels, evaporative shower towers and phase change materials. Five shower towers on the exterior of the building evaporatively cool water which is used to remove heat from the phase change material, and then to cool the water that travels through the chilled beams and panels. Each day, 100,000 litres of water is mined from the city's sewer line and filtered for use in the evaporative cooling system and as a non-potable water source.

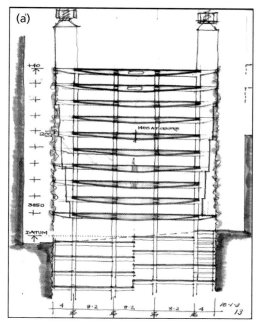

Source: (a) Courtesy of Mick Pearce; (b) Photograph by Diana Snape

Figure 2.17 *(a) CH2 building early concept sketch from the CH2 Charrette Workshop and (b) CH2 – the built result*

- The high thermal mass of the building, along with shading mechanisms on the sun-exposed sides of the building effectively prevent heat from penetrating the building during the day, reducing reliance on air-conditioning. The western facade has louvres made from recycled timber that move according to the position of the sun and are powered by photovoltaic roof panels (as shown in Figure 2.17). Windows on the northern and southern facades are automatically opened at night to purge the building with fresh, cool air.
- The building has a 'one pass' system where occupants receive 100 per cent fresh air, achieved through innovative use of the building's facades. The north-facing facade has ten dark-coloured air ducts that absorb heat from the sun, causing hot air to rise and in doing so draw stale air up and out of the building. The south facade has light-coloured ducts that draw in fresh air from the roof and distribute it down through the building.
- Light shelves inside and outside of the building shell reflect light onto the ceiling, providing diffused natural light.
- Artificial light levels are kept at a minimum to conserve energy, and high-frequency ballast lighting is used within the building while task lighting is located at work areas.

- Highly energy-efficient electrical goods are used throughout the building. (The heat loadings of these electrical goods were accounted for in the heat loading calculations for the building, which were used to determine the air-conditioning needs of the building).

According to the Melbourne City Council, CH2 has achieved 72 per cent reduction of mains water through a combination of water efficiency, rainwater harvesting, water recycling and sewer mining.[176] Water efficiency measures include the highest standard water-efficient shower heads, taps, toilets and appliances, and using recycled water in the building's cooling towers. The building has been designed to collect the maximum amount of rainwater and it is stored in the basement. CH2 has also innovated by investing in a blackwater treatment plant[177] that enables the treatment of not just the blackwater (toilet) and greywater (showers and basins), but also sewerage 'mined' from the sewer below the street next to CH2. CH2 is demonstrating that, since sewerage is made up of approximately 95 per cent water, it can be a source of usable water. This approach is treating as much as 100,000 litres of wastewater to Class A standards per day to provide 100 per cent of CH2's non-drinking water for toilet flushing, cooling and irrigation.[178] In addition, any surplus water produced through this water re-use and treatment plant can be piped and used by other buildings.

Other new construction examples from around the world

From the rapidly expanding literature of green building examples, notable commercial buildings of varying size and use demonstrate a variety of energy efficiency opportunities (see Table 2.2).

Table 2.2 *Factor Five office/commercial new buildings from around the world*

Sohrabji Godrej Green Business Centre ('CII-Godrej GBC'), Hyderabad, India[181]

This 1900m² (20,450ft²) building was the first outside the US to achieve a LEED platinum rating from the United States Green Building Council, in 2003. The building is an example of a public–private partnership, as a joint initiative of the Government of Andhra Pradesh, Confederation of Indian Industry (CII) and House of Godrej, with the technical support of the United States Agency for International Development (USAID).
–   The building uses 55 per cent less energy than a conventional building, with 90 per cent of the spaces having daylight access and views to the outside.
–   The building has a roof garden covering 60 per cent of the roof, which provides insulation, and two air-conditioning towers which cool incoming air by 7 to 8°C, by spraying water which is fed into the air-conditioning system, further lowering cost. Of the remaining energy demand, approximately 16 per cent is met by rooftop solar panels of capacity 24kW.
–   The building is made of 77 per cent recycled construction material and sustainably harvested new wood, and the recycled timber louvres are controlled by photovoltaic cells.
–   Wastewater is recycled through 'root zone treatment', and low-flush toilets reduce municipal water supply by an additional 35 per cent.

China's Ministry of Science and Technology 'Accord 21 Office Building', Beijing, China[179]

This 3600m² (39,000ft²) building achieved LEED gold certification in 2005, as the first LEED-certified project in China and one of the greenest building projects in the world. The building is an international effort between the Chinese Ministry of Science and Technology and the US Department of Energy, and is managed by the US-based National Resources Defense Council.
–   The building uses 70 per cent less energy while producing over 15 per cent of its energy from renewable energy sources such as solar panels and heat recovery.
–   Lighting is 'intelligent', adjusting the level of artificial lighting to take into account the amount of natural light.
–   Double-pane, argon-filled windows are used, which reduce heating and air-conditioning costs by limiting the transfer of heat through glass.
–   The elevators adjust their energy use to match the passenger load.
–   A variable flow air-conditioning system saves energy during periods of low demand.
–   The building has a rooftop garden, with seating areas, grass, trees and shrubs, which insulates the building.
–   The building also uses 60 per cent less water, or 10,000 tons per year, by storing 70 per cent of the rain that falls on it.
–   During construction, energy was saved by buying locally produced materials whenever possible, and 75 per cent of the building waste from construction was recycled.

Pacific Controls Headquarters, Dubai, United Arab Emirates[180]

This 11,150m² (120,000ft²) LEED platinum-rated building at the Techno Park in Dubai was, in 2007, the first and only certified green building in the Middle East, and the 16th worldwide.
–   Photovoltaic panels cover the roof of the building, meeting the daytime lighting needs, and shading the roof from heat gain into the building. The building also uses a solar thermal system to provide 25 per cent of the building design cooling load (i.e. fresh air cooling), where a solar collector farm of hot water panels produces hot water at 90°C to run a 100 ton absorption chiller.
–   Water is treated onsite and used for greywater irrigation. One tank stores the sewage which is then treated and stored in a second tank as greywater for later use in irrigation or as make-up water for the mechanical plant.
–   All energy consumption is monitored and tracked in real time to ensure the consumption is optimized and targeted costs are achieved.

Table 2.2 *continued*

Pusat Tenaga Malaysia's (PTM) Net Zero Energy Office (ZEO) Building, Selangor, Malaysia[182]

This 4000m² (43,000ft²) administration and research office building was completed in 2007, as the first zero-energy office building in South-east Asia. It does not use fossil fuel as an energy source, and has achieved 'zero net energy' through a combination of features including:

- Effective passive solar design; a step-in design wherein each floor is shaded by a slightly larger floor above; super-windows; skylights; light shafts and shelves; a highly reflective ceiling that diffuses daylight deep into the building; insulation; cool water pipes embedded in the concrete slabs on each floor; efficient lighting; an air-conditioning system with CO_2 sensors to control outside air intake; and a heat recovery system.
- Four building-integrated photovoltaic (BIPV) systems – on two building roofs, a car park roof and an atrium – generate solar electricity which is either consumed or sold to the grid. The super-energy-efficient features of ZEO reduce the consumption to 286kWh per day, which is covered by the BIPV system.
- The building also has a rainwater collection system for toilet flushing and irrigation.

Lawrence Berkeley National Laboratory

Energy costs in research facilities can be staggering – today's scientific facilities can be more than 100 times more energy intensive than conventional buildings,[183] and only 1–3 per cent of these buildings are designed to be 'green'.[184] According to Evan Mills from the Californian Lawrence Berkeley National Laboratory (LBNL), 'The potential for energy savings is routinely affirmed by benchmarking investigations that reveal energy intensity variations of Factor Five or more for (scientific) facilities supporting similar activities and providing similar or greater levels of services, reliability, comfort, and safety'.[185] The LBNL is an US$85 million, six-storey, 8800m² (94,500ft²) steel and glass building, completed in 2006, which achieved a LEED gold rating through extensive green and energy-efficient features and renewable power purchases. LBNL estimated the CO_2 emissions of this building to be 85 per cent less than standard practice, which includes aggressive environmentally conscious California building codes.

Elsewhere, the NREL's Science and Technology Facility, and laboratories at the University of California (Santa Barbara and Davis) have achieved the highest LEED platinum rating while saving approximately US$90,000/year in energy costs and significantly improving the working environment.[186]

Source: Compiled by TNEP, sources as noted within the table text

Best practice case studies – Building retrofit and refurbishments

In the search for retrofit examples, the authors found only a small handful of significant documented examples internationally over the last decade. This is perhaps an indication of the emergent nature of building retrofits, in comparison to new buildings. Here we consider an office building retrofit in Australia, a multiple-building retrofit project in India and a hotel retrofit in the US.

60L Building, Australia

The 3375m² (36,328ft²) building retrofit at 60 Leicester Street, Carlton, in Melbourne Australia ('60L'), involved an existing three-storey brick, timber and concrete office building (originally erected in 1876), and the integrated construction of a new four-storey structure. Completed in 2002, the 60L building provides one of the best-documented examples of an integrated design

Source: Courtesy of Alistair Mailer, The Green Building Partnership

Figure 2.18 *Features of the 60L Building retrofit, showing the street frontage, rainwater storage and treatment system, and the building's thermal chimneys and roof garden*

process that has led to large-scale reductions in energy and water consumption. The retrofitted building uses only 30 per cent of the energy, and 25 per cent of the water used by a conventional office building of similar size and class, achieving an 80 per cent reduction in the energy used for lighting compared with a typical commercial building of its size.[187] To address embodied energy within the building, the retrofit used significant quantities of recycled materials, including timber for floors, doors and window frames, new concrete, reinforcing steel and second-hand bricks, and new materials were selected based on their potential to be recycled at the end of their life.

The significant improvement in sustainable outcomes of the design process may be attributed to the involvement of all critical players, as well as the provision of a prescriptive green specification document that was provided to the builder by the developers.[188] The design process also included a series of design charrettes that occurred over four months.[189] Unlike standard design charrettes of the time, the 60L charrettes featured significant client involvement from The Green Building Partnership and the Australian Conservation Foundation, who were to become the principal tenants. In addition, all building tenants were required to sign a 'green lease' which requires conformance with the building's Environmental Management Plan and informs the tenants of how to interact with the building to ensure its sustainability features are maximized. The building owner provides additional information to tenants, to assist with minimizing tenancy environmental footprints, including information required to source efficient office and kitchen appliances. There have been over six years of building operation since the retrofit, and according to The Green Building Partnership's Project Manager, Alistair Mailer, 'the building continues to demonstrate the practicality of designing commercial office buildings with a significantly reduced environmental footprint, within the commercial budget, together with provision of a healthy, pleasant and more productive work place'.[190]

Design features of the retrofitted building include:

- Hybrid passive/active ventilation and air-conditioning for tenancies without a central air-conditioning plant, using thermal chimneys to induce natural ventilation in conjunction with automated ventilation louvres controlled by the building automation system, ensuring the building internal temperatures fluctuate within a 19–26°C thermal control band.
- Purchasing mains power supply sourced from green power, with solar panels supplementing mains energy supply.
- A central atrium and six light wells on the building's north and south perimeter walls, which draw in natural daylight, also providing ventilation to the building.[191]
- Light shelves and light-coloured ceilings assist the reflection and diffusion of natural light into the building interior, and occupants adjust windows and some of the louvres to increase user comfort, reducing reliance on air-conditioning.

60L uses 75 per cent less water than a standard commercial/office building through a variety of measures, including: minimizing the demand for water by providing water-efficient fixtures and fittings, including waterless urinals and low flush-volume toilet pans; using collected rainwater (treated to potable standard) as the principal source of water used in the building; and onsite treatment and re-use of greywater (basins and sinks) and blackwater (sewage) streams to produce reclaimed water for flushing toilets, irrigating the roof garden, and for the central water feature in the atrium.[192] The designers say that in an average rainfall year, only the water required for testing the fire sprinkler system should require the use of mains water.

Tune-Up Project, India

Australian company Szencorp through its subsidiary ECS, is finding smart ways to achieve significant building energy savings in India, through a financing project supported by the Australian government through the Asia-Pacific Partnership on Clean Development and Climate.[193] The 'Building

Figure 2.19 *(a) Holy Family Hospital, Delhi; (b) National Museum, Delhi; (c) National Thermal Power Corp Building, Delhi*

Tune-Up' project aims to upgrade a number of existing buildings in and around Delhi using energy performance contracting to provide a guarantee of the energy savings expected on a project.[194] The upgrades will draw on Australian expertise and integrate renewable technology including solar thermal air-conditioning where applicable. Performance guarantees will be provided to ensure that the expected outcomes are realized, which will also enable Indian banks to provide third party financing (backed in part with Asian Development Bank assistance). In the immediate term, the project conservatively estimates that it will reduce greenhouse gas emissions in participating commercial buildings by over 50 per cent, through no-cost/low-cost measures and cost-effective retrofits. The larger programme goal is to influence government and business policies, programmes, and building portfolio management practices to include building performance monitoring and recognition activities. The building retrofit comprises 12 buildings, including iconic sites such as Parliament House, the Vigyan Bhawan Complex, the Supreme Court and those shown in Figure 2.19.

With the modelling and retrofit specifications completed, the refurbishments are expected to be completed by 2011. Szencorp's Group Manager of Corporate Affairs, Mark Lister, reflected to the authors that:

> *This project is an exciting milestone in industry taking up commercial building retrofits, because countries like India have such potential for energy savings, and are experiencing strong demand growth. Creating the funding model and business case for retrofitting in markets such as these can be difficult, but can also be highly influential in creating meaningful energy reductions as well as pioneering replicable models for further rollout. It's also an opportunity to transfer the skills and frameworks from more developed markets like Australia to places where energy efficiency is still an emerging concept, and to create new export markets in high quality green jobs.[195]*

Saunders Hotel Group, US

The Saunders Hotel Group is a third generation, family business that owns and operates three properties in Boston. It is the first such group to retrofit their hotels to become climate neutral, through a combination of energy efficiency initiatives, and purchasing renewable energy. The company is certified by The Climate Neutral Network as the first hotel group in the world to offer climate neutral rooms. It is also the first hotel company to offset the air pollution and carbon emissions of its electricity. Saunders Hotel Group has implemented a number of energy efficiency features in one of its 10,000m² (106,560ft²), eight-storey, 208-suite Comfort Inn & Suites in Boston, originally constructed in 2000. These features include:[196]

- low-energy windows;
- super-efficient boilers and heat pumps;
- state-of-the-art, infrared motion sensors for HVAC in all guest rooms;
- motion sensors for lighting in intermittent or low-traffic areas;
- compact and fluorescent bulbs (saving 58,000 kilowatts each year);
- Energy Star-rated office equipment and televisions;
- motion sensors on vending machines – which saves an additional 21,000 kilowatts per year.

Other features include: an ionization cleaning system for the swimming pool, which eliminates the use of chlorine; and compressed natural gas shuttle vans, which provide transport to Logan International Airport. The hotel has achieved 40 per cent energy efficiency and is climate neutral, and in 2004 the building received an award for energy efficiency and good environmental practices from the United States Environmental Protection Agency (US EPA).[197]

Other retrofit examples from around the world

From the rapidly expanding literature of green retrofitted building examples, notable commercial buildings of varying size and use demonstrate a variety of energy efficiency opportunities.

A whole systems approach to Factor Five in commercial buildings

IPCC Strategy One: Energy efficiency opportunities
Heating, ventilation and air-conditioning (HVAC) systems

Heating, ventilation and air-conditioning (HVAC) is responsible for a signifi-cant proportion of energy consumption in commercial buildings around the world, representing 30 per cent in the US in 2003 (electricity),[198] 56 per cent in the EU in 2001 (electricity)[199] and 61 per cent in China in 2000 (all sources).[200] The requirement for HVAC can be significantly reduced using several features related to building orientation, the building envelope and the building's form, taking advantage of opportunities for passive heating, cooling and ventilation, most of which are low-cost options if integrated in the earliest stages of

Table 2.3 *Factor Five office/commercial building retrofits from around the world*

Renewable Energy House, Belgium

The Renewable Energy House is a 2000m^2 (21,500ft^2) office building that was originally built in 1885 in Brussels, Belgium.[201] The building now uses half of the energy of a typical building of its type, costs 70 per cent less to run compared to before the retrofit, and demonstrates the application of many types of renewable energy technology, including: an 80kW boiler to meet most of the heating demand;[202] 25kW heat pumps to meet the rest of the heating demand; a 60m^2 solar hot water system with 5000 litre storage; a 37.5kW thermally driven cooling system; rooftop and window solar panels; a highly efficient ventilation system with 85 per cent heat recovery; highly efficient lighting; 15cm mineral wool insulation; and double glazing on the windows.

Hudiksvall District Courthouse, Sweden

Hudiksvall District Courthouse is a 2000m^2 (21,500ft^2) office building that was originally built in 1909 in Hudiksvall, Sweden.[203] The building's energy use has been reduced by 132MWh per year through a combination of measures, including: reducing heating energy demand by 105MWh per year or 30 per cent; achieving 80 per cent heat recovery and thus helping to reduce ventilation electricity demand by 13MWh per year or 68 per cent; using a computer control system to manage heating and ventilation power consumption; and improving the insulation. The building's heating energy requirements, which were originally met by burning oil, are now met by district heating, which uses 99.7 per cent renewable fuels.

The Barton Group's Headquarters, US

The Barton Group's Headquarters is a three-storey, 1500m^2 (16,000ft^2) brick building that was originally built in 1865 in Glens Falls, New York and retrofitted in 2007.[204] The building, which has achieved a LEED platinum rating, is 49 per cent more energy efficient than stipulated by the New York State building code, and sources all of its electricity from wind power. The building also has several resource-efficient features, including: a geothermal system for internal temperature control; a green roof and greywater system; preferred parking for cyclists and hybrid vehicles; and office furniture with recycled content. During the building's retrofit, 97 per cent of the structure and shell was re-used and over half of construction waste was recycled, and the building also includes the state's first green elevator, which uses far less power than other elevators and was constructed using recycled material.

Metrotower Office Complex, British Columbia

Based on the findings of a comprehensive energy audit in 2003 supported by BC Hydro, the Metrotower Office Complex, in Burnaby, British Columbia (Canada) undertook a C$1.1 million (US$750,000) lighting upgrade, replacing the existing double T12 fluorescent light tubes with single T8 tubes and a reflector. On average the upgrade reduced the energy use for each unit by almost half while delivering the equivalent light. The lighting is now computer controlled to avoid unnecessary lighting. According to the buildings manager, Ivanhoe Cambridge, 'an estimated saving of 2.8 million kilowatt-hours of electrical energy was realized from the lighting retrofit. This translated to on-going annual savings of $150,000'.[205] The building's energy conservation programme also includes a number of complementary activities such as smart controls for lighting and HVAC, chilled water closed-loop systems, efficient motors and variable speed drives, low-energy reflective glass, and window blinds.

Table 2.3 *continued*

Szencorp Building, 40 Albert Road, Australia

The 1200m² (13,000ft²) five-storey office building, built in 1987, became the first commercial 6-star Green Star (i.e. 'World Leadership Status') refurbishment in Australia, with a number of Australian 'firsts', including a DryKor air-conditioning unit which uses desiccant technology to dry and cool the office space simultaneously, and a ceramic fuel cell to provide heat and electricity. In the year following the refurbishment, the building achieved a 61 per cent reduction in energy use, and an 82 per cent water saving, compared to the industry average.[206] Following fine-tuning in the second year, this increased to 71 per cent saving in energy and 90 per cent savings in water use.[207] Water consumption is minimized at each end-use point by using the latest in controlled-flow shower heads and taps, some of them sensor activated only. Toilets are dual-flush design and urinals are waterless. Greywater is collected, treated and re-used for toilet flushing. This is complemented with a rainwater harvesting system providing 4400 litres of rainwater storage to provide much of the building's water needs.[208]

Wal-Mart building retrofits – Upgrading 113 stores in China

In addition to the new building energy efficiency initiatives, Wal-Mart is achieving significant energy efficiency savings across its American and international stores. In 2007 Wal-Mart retrofitted its low- and medium-temperature refrigerated display cases in over 500 US stores and installed energy-saving LED lighting, which resulted in up to two-thirds estimated energy savings compared with fluorescent technology.[209] Occupancy sensors and LED-dimming capabilities were also installed to reduce the time the LED refrigerated display cases are at full illumination levels – reducing the hours from 24 to approximately 15 hours a day. Wal-Mart estimates the energy cost savings of the retrofit to exceed US$2.6 million annually. After opening its first energy-efficient location in Beijing in 2008, Wal-Mart is planning energy efficiency upgrades for all 113 of its Chinese stores within the next five years.[210] Compared to a typical store in 2005, the new Beijing store will consume 23 per cent less electricity and 17 per cent less water annually. Upgrades for other stores will include: LEDs for major lighting; motion sensors to control lighting during non-peak hours and in low-traffic areas; sliding glass doors in refrigerators and coolers; and treatment and re-use of water running from the refrigeration system.

Source: Compiled by TNEP, sources as noted within the table text

design.[211] According to a study by the Californian Energy Commission, 'By applying the integrated design principles ... the energy consumption of buildings with small HVAC systems can be reduced by 25 to 35 per cent without incurring significant increases in capital costs.'[212] The study reviewed the operation of 75 buildings and 215 rooftop HVAC units in California and identified several issues with HVAC systems that increase energy consumption, including: economizers not operating properly (63 per cent); improper refrigerant charge (46 per cent); low air flow (39 per cent); cycling fans during unoccupied periods (38 per cent); fans running during unoccupied periods (30 per cent); simultaneous heating and cooling (7 per cent); and inadequate ventilation air (7 per cent).[213] The study highlighted a range of options for reducing the consumption of HVAC systems, as shown in Figure 2.20.

According to the UK Carbon Trust, 'Heating, ventilation and air conditioning can account for the majority of money spent by an organisation on energy. Making even small adjustments to systems can significantly improve the working environment and at the same time, save money.'[214] Achieving

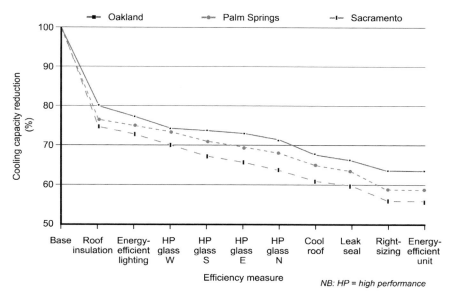

Source: Based on data from the Public Interest Energy Research Program, State of California Energy Commission

Figure 2.20 *The impact of integrated design*

significant reductions in the energy consumption of HVAC units involves the implementation of a range of complementary actions, including load management, new HVAC unit selection, commissioning and maintenance, for instance.[215]

Load management
There are a number of options for reducing the heating and cooling load, related to both the building structure and the HVAC system itself, including the following:

- *Building orientation and external facades*: The orientation of the building can affect the solar gain and hence the level of heating from the sun within the building space. Combined with fixed horizontal shading on the sun-facing facade and adjustable vertical shading devices for east and west facades, and low solar heat gain coefficient windows,[216] the solar gain can be minimized.
- *Windows*: Once the building orientation and external facades are appropriately designed the next area to reduce heat transfer is the windows. Single-glazed windows can transfer a large portion of incident infrared (heat-containing) light wavelengths, which is usually undesirable. However, there are window technologies that allow large-area windows to transfer relatively little heat. For example, gas-filled double- and triple-glazed windows (usually using either air, argon or krypton gas) reduce heat (and noise) transfer because the gas has a lower thermal conductivity (and

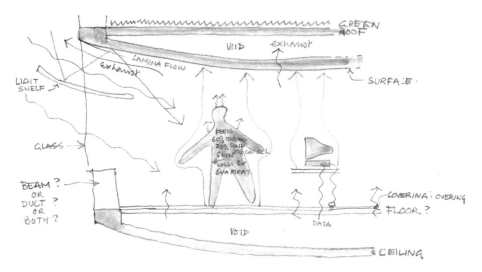

Source: Courtesy of Mick Pearce

Figure 2.21 *Designer's sketch of interior heat generation considerations for Melbourne's Council House II*

acoustic transmittance) than the glass. An alternative or addition to multiple glazed windows are spectrally selective windows and films, which reject up to 98 per cent of infrared wavelengths and 99 per cent of ultraviolet wavelengths, while transmitting up to 70 per cent of visible wavelengths, similar to that used for car window tinting. Such technologies have been described in the technical appendices to the book *Natural Capitalism* as 'probably the single most important technology for making possible very energy-efficient, cost-effective, and delightful buildings.'[217] There are several emerging window technologies that can assist to further optimize energy consumption, including photo-chromic glass, thermo-chromic glass, electro-chromic glass and liquid crystal film.[218] In addition, heat transfer across the window and building framing can be reduced by minimizing thermal bridges, such as metal beams and studs, which are good thermal conductors.

- *Roofs*: In hot climates, heat transfer through the roof can be minimized by painting the roof a light colour (reflectivity greater than 0.65), preferably white, or by painting the roof with heat-reflective paint. Heat gain through any external building surface is directly proportional to the temperature difference across that surface,[219] and in the case of a roof on a commercial building, the temperature difference ranges from 10°C for light-coloured roofs to up to 45°C for dark-coloured roofs.[220] Unpainted galvanized roofs, while good reflectors of visible light wavelengths, are also good absorbers of the infrared (heat-containing) wavelengths and are thus not a good option for large roofs. In addition to reducing the cooling load, light coloured roofs and exterior walls also reduce the temperature of the surroundings, which is more pleasant for pedestrians and local wildlife.

*   *Exterior ground surfaces*: In hot climates, heat in the immediate surroundings of the building can be reduced by minimizing paved and concreted ground areas. Where paving and concreting is used, high reflectivity finishes will absorb less heat. However, note that some high reflecting ground covers also produce undesirable glare.[221]

*   *Indoor conditions*: Inside the building heat is generated by lighting, equipment and people, and this load needs to be incorporated into the design load, as in CH2. In addition the interior air temperature needs to be closely matched to the requirements as it is possible to save as much as 10 per cent a year on heating and cooling costs by simply turning the thermostat back 10–15 per cent.

*   *Natural ventilation*: Using natural ventilation, particularly the purging of hot air at night, reduces energy consumption by using passive cooling and/or high-efficiency fans and motors only when required.[222] Undesired air infiltration and exfiltration can be prevented by weather-stripping doors, using sealing gaskets and latches on operable windows, and filling holes in sills, studs and joists.[223]

*   *HVAC distribution systems*:[224] Clean fans, filters and air ducts can improve efficiency by up to 60 per cent.[225] There is often pressure to minimize distribution system capital cost because the installed cost can approach the HVAC unit cost,[226] but failing to optimize the distribution system performance efficiency usually results in higher long-term costs and poor indoor comfort. Distribution system energy losses can be minimized by reducing resistance to air movement, and hence pressure drop, resulting in energy consumption, through good ductwork design. Reducing resistance in ductwork involves minimizing pressure drop by: creating low air velocities; using low-loss fittings; designing central plant air filters to balance filtration efficiency and pressure drop; maintaining central plant air filters; and minimizing duct lengths by carefully positioning the plant room and HVAC units.[227] For example the design of bends in the ducting can have a significant effect on the pressure drop through the system, as shown in Figure 2.22.

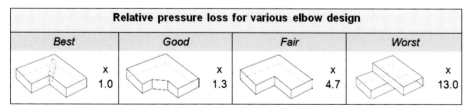

Source: Based on the work of the Architectural Energy Corporation

Figure 2.22 *Comparing pressure drop across various square elbow designs*

- *HVAC control systems:*[228] Control systems that are adequately commissioned and programmed reduce HVAC energy consumption by ensuring that the right amount of air-conditioning is provided when and where it is required. There are several types of control systems available for HVAC systems, such as: time switches that activate and deactivate the system,[229] and that can learn to auto-adjust to deliver reduced operating times of 5–10 per cent; and thermostats that control both the unit and ventilation fans.[230] Thermostat location is also an important consideration because poorly located thermostats can increase energy consumption substantially. Thermostats provide accurate readings when located on an interior wall (which is nearer to the average space temperature than exterior walls), or near a return duct (where flow is constant and unrestricted). Thermostats will provide inaccurate readings when located in direct sunlight, near artificial heat sources such as office and refrigeration equipment, or when isolated behind doors or curtains. Locating multiple thermostats in the same space with conflicting air-conditioning set points will make HVAC systems work against each other and thus increase energy consumption.[231]

New HVAC unit selection

If upgrading the HVAC system, or needing to choose a new system as part of the design of a new building, after reducing the heating and cooling load as much as possible using a combination of the above features, the next step is to select the right type and size of system. Selecting the right type and design for a HVAC system depends on the size and design of the building, the interior heating and cooling requirements, and the exterior climate. These factors determine the calculated sensible and latent heating and cooling loads and supply-air flow rate. When selecting the system it is important to choose the most energy-efficient type within budgetary constraints. Energy-efficient units are up to 30 per cent more efficient than standard efficiency units and are available in most size ranges.[232] Energy-efficient units differ from standard efficiency units in several ways; for instance, they typically incorporate larger condenser and evaporator coils, more efficient compressors, enhanced insulation,[233] and thermostatic expansion valves, which make units more tolerant to variations in refrigerant charge.[234] Some units also use electronic ignition devices rather than gas-burning pilot equipment.[235] In *Natural Capitalism*, the authors outline a range of new insights, based on the work of Professor Luxton and Eng Lock Lee, that when brought together can transform HVAC design and lead to significant energy efficiency savings for the system itself.[236]

Commissioning and adequate staff training are vital to ensure that the building services equipment operates as intended by the design team. Commissioning is a quality assurance process that ensures HVAC systems operate as intended. Commissioning is integrated into the entire development process, from design to construction, testing, post-occupancy and handover.[237] The post-occupancy commissioning phase provides an opportunity to test and adjust the HVAC system over a range of operating loads, especially the most common load for the building. Once the building has been built and the system has been installed and properly commissioned, ongoing monitoring and maintenance are key steps to further fine-tuning energy savings and ensuring that the system is running as well as possible. Thorough maintenance procedures assist in maintaining HVAC system energy efficiency and occupant comfort, as well as maximizing equipment life and minimizing component failure.

Heat recovery systems
Heat exchange technology can be used to recover heat in winter and coolth in summer. Heinz Shilling, of German firm SEW reports to the authors that:

> *SEW has developed a super-efficient system that exchanges about 90 per cent of the heat by letting streams of air or gas run in one direction and streams of fluids (or gas again) in the other. Because of the efficiency of the system, even very small temperature differences can be harnessed... The figure provided [Figure 2.23] shows the construction arrangement for heating air from 10°C to 28°C by cooling water from 30°C to 12°C, where the heat equivalent of 50 kilowatt-hours of heat or coolth can be*

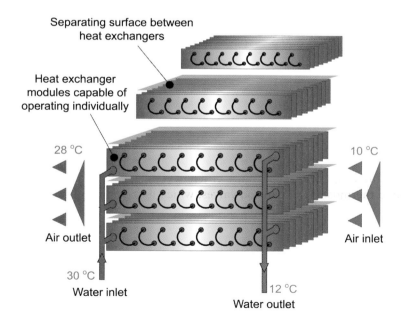

Source: Provided by Heinz Schilling

Figure 2.23 *Heat exchange by layers of opposite streams of air and water (GSWT®). Incoming air of 10°C can be heated to 28°C by cooling water from 30°C to 12°C* *recovered with 1 kilowatt-hour of electricity. The process is known as 'heat-recycling' and the patented technology is called 'heat exchange by layers of opposite streams' (Gegenstrom-Schicht-Wärmeaustauscher) or GSWT.*

Shilling went on to report that:

The modular design allows for a variety of sizes and functions in heating, cooling and air-conditioning. The insulation layers between the flat modules make separated operations of the modules possible but also remove moisture from the system. The modules are easy to clean and can be filled, emptied, and locked off individually.[238]

According to Shilling, to further enhance the cooling and/or heating efficiency of buildings the GSWT modules can be combined with numerous other functions, including, for example, adiabatic evaporation cooling between the stream of used air and the heat exchanger. The system is particularly efficient for summer cooling in rather dry areas where night temperatures tend to be low, allowing the feeding into the system of the cold at night. Combined heat and power units can be coupled into the system, enhancing the combined economic efficiency. The SEW technology considerably reduces the sizes of heating and cooling systems and correspondingly reduces costs, in addition to reductions in fuel and power cost.

Indoor lighting

Indoor lighting is responsible for a significant proportion of energy consumption in commercial buildings around the world, representing up to 8 per cent in China in 2000 (all sources),[239] 14 per cent in the EU in 2001 (electricity)[240] and 37 per cent in the US in 2003 (electricity).[241] As demonstrated in the case studies above, the energy used for indoor lighting can be significantly reduced through the use of modern lights, effective methods to reduce lighting needs, and through effective lighting control. According to the IPCC:

Lighting energy use can be reduced by 75–90 per cent compared to conventional practice through (i) use of the most efficient lighting devices available; (ii) use of day-lighting with occupancy and daylight sensors to dim and switch off electric lighting; and (iii) use of such measures as ambient/task lighting.[242]

The most cost-effective activity to reduce energy consumption in existing buildings is retrofitting them with modern energy-efficient lamps, with payback periods in the order of 1–3 years.[243] There are also several technological control solutions, including: rewiring, key lock switches, time-switched lights (push-button or time delay switches, lighting controllers), voltage reduction technology, and occupancy sensors (i.e. passive infrared, ultrasonic, microwave, photo).[244]

> *Since the early 1980s, 40 watt fluorescent tubes with ballasts that use 12 watts or more installed in light fittings that absorb around half the light produced and are switched in large banks have been replaced by 36 watt tubes with low loss ballasts (typically 6 watts or less) in more efficient fittings that deliver 60 per cent or more of the light generated. A new generation of triphosphor lamps (25 per cent more efficient than traditional 36 watt tubes) with very low-loss electronic ballasts in even more efficient fittings and with occupancy and/or daylight sensors and automated control systems is now capturing increasing market share and will soon become the de facto standard... As lighting is typically replaced every 15–20 years, there is potential for a significant improvement in performance of existing buildings over the next decade, as outdated equipment is replaced. Display and feature lighting, particularly in foyers and retail facilities, has increased, along with outdoor lighting. In many cases, these activities use inefficient lamps such as low voltage halogens. Further, bright, inefficient lights generate substantial heat and radiant discomfort for those located under them: so air-conditioning requirements increase. More efficient lighting options for feature lighting are emerging, such as smaller output metal halide lamps, and solid state (LED) lighting is expected to play an increasing role over time.*
>
> Alan Pears, The Allen Consulting Group, 2004[245]

The following provides a range of solutions highlighting the Factor Five potential (when combined) within the main issues related to indoor lighting – that is, new technology for lamps, day-lighting, and appropriate lighting levels.

New technology for lamps

New generation triphosphor fluorescent lamps are 25 per cent more efficient than the traditional 36 watt monophosphor fluorescent tubes (CFLs),[246] and light emitting diodes (LEDs) are solid state light emitters, which are currently cost-effective in specific applications where there is a requirement for long lifetime, high durability, very low profile and highly directional output.[247] According to Lester Brown:

> *The energy saved by replacing a 100-watt incandescent bulb with an equivalent CFL over its lifetime is sufficient to drive a Toyota Prius hybrid car from New York to San Francisco. Over its lifetime, each standard (13 watt) CFL will reduce electricity bills by roughly $30 ... last 10 times as long ... and reduce*

energy use by the equivalent of 200 pounds of coal. An even newer lighting technology – light-emitting diodes or LEDs – uses only one fifth as much electricity as the old-fashioned incandescent bulbs.[248]

Brown goes on to point out that:

Shifting to CFLs in homes, to the most advanced linear fluorescents in office buildings, commercial outlets, and factories, and to LEDs in traffic lights would cut the world share of electricity used for lighting from 19 per cent to 7 per cent. This would save enough electricity to avoid building 705 coal-fired power plants. By way of comparison, today there are 2370 coal-fired plants in the world.[249]

Day-lighting

Day-lighting is the practice of bringing natural light into a building and distributing it to provide illumination.[250] This method of lighting reduces the reliance on artificial lighting and thus reduces energy consumption and energy costs, but can also increase undesired solar gain and glare. According to the IPCC:

A number of recent studies indicate savings in lighting energy use of 40 to 80% in the day-lighted perimeter zones of office buildings.[251] The management of solar heat gain along with day-lighting to reduce electric lighting also leads to a reduction in cooling loads. Lee et al[252] measured savings for an automated Venetian blind system integrated with office lighting controls, finding that lighting energy savings averaged 35% in winter and ranged from 40 to 75% in summer.[253]

There are a series of day-lighting guidelines and technologies that assist in optimizing daylight illumination, solar gain and glare, including:[254]

- *Higher angles of daylight illumination*: Bringing daylight into the building core can be achieved using top-mounted apertures such as clerestories, light shelves and roof monitors (see Figure 2.24). Windows not fitted with light shelves or venetian blinds can be a source of unacceptable brightness levels and excessive contrast ratios of background to foreground.
- *Avoid direct sunlight*: Direct sunlight can cause unacceptable contrast ratios, disability glare or veiled reflection. However, direct sunlight can be pleasant and stress-relieving to occupants in non-task zones.
- *Filter the daylight*: Daylight can be diffused and distributed and its intensity reduced using trees, plants, draperies, screens, translucent shades and light-scattering glazing.

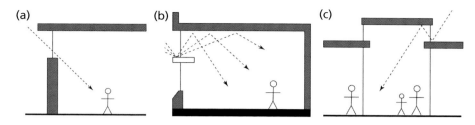

Source: Based on Abraham (1996)[255]

Figure 2.24 *(a) Clerestory; (b) light shelf; (c) roof monitor*

- *Bounce daylight off surrounding surfaces*: Daylight can be reflected and distributed throughout the building interior using light shelves, louvres, blinds and vertical baffles. In general, softer light sources reduce eye strain while scattered light reduces shadows.
- *Integrate daylight with other building systems*: Day-lighting systems are most effective when their operation is integrated with that of other systems, such as HVAC, natural ventilation, passive heating and cooling, acoustic control systems, electrical lighting systems incorporating occupancy sensors, photocells and dimmable electronic ballasts, and building energy management systems.

In addition to reducing energy consumption and energy costs, day-lighting has also been shown to improve personnel productivity, reduce errors, reduce absenteeism and increase retail sales.[256] Estimates across a variety of commercial buildings indicate that while operating and maintenance costs (about half of which are energy costs) contribute to 2 per cent of total annual operating costs, personnel costs contribute to 78–89 per cent.[257] Thus, a 1 per cent increase in personnel productivity can almost offset the entire energy budget.

Appropriate lighting levels

Matching the lighting levels to the requirement, rather than over-lighting, will assist in reducing energy consumption and in providing comfortable workplaces. The simple method to reduce energy consumption is to avoid having lights on when there is ample daylight or in unoccupied zones. One of the latest research innovations in improving lighting energy efficiency is spectrally enhanced lighting, which focuses on increasing the correlated colour temperature of a lamp, and makes the light appear brighter for the same lighting intensity.[258] In addition, according to the IPCC:

> *A simple strategy to further reduce energy use is to provide a relatively low background lighting level, with local levels of greater illumination at individual workstations. This strategy is*

referred to as 'task/ambient lighting' and is popular in Europe. Not only can this alone cut lighting energy use in half, but it provides a greater degree of individual control over personal lighting levels and can reduce uncomfortable levels of glare and high contrast.[259]

Office equipment

Office equipment is responsible for a significant proportion of energy consumption in commercial buildings around the world, representing 7 per cent in the US in 2003 (data not identified for China and Europe).[261] Estimates from the UK suggest office/client equipment is the fastest growing energy consumer in business, consuming about 15 per cent of total electricity used in offices and expected to increase to 30 per cent by 2020.[262] Figure 2.25 shows the estimated energy consumption of various items of IT equipment as a percentage of total IT energy consumption in the US.

The following briefly overviews, and provides references for, a range of solutions highlighting the Factor Five potential (when combined) within the main issues related to office equipment – assessing opportunities for reduced use or consolidation, selecting the appropriate equipment, using power management strategies, using low-energy equipment, and continuous management and monitoring. Also refer to the online sector study on the IT and communication sector at www.factorfiveonline.info.

Assess and consolidate

Operating equipment only when necessary and removing unnecessary equipment in order to reduce the costs, energy and materials consumption. For

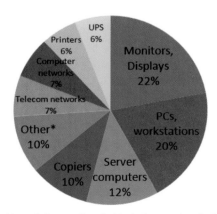

Note: 'Other' includes fax machines, desktop and handheld calculators, point of sale (POS) terminals, electric typewriters, automated teller machines (ATMs), scanners, very small aperture terminals (VSATs), supercomputers, voicemail systems, smart hand-held devices and dictation equipment. UPS = uninterruptible power supply.
Source: Based on data from Roth et al (2002)[260]

Figure 2.25 *Estimated energy consumption of various items of IT equipment as a percentage of total IT energy consumption in the US*

example, it is common to find opportunities to consolidate desktop computers, imaging equipment and supplies inventory within a building, particularly when one company may be spread over a number of floors.[263]

Select the appropriate equipment

Often the energy consumption of equipment can be reduced at no cost by simply using the right-sized item. There are also specific features to consider for most common items of equipment – computers, printers, photocopiers and combined machines – such as standby, duplex and draft printing.[265]

Power management strategies

In an average office, many items of office equipment are on for a large portion of time while not engaged in tasks. Power management strategies reduce energy consumption by turning off client equipment when they are least likely to be used. Generally, turning off client equipment after hours can reduce power consumption by about two-thirds, while a combination strategy of setting them to consume minimal power when in use and setting them to turn off after just a few minutes of inactivity can reduce power consumption by about an additional third.[266] Power management options in modern client equipment usually rely on the function of both hardware and software – that is, processor, chipset, system BIOS, operating system and processor driver.[267] Figure 2.26

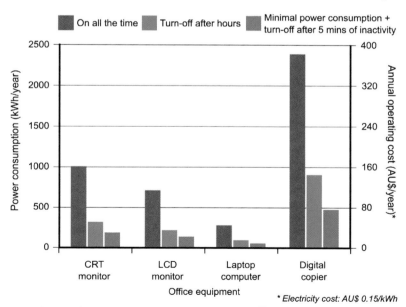

Source: Based on data from the Ministerial Council on Energy (2003)[264]

Figure 2.26 *Comparison of power consumption and operating costs of office equipment with no power management, with simple power management and with aggressive power management*

shows the effect on power consumption and operating costs of common client equipment with no power management and with the two power management strategies described above.

Low-energy client equipment

There is a range of component options for many items of IT equipment and these components can have quite varied energy consumption despite providing the same services. There are low-energy technologies for common IT equipment components such as processors, monitors, power supplies, storage memory and computers. Indirect energy consumption can also be reduced using internet communication technologies, which can provide common communication services, such as face-to-face meetings via videoconference[268] and phone calls,[269] and enable new employment and operations models without the associated travel and serviced infrastructure.[270] Internet communication technologies can also enable remote access to targeted or costly information services, such as processing power, storage and software.

Management and monitoring

Continuously managing and monitoring the client environment for opportunities to reduce energy and materials consumption can potentially reduce energy consumption and costs. These opportunities may include: replacing inefficient client equipment when cost effective, and ensuring appropriate end-of-life processing of the replaced equipment; recycling spent print cartridges; monitoring and reporting energy and material consumption; introducing or updating sustainable purchasing and procurement policies;[271] and scheduling non-critical, high-energy activities out of peak periods.[272]

IPCC Strategy Seven: Materials efficiency – water

All commercial buildings use water across a variety of uses as shown in Figure 2.27. The main areas of water usage are not simply amenities (37 per cent) – toilets, kitchenettes, showers – as most would assume but also cooling towers use 31 per cent, and 26 per cent is usually being lost due to leakage somewhere in the building.[273] These three areas make up over 90 per cent of commercial buildings water usage. Hence here we focus on how to achieve Factor Five in each of these three areas.

Case studies featured previously in this Sector Study, such as 60L, Szencorp Headquarters, and the Melbourne City Council CH2 building, showed that Factor Five water productivity improvements are possible. These buildings are virtually water self-sufficient and the water productivity initiatives have been shown to also improve energy productivity. Currently most of the water used in cities requires the storage, treatment and pumping of water from dams, which requires energy. If instead buildings use onsite rainwater, or treated and re-used greywater and blackwater, to meet their water needs, there is the potential to significantly reduce the energy consumption of city water treatment and distribution systems. Also, as shown in Figure 2.27, cooling towers used to air-

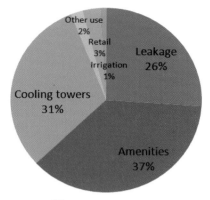

Source: Based on data from DEWHA (2007)[274]

Figure 2.27 *Typical commercial building office water usage patterns*

condition commercial buildings are a major user of water for this sector. So, just as there was in residential buildings, again there is a strong nexus of mutually reinforcing energy- and water-saving opportunities in the commercial building sector. Specifically the following general strategies can be applied to commercial buildings to achieve Factor Five improvements in water productivity, which also have energy-saving benefits.

Improving water efficiency in amenities

Toilets, taps, showers and water appliances are all common sources of water use and wastage, along with maintenance costs in offices, public buildings and households. As explained for residential buildings, there are significant opportunities to improve water efficiency in all these areas:[275]

- Dual-flush toilets are capable of reducing water usage by 67 per cent compared with conventional high-flow models. Waterless urinals are becoming increasingly common in office/commercial buildings. These have been used in Europe and the US for over 10 years now with annual water savings of 170,000 litres per annum, with manufacturers now offering options that allow any type of flushing toilet to be converted into a waterless urinal.
- Various shower-head designs exist to reduce water consumption by up to 75 per cent by using a combination of high pressure and innovative orifice design.
- Alternative tap/faucet devices exist that can reduce flow rates by up to 70 per cent, this is particularly important as it can lead to significant reductions in energy costs for water heating and subsequent greenhouse gas emissions.

Saving water in water cooling systems (based on cooling towers)

Many commercial and public buildings, and in particular larger buildings, have water cooling systems which use cooling towers. It is estimated that there are approximately a million cooling towers in operation globally.[276] They can account for up to 30 to 40 per cent of a building's water use. Water cooling systems process and remove heat from the building, essentially by evaporating water. The evaporation of one kilogram of water absorbs more heat (2257kJ at atmospheric pressure) than any other molecular liquid, which enables the cooling system to remove significant amounts of heat from a building. In a building with 10,000m² of floor space, roughly two million litres of water will be evaporated each year using water-cooled systems.[277] The first step then to reduce water usage in this area is to reduce the size and time of operation of water-cooled systems in buildings through reducing the cooling loads needed to maintain a comfortable ambient temperature in the building. As explained earlier, it is possible to reduce cooling loads in buildings significantly – and hence significantly reduce the associated water consumption.[278] Also, considerable savings can be achieved by reducing the overflow that occurs in a cooling tower when the level of water exceeds a predetermined height. This overflow water simply flows into stormwater drains and is wasted, and this wastage can be as much as 40 per cent of the water used.[279]

Alternatives to water cooling systems with cooling towers

The main alternatives to water cooling systems are dry cooling systems, which do not use any water at all but tend to use more energy than water cooling systems.[280] A new hybrid dry air/water cooling system, developed by Muller Industries Australia, enables reductions in water usage of around 80 per cent while still being almost as energy efficient as water-cooled systems, using air to cool in ambient temperatures and only using water under extreme conditions.[281] The system – the Muller 3C Cooler – is designed so that it can be retrofitted, easily replacing water-cooled systems and their water cooling towers. The cooler consumes 30 per cent less energy than other air-conditioning systems,[282] and uses only slightly (5–10 per cent) more energy compared to water-cooled systems. It also delivers a sizeable 7dBA noise reduction.

Also, cooling towers are open systems which make ideal conditions for the propagation of the Legionella bacteria. The 3C on the other hand is a closed system thus eliminating this risk. This provides hospitals and public buildings with the security of knowing that their air-conditioning system cannot ever cause Legionella disease. As recently as 2000, there was a Legionella outbreak at one of Melbourne's main indoor tourist attractions, the Melbourne Aquarium. Four people tragically died and 95 people were hospitalized. The source of the Legionella outbreak was the Aquarium's cooling towers.[283] Currently there are over 600 installations of the Muller 3C Coolers across Australia, and others in the UK, France and Asia. The cooler has been used in a range of applications, including hospitals, commercial office buildings and government buildings. Another innovation, the Muller Dricon, is designed to be used instead of evaporative condensers to supply cool air for refrigeration. Coles supermarkets in Australia are using this technology to reduce water usage in their refrigeration air cooling systems. The Muller 3C and the Dricon can use rainwater and greywater, enabling them to further reduce commercial buildings' water usage from mains water. Melbourne University's new Faculty of Economics and Commerce building is an example of this approach. They claim that the 12-storey building delivers carbon reductions of 73 per cent and water use reductions of up to 90 per cent. The building achieves this through reducing cooling demand by utilizing natural ventilation, using chilled beam cooling technology, and by the installation of Muller 3C Coolers combined with rainwater harvesting and greywater re-use.[284]

Addressing sources of leakage

Office and public building hydraulic systems and equipment are prone to leakage, especially if the local network pressures are high. Leakage losses of 10–30 per cent are not uncommon.[285] A relatively small leak of 2L per minute will result in a loss of roughly a million litres per annum. In a large commercial office building even just 5–10 such small leaks will result in significant water losses that can go undetected if organizations simply rely on a total consumption figure in their water bills.[286] Water metering needs to be undertaken periodically to check for leaks.

Using these three strategies above – water efficiency in amenities, reducing water losses from cooling towers, and stopping leakages – alone can achieve 75 per cent savings in water. But, as shown by the case studies earlier in this sector, commercial buildings can further reduce their dependency on mains water through sourcing water onsite through rainwater harvesting, greywater/blackwater treatment and re-use and even sewer harvesting. An integrated whole system approach applying these strategies, enables Factor Five reductions in mains water usage to be achieved.

Notes

1   OECD (2003b).
2   ibid.
3   Kenway et al (2008).
4   IPCC (2007).
5   ibid.
6   International Energy Agency (IEA) (2006) 'Electricity/Heat in World in 2006', www.iea.org/Textbase/stats/electricitydata.asp?COUNTRY_CODE=29&Submit= Submit, accessed 23 February 2009.
7   EIA (2006) cited in IPCC (2007).
8   Zhou (2007) cited in IPCC (2007).
9   IEA (2003) cited in Bertoldi and Atanasiu (2007).
10   Waide et al (2004) cited in Bertoldi and Atanasiu (2007).
11   Communities and Local Government (2008).

12   Energy Saving Secrets (undated) 'BedZED: the UK's Biggest Eco Community',
      www.energysavingsecrets.co.uk/bedzed-the-uks-biggest-eco-community.html,
      accessed 12 May 2009.
13   Monbiot (2007).
14   Koerner (2008).
15   Cost Efficient Passive Houses as European Standards initiative (CEPHES) is a
      project involving the construction and scientific evaluation of housing units built
      to Passive House standards in five European countries.
16   Schnieders (2003).
17   Determined by measurements, extrapolated for a whole year and normalized to
      20°C indoor temperature.
18   Piebalgs (2006).
19   PEP (2006).
20   Feist (1996).
21   For more information see Aspen Publishers (2004).
22   Concordia Language Villages (undated) 'Design and Architecture',
      http://waldseebiohaus.typepad.com/biohaus/design.html#top, accessed
      21 February 2009.
23   IEA (2003); Waide et al (2004) cited in Bertoldi and Atanasiu (2007).
24   Zhou (2007) cited in IPCC (2007).
25   EIA (2006) cited in IPCC (2007).
26   Pears (1998).
27   For further information refer to Smith et al (2007) Lecture 9.1; IPCC (2007).
28   IPCC (2007).
29   ibid.
30   For more information see Smith et al (2007) Lecture 2.3.
31   Sherman and Jump (1997); O'Neal et al (2002); Francisco et al (2004) cited in
      IPCC (2007).
32   Pears (2005).
33   For further information refer to Fraunhofer Institute for Solar Energy Systems
      (2000).
34   Clinton Climate Initiative (2008) 'C40 Cities: Buildings, Freiburg, Germany',
      www.c40cities.org/bestpractices/buildings/freiburg_housing.jsp, accessed 8
      January 2009.
35   Wigginton and Harris (2002) pp143–148.
36   Zhou (2007) cited in IPCC (2007).
37   IEA (2003); Waide et al (2004) cited in Bertoldi and Atanasiu (2007).
38   EIA (2006) cited in IPCC (2007).
39   Lovins et al (2002) p99.
40   Lawrence Berkeley National Laboratory (2004) cited in IPCC (2007).
41   International Energy Agency (IEA) (2004) cited in IPCC (2007).
42   East (2006).
43   Pears (2004b) see Appendices.
44   ibid see Appendices.
45   von Weizsäcker et al (1997) pp41–44.
46   Pears (2004b) see Appendices.
47   ibid.
48   von Weizsäcker et al (1997) pp41–44.
49   Eco-Kettle (undated) 'The Eco Kettle: Exactly The Right Amount of Water Every
      Time You Boil!', www.ecokettle.com/ECOKETTLE.htm, accessed 14 May 2009.
50   ibid.

51   Morphy Richards (undated) 'Toaster', www.morphyrichards.co.uk/
      ProductDetail.aspx?Product=44943, accessed 14 May 2009.
52   Goorskey et al (2004).
53   For further information refer to Lawrence Berkeley National Laboratory
      (undated) 'Standby Power', http://standby.lbl.gov/standby.html, accessed 8
      January 2009.
54   Monbiot (2007) p77.
55   Rocky Mountain Institute (2007).
56   IEA (2003); Waide et al (2004) cited in Bertoldi and Atanasiu (2007).
57   EIA (2006) cited in IPCC (2007).
58   Zhou (2007) cited in IPCC (2007).
59   IPCC (2007).
60   Pears (2004b) pp134–140.
61   Riedy et al (2008) see '6.5 Hot water service'.
62   Rocky Mountain Institute (2004).
63   ibid.
64   OECD (2008) 'OECD Family Database: OECD – Social Policy Division –
      Directorate of Employment, Labour and Social Affairs',
      www.oecd.org/dataoecd/62/22/41919509.pdf, accessed 14 May 2009.
65   But if it is assumed that the household is not using efficient AAA shower heads
      and instead are using inefficient shower heads, then 30 litres will not be enough.
66   Zhou (2007) cited in IPCC (2007).
67   EIA (2006) cited in IPCC (2007).
68   IEA (2003); Waide et al (2004) cited in Bertoldi and Atanasiu (2007).
69   Garg and Bansal (2000); McCowan et al (2002).
70   Gumbel (2008).
71   Brown, L. (2008) pp215, 217–218.
72   EIA (2006) cited in IPCC (2007).
73   IEA (2003); Waide et al (2004) cited in Bertoldi and Atanasiu (2007).
74   Brown, L. (2008) p219.
75   von Weizsäcker et al (1997) pp34–35.
76   Sun Frost (undated) 'Sun Frost: The world's most elegant refrigerators are also
      the most energy efficient!', www.sunfrost.com/Sunfrost_refrigerators.pdf,
      accessed 8 October 2008.
77   Goorskey et al (2004).
78   Harrington and Holt (2006) p12.
79   Arcelik (2008) 'Arçelik was the Only Turkish Company in UN Conference',
      Arcelik Press Release, www.arcelikas.com.tr/Cultures/en-US/MedyaIliskileri/
      KurumsalHaberlerBasinBultenleri/News8.htm?LANGUAGE=en-US&
      MENUID=3, accessed 15 May 2009.
80   Pears (2009).
81   ibid.
82   von Weizsäcker et al (1997) pp35–36.
83   ibid.
84   ibid.
85   Pears (2009).
86   People and Planet (2008) 'People and Water: Water Use',
      www.peopleandplanet.net/doc.php?id=593&section=14, accessed 18 April 2009.
87   Safe Drinking Water Foundation (2004).
88   UNESCO (2000).
89   ibid.

90   Stasinopoulos et al (2008).
91   Kenway et al (2008).
92   Stasinopoulos et al (2008).
93   Kenway et al (2008).
94   Troy (2008).
95   Department of Environment, Water, Heritage and the Arts (DEWHA) (2009).
96   Department of Environment, Water, Heritage and the Arts (DEWHA) (2009).
97   Troy (2008).
98   Hargroves and Smith (2005).
99   This figure is substantially lower than the average Australian household water consumption of 282L/person/day.
100 NSW Health Department (2001) p12.
101 Ecological Homes (2002).
102 Mobbs (1999).
103 Bowmer (2004).
104 ibid.
105 Department of Environment, Water, Heritage and the Arts (DEWHA) (2009).
106 UNESCO (2000).
107 International Energy Agency (2006) 'Electricity/Heat in World in 2006', www.iea.org/Textbase/stats/electricitydata.asp?COUNTRY_CODE=29& Submit=Submit, accessed 23 February 2009.
108 Peon et al (2005).
109 ibid.
110 Mills (2005).
111 Peon et al (2005).
112 ibid.
113 International Energy Agency (IEA) (2006a).
114 Mills (2005).
115 Mills (2000).
116 Peon et al (2005).
117 Light Up the World Foundation (undated) website, www.lutw.org, accessed 4 February 2009.
118 Gupta (2009).
119 Gupta (2003).
120 International Energy Agency (IEA) (2006b).
121 World Health Organization (WHO) (2004).
122 Ramanathan and Carmichael (2008).
123 University of California (2008).
124 ibid.
125 REN21 (2005).
126 Brown, L. (2008).
127 Grameen Shakti (2007) 'Dipal Chandra Barua, Solar Power Pioneer wins Zayed Future Energy prize', www.gshakti.org/, accessed 27 February 2008.
128 US Department of Energy (2009) 'Department of Energy and Commercial Real Estate Executives Launch Alliance to Reduce Energy Consumption of Buildings', www.energy.gov/news2009/7251.htm, accessed 23 April 2009; USA EPA (undated) 'Facts About Energy Use in Commercial and Industrial Facilities', www.energystar.gov/ia/business/challenge/learn_more/FastFacts.pdf, accessed 23 April 2009.
129 Department of Environment and Water, Heritage and the Arts (DEWHA) (2007).
130 Todesco (2004) ppS42–S47.

131 Harvey (2006).
132 IPCC (2007).
133 International Energy Agency (2006) 'Electricity/Heat in World in 2006', www.iea.org/Textbase/stats/electricitydata.asp?COUNTRY_CODE=29& Submit=Submit, accessed 23 February 2009.
134 Energy Information Administration (EIA) (2008) 'Table E3 – Electricity Consumption (Btu) by End Use for Non-Mall Buildings, 2003', www.eia.doe.gov/emeu/cbecs/cbecs2003/detailed_tables_2003/2003alltables/ set20.pdf, accessed 12 May 2009.
135 Zhou et al (2008) p22.
136 Janssen (2004) p37.
137 Kennett (2009).
138 Engineers Australia (2001).
139 California's building efficiency standards (along with those for energy-efficient appliances) have saved more than US$56 billion in electricity and natural gas costs since 1978. It is estimated the standards will save an additional US$23 billion by 2013, www.energy.ca.gov/title24/, accessed 25 March 2009.
140 *Environment News Service* (2006).
141 ibid.
142 World Business Council for Sustainable Development (WBCSD) (2009) p7.
143 Kornevall (2008).
144 Griffith et al (2007) p8.
145 ibid.
146 BOMA (2009) 'BOMA, CCI Deliver Pioneering Energy Efficient Retrofit Solutions to Commercial Real Estate,' BOMA Press Release, 6 January 2009.
147 Global Reporting Initiative (2009) 'Construction and Real Estate', www.globalreporting.org/ReportingFramework/SectorSupplements/ ConstructionandRealEstate/ConstructionAndRealEstate.htm, accessed 29 March 2009.
148 Lamprinidi and Ringland (2008).
149 WBCSD (2007) 'Global Survey Shows "Green" Construction Costs Dramatically Lower Than Believed', Press Release, WBCSD, 21 August 2007.
150 *Environment News Service* (2006).
151 *China Daily* (2008).
152 Collier (2008).
153 Bureau of Energy Efficiency (BEE) (undated) 'About Us', www.bee-india.nic.in/ index.php?module=Company&id=1, accessed 20 March 2009.
154 Mathur (2007).
155 Bureau of Energy Efficiency (undated) 'Energy Conservation Building Code', www.bee-india.nic.in/ecbc.php, accessed 23 March 2009.
156 Hargroves and Smith (2005) pp352–361; World Business Council for Sustainable Development (WBCSD) (2009) p7.
157 Eichholtz et al (2008).
158 Romm and Browning (1998).
159 ibid.
160 Kats (2003).
161 Australian Greenhouse Office (1999).
162 Romm (1994) cited in Hawken et al (1999) Chapter 6.
163 Stephens et al (2007).
164 Som.com (2008) 'Pearl River Tower', www.som.com/content.cfm/ pearl_river_tower, accessed 23 March 2009.

165 Frechette and Gilchrist (2009).

166 Traum (2007).

167 Frechette and Gilchrist (2008).

168 Demos and Tkaczyk (2009).

169 MSNBC (2009).

170 *Green News* (2008).

171 Extract adapted from Smith et al (2007).

172 Fortmeyer (2008).

173 City of Melbourne (2007).

174 Paevere and Brown (2008) p20.

175 Department of Environment and Water Resources (2007).

176 Melbourne City Council (undated) 'CH2: Water Conservation', www.melbourne.vic.gov.au/info.cfm?top=171&pa=4112&pa2=4091&pg=4077, accessed 23 March 2009.

177 ibid.

178 ibid.

179 NRDC (undated) 'China's Greenest Building', www.nrdc.org/international/ chinagbldg/page2.asp, accessed 23 March 2009; Marquand, R. (2006); NRDS (undated) 'Building Green from Principle to Practice: Accord 21 Office Building', www.nrdc.org/buildinggreen/strategies/default.asp, accessed 23 March 2009.

180 PRWeb (2007) 'Pacific Controls HQ Building Wins Prestigious Buildy Award for Best Intelligent Building at Builconn 2007, in Chicago, Illinois, USA', PRWeb Press Release, 12 June 2007.

181 Confederation of Indian Industry (undated) 'CII–Sorabji Godrej Green Business Centre', http://greenbusinesscentre.com/aboutus.asp, accessed 23 March 2009; Jafri (2004); Green Growth (2008); Srinivas (undated).

182 Yoong (2008) pp65–67.

183 Mills et al (2007) cited in Mills (2009).

184 Grant (2007).

185 Mills (2009).

186 Grant (2007).

187 Australian Conservation Foundation (2005).

188 City of Melbourne (undated) 'AusIndustry Research Papers – Study 8: The Building Structure and the Process of Building', www.melbourne.vic.gov.au/rsrc/ PDFs/CH2/Study8TechnicalPaper_updated.DOC, accessed 11 October 2007.

189 Mailer (2007); Hes, D. (undated) 'Greening the Building Life Cycle: Life Cycle Assessment Tools in Building and Construction 60L Green Building', http://buildlca.rmit.edu.au/CaseStud/60L/60L.html, accessed 20 March 2009.

190 Mailer (2009).

191 Department of Environment and Water Resources (2007).

192 Case study summarized at 60L Green Building (undated) website, www.60lgreenbuilding.com/, accessed 9 August 2008; Department of Environment and Water Resources (DEWR) (2007).

193 Australian Pacific Partnership (2007) 'BATF-07-39 Project 39. Australian-Indian building tune-ups', www.asiapacificpartnership.org/pr_buildings_ appliances.aspx#BATF_Project_21, accessed 23 March 2009.

194 Szencorp (2008) 'Szencorp Announces Building Tune-Up Program in India', www.ourgreenoffice.com/news_archive.html, accessed 23 March 2009.

195 Lister (2009).

196 Energy Star (undated) 'Energy Star Labelled Building Profile: Comfort Inn and Suites, Boston/Airport', www.energystar.gov/index.cfm?fuseaction=LABELED_

BUILDINGS.showProfile&profile_id=1000242, accessed 23 March 2009.
197 US EPA (2004) 'Boston's Saunders Hotel Group Awarded for Energy Efficiency and Good Environmental Practices', Press Release 18 November 2004, US EPA.
198 Energy Information Administration (2008) 'Table E3 – Electricity Consumption (Btu) by End Use for Non-Mall Buildings, 2003', www.eia.doe.gov/emeu/cbecs/cbecs2003/detailed_tables_2003/2003alltables/set20.pdf, accessed 12 May 2009.
199 Janssen (2004) p37.
200 Zhou et al (2008) p22.
201 Dymond (2006); GreenBuilding (2006) p10.
202 Pellets are sawdust compressed into cylinders of circumference about 1cm and length about 2cm. The pellets are fed into the boiler and are replaced 2–3 times per year.
203 GreenBuilding (2006) p7.
204 Del Percio (2009).
205 Ivanhoe Cambridge (2007).
206 Based on a survey of 117 existing Melbourne office buildings undertaken by Sustainability Victoria in 2000, the average base building office energy use is 600MJ/m^2 – Sustainability Victoria (2008).
207 Sustainability Victoria (2008).
208 The Department of Environment, Water, Heritage and the Arts (DEWHA) (2007); Department of Environment and Water Resources (DEWR) (2007).
209 Energy Resource (2006).
210 *China Daily* (2008).
211 Burke (1996).
212 State of California (2005).
213 Architectural Energy Corporation (2003) p2.
214 Carbon Trust (2006).
215 Adapted from Smith et al (2007) Lecture 2.3.
216 ibid.
217 Hawken et al (1999) Appendix 5C.
218 Abraham (1996).
219 ASHRAE (1997) p27.5.
220 Merritt and Ricketts (2001) pp13, 38.
221 Smith et al (2007) Lecture 2.3.
222 Jacobs (2003) pp37, 59–60.
223 Smith et al (2007) Lecture 2.3.
224 For further detail see Smith et al (2007) Lecture 2.3.
225 Carbon Trust (2006).
226 Architectural Energy Corporation (2003) p10.
227 Jacobs (2003) pp49–54, 57.
228 For further detail see Smith et al (2007) Lecture 2.3.
229 Architectural Energy Corporation (2003) p13.
230 Jacobs (2003) p63.
231 ibid.
232 Australian Greenhouse Office (2005b) p33.
233 Architectural Energy Corporation (2003) p8.
234 Jacobs (2003) p38.
235 Sustainability Victoria (2006).
236 Hawken et al (1999) Appendix 5G.
237 Penny (2004).

238 Contribution from Heinz Shilling on invitation from the authors, translated from the German by Ernst von Weizsäcker.
239 Zhou et al (2008) p22.
240 Janssen (2004) p37.
241 Energy Information Administration (EIA) (2008) 'Table E3 – Electricity Consumption (Btu) by End Use for Non-Mall Buildings, 2003', www.eia.doe.gov/emeu/cbecs/cbecs2003/detailed_tables_2003/2003alltables/set20.pdf, accessed 12 May 2009.
242 IPCC (2007).
243 Sustainability Victoria (undated) 'Energy Efficiency Lighting: Fact Sheet', www.sv.sustainability.vic.gov.au/, accessed 23 March 2009.
244 Australian Greenhouse Office (2005a).
245 Pears (2004b) pp152–153.
246 ibid.
247 Gauna and Page (2005) pp3–4.
248 Brown, L. (2008) pp215, 217–218.
249 ibid.
250 Abraham (1996).
251 IPCC (2007) 'Residential and Commercial Buildings', cited in Rubinstein and Johnson (1998); Jennings et al (2000); Bodart and Herde (2002); Reinhart (2002) pp309–322; Atif and Galasiu (2003); Li and Lam (2003).
252 Lee et al (1998).
253 IPCC (2007) p402.
254 For further information see Smith et al (2007) Lecture 2.2.
255 Abraham (1996).
256 Romm and Browning (1998); Heschong Mahone Group (1999); Kats (2003) p64; Madew (2006) pp55–56.
257 Center for Building Performance and Diagnostics, Carnegie Mellon University, cited in US General Services Administration (GSA) (1999) p32; Whole Building Design Guide Productive Committee (2007).
258 Gordon et al (2006).
259 IPCC (2007) p402.
260 Roth et al (2002) cited in Ministerial Council on Energy (2003) p7.
261 Energy Information Administration (EIA) (2008) 'Table E3 – Electricity Consumption (Btu) by End Use for Non-Mall Buildings, 2003', www.eia.doe.gov/emeu/cbecs/cbecs2003/detailed_tables_2003/2003alltables/set20.pdf, accessed 12 May 2009.
262 Carbon Trust (2006) p3.
263 Kong (undated).
264 Ministerial Council on Energy (2003) pp17–19.
265 Carbon Trust (2006) p3.
266 ibid.
267 Hewlett-Packard Development Company (2007b).
268 Hewlett-Packard Development Company (2007a).
269 Australian Computer Society (2007) 'ACS Reveals ICT's Carbon Footprint – Calls for Energy Star Rating for IT Products as Part of a Green ICT Industry Policy', Media Release, Australian Computer Society.
270 Australian Computer Society (2007) 'ACS Reveals ICT's Carbon Footprint – Calls for Energy Star Rating for IT Products as Part of a Green ICT Industry Policy', Media Release, Australian Computer Society; Taylor, P. (2008).
271 Kong (undated).

272 Australian Computer Society (2007) 'ACS Reveals ICT's Carbon Footprint – Calls for Energy Star Rating for IT Products as Part of a Green ICT Industry Policy', Media Release, Australian Computer Society.

273 Department of Environment, Water, Heritage and the Arts (DEWHA) (2007).

274 ibid.

275 ibid.

276 Harfst (2008).

277 Pears (2009).

278 ibid.

279 Sydney Water (2007).

280 Department of Environment, Water, Heritage and the Arts (DEWHA) (2007).

281 Australian Institute of Refrigeration, Air-Conditioning and Heating (AIRAH) (2003).

282 Save Water (2007) 'Product Innovations: Winner – Muller Industries', www.savewater.com.au/programs-and-events/savewater-awards/past-winners-finalists/200607-winners/product-innovations, accessed 8 May 2009.

283 Australian Institute of Refrigeration, Air-Conditioning and Heating (AIRAH) (2005).

284 Muller Industries (2009) '5 Stars for Melbourne University', www.mullerindustries.com.au/home/newsApr2009_2.shtml, accessed 8 May 2009.

285 Department of Environment, Water, Heritage and the Arts (DEWHA) (2007).

286 ibid.

3

The Heavy Industry Sector (Steel and Cement)

1 The steel industry

The potential for Factor Five improvements in steel production resource productivity

The majority of steel produced globally, some 1300Mt in 2007,[1] is manufactured in a small number of countries, each with access to similar processing technologies. This would suggest that in such a competitive and expanding global market – growing 8.3 per cent between 2005 and 2007[2] – most of the opportunities to reduce operating costs would already be captured and the energy intensity of steel making should be fairly even. However, this does not appear to be the case, with the average energy required to produce a ton of steel in 1995 varying from as little as 18GJ/t in Germany to as much as 37GJ/t in China, suggesting significant opportunity for improvement.[3] According to the International Iron and Steel Institute (IISI) the US has the most energy-efficient steel industry in the world, using an average of only 12GJ per ton of steel produced in 2006.[4] Using a baseline of the average energy intensity of the major producers in 1995 of 27.9GJ/t – the year with the most comprehensive data found, as shown in Table 3.1 – the US average equates to an energy productivity improvement of just under 60 per cent.

This Sector Study will outline the main methods used to achieve such improvements, and outline a number of further improvements that can deliver greater than Factor Five – up to 93 per cent – energy productivity improvements in the steel industry. Such significant improvements are achieved by switching to a state-of-the-art electric arc furnace system that processes recycled steel (including options such as improved process control, oxy-fuel burners, DC-arc furnaces, scrap pre-heating and post-combustion processes), adopting leading practices such as net shape casting, implementing options such as energy monitoring and management systems for energy recovery and distribution between processes, and preventative maintenance. Further, using

Table 3.1 *Performance of the major steel-manufacturing countries in 1995*

Country	Steel produced in 2008[5] (Mt)	1995 baseline energy intensity (GJ/t) in 1995	Percentage EAF used in 1995 (rather than BOF)
China	502.0	36.7	20
Japan	120.2	22.0	22
US	91.5	23.0	26
Russia	68.5	25.0[6]	34.8[7]
India	55.1	37.3	32
Germany	45.8	18.0	17
Brazil	33.7	23.1	20
France	17.0	22.5	24
Mexico	17.0	22.6	65
Poland	9.0	32.0	28
Average		27.87GJ/t	29.5% EAF

Source: Compiled from IISI (2008),[8] Martin et al (1999a),[9] Worrell (1999)[10]

recycled steel in electric arc furnaces not only improves energy productivity but also materials and water productivity.[11]

With proof that such a level of energy productivity is possible it is vitally important that at least 12GJ/t is achieved across the global sector, as the sector accounts for about 7 per cent of anthropogenic emissions of CO_2 and is growing.[12] This is especially true in the rapidly expanding steel industries in China, Japan and across the European Union. According to the UN, by 2006, China's steel industry electricity usage had reached 328 billion kWh, compared to 112.6 billion in 2000,[13] and representing 11 per cent of China's 2006 total electricity use.[14] The main opportunities lie in improving the efficiency of existing steel-making processes and upgrading processes to more efficient alternatives, along with options for fuel switching, onsite heat recovery and changing feedstock (including dramatically increased levels of recycling). Steel making is a complex process involving a number of alternative processes. Hence, in this Sector Study we present a simplified summary to demonstrate that there is significant opportunity for improvement in this sector, and refer readers to greater explanation and detail in various reports and references.

Steel making globally is done using two main types of furnaces, either a basic oxygen furnace (BOF) or an electric arc furnace (EAF). However, as pointed out in Factor Four,[15] the energy performance of the two processes varies greatly, quoting a study by Liedtke et al[16] which stated that:

> electric arc steel furnaces use one-tenth of the fuel, one-eighth of the water, one fifth of the air and less than one-fortieth of other materials compared with traditional basic-oxygen blast furnace steel plants.

When the fact that EAF uses 30 per cent more electricity than BOF is considered, this results in an overall efficiency improvement being a Factor of 4.

On average, the energy intensity of steel manufactured using a BOF is more than twice that of an EAF.[17] Furthermore, as the OECD explained in 2008,[18] the relatively new EAF technology emits over four times less CO_2 per unit of steel produced than BOF technology.

Both technologies have potential for improvement; however, on the whole the EAF process provides the greatest opportunity for energy productivity improvements. The work of world leading energy efficiency expert and member of the IPCC Mitigation Working Group, Ernst Worrell, shows that the productivity of the EAF process has been significantly improved since 1965, with 50 per cent reductions in energy intensity achieved by 1990 in best practice plants.[19] Further investigations in 2004 led Worrell to conclude that this could be further improved by another 50 per cent, saying that for an EAF process, 'a typical mid 1990s energy requirement was 550kWh per ton of product, but best practice is now considered to be around 300kWh, with "ideal" theoretical performance around 150kWh.'[20]

A potential concern with the EAF process is that it is designed to re-manufacture scrap steel, and hence relies on an ongoing supply of scrap, as opposed to the BOF process which can run without any recycled steel, and is in fact only able to process up to 30–35 per cent scrap.[21] The benefit of using scrap is that according to the Bureau of International Recycling, steel requires only approximately 26 per cent of the energy needed for virgin production.[22] However, the availability of scrap steel in the near future is not likely to be a limitation, with the IISI estimating in 2006 that 37 per cent of the crude steel produced globally was from recycled steel.[23] This is further supported by a study by the US Department of Interior and the US Geological Survey in 1998 that concluded that by 2010 EAF plants would produce the majority of steel in the world.[24] But, in the case that sufficient inputs of scrap steel are not available, a process to create direct reduced iron (DRI) can be added to the EAF process, as shown in Figure 3.1, where 30–50 per cent scrap steel can be used. In this case, where a DRI process is required to top up levels of scrap steel, the process has the same or a little more overall energy intensity of a BOF; however, as this energy is sourced primarily from natural gas rather than coal and oil the EAF/DRI process still delivers 50 per cent reductions in greenhouse gas emissions compared to a BOF process.[25] Hence there is a strong case to phase out BOF processes and use the EAF process, even if it means the incorporation of a DRI process.

However, in rapidly emerging countries that are constructing significant amounts of new infrastructure, such as China, it may be the case that in the coming 10–15 years the yield of scrap from infrastructure turnover will be much lower than that experienced in Europe and the US. China is, however, importing scrap, and even though China's imports of scrap steel have increased significantly, from an estimated 3.3Mt in 2007 to 20.3Mt in 2008, this is still much less than the gross production for over 500Mt that year in China.[26] Considering this it may be wise to implement a staged approach leading to a steel sector dominated by EAF. In such a staged approach an initial step would

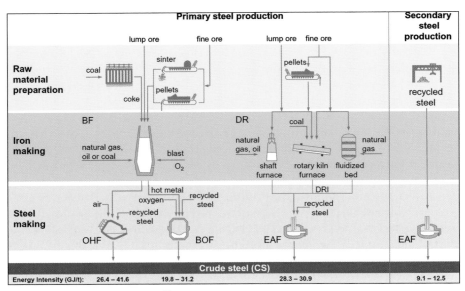

Source: World Steel Association (2008)[27]

Figure 3.1 *Energy intensity of various steel-making processes (1) BOF process (58 per cent of global operations[28]), (2) EAF/DRI process (7 per cent) and (3) EAF process (27 per cent)*

be to capitalize on opportunities to reduce the energy intensity of the existing BOF plants by using processes that eliminate the need for a coke oven or a sinter plant, harnessing co-generation and renewable energy options, and using plastic/biomass feedstock replacements. Then, while improving BOF, shift new plants to DRI/EAF in preparation for the availability in the future of appropriate levels of scrap steel (by infrastructure turnover or import). Even if a DRI/EAF process is used that uses minimal scrap steel in the short term the greenhouse gas emissions can be reduced by 50 per cent compared to BOF. Although rapidly emerging countries are constructing vast amounts of civil infrastructure, and the future will see an abundant supply of scrap steel, the BOF process can only use up to 30 per cent of this, which means that the opportunities of using scrap will not be captured to underpin the economic security of the sector. This, together with the increasing greenhouse gas emissions liability, presents a real threat to the sector.

As can be seen in Table 3.1, the largest steel-producing nations of the world have on average only around 30 per cent EAF, providing significant opportunity for improvement. This is best illustrated by the fact that the eighth largest steel producer, the Ukraine, uses EAF for less than 2 per cent of total crude steel output.[29] Hence, EAF technology is not only a significant opportunity for the sector to reduce energy demand and greenhouse gas emissions, it could also help boost market demand for recycled steel. And this is not the end of the innovation in this sector. For instance, consider the new process of 'near net shape casting' which involves, as the name suggests, steel being cast as close to its intended form as possible to minimize machining and finishing. According to Worrell et al,[30] if by 2025 40 per cent of US steel is cast using this new process this would result in an estimated primary energy saving equivalent to 10 per cent of total projected primary energy use in the iron and steel industry, and that if there was an uptake of 100 per cent by 2025, this would be the equivalent of an approximately 25 per cent energy productivity improvement across the US steel-making industry.[31] This, on top of the significant achievement to deliver steel at an average of 12GJ/t, would deliver steel at 8GJ/t – nearly a Factor Five improvement (72 per cent) on the average intensity of the major producers in 1995.

Further to this, a study by the US Environmental Protection Agency (US EPA) highlighted a number of potential improvements that are 'technically available but that may not be economically viable in all situations', including: installation of energy monitoring and management systems for energy recovery and distribution between processes; preventative maintenance; and improvements in the EAF process such as improved process control, oxy-fuel burners, DC-arc furnaces, scrap pre-heating and post-combustion processes. The study stated that these technologies could deliver steel at 2GJ/t,[32] an improvement of 93 per cent, or Factor 10. The OECD in 2008 argued that such a technical transition may prove to be the key reason why the steel industry globally will be able to adapt over time to a carbon price signal, either through a carbon tax or emissions trading scheme.[33]

Best practice case study – Nucor Corporation

Nucor is the biggest steel maker and steel recycler in the US, and, by using the EAF process, has recycled over 19Mt of scrap steel in 2008, to deliver 80 per cent of their steel from recycled feedstock. Also, since 2003, Nucor further innovated their process to reduce the amount of energy needed to produce each ton of steel by an additional 17 per cent. Nucor also installed the first commercial near net shape casting facility at its Crawfordsville plant in Indiana,[34] which was developed by Nucor working with BHP (Australia) and IHI (Japan).[35] Hence compared to the traditional BOF process that requires on average 60–70 per cent more energy, the Nucor EAF process at their Crawfordsville plant is now delivering steel at close to a Factor Five more energy efficiency than BOF competitors. Nucor has also made a significant contribution to broadening the range of steel products which can be produced from EAF mills.[36] Historically, EAF mills had focused on the production of steel bars and structural steel beams, while larger BOF producers have focused on sheet steel production. Nucor showed in 1987, that it was possible to produce sheet steel from an EAF plant – which had previously been thought impractical.[37] In 1995 Nucor showed that EAF mills could also produce speciality steel, and more recently, the Crawfordsville plant has been modified to be able to also produce thin slab stainless steel – again previously thought to be 'impossible' for an EAF mill.[38]

As the EAF process can now produce virtually all types of steel products, such innovations in the process, pioneered by Nucor, mean that these much smaller and cheaper plants have the potential to replace most BOF plants around the world. This would allow Factor Five gains across the sector/industry as a whole and drive the market for steel scrap – hence driving design for recovery of a range of products and infrastructure. Nucor is also investing in EAF/DRI plants to diversify their feedstock options, enabling them to have the flexibility of producing EAF steel from either 100 per cent scrap, or DRI steel made from a combination of iron ore and scrap.[39] Hence, as the EAF process can make steel cheaper, faster and more efficiently compared to the BOF processes, they are highly attractive in periods of economic downturn, allowing Nucor to be not only one of the most profitable steel companies in the US, but also the only company in the sector to maintain its workforce, with all staff taking a 50 per cent pay cut during the 2008–2009 global financial crisis, despite over 25,000 worker layoffs in the steel sector in the US.[40]

A whole system approach to Factor Five in the steel industry

IPCC Strategy One: Energy efficiency opportunities

While producing an in-depth analysis of the US iron and steel industry in 1999, the researchers at the Ernest Orlando Lawrence Berkeley National Laboratory found that there are at least 48 specific energy efficiency technologies and measures available to improve the energy productivity of the steel industry, applicable to both BOF and EAF, as shown in Table 3.2.

Based on these opportunities the energy productivity of both of the current forms of steel furnaces can be improved, specifically:

Basic oxygen furnace (BOF)

The 'Hismelt' process[41] can reduce the energy intensity of a BOF process by up to 50 per cent, as it allows the smelting reduction process to be undertaken without the need for a coke oven or a sinter plant, and can run on cheap non-coking coals. This is particularly important to allow greater flexibility in the output levels of the process, as according to the Institute of Materials, Minerals and Mining, 'running traditional oxygen blast furnaces is expensive, as they are inflexible and generally uneconomic to run at anything less than full capacity'.[42] Hence such innovations can significantly reduce both the operational and upfront capital costs, allowing the process to more cost-effectively vary its output to optimize production with market price signals.[43] As the *Australian Business Review Weekly* states, 'At its current level of development, [the Hismelt process] is over 50 per cent more efficient than many blast furnaces in operation today.'[44] However, even if processes such as Hismelt can reduce the energy intensity of BOF by up to 50 per cent, this can be matched and exceeded by improvements to the EAF process.

Table 3.2 *State-of-the-art energy efficiency measures in the US iron and steel industry*

Steel making using a BOF-based process	Steel making using an EAF-based process
Iron ore preparation (sintermaking)	*Electric arc furnace (EAF)*
Sinter plant heat recovery	Improved process control (neural networks)
Use of waste fuels in the sinter plant	Flue gas monitoring and control
Reduction of air leakage	Transformer efficiency measures
Increasing bed depth	Bottom stirring/gas injection
Improved process control	Foamy slag practices
	Oxy-fuel burners/lancing
Coke making	Post-combustion
Coal moisture control	Eccentric bottom tapping (EBT)
Programmed heating	Direct current (DC) arc furnaces
Variable speed drive on coke oven	Scrap pre-heating
gas compressors	Consteel process
Coke dry quenching	Fuchs shaft furnace
	Twin shell DC arc furnace
Iron making – blast furnace	
Pulverized coal injection (medium and high levels)	
Injection of natural gas	
Top pressure recovery turbines (wet type)	
Recovery of blast furnace gas	
Hot blast stove automation	
Recuperator on the hot blast stove	
Improved blast furnace control	
Steel making – basic oxygen furnace (BOF)	
BOF gas and sensible heat recovery (suppressed combustion)	
Variable speed drive on ventilation fans	

Casting and rolling (for both options)	
Casting	*Rolling*
Adopt continuous casting	Hot charging
Efficient ladle pre-heating	Recuperative burners in the reheating furnace
Thin slab casting	Controlling oxygen levels and variable speed drives on combustion air fans
	Process control in the hot strip mill
	Insulation of furnaces
	Energy-efficient drives in the hot rolling mill
	Waste heat recovery from cooling water
	Heat recovery on the annealing line (integrated only)
	Automated monitoring and targeting system
	Reduced steam use in the pickling line

Overall measures
(measures apply to both BOF and EAF plants)

Preventative maintenance
Energy monitoring and management systems
Variable speed drives for flue gas control, pumps, and fans
Co-generation

Source: Worrell et al (1999)[45]

Electric arc furnace (EAF)

For the EAF process for instance, in the case that 100 per cent of the feedstock is not able to be supplied by recycled steel, the process to create DRI can also be improved on current practice. The DRI process reduces iron by heating iron ore (generally having 65–70 per cent iron) to a temperature high enough to burn off the carbon and oxygen content (a process called 'reduction'), but below the melting point of iron (1535°C or 2795°F). The output is in the form of pellets or briquettes (known as hot briquetted iron or HBI) and contains 90–97 per cent pure iron, the rest being mainly carbon with trace amounts of other impurities. An example of the latest innovations in DRI is FINEX.[46] In a FINEX process the sintering and coke-making steps are eliminated, resulting in substantial cost and energy savings, along with reductions in air pollution – with the emission of sulphur oxides (SO_x) and nitrogen oxides (NO_x) falling to 19 per cent and 10 per cent, respectively.[47]

However, other than improving the existing furnaces, according to Larry Kavanagh, Vice President of Manufacturing and Technology for the American Iron and Steel Institute (AISI),[48] the greatest potential for reducing the energy intensity of steel making lies with the development of new transformational technologies and processes. An example of such transformational R&D efforts is that of molten oxide electrolysis. Researchers from the MIT Department of Materials Science and Engineering have pioneered a process to manufacture steel that provides the potential to eliminate greenhouse gas process emissions. According to Kavanagh, 'What sets molten oxide electrolysis apart from other metal-producing technologies is that it is totally carbon-free, and hence generates no carbon dioxide gases – only oxygen.'[49]

> *I now can confirm that in molten oxide electrolysis we'll see iron productivities at least five times that of aluminum, maybe as high as 10 times. This changes everything when it comes to assessing technical viability at the industrial scale.*
>
> Professor Donald Sadoway, MIT, 2006[50]

IPCC Strategy Two: Fuel switching

In the steel-making process, up to 90 per cent of the energy requirement is met by coal; however, waste plastic may become a viable alternative.[51] Researchers at the University of New South Wales have shown that waste plastic can be used to offset coal requirements by up to 30 per cent.[52] The research also shows that not only does the plastic replace coal as a carbon source, it also acts as a fuel, reducing the power requirements for the furnace. Professor Veena Sahajwalla reflects that:

> *if you look at its chemical composition, even something as simple as polyethylene that we all use in our day to day lives, has about 85 per cent carbon and 15 per cent hydrogen, so it's simply a carbon resource... So if you put the two and two together it*

would lead to a win–win situation for both plastics and the steel industry.[53]

According to AISI, such research may be expanded to uncover similar opportunities for the use of other waste products such as rubber, oils and car tyres, as long as emissions are controlled.[54]

Another promising advance in fuel switching for the steel industry is hydrogen flash smelting. Researchers from the University of Utah are researching the potential to use hydrogen as a fuel for steel making, and hence reduce the greenhouse gas emissions. According to AISI, 'Hydrogen Flash Smelting is a process during which iron is separated from iron ore ("smelting") at a high temperature (above 1300°C) and at very fast reaction times'.[55] However, research director, Dr Sohn, cautioned AISI that the research is in its early stages of development but, 'what has been demonstrated thus far is encouraging'.

Other alternatives include coal gasification and the use of charcoal as a replacement for coke. Studies have shown that if coke is fully replaced by charcoal, then fossil fuel consumption and greenhouse gas emissions can be reduced by over 60 per cent.[56]

IPCC Strategy Three: Heat and power recovery

In the steel industry, most co-generation operations (explained in Chapter 1) incorporate conventional systems such as steam boilers and steam turbines. However, there are now specially adapted turbines which can burn low-calorific-value off-gases such as coke oven gas, blast furnace gas and BOF gas, which are produced in significant quantities in steel plants. While EAFs typically use mostly electricity, co-location of an EAF with other industries that require heat means a shared co-generation facility can be used. Combined cycle gas turbines can be also used to self-generate some of the electricity used in the steel and iron industries.[57] Researchers at the McMaster University in Ontario, Canada, have now demonstrated at pilot scale the potential of a new form of steel furnace, the paired straight hearth furnace. This new process provides the opportunity for heat capture from one part of the process, off-gas from the oxygen melter, to be used to power another, the hearth furnace.

IPCC Strategy Four: Renewable energy

Unlike the BOF process that currently relies on natural gas, oil or coal for energy the EAF process can source 100 per cent of its energy needs from renewable forms of electricity generation. In addition the steel industry provides significant value to the renewable energy industry as according to WorldSteel:

> *Stainless steels play a key role in converting solar energy into electricity or hot water. They are used as a base for solar thermal-panels and in pumps, tanks and heat exchangers. A steel pile is the main component of a tidal turbine ... [and] steel is also used to fabricate wave energy devices. The steel used is formulated to*

withstand the harsh marine environment, and steel is the main material used in onshore and off-shore wind turbines. Almost every component of a wind turbine is made of steel, from the foundation, to the tower, gears and casings.[58]

IPCC Strategy Five: Feedstock change

This part has been contributed, on invitation from the authors, by Dr Roland Geyer, Assistant Professor for Industrial Ecology, Production and Operations Management at the Bren School of Environmental Science and Management, University of California, Santa Barbara (supported by PhD student Vered Doctori-Blass).

The life-cycle energy requirements for one metric ton of primary steel sections is 37GJ.[59] This number includes manufacture (assuming production from iron ore with a BOF process), fabrication, erection on site, demolition and landfill. However, as pointed out above, if we instead assume that sections are made in an EAF process using scrap recovered from construction and demolition waste, the life-cycle energy requirements decrease to 18GJ/t, a 50 per cent increase in energy productivity. The reason is simply that remelting scrap requires 25–35 per cent of the energy needed to reduce and refine iron ore, assuming closed-loop recycling of steel sections into steel sections. However, some argue that calculations of life-cycle energy requirements should include energy that is consumed to produce the recycled content in the first place, while others maintain that it should account only for end-of-life recycling, while recycled content is irrelevant.[60] In any case, it is clear that steel recycling, just as all metal recycling, offers tremendous productivity gains, as long as irreversible contamination is avoided.

The life-cycle energy requirements of re-using steel sections reclaimed from decommissioned structures is just over 7GJ/t. This is a stunning improvement in energy productivity, just over 80 per cent, or Factor Five, relative to primary steel sections. The 7GJ/t includes section recovery via deconstruction, refabrication of the reclaimed sections and erection on site. To be able to re-use building components rather than recycle them, buildings have to be deconstructed rather than demolished, which requires increased time and costs. Whether a contractor chooses to deconstruct a building and reclaim the sections, or demolish it and recycle the steel depends on the price difference between section scrap and reclaimed sections, and the time available to complete the project. In 2008, demolition contractors were able to sell reclaimed sections for around £300 per metric ton, while scrap prices ranged from £120 to £260 per metric ton.[61] Reclaimed steel sections were then resold from salvage yards for £350–£600 per metric ton, while newly produced steel sections cost £800–£900 per metric ton. In principle, reclaimed steel sections offer the double-dividends of dramatic energy savings and substantial cost savings.

These apparent double-dividends raise the question of why currently only around 10 per cent of the recovered steel sections in the UK is re-used. A host of reasons for the low re-use rate has been identified, which all indicate that, while re-use has the potential for combining enormous productivity gains with significant cost savings, it also faces many more obstacles than recycling. Demolition contractors need to be given the time to deconstruct rather than demolish buildings, while either the revenue from reclaimed building components needs to justify the higher cost of deconstruction, or the cost of steel needs to incorporate the carbon price. Buildings are typically not designed for deconstruction, as can be seen by the increased use of wet bonding methods to bond concrete to steel sections, rather than using nuts and bolds. This re-use is further complicated by the fact that the exact specification needs to be met with the re-used steel section, something that is much easier to specify for new sections of recycled steel. The markets for reclaimed steel sections are currently local, small-scale and suffer from poor flow of information. Matching time and location of supply and demand is thus challenging. There is also some evidence that potential suppliers of reclaimed steel sections underestimate potential demand, while the potential users of steel sections underestimate potential supply. The use of modern information technology to build an online clearing house for reclaimed building components thus has tremendous potential to remove many of the information barriers to increased re-use and unleash the environmental potential of re-use.

IPCC Strategy Seven: Material efficiency (water)

In steel making, water is used primarily for cooling both the coke and the metal, as well as dust suppression and steam generation. As mentioned above, *Factor Four* quoted a study by Liedtke and Merton[62] which found that 'electric arc steel furnaces (EAF) use ... one-eighth of the water ... compared with traditional basic-oxygen blast furnace (BOF) steel plants.'[63] However, the BOF process can also significantly reduce water consumption. For instance BlueScope Steel's Port Kembla Steelworks have shown that greater than 80 per cent improvements in water efficiency can be achieved in BOF steel making. Over ten years ago BlueScope Steel was using 55ML/d of water and by the end of 2005, through investment in water efficiency improvements and recycling schemes, was using only 9ML/d of fresh water – an 84 per cent improvement.[64] Furthermore, steel facilities are often situated close to the ocean for shipping access and can utilize seawater for many aspects of cooling, which reduces the amount of fresh water needed. CST, a subsidiary of Arcelor in Brazil, uses seawater for 96 per cent of the total water used for steel manufacturing in their plant.[65] In regards to water pollution, Saldanha Steel (Pty) Ltd, a subsidiary of Mittal Steel South (MSS) Africa Ltd, has shown that it is possible for the steel industry to achieve zero water pollution levels by building a zero-effluent plant in 1998–1999. The Saldanha region of South Africa has a RAMSAR wetland, the Langebaan Lagoon. To address environmental concerns, MSS built a zero-effluent plant and installed technologies to treat and re-use water in order to minimize water consumption, for example, 'reverse osmosis technology was installed to allow effluent from all open and closed cooling systems to be re-used'.[66]

2 The cement industry

The potential for Factor Five improvements in cement manufacturing resource productivity

Conventional concrete is second only to water as the commodity most used by humanity today – currently at approximately 2.5 billion tons per year (Gt/y) and growing. Typically, concrete is comprised of a mixture of materials such as limestone, clay, sand and/or shale (referred to as cement) that is bound to various aggregates when mixed with water. Valued at US$181 billion in 2008, output from the cement industry is expected to grow by 4.7 per cent annually through to 2012, with a projection of five billion tons of cement produced per year by 2030, as shown in Figure 3.2.

China is by far the largest producer of cement in the world (1.36Gt in 2007),[67] increasing its production by 13 per cent between 2000 and 2006.[68] In 2008 China was responsible for producing roughly half of the total global output of cement, with the next three largest producers (India, Japan and the US) combined accounting for just under 20 per cent of the remaining production.[69] Market research predicts that product demand in India (the second largest cement producer), will climb at the fastest rate of any major market; also that the smaller industries being rapidly developed in Indonesia, Malaysia, Nigeria, Vietnam and the United Arab Emirates are expected to increase supply by more than 7 per cent per year.[70] Such growth trends within the industry are expected based on the significant levels of growth in infrastructure around the

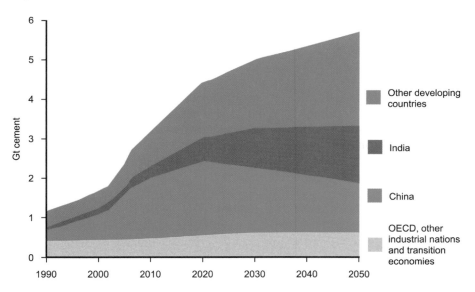

Source: Based on estimates by the World Wildlife Foundation (with sources of data listed in Müller and Harnisch (2008)[71])

Figure 3.2 *Cement production in industrialized and developing countries*

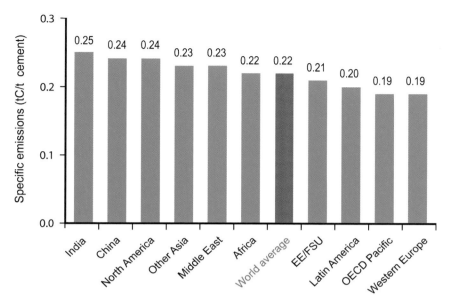

Source: Based on data from Worrell et al (2001)[72]

Figure 3.3 *Carbon intensity of cement production in different regions (tons of carbon per ton of cement)*

world; however, as the sector is energy intensive, if levels of greenhouse gas emissions are to be reduced the method for creating cement will need to be significantly improved.[73] The industry is responsible for between 5 per cent[74] and 8 per cent[75] of CO_2 emissions alone, having produced some 1.8 billion tons (Gt) of CO_2 in 2005. Figure 3.3 summarizes the variability in carbon emissions for cement production by country and region, with the world average being 0.22 tons of carbon per ton of cement. As can be seen in the figure, these carbon emissions do not directly relate to the wealth of the country, with North America's average emissions worse than that of some of the emerging economies.[76]

Given the large scale of building construction in China the cement sector is responsible for approximately 25 per cent of all such emissions in the country.[77] However, even within developed countries, the cement industry is still a large contributor by proportion. For example, in the US, cement is still the second largest source of industrial CO_2 emissions (44Mt in 2007), growing by 34 per cent since 1990.[78] With regard to energy consumption, the thermal energy intensity for cement production (i.e. in the kiln) ranges from country to country, with Japan having the most efficient cement industry at 3.1GJ/t, using predominantly dry kilns which feature pre-heaters and pre-calciners. China has improved from 4.7GJ/t in 2000 to 3.9GJ/t in 2006 with the production of a number of new kilns; however, its industry is still comprised of approximately 45 per cent of the older, relatively energy-intensive small-scale vertical shaft kilns which can consume as much as 6.1GJ/t of cement. The electricity costs for cement production are also quite variable, and as cement tends to be manufactured in the countries where it is being used, energy intensities also tend to reflect the industry's response to local energy prices to some degree. For example, Japan, which imports nearly all of its energy, has the lowest cement-manufacturing energy intensity of any country in the world.[79] In contrast, the energy consumption of cement in China is currently 1.3 times that of advanced production techniques at 110kWh/t cement (128kg standard coal/t cement).[80] Cement manufacture is such an energy-intensive industry in China that the 12 billion tons produced annually[81] consumes 6 per cent of China's total energy supply (compared with 0.33 per cent in the US[82]). India, as the second largest producer of cement, averages 100kWh/t cement, sharing a similar problem of outdated technologies and a proliferation of smaller, inefficient plants.[83]

Clearly with such a range of performance figures for emissions, and thermal and electrical energy intensity across various cement industries, there is significant potential to improve the overall performance of this sector. Understanding this opportunity, leading concrete companies are already implementing energy efficiency strategies and achieving sizeable emission reductions. For example, cement company Cemex has strong sustainability drivers in moving the 100-year-old company forward, including a target of 25 per cent reduced CO_2 emissions by 2015.[84] Swiss cement company, Holcim, is also receiving market recognition for its efforts in composite cements, improving thermal energy efficiency and process technology, and optimizing fuel composition (including the use of waste as fuel). Since 2004 Holcim has been named 'Leader of the Industry' each year in the Dow Jones Sustainability Index (DJSI). The company's global average net CO_2 emissions have also decreased by 18.7 per cent relative to 1990 (not including power generation).[85] Such efforts are commendable; however, they will not move the sector towards Factor Five.

Factor Four did not investigate opportunities in the cement sector as much of the required innovation was not available in 1997. It is the recent innovations based on decades of R&D that are enabling new cements – geopolymers – to achieve significant verified energy savings. In this Sector Study, we examine emerging opportunities for achieving significant improvements in the energy productivity of the cement industry, beginning with a brief description of the most prevalent cement used today – Portland cement. We then focus on an innovation called 'geopolymer cement' which appears best placed to achieve Factor Five levels of reductions in energy intensity and CO_2 emissions over the coming decades. Coupled with other innovations in kiln design, materials efficiency, fuel switching and carbon capture and storage, there may even be the potential for Factor 10 reductions in emissions and energy intensity.

The most common form of cement, 'calcium-silicate' cement, is currently made by heating limestone (calcium carbonate) with small quantities of other materials (such as clay) to temperatures in the order of 1450°C, requiring a kiln temperature in the order of 1850°C. The resulting hard substance, called 'clinker', is then ground with a small amount of gypsum into a powder to make what is commercially known as 'Portland cement' (named so by Joseph Aspdin in 1824 as the concrete produced resembled the limestone on the Isle of Portland, in the English channel). This method for producing cement has remained roughly the same since it was patented in 1824.[86] Approximately 50 per cent of the greenhouse gas emissions from Portland cement are produced from the reaction that converts limestone to calcium oxide (limestone + silica → Portland cement + carbon dioxide) – with 0.36–1.09 ton of CO_2 released for every ton of cement produced, depending on variables such as the type of process and the clinker/cement ratio.[87] Of the remaining emissions, approximately 40 per cent are produced from the combustion of fossil fuels onsite, such as coal and coke to heat and process the component materials.[88] Then a small proportion of emissions (up to 10 per cent) arises equally from the emissions generated by the electricity used onsite (for grinding raw materials and then grinding the cement), and from the transport of raw materials.

Research shows that both the energy- and process-related CO_2 emissions from current methods of Portland cement manufacture can be reduced by at least 30 per cent globally[89] – with much of this achieved though shifting from 'wet' to 'dry' manufacturing processes (also reducing water consumption). The use of dry kilns has grown from 12 per cent of Chinese capacity in 2000 to 53 per cent in 2005, with 450Mt capacity installed over the five-year period. Improvements are also made through slight process changes and by mixing supplementary cementitious materials, such as blast furnace slag and coal fly ash (known as pozzolanic materials) in with Portland cement.[90] An extensive 2008 report[91] claimed that greater improvements could be made with Portland cement but it relied heavily on carbon capture and storage, and the increasing use of bio-fuels, both of which are yet to be proven to scale and have significant complicating factors. Hence, although 30 per cent is a significant improvement, in order to address the growing energy demand and greenhouse gas emissions from the sector it will need to be significantly increased. However, to date there is no evidence to support such an achievement in Portland cement manufacture, with such improvements only becoming feasible through the use of 'alternative' forms of cement, including sulfo-aluminate cement, magnesium-phosphate cement and alumino-silicate (geopolymer) cement. A full description of all the research currently under way on alternative cements is beyond the scope of this book, other than to highlight that:

- *Sulfo-aluminate cement* reduces the overall greenhouse gas emissions of the concrete by just under 30 per cent, compared to Portland cement.[92] This is due in part to the slightly lower temperature of up to around 1300°C (from 1450°C), and the reduced content of calcium oxide in the process. However, as this process is reliant on blast furnace slag as a feedstock, its potential to replace calcium-silicate cements (Portland cement) is considered to be limited.[93]
- *Magnesium-phosphate cement* theoretically reduces the overall greenhouse gas emissions of the concrete by about 70 per cent, compared to Portland

cement. This is primarily due to a reduction in temperature to around 650°C which reduces overall emissions by up to 30 per cent,[94] combined with the fact that its proponents claim that, even though its process emissions per ton are slightly greater than that for Portland cement,[95] the concrete can absorb much more CO_2 than Portland cement soon after setting as part of a carbonation process.[96] However this claim has not been substantially verified.

- *Alumino-silicate (geopolymer) cement* reduces the overall greenhouse gas emissions of the concrete by 80 per cent, compared to Portland cement,[97] depending on formulation variations, as it requires lower temperatures, and has no direct process emissions of CO_2.[98] This form of cement is usually formed by alkali-activation of a coal fly ash, calcined clays (including kaolinite) and/or metallurgical slag, and hence – unlike Portland cement – does not rely on lime (calcium carbonate).[99] Typically this process also has a lower temperature of around 750°C, resulting from the fact that the process does not require a high-temperature calcination step. However, the process can be undertaken commercially at room temperature.

Considering the areas of research above, the geopolymer based alumino-silicate cement has emerged as the most promising, commercially viable alternative to calcium-silicate (Portland) cement for immediate application to address both emissions and energy intensity, with the potential for at least 80 per cent improvements. Hence, we now provide more detail on this innovation, including a case study of a company that is commercializing an alumino-silicate cement product, followed by a summary of the main strategies to reduce emissions also from the Portland cement sector.

Geopolymers are formed by reaction of an alumino-silicate powder with an alkaline silicate solution, the molecular structure of which makes them an ideal substitute for Portland cement. Although based on pozzolans (natural or man-made materials such as fly ash, slag or clays) geopoloymers use sodium hydroxide or sodium silicates to activate the pozzolans, rather than lime, hence eliminating the process-related carbon emissions of the Portland cement process (some 50 per cent of the overall emissions).[100] This, together with the lower kiln temperatures mentioned above, means that CO_2 emissions may be as low as 10–20 per cent of those of Portland cements, provided the pozzolan material itself does not have to be specially produced.[101] Many by-products from industry can be used as feedstocks for geopolymer cement, including fly ash, mine tailings and bauxite residues. Variations in the ratio of aluminium to silicon, and alkali to silicon, produce geopolymers with different physical and mechanical properties.[102] Even if the availability of fly ash is reduced – say from the inevitable future reduction in the use of coal-fired power plants – pozzolans can then be sourced from clays and metallurgical slag.

According to CSIRO, Australia's leading science research organization, alumino-silicate cement can be used for every major purpose for which

Note: Volcanic ash, similar to today's fly ash from coal-fired power stations, was used extensively in the construction of Roman structures including the Colosseum, which was constructed in 100AD, giving Roman cement a similar chemistry to modern geopolymers
Source: Courtesy of Karlson and Stacey Hargroves

Figure 3.4 *The Colosseum, Rome*

calcium-silicate cement is currently used.[103] Broadly speaking, geopolymer cements set quickly (ten hours at −20°C, and up to 60 minutes at +20°C), are at least as strong as Portland cement (reaching 90MPa – megapascals – at 28 days, and 20MPa after four hours), and have greater structural fire resistance.[104] CSIC, Spain's largest public research organization, tested the concrete from geopolymer cement as railway sleepers, and according to materials scientist Angel Palomo, of the Eduardo Torroja Institute in Madrid, they passed 'with high marks'. Palomo stated that, 'From an engineering point of view a sleeper is a very complex element, which is also subjected to very aggressive mechanical conditions and weather extremes... The material is good enough for sleepers, so it will be good enough for many building parts.'[105]

For these reasons, 'alumino-silicate' cement stands to provide an attractive alternative to Portland cement in the coming decades as the world seeks to reduce its greenhouse gas emissions and energy demand.[106] In the past, the main concern with geopolymer cement was the lack of long-term durability data (i.e. 20+ years) for the product's performance.[107] This form of concrete, however, has a long history, having been identified as being used by ancient civilizations – including in Ancient Rome more than 2000 years ago to build a range of load-bearing structures, such as aqueducts and sizeable structures such as the Roman Coliseum;[108] however, this knowledge was subsequently lost. Key elements of modern Portland cement techniques and processes were then invented by chemists of the 18th and 19th centuries, although, in contrast to the long-standing Roman buildings, modern cement decays and is unable to continue to carry load within decades.

The alumino-silicate form of cement manufacture, used by the ancient Romans, was rediscovered by a Ukrainian research team led by scientist Victor Glukhovsky who responded to a shortage of cement in the former Soviet Union in the 1960s by making geopolymers using a process of alkali-activated blast furnace slag. This concrete was widely used in the Ukraine for the construction of apartment blocks, railway sleepers, pipes, drainage and irrigation channels, flooring for dairy farms, and pre-cast slabs and blocks;[109] however, due to the Cold War, their findings were inaccessible for many years. In the following years, little detail on this work has been published in English, other than two sets of conference proceedings from 1994[110] and 1999,[111] and a 2006 book reviewing alkali-activated cements and concretes.[112] In 2007 an Australian research team from the University of Melbourne's chemical engineering school collaborated with the Glukhovsky's Scientific Research Institute for Binders and Materials to understand why geopolymers are so durable. Their research, published in 2008, explained in detail why the chemistry of geopolymers makes them so strong and stable, providing the much needed scientific explanation of their longevity.[113]

In summary, the research found that the chemistry and structure of geopolymer cement allows the production of a concrete that is more resistant to chemical attack, and that has reduced levels of internal deterioration. Specifically, geopolymer concretes have high resistance to two of the main mechanisms of concrete degradation associated with ageing – sulphate and chloride attack. The lower level of calcium in geopolymers compared to Portland cement is generally beneficial for sulphate resistance, as the formation of the expansive compounds responsible for sulphate degradation of Portland cement generally requires the presence of significant levels of available calcium.[114] The permeability of the geopolymeric binder phase has also recently been shown to be lower than that of Portland cements, which reduces chloride permeability and hence the rate of chloride attack on steel reinforcing, thereby increasing the lifespan of composite members.[115] This is a significant advantage, as one of the main reasons why old concrete structures fail is due to corrosion of steel reinforcement embedded in the concrete.

The potential for geopolymers to replace a significant percentage of Portland cement cost effectively exists partly because geopolymers can be made using a large proportion of fly ash at room temperature. Such a solution would address greenhouse gas emissions, reduce energy demand and contribute to solving the major waste problem of fly ash disposal. Fly ash has been successfully used as a mineral admixture component of Portland 'blended' cement for nearly 60 years, but still only consumes about 10 per cent of fly ash production. About another 10–15 per cent is used for construction, building materials and beneficiation applications to produce lightweight concrete products. The remaining 75–80 per cent of ash is disposed of as waste materials, with power stations having significant environmental issues relating to the disposal of such large volumes.[116] Hence, fly ash has the potential to meet at least the short- to medium-term demand of increasing geopolymer production. Geopolymers can also be made out of slag wastes from steel production at low temperatures, which provides a waste disposal solution for significant quantities of such waste produced globally. In the longer term, the availability of suitable pozzolans would need to be addressed in some locations, where fly ash, slag or other potential ingredients are not available. The other main ingredient in geopolymers is sodium hydroxides or silicates, which are required as activators, and thus more plants would need to be produced to manufacture these chemicals as the geopolymer industry expands.[117]

We now consider a case study of an Australian company commercializing a geopolymer concrete, which has emerged from more than a decade of research and collaboration.

Best practice case study – Zeobond (alumino-silicate cement)

Although limestone is ubiquitous, has low extraction costs and performs very well as an element of cement, its high energy requirement for transportation and processing (in addition to its high carbon content) makes it problematic as a core ingredient of cement.[118] Professor Jannie van Deventer (former Dean of Engineering, The University of Melbourne and expert in geopolymer technology) is the Founder and Director of ZeoBond Pty Ltd, an Australian-based company that provides an alternative to limestone-based cement, using a process of geopolymerization to convert recycled waste into cement, producing 80 per cent less CO_2.[119] After a decade of research on geopolymers, Zeobond was formed in 2008 to commence commercial supply of their geopolymer concrete product called 'E-Crete™' – a geopolymer cement that actually forms at room temperature, requiring no kiln, and using fly ash as the main feedstock. In 2009, Zeobond laid the first slab of E-Crete and is in negotiations for production in North America and several countries in South-east Asia.[120] According to Zeobond Director Peter Duxson, Zeobond can make a range of geopolymer products for only 10 per cent more cost than Portland cement at the smallest commercial scale, and using existing supply chains, which is an 'excellent starting position, as the scale of commercialization is increased and more is invested in the supply chains, we expect the costs of making geopolymer cements to come down significantly'.[121]

According to Zeobond, E-Crete can be cheaply made, based on several types of clay and industrial waste and a few common sedimentary rocks. Generally when high volumes of ash and slag are used to replace Portland cement in concrete the curing of the concrete is adversely affected. For instance, these blended concretes typically have low early strength, take a long

Source: Courtesy of Zeobond

Figure 3.5 *Zeobond demonstration plant*

time to achieve an initial set, and do not achieve their nominal strength for more than 28 days. E-Crete avoids these negative effects associated with use of slag and ash (using proprietary technologies), and in the process creates identical or even better strength development profiles than a pure Portland cement-based concrete. In addition the shrinkage of E-Crete is similar or less than supplementary cementitious material (SCM) blends, and has a very low heat generation that results in only a few degrees temperature rise in large volume slabs. The concern that geopolymers are difficult to handle due to unpredictable setting times has been resolved using proprietary technology, permitting geopolymer concrete to be mixed using the same process as for Portland cement – by adding aggregates and water onsite. The setting time of geopolymers can also be manipulated much in the same way as Portland cement-based concrete. These traits of E-Crete lend themselves to use in applications where both speed and high quality are needed.[122]

A life-cycle analysis undertaken by Australian researchers in 2007 identified that geopolymer cement can reduce energy consumption by over 85 per cent compared to the Portland cement process, at approximately 200MJ, compared to approximately 1550MJ using Portland cement, for $1m^3$ of

Table 3.3 *Energy use to make one cubic metre of concrete*

Input energy	Indicative energy requirements for 1m³ of concrete (2220kg)	
	Portland cement (calcium-silicate) (approximately 1550MJ)	Zeobond cement (geopolymer) (approximately 200MJ)
Electricity	150MJ, comprising: 2.1MJ – fine sand (160kg) 11.6MJ – coarse sand (700kg) 16.6MJ – crushed river gravel (1t) 0MJ – fly ash [waste product] (80kg) 118.7MJ – cement (280kg) 1.0MJ for manufacture (process)	32MJ to produce aggregates for the concrete (including the energy involved in making chemical activators)
Coal	375MJ to produce the cement (280kg)	Nil
Natural Gas	375MJ to produce the cement (280kg)	Nil
Diesel	135.5MJ comprising: 7.7MJ/160kg of fine sand 52.6MJ/700kg coarse sand 75.2MJ/ton of crushed river gravel	189.3MJ comprising: 143MJ to produce aggregates for the concrete 46.3MJ to run a plant to produce the concrete

Source: Net Balance Foundation (2007)[123]

concrete, summarized in Table 3.3.[124] With regard to carbon emissions, Zeobond's geopolymer concrete emissions were estimated at approximately 115kg, mostly from transportation and grinding, while the Portland cement-based concrete emissions were approximately double, at 300kg for 1m³ of concrete. In regard to water consumption, the making and use of geopolymers requires approximately as much water as Portland cement throughout the entire life cycle.[125]

Trialling and evaluation of other geopolymers by the Geopolymer Institute, based in France, shows equal or better structural performance of geopolymer concrete, with documented benefits including:[126]

> *good abrasion resistance, particularly when mixed with PTFE [Polytetrafluoroethylene] filler, rapid controllable setting and hardening, fire resistance (up to 1000°C) and no emission of toxic fumes when heated – either in the form of a carbon fibre/geopolymer composite or as a pure geopolymer (e.g. a geopolymeric coating on an exposed surface), a high level of resistance to a range of different acids and salt solutions, not subject to deleterious alkali–aggregate reactions, low shrinkage and low thermal conductivity; high adhesion to fresh and old concrete substrates, steel, glass, ceramics, high surface definition that replicates mould patterns; and inherent protection of steel reinforcing due to high residual pH and low chloride diffusion rates.*[127]

The success of Zeobond provides further evidence of the ability of commercial geopolymers to replace ordinary Portland cement. Whereas Europe's highly prescriptive standards and validation procedures for concrete products limit commercialization potential in the short term, Australia does not have EU-style regulatory standards – allowing cement manufacturers to trial progressively larger demonstration structures with commercial potential. In the US, the approval process for new materials is also more flexible than Europe. Hence it is important that the cement industries in countries such as Australia and the US take the lead in using geopolymer cements to further demonstrate their suitability to the rest of the world.

A whole system approach to improving cement-manufacturing resource productivity

The examples provided so far have outlined feasible opportunities for the cement industry to improve its energy productivity by simultaneously expanding the production of less energy-intensive geopolymer cement, and improving the energy productivity of Portland cement.[128] While a transition to higher percentages of geopolymer cement can be made rapidly, cement will still be produced using the Portland cement method for at least several decades to come. While this transition occurs, it is important that existing Portland cement plants are made as efficient as possible. Hence, this Sector Study concludes by discussing a range of strategies for improving cement plant productivity and opportunities for retrofitting them to make geopolymer cements. Overall, the IPCC finds that greenhouse gas emissions could potentially be reduced by 30 per cent, as well as improving energy productivity in Portland cement production, although this percentage varies between 20 and 50 per cent for different regions.[129] But, as we will show, Portland cement plants can be retrofitted to make geopolymer cement and achieve far higher energy productivity gains. Here we group these opportunities in the order of the IPCC's considerations as outlined in Chapter 1, comprising: energy efficiency improvements (up to 40 per cent); fuel switching (up to 40 per cent); heat recovery (up to 25–30 per cent); feedstock changes, such as using slag from steel production, fly ash from coal production and natural pozzolans (more than 7 per cent);[130] and materials efficiency, including water.

IPCC Strategy One: Energy efficiency (existing plants)

After the invention of pre-heater/pre-calciner technology in the 1970s, Japanese producers reduced the energy intensity of clinker production from 5.0GJ/t to 3.1GJ/t by 2002, and they are now the most efficient in the world, with China estimated to reach the Japanese benchmark by around 2030.[131] Benchmarking and other studies have demonstrated a technical potential for up to a 40 per cent improvement in energy efficiency in the global cement industry, dominated by Portland cement, through upgrades to existing plants.[132] The countries with the highest potential are the ones still using

Table 3.4 *Opportunities for energy-efficient practices and technologies in cement manufacture (existing plants)*

Raw materials preparation

- Efficient transport system
- Raw meal blending systems (dry process)
- Conversion to closed-circuit wash mill
- High-efficiency roller mills (dry cement)
- High-efficiency classifiers (dry cement)

Clinker production (wet)	*Clinker production (dry)*
- Kiln combustion system improvements - Kiln shell heat loss reduction - Use of waste fuels - Conversion to modern grate cooler - Optimize grate coolers - Conversion to pre-heater, pre-calciner kilns - Conversion to semi-wet kilns	- Kiln combustion system improvements - Kiln shell heat loss reduction - Use of waste fuels - Conversion to modern grate cooler - Heat recovery for power generation - Low pressure-drop cyclones for suspension pre-heaters - Long dry kiln conversion to multi-stage pre-heater kiln - Optimize grate coolers - Long dry kiln conversion to multi-stage pre-heater, pre-calciner kiln - Addition of pre-calciner to pre-heater

Finish grinding (applies to wet and dry cement production)

- Improved grinding media (ball mills)
- High-pressure roller press
- High-efficiency classifiers
- Improve mill internals
- Use of gas engines to replace electric motors

General measures

- Preventative maintenance (insulation, compressed air losses, maintenance)
- Reduced kiln dust wasting
- Energy management and process control
- High-efficiency motors and appropriate motor sizing
- Efficient fans with variable speed drivers
- Improved aerodynamic design of air flow paths
- Upgrade to state-of-the-art refractory material (for the thermal insulation of the kiln)

Source: Martin et al (1999)[133]

outdated technologies, like the wet process clinker. In 2006, the US EPA developed a cement industry 'energy performance indicator' (EPI) through its Energy Star Industrial Focus program, in collaboration with the Portland Cement Association and the Argonne National Laboratory. The EPI scores the energy efficiency of a plant, allows it to compare its performance with the rest of the industry, and 'helps cement plant operators identify opportunities to improve energy efficiency, reduce greenhouse gas emissions, conserve conventional energy supplies, and reduce production costs'.[134] In 1999 researchers Martin, Worrell and Price[135] found that 30 energy efficiency opportunities still existed in American plants, with opportunities in every production step in the cement-making process, as summarized in Table 3.4.

In particular, improving the thermal efficiency of kilns has a significant potential to reduce energy consumption and related emissions. This includes retrofitting or building new rotary kilns with pre-calciner and suspension pre-heaters, and upgrading to state-of-the-art refractory material for lining the kiln, which can save up to 0.5GJ/t.[136]

Kiln technologies

Cement production technologies involve two basic processes, 'wet' and 'dry'. The wet process was developed to improve chemical uniformity of the raw materials, a deficiency in original dry kilns. Wet production technologies use high-moisture raw limestone feed, which allows for better control of the chemistry and texture of the cement, but it also requires on average 35 per cent more energy due to the need to evaporate the water. Technological improvements in the grinding of raw materials gradually improved the chemical uniformity of the clinker, enabling producers to return to the dry process and benefit from its lower energy and water consumption. Shifting from 'wet' to 'dry' Portland cement-making processes is the main way that water consumption can be reduced; however, modern dry process operations do require retrofitting to use modern crushing and grinding equipment.[137] With these changes in technologies over the last 200 years, there are now a variety of cement plants in existence with varying performance in energy consumption (i.e. 'energy intensity'), as shown in Figure 3.6.

By 2004 most countries were starting to realize the benefits of larger plants and dry kiln processes, with large- and medium-scale plants accounting for 63 per cent of global production and dry kilns accounting for around 45 per cent of total output, resulting in a decline in energy intensity for clinker production from about 5.4GJ/t in 1990 to 4.5GJ/t clinker. It is estimated that cement from

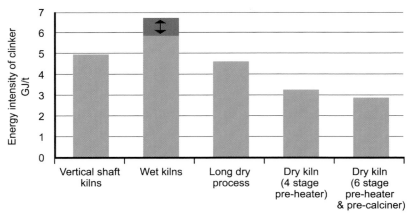

Note: For wet kilns, the arrow represents the range of energy consumption for different wet kiln types
Source: Based on the findings of FLSMidth (2006)[138]

Figure 3.6 *Energy intensity of clinker in the major kiln types in use around the world*

large-scale dry kilns should reach 80 per cent of global production by 2010 and 95 per cent by 2030, which would result in significant energy savings.[139] Further energy savings can be achieved with air entering the kiln being condensed and pre-heated to minimize the moisture content. Additional drying of the raw materials can also be carried out at very low costs using the hot exhaust gases or even solar radiation. It is projected that a shift to pre-heaters and pre-calciners will provide $0.6GtCO_2$ reductions by 2030, mostly in China.[140]

Electrical energy efficiency of grinding

Grinding is the largest electricity demand in the cement industry, averaging about 100kWh/t, which is mostly used for grinding raw input materials, and in grinding the clinker into cement.[141] Current best practice is 80–90kWh/t, but the energy efficiency of grinding is still only 5–10 per cent, with most of the energy converted to heat. There has been a slight downwards trend in electricity consumption, although in some countries it has increased. Figure 3.7 shows how the transition in the cement industry to better electrical energy efficiency has progressed in India, with retrofits and new plants involving various process innovations since 1960. The country has experienced a 50 per cent improvement up to 2000, after an initial period of decreasing performance. According to the Director General of the Indian National Council for Cement and Building Materials, Mr Shiban Ji Raina:

> *Energy conservation measures are cost effective and can bring about considerable improvement in cost-economics of cement manufacture. The government efforts can result in further large-scale rationalization in energy use efficiency of industry through*

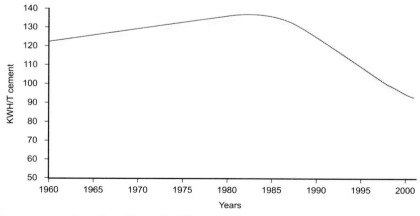

Source: Based on the findings of Raina (2002)[142]

Figure 3.7 *Trend of electrical energy consumption in the Indian cement industry (TPD refers to tons per day)*

*a well-defined and judicious implementation of the provisions of
the [2002] energy efficiency bill passed by the parliament.*[143]

However, perhaps the greatest opportunity for improvements to existing plants
comes from retrofitting to produce geopolymer cement. Although literature on
the costs of such a transition is not yet available, according to researcher Peter
Duxson:

> *In the short term cement companies can shift to geopolymers
> made from fly ash at room temperature to meet new demand. In
> time, much of the same equipment from existing cement plants
> can then be retrofitted to make geopolymer cement. Kilns can be
> retrofitted for lower temperature treatments at a time when the
> types of geopolymer cements being made will require 700°C
> treatment. Since Portland cement companies already have equip-
> ment that processes materials, grinds them into a powder and
> transports the materials around, this can all be used in transition-
> ing to geopolymer cement manufacture.*[144]

IPCC Strategy Two: Fuel switching

As the clinker production process for Portland cement involves kilns operating
at a high temperature, fuel switching is a way to reduce the demand for fossil
fuels while reducing waste stockpiles. For example, coal or gas may be replaced
with waste products such as used tyres, demolition timbers, used oil, carbon
anode dust, aluminium spent cell liners and solvent-based fuels.[145] This use of
waste as alternative fuel in cement kilns can contribute to lower overall CO_2
emissions, if fossil fuel use is displaced with alternative fuels that would otherwise have been incinerated or landfilled. However, such substitution needs to
be accompanied by strict air pollutant monitoring. Biomass could also be used
as substitutes for carbon-intensive fuels for cement kilns, particularly in regions
that also produce agricultural or forestry waste, or where fast-growing biomass
is possible (and which does not compete with food production). The use of
biomass is still quite low, at less than 5 per cent in most developing countries,
even with almost 40 per cent substitution in Brazil.[146] In India, biomass-based
co-generation is well established in the paper, sugar and chemical sectors but a
suitable technology has not yet been mainstreamed in the country's cement
industry.[147]

IPCC Strategy Three: Heat and power recovery

Given the high temperature of exhaust gases from modern cement plants
(around 350°C), there is significant potential for plants (including Portland
cement, blended cements and geopolymer cements) to use recovered lost heat
to achieve reductions in fuel consumption. In practice, 20–45kWh can be
recovered for each ton of cement produced, using large-scale dry kilns that
have a capacity of 2000 tons per day or more.[148] According to the

International Energy Agency (IEA), even in cases where modern pre-heater and pre-calciner kilns have low useful heat outputs due to the pre-heaters, there are still opportunities to economically recover heat and produce electricity.

For example, the highly energy-efficient cement plants in Japan generate around 10 per cent of their electricity needs from heat recovery, by using co-generation, or combined heat and power technology,[149] as outlined in Chapter 1. The Chinese cement industry estimates a potential reduction of 35–40kWh/t clinker (30–40 per cent) from co-gen.[150] So far, only Japan has taken up a significant part of this potential, perhaps explained by the high electricity prices that make such energy recovery economical. Co-gen can be particularly important for regions with a carbon-intensive electricity supply, and which have additional issues with low-quality and irregular power. In India, the National Council for Cement and Building Materials studies indicate that in plants using dry processes, almost 40 per cent of the total heat input is rejected as waste heat from the pre-heater and exit gases, which could otherwise be used for electric power generation. According to the Council, many combinations are possible, with co-generation technologies in existing plants having the potential to generate up to 25–30 per cent of a plant's power requirement. Waste heat could also be used directly by local consumers including residential areas, offices and other neighbouring industries, for heating purposes.

IPCC Strategy Five: Feedstock change

In producing standard Portland cement, the production of clinker is responsible for most of the process emissions and the majority of the energy-related emissions. As discussed earlier in this study, these emissions can be reduced by partly replacing the conventional limestone feedstock with SCMs such as blast furnace slag, fly ash from coal-fired power stations or natural pozzolans, creating what is known as 'blended cement'. The IEA estimates that it might be possible to reduce clinker production by 300Mt per year, resulting in a reduction of CO_2 emissions by about 240MtCO$_2$ per year, if the industry makes better use of clinker substitutes, in particular granulated blast furnace slag, steel slag, fly and bottom ash, and natural pozzolans.[151] Globally approximately only 7 per cent of cement currently uses additives and SCMs, mainly in continental Europe and China, but not as much in the US and UK.[152] This is due in part to regulatory limitations, in addition to the location of feedstock being too far away from the cement-manufacturing locations.

However, such reductions within the realm of Portland cement and blended cement manufacture are still incremental, and significant further gains are possible with the production of geopolymer cements that can either substitute parts of the Portland cement clinker, or replace it. According to Müller and Harnisch, if new alternatives to Portland cement could account for 20 per cent of the market (i.e. more than double) by 2030, they would lead to a 10 per cent decrease in CO_2 emissions from the sector. The amount of fly ash globally that could be used for geopolymers is immense and geopolymers would solve a major waste problem for power stations and metal industries.[153]

IPCC Strategy Seven: Material efficiency (water and materials)
Water productivity
A relatively simple way for the cement industry to reduce water usage is by retrofitting the remaining 'wet' Portland cement manufacturing plants into 'dry' plants. As discussed previously, the cement industry is shifting in this direction, driven mainly by the imperative to reduce energy costs and greenhouse gas emissions, and this will also significantly reduce the overall water consumption by this sector. Geopolymers use approximately the same amount of water through their life cycle as dry Portland cement. Both use significantly less water than the 'wet' Portland process, and as this process is phased out, and more cement companies shift to geopolymers, total water usage for the cement industry will be reduced.[154]

Materials productivity
Finally, in addition to the innovations possible with feedstock substitution, the building industry also has the potential to use its materials more efficiently. While research shows that recycling cement into aggregate does not lead to any significant greenhouse gas savings (unless there is reduced transportation of raw materials), there are a number of other mechanisms for reducing material use (and subsequently energy use and emissions), including:[155]

- allowing alternative products in tender specifications that meet the design requirements rather than stipulating a particular form of cement;
- restricting the construction of small-scale cement-manufacturing plants, to promote economies of scale and higher-quality outcomes which can be achieved with the larger plants;
- using concrete more efficiently in construction, supplementing with other less carbon-intensive materials where practical;
- extending the lifespan of buildings.

Notes

1   International Iron and Steel Institute (2008).
2   ibid.
3   A GJ, Gigajoule, is one billion joules.
4   International Iron and Steel Institute (2008).
5   World Steel Association (undated) 'Crude Steel Statistics Total 2008', www.worldsteel.org/?action=stats&type=steel&period=latest&month=13& year=2008, accessed 24 March 2009; World Steel Association (2009) 'World crude steel production decreases by 1.2% in 2008', www.worldsteel.org/?action=newsdetail&id=257, accessed 24 March 2009.
6   Yamaguchi (2005).
7   Central Institute of Information & Techno-Economic Research for Steel Industry (undated).
8   International Iron and Steel Institute (2008).
9   Martin et al (1999a).
10 Worrell et al (1999).

11   Liedtke and Merten (1994).
12   IPCC (2007) see 'Industry'.
13   Qun (2007).
14   UN Data (2008) 'UN Statistics Division: China – Electricity Data',
      http://data.un.org/Data.aspx?d=EDATA&f=cmID%3AEL%3BtrID%3A1211,
      accessed 22 March 2009.
15   von Weizsäcker et al (1997) pp79–80.
16   Liedtke and Merten (1994).
17   Zhu (2008).
18   OECD (2008).
19   Worrell highlights improvements such as oxygen lancing, water cooling, control
      systems, scrap pre-heating and pneumatic steering.
20   Worrell (2004).
21   De Beer et al (1998).
22   Bureau of International Recycling (undated) 'About Recycling',
      www.bir.org/aboutrecycling/index.asp, accessed 4 April 2009.
23   International Iron and Steel and Institute (2008).
24   Fenton (1998).
25   OECD (2003a) p14.
26   Chinamining.org (2009) 'China's import of scrap steel in 2009',
      www.chinamining.org/Statistics/2009-03-20/1237533045d22790.html,
      accessed 25 March 2008.
27   World Steel Association (2008) 'Fact Sheet: Steel and Energy',
      www.worldsteel.org/pictures/programfiles/Fact%20sheet_Energy.pdf, accessed
      20 March 2009.
28   OECD (2003a).
29   US Department of Commerce (2000) Chp 6.
30   Worrell et al (2004).
31   ibid.
32   US Environmental Protection Agency (2007).
33   OECD (2008).
34   Worrell et al (2004).
35   ibid.
36   Boyd and Gove (2000).
37   ibid.
38   ibid.
39   Nucor Corporation (2007).
40   60 Minutes (2009).
41   Harris (2007).
42   Institute of Materials, Minerals and Mining (2002).
43   ibid.
44   Minerals Council of Australia (2007).
45   Worrell et al (1999).
46   World Steel Association (2008).
47   ibid.
48   Kavanagh (2007) cited in US Environmental Protection Agency (2007).
49   ibid.
50   Thomson (2006).
51   Okuwaki (2004).
52   Ziebek and Stanek (2001).
53   Blanch (2004).

54 American Iron and Steel Institute (2005).
55 American Iron and Steel Institute (2008).
56 Ferret (2005).
57 Stubbles (2000); International Iron and Steel Institute (IISI) (1998); Hamilton et al (2002).
58 World Steel Association (2008) 'Fact Sheet: Steel and Energy', www.worldsteel.org/pictures/programfiles/Fact%20sheet_Energy.pdf, accessed 20 March 2009.
59 Geyer (2004).
60 Atherton (2007).
61 Astle (2008).
62 Liedtke and Merten (1994).
63 ibid.
64 Hird (2005).
65 International Iron and Steel Institute (2005).
66 ibid.
67 Wang (2008).
68 National Bureau of Statistics of China (2007) cited in Garnaut (2008b) Chp 3.
69 US Geological Survey (2006) cited in International Energy Agency (IEA) (2007a) Table 6.2.
70 Fredonia Group Inc (2008).
71 Müller and Harnisch (2008) Figure 1.a.
72 Worrell et al (2001) Table 6.
73 Nakicenovic and Swart (2000) Chp 5.
74 USGS (2006) cited in International Energy Agency (IEA) (2007a) p139.
75 Price et al (2006); Vattenfall AB (2007); Netherlands Environmental Assessment Agency (2007).
76 Müller and Harnisch (2008) piii.
77 Wang (2008) p9.
78 US Environmental Protection Agency (2009a) Section 4.1.
79 Worrell et al (2001).
80 Cho and Giannini-Spohn (2007); Wang (2008) p9. This research brief was produced as part of the China Environment Forum's partnership with Western Kentucky University on the US AID-supported China Environmental Health Project.
81 Wang (2008) p9.
82 National Ready Mixed Concrete Association (2008) Figure 4 – '2005 US CO_2 Emissions by Category', p6.
83 Raina (2002).
84 Cemex (2006).
85 Holcim (2008) 'Holcim sets benchmark in sustainability again', Holcim Press Release, www.holcim.com/CORP/EN/id/1610647952/mod/6_1/page/news.html, accessed 2 April 2009; Holcim (undated) 'Innovative products, including composite cements', www.holcim.com/CORP/EN/id/1610653472/mod/7_2_2/page/editorial.html, accessed 2 April 2009.
86 CN Cemnet (2009) 'What is Cement?', www.cemnet.com/cement-history/portland-cement.aspx, accessed 2 April 2009.
87 Hendriks et al (2004).
88 Martin et al (1999b) p42.
89 Humphreys and Mahasenan (2002) 'Substudy 8: Climate Change'; Kim and Worrell (2002).

90   Duxson (2008).
91   Müller and Harnisch (2008) pii.
92   Alaoui et al (2007).
93   Duxson (2008).
94   Swanson (undated) 'Building Biology Based New Building Protocol: Magnesium Oxide, Magnesium Chloride, and Phosphate-based Cements', www.greenhomebuilding.com/pdf/MgO-GENERAL.pdf, accessed 4 March 2008.
95   Duxson (2008).
96   Pearce (2002).
97   Duxson et al (2007); Duxson (2008).
98   Davidovits (2002).
99   Provis and van Deventer (2009).
100 Müller and Harnisch (2008) p34.
101 Müller and Harnisch (2008).
102 CRC for Sustainable Resource Processing (2008) 'Geopolymers Program', www.csrp.com.au/projects/geopolymers.html, accessed 18 April 2009.
103 CSIRO (undated) 'Geopolymers: Building Blocks of the Future', www.csiro.au/science/ps19e.html, accessed 4 September 2008.
104 Zongrin et al (2004).
105 Nowak (2008).
106 Geopolymer Institute (undated) 'Cements, Concretes, Toxic Wastes, Global Warming', www.geopolymer.org/science/cements-concretes-toxic-wastes-global-warming, accessed 4 September 2008; CSIRO (undated) 'Geopolymers: Building Blocks of the Future', www.csiro.au/science/ps19e.html, accessed 4 September 2008; Net Balance Foundation (2007).
107 Duxson (2008).
108 Phillips (2008).
109 Shi et al (2006).
110 Glukhovsky (1994).
111 Krivenko (1999).
112 Shi et al (2006).
113 Xu et al (2008).
114 Zeobond E-Crete (undated) 'FAQ', www.zeobond.com/faq.htm, accessed 30 March 2009.
115 Yong et al (2007).
116 Drechsler and Graham (2005).
117 Davidovits (2002).
118 Houghton (2005).
119 Zeobond (2008) 'Zeobond to Present at Premier European Green Conference', Zeobond Press Release, 13 February 2008.
120 Duxson (2008).
121 Duxson (2009b).
122 Zeobond (2008) 'Zeobond to Present at Premier European Green Conference', Zeobond Press Release, 13 February 2008.
123 Net Balance Foundation (2007).
124 Net Balance Foundation (2007). This assumed a similar life for the two products, similar transport for the raw product (40km return trip), the final product (20km return trip) on a 30 ton truck with a 28 ton load, and a similar end-use.
125 Duxson (2009b).

126 Duxson et al (2007); Geopolymer Institute (undated) 'Technical Data Sheet for Geopolymeric cement type', www.geopolymer.org/science/technical-data-sheet, accessed 5 March 2009.
127 Davidovits (1991); Miranda et al (2005); Muntingh (2006).
128 Humphreys and Mahasenan (2002) 'Substudy 8: Climate Change'; Kim and Worrell (2002); International Energy Agency (2006c).
129 Kim and Worrell (2002); Humphreys and Mahasenan (2002).
130 Kim and Worrell (2002).
131 Vattenfall AB (2007) p20.
132 Kim and Worrell (2002).
133 Martin et al (1999b).
134 US Environmental Protection Agency (2007) Table 24.
135 Martin et al (1999b).
136 Price (2006) cited in Müller and Harnisch (2008) p19.
137 US EPA (2007) Section 3.2 Cement, pp3–12.
138 FLSMidth (2006).
139 International Energy Agency (IEA) (2007a) p153.
140 Vattenfall AB (2007) pp15–17.
141 International Energy Agency (IEA) (2007a) p157.
142 Raina (2002).
143 Raina (2002).
144 Duxson (2009a).
145 IPCC (2007) see 'Industry'.
146 Raina (2002).
147 ibid.
148 Müller and Harnisch (2008) pp2, 23.
149 Japan Cement Association (JCA) (2006) cited in International Energy Agency (IEA) (2007a) p154.
150 Cui and Wang (2006); International Energy Agency (IEA) (2007a) p154.
151 USGS (2006) cited in International Energy Agency (IEA) (2007a) p139.
152 IPCC (2007) 'Industry', pp1313–1320.
153 Müller and Harnisch (2008).
154 Duxson (2009a).
155 Duxson (2008).

4

The Agricultural Sector

We focus next on identifying Factor Five opportunities in the agricultural sector because this sector currently has a significant global ecological footprint. As this Sector Study will show, this sector is responsible for 18 per cent of global greenhouse gas emissions and 70 per cent of all freshwater withdrawals. However, the sector is also one of the most vulnerable to climate change – largely through reduced water availability and drier climates, which will hit those regions the hardest that depend on fresh water from annual snow or glacier melt. The potential negative impacts of climate change on the agricultural sector and in rural areas could be very serious because, according to the International Labour Organization in their 2005 World Employment Report, '75 percent of the world's poor live in rural areas, and agriculture employs 40 percent of workers in developing countries'.

This Sector Study seeks to complement the book *Factor Four* by providing a comprehensive overview of this sector's major resource productivity opportunities, beginning with energy and then focusing on water. *Factor Four* looked at ways to improve resource productivity in the agricultural sector in a number of ways, including new paradigms of agriculture that have the potential to achieve Factor 10–100 improvements in resource productivity for this sector. *Factor Four* discussed the exciting research of The Land Institute, led by Wes Jackson, to develop perennial grain crop agricultural systems to replace current annual grain crop systems, along with examples of organic bio-intensive farming around the world. *Factor Four* also discussed a number of case studies showing that the 'food miles' from the transportation of food, from the farm gate to the supermarket, had grown to ridiculous proportions and thus could be reduced. In terms of water productivity and agriculture, *Factor Four* pointed out that water efficiency savings through subsurface drip irrigation can be significant. This is an important enabling technology to assist humankind to meet our food needs with increasingly less water, as predicted by the IPCC, due to climate change. However, advanced efficient irrigation systems require more energy to pump the water through their pipes compared to flood irrigation, which typically uses flood plains or channels to move the water. Hence in this chapter we show that drip irrigation can be complemented by five other water productivity strategies – some that require no energy and others that reduce energy usage in irrigation thus enabling irrigation to be more easily powered by renewable energy sources. The strategies outlined in this chapter enable a simultaneous Factor Five improvement in both energy and water productivity on the farm.

Energy and water usage on the farm is but one input into the food that you buy. This chapter is extended through an online Sector Study on 'the food and hospitality industry', that provides an analysis of resource productivity opportunities from the 'paddock to the plate' to demonstrate the significant opportunities for improving resource efficiency through the entire supply chain. The study follows a progression from the farm (focusing on dairies), to food processes (focusing on bakeries), to supermarkets, to restaurants, and then to fast food outlets. Each step of the journey highlights key aspects of what would be covered in a full life-cycle approach to improve resource productivity, in particular the energy/water nexus opportunities.

1 The potential for Factor Five improvements in agricultural energy productivity

It is perhaps ironic that the impact from climate change on agricultural production will be increased by the industry itself, as one of the largest emitters of greenhouse gas emissions. According to a 2006 UN Food and Agricultural Organization (FAO) report, animal farming contributes more greenhouse gases than transportation worldwide (18 per cent versus 13.5 per cent).[1] Farming – from beef, pig and poultry to dairy and crops – has become increasingly mechanized, requiring significant energy inputs at particular stages of the production cycle to achieve optimum yields.[2] Energy is used directly as fuel or electricity to operate machinery and equipment, to heat or cool buildings, for lighting, and indirectly in the fertilizers and chemicals produced off site.

As the UK Carbon Trust reports, there are many areas where energy is being wasted in agriculture, from lighting, heating, ventilation, air circulation and refrigeration equipment to inefficient water irrigation and use.[3] For example, in America, even though farms have doubled their direct and indirect energy efficiency since 1978, farming still uses perhaps ten times as much fossil fuel energy in producing food as it returns in food energy,[4] and within the Asian region, India and China account for more than 80 per cent of the agricultural energy consumed.[5] In India, in particular, the total energy input – including seed, fertilizer and agrichemicals – has increased more than six times over the past three decades.[6] In China, the energy input for crop farming has increased by 2.5 times, and animal-farming energy input has increased by 1.8 times over a similar period.[7] Energy-intensive industries that have the opportunity to make significant efficiency improvements are summarized in Table 4.1.

Savings of up to 30 per cent can be achieved through better understanding of the farm's energy usage – whether in the field or in buildings – using control

Table 4.1 *Some major areas of energy usage in different agricultural systems*

Activity	Major areas of energy consumption
Pig farming	Animal feeding systems; maintenance of living conditions; building services and environmental protection; waste management; and emissions control.
Poultry farming	Animal feeding systems; maintenance of living conditions, including heating/cooling; and cleaning.
Dairy	Generally split amongst cooling, water heating and general power for lighting and pumping.
Crops	Irrigation; harvesting; crop storage; and drying.
Grain stores	Harvesting; crop storage; and drying.

Source: UK Carbon Trust (2006)[8]

systems to ensure the minimum amount of energy is being used to achieve the desired results. In addition, the structure of these buildings, the materials they are made from and the levels of insulation will all have a direct impact on the amount of energy used for heating, ventilation and cooling, as presented in Chapter 2. Here we will explore how conventional farming can achieve Factor Five improvements in energy productivity through a combination of direct and indirect initiatives plus investment in renewable energy options. There is significant potential for the agricultural sector to not only source its energy from biomass waste steams and renewable energy sources, but also to produce excess low-carbon electricity to sell to the grid. This is possible if farms utilize conversion of waste manure from livestock, waste woody biomass, wind or solar for electricity.

A whole system approach to Factor Five in agricultural energy productivity

As the world's food and materials requirement continues to increase alongside population growth and changing diet preferences, there is great potential to review and renew agricultural practices and systems to be less energy intensive. Given the significant differences in labour availability, types and volumes of crop or animals farmed, and geography around the world, these systemic opportunities are likely to be highly variable, requiring contextually sensitive solutions. For example, China has a strong focus on the production and domestic supply of vegetables, which yields high quantities per unit of land, making efficient use of scarce land resources and resulting in a low energy product. China also has a high availability of human labour, with 300 labourers available for every 100ha of farmland compared with the world average of 82, and the American average of two, and a low use of mechanized equipment, with approximately 6 tractors per 1000ha, compared with the world average of 18, and the American average of 27.[9] However, China uses approximately 2.5 times more fertilizer than the world average, at approximately 270kg/ha, and has an energy-intensive meat industry – as the world's second-largest poultry producer, third-largest beef producer, and producing nearly half of the world's pork (47 per cent).[10] Hence, for China, fertilizer has the potential to be increasingly sourced from high-nutrient agricultural waste from these industries in addition to composted urban waste – making use of the available human labour – rather than energy-intensive chemical manufacture. China also has the potential to build on its existing status as the major biogas producer (discussed below) through scaling up and commercializing such effluent and waste re-use opportunities, and making energy from the composting processes to further reduce the net energy requirements per unit of food production.

In the following paragraphs we consider the IPCC strategies for improved productivity with respect to energy use in food production, noting innovations in China, Europe, Australia and America that are achieving Factor Five improvements.

IPCC Strategy One: Energy efficiency

Table 4.2 summarizes a variety of ways farms can significantly reduce direct and indirect energy consumption and become net renewable electricity and energy exporters.

IPCC Strategy Two: Fuel switching
Switching to biogas

The agricultural sector has a number of unique and potentially lucrative options for onsite energy generation – such as processing enormous quantities of manure to create methane that can be combusted to create electricity. Methane is a product of an anaerobic digestion process which uses microorganisms to break down organic material in the absence of oxygen, producing the gas, and a rich fertilizer. And as the global warming potential of methane is 21 times that of CO_2 even though this process creates CO_2, the overall effect is a significant reduction in greenhouse gas emissions.[11] It is hence considered a significant part of the solution to managing agricultural waste while also producing a valuable alternative fuel source to fossil fuels. Other options include gasifying waste woody biomass from vegetation, or cellulose from pastures and grasses, with the by-product from the gasification process being charcoal (referred to as 'biochar') which can be used to improve soil productivity and carbon storage.

Farmers can then benefit from reduced operating costs through switching to methane for vehicle fuel, heating and electricity generation, and can return the natural fertilizer to the farm, as well as avoid the greenhouse gas emissions from the decomposing waste.[12] The UK Carbon Trust estimates that dairy anaerobic digesters could produce 4–5kWh per cow per day, which is significant when considering large-scale farms with in the order of 15,000–100,000 cows, pigs and chickens at some operations.[13] In Germany there are already more than 2700 agricultural anaerobic digestion plants installed, benefitting from a relatively high population density with good transport infrastructure in place which enables easy feedstock supply. In contrast, as of February 2009,

Table 4.2 *Potential areas of energy savings and renewable energy production*

Activity	Innovation potential
Irrigation	A study by Kansas State University found that, on average, irrigation systems could use 40 per cent less energy if they were properly sized, adjusted and maintained.[14] Reducing the energy requirement makes sourcing the energy from renewable energy sources such as wind and solar more viable. Farms can also create power through the use of anaerobic digester technologies to turn manure into electricity.[15]
Heating	Heating is often the greatest energy cost in agriculture, with at least 30 per cent reductions in energy needs available through the implementation of some simple energy-saving measures.[16] More advanced strategies of heat recovery can achieve 80 per cent energy improvements in some agricultural sectors.
Drying crops	All major crops, as well as fruit, are stored and dried, often by gas-fired systems that can be substituted with electric systems powered by low- to no-carbon renewable energy, hence all but eliminating emissions.[17]
Lighting	Lighting can account for 20 per cent of energy used in agriculture and, as electricity is relatively expensive, advances as outlined in Chapter 2 could save over 50 per cent of total energy costs.[18]
Building design	Agricultural buildings range from new, purpose-built storage facilities to old farm buildings that may have stood for hundreds of years. Better building design, as outlined in Chapter 2, can assist to reduce the amount of energy needed for heating, air ventilation and lighting.[19]
Refrigeration	In some agricultural sub-sectors, particularly dairy farming, refrigeration accounts for a significant proportion of overall site energy costs.[20] Purchasing the most energy-efficient refrigeration equipment can save up to 50 per cent, as outlined in the online Sector Study on the food and hospitality industry.
Fertilizer and pesticide use	Farms can reduce the amount of indirect energy linked to the use of pesticides and fertilizers through biological control of pests, companion planting and other ecological strategies to reduce pest damage. Farmers can also reduce artificial fertilizer usage through utilizing recycled organic fertilizers which are made from organic waste that would otherwise go to landfill. This achieves a significant reduction in energy consumption in this area because it takes 30GJ/ton of energy to make artificial nitrogen-based fertilizers through the Haber process (more than a ton of cement or steel), whereas recycled organics can be turned into organic composts with negligible energy inputs. Organic fertilizers produced from organic recycling increases organic levels and microbial density in the soil, also enabling soil carbon sequestration to be increased.
Conservation tillage	Conservation tillage and zero tillage are increasingly being adopted to reduce the use of energy and to increase the carbon storage in soils. Zero tillage can achieve 90 per cent erosion reduction compared with a system of intensive tillage, conserving soil, water and soil organic matter. Effectively implemented, the system reduces costly inputs, such as time and fuel, while maintaining or improving crop yields and profits.[21] Other benefits include reduced soil compaction, utilization of marginal land, some harvesting advantages and conservation compliance. Combining the use of organic fertilizers and conservation tillage enables farmers to increase soil carbon in their soils. The IPCC 4th Assessment estimates that the global technical mitigation potential from agriculture (excluding fossil fuel offsets from biomass) by 2030 is ~5500–6000MtCO$_2$-eq/yr with soil carbon sequestration (enhanced sinks) being the main mechanism – contributing 89 per cent of this technical potential.[22]

Source: Compiled by TNEP with sources as noted within the text

the US EPA AgSTAR programme estimates that there are only 125 farm-scale digesters operating at commercial livestock farms in the US, which generate about 244,000MWh of electricity per year.[23] Hence the potential for growth of anaerobic digesters in the US is significant.

Anaerobic digesters also have a strong uptake in the developing and rapidly emerging economies of the world, including:

- *China*: China is now the biggest biogas producer and user in the world, with around 18 million farm households using biogas, much of which was installed within the last 30 years. There are also 3500 large and medium-scale anaerobic digestion plants with the capacity to produce 230 million cubic metres of biogas per year.[24] For example, an industrial-scale chicken farm (3 million chickens) north of Beijing has installed the country's first chicken manure-biogas plant, using the 220 tons of manure and 170 tons of wastewater each day to produce 14,600MWh of electricity a year, as well as providing heat for the farm, saving US$1.2 million each year in electricity.[25]
- *Thailand*: In Thailand biogas engines have helped keep pig farms viable after rising costs and falling pork prices have challenged the survival of farms. Thailand's Ministry of Energy has set a target of building 1540 100MW biogas plants by 2011 using sewage, manure or grass as the feedstock.[26] For comparison, India produces about 500Mt of crop residue annually, of which 25 per cent is available for energy generation in the rural sector, approximately 12,500MW.[27]
- *Philippines*: Maya Farms in metropolitan Manila is one of the pioneers of large-scale biogas applications in developing countries. Manure from 22,000 pigs is fed into digesters which produce 1700m³ (66,000ft³) of biogas per day. The biogas is used as a fuel for the processing plants, as a petrol substitute in a variety of equipment and machinery, and in motors to generate electricity which is used onsite. The slurry from the biogas manufacturing process is separated into liquid and solids, with the liquid being used for crop fertilizers and fish pond feed, while the solids are re-fed to the pigs, cattle and ducks (providing 10–15 per cent of the total feed for the pigs and cattle, and 50 per cent of the feed for the ducks).[28]

However, even with such examples of implementation there is still great potential for an increase in the uptake, as well as innovation in the application, of anaerobic digestion systems. For example, in China there is still an estimated 580 million ton/year agricultural (manure) and agro-industrial biodegradable wastes and wastewater thought to be available as potential sources from which biogas can be produced to supply renewable energy.[29] In the US, researchers at the University of Texas, Austin have demonstrated the biogas potential of the one billion tons of cow manure produced each year in America, which would otherwise be a powerful emitter of greenhouse gas emissions (51 to 118 million tons of CO_2 equivalent) where it is left to decompose. This manure could be used to create biogas, generating electricity through micro-turbines that could supply the equivalent of 3 per cent of the total US electricity demand.[30]

Second generation bio-fuels

Increasingly, agricultural crops and residues are seen as sources of feedstocks for energy to displace fossil fuels. A wide range of materials has been proposed for use, including grain, crop residue, cellulosic crops (e.g. switchgrass, sugarcane) and various tree species which can be burned directly or processed further to generate liquid fuels such as ethanol or diesel fuel.[31] Currently, around 60 per cent of world ethanol supplies are produced from sugar, primarily in Brazil, with most of the balance made from grains. Second generation bio-fuels (referring to the improved process for creating bio-fuels that includes wood- and fibre-based feedstock), are an improvement from first generation bio-fuels as they did not achieve significant greenhouse gas savings, and negatively affected the supply and price of food. However, second generation bio-fuels still have the potential, if poorly managed, to affect food production and sales. They may also result in minimal reductions in net emissions or even, in some cases, higher total emissions than fossil fuels, especially where crops and processing have high non-renewable energy requirements or where forest is cleared for feedstock production, such as for palm oil in Asia. Hence, landuse competition and environmental impacts are important considerations when planning to use crops for fuel production.

In general, non-food feedstocks outperform food-based feedstocks on energy, environmental and economic criteria.[32] For instance, trees, other woody plants, various grasses and forbs (weeds) and algae can all be converted into hydrocarbons or cellulosic ethanol, and may be produced on poor agricultural lands with little or no fertilizer, pesticides or energy inputs. Hence, these second generation bio-fuels, such as ethanol, biodiesel, butanol, methanol and methyltetrahydrofuran (MTHF), are being developed with the potential for Factor 10 improvements in greenhouse gas emissions.[33] Such technologies could also greatly expand potential 'bio-energy' supplies, using bio-refineries to create a range of high-value bio-based products, with bio-fuel and energy as co-products. In many cases these second generation technologies are able to use the same feedstock to produce either bio-electricity or liquid bio-fuels, creating additional opportunities but also the potential for competition across these markets.[34]

IPCC Strategy Four: Renewable energy

Agriculture holds enormous potential to take advantage of a combination of renewable energy technologies and various energy-related innovations, from small- to large-scale agriculture across developing and developed countries. There are numerous renewable energy options in addition to the biogas options discussed above, including wind, solar (solar thermal and solar PV), water, geothermal and biomass. Farmers around the world have long used wind power to pump bore water and provide energy for the pumping required by irrigation systems. India has a long history of combining renewable energy sources, including: solar drying of products;[35] windmills for water lifting; solar energy for crop drying;[36] and upgrading watermills by replacing wooden runners with precision-made metal ones.[37] Examples of opportunities related to solar, wind and water energy include the following:

- *Solar bore and surface water pumping – photovoltaic systems*: Although current prices for solar panels make them too expensive for most crop irrigation systems, photovoltaic systems can be economical for remote livestock water supply, pond aeration and small irrigation systems. There are estimated to be around 10,000 solar-powered surface and bore water pumps in use globally, with potential for further use.[38]
- *Solar heating and drying*: The agricultural sector is ideally positioned to use solar energy for lighting, heating and drying in buildings and on the land. Solar heating and drying technology can vary but essentially comprises an enclosure or shed, screened drying trays or racks, and a solar collector. Gas-fired crop drying is widely used to process crops such as fruit, wheat and rice, for which solar thermal energy can be substituted. Solar-drying equipment can dry crops faster and more evenly than leaving them in the field after harvest, with the added advantage of avoiding damage by birds, pests and weather.[39]
- *Wind power*: The use of water-pumping windmills was a major factor in the expansion of farming and ranching activities in places such as Europe, North America and Australia. Windmills also helped to create productive land in the Netherlands by providing a cost-effective method for drawing down the water table. In addition, farmers and ranchers are now in a unique position to benefit from the growth in the wind power industry, to power more on-farm operations and to create another revenue stream for their land.[40] The typical costs[41] in setting up a wind turbine may be beyond the individual capacity of farmers, in which case either 'renting' land to wind utilities or pooling resources through community wind farm cooperatives may be attractive options.
- *Water power*: A watermill uses a water wheel or turbine, either horizontally or vertically (which is much more energy efficient), to drive a mechanical process. The force of the water's movement drives the blades of a wheel or turbine, which rotates an axle that drives machinery. By the early 20th century, watermills became commercially obsolete in developed countries due to the availability of cheap electrical energy, with only smaller rural mills operating commercially into the 1960s. However, watermills are still widely used in developing countries for processing grain, with an estimated 25,000 watermills operating in Nepal ('*ghattas*'), over 200,000 in India ('*gharats*' or '*panchakis*'), and many more in the mountainous regions of China, Pakistan and Turkey.[42] Many of these are still of the traditional style, but some have been upgraded by replacing wooden parts with metal ones to more than double the mill's productivity.

IPCC Strategy Seven: Material efficiency

Soil quality is of fundamental importance, as farming can deplete soils, and nitrogen fertilizers can pollute waterways leading to algal blooms. At the same time, at the other end of the process, organic material makes its way into landfills, which are fast becoming one of the largest long-term problems facing urban society today, taking space, devaluing property, polluting waterways, creating greenhouse gas emissions and contaminating land. Hence, 'soil' provides a common reference to consider waste management, soil management, and product and packaging design. Conventional agriculture today is essentially a mineral extractive industry that progressively removes from the soil not only the organic fraction, but also minerals and trace elements. All of this material is either exported or carried into the cities where it is processed through people and, passing through a waste management system, ends up in either landfills or sewage treatment plants, subsequently re-entering waterways and land as pollutants.[43] It is ironic that the greatest 'contaminant' ending up in landfill is organic material. If this organic material could be safely returned to the farm, landfill volume and contamination issues could be significantly addressed, and nutrients and minerals could be returned to the soils.

Specifically, organic recycling to produce fertilizer enables levels of organics in the soil, along with the microbial density, to be increased. Soils function well when they have a balance of key nutrients such as carbon, nitrogen, phosphorus and potassium. Enriching soils, through organic recycling, adds these important nutrients back into soils and thus enables soils to then also be able to sequester and store more carbon long term. According to the IPCC:

> *Agricultural ecosystems hold large carbon reserves, mostly in soil organic matter... Any practice that increases the photosynthetic input of carbon and/or slows the return of stored carbon to CO_2 via respiration, fire or erosion will increase carbon reserves, thereby 'sequestering' carbon or building carbon 'sinks'. Many studies, worldwide, have now shown that significant amounts of soil carbon can be stored in this way, through a range of practices.[44] Significant amounts of vegetative carbon can also be stored in agroforestry systems or other perennial plantings on agricultural lands.[45]*

The IPCC's 3rd Assessment, published in 2001, estimated that improved soil health and productivity can allow increases in soil carbon at an initial rate of around 0.3 tons of carbon/ha/yr.[46] The potential of carbon sequestration through soil carbon, on a global scale, is about 0.6 billion to one billion tons per year.[47] The IPCC then estimated in their 4th Assessment that:

> *the global technical mitigation potential from agriculture (excluding fossil fuel offsets from biomass) by 2030 is between*

~5500–6000MtCO$_2$-eq/yr with soil carbon sequestration (enhanced sinks) the main mechanism contributing 89% of this technical potential.[48]

Thus soil carbon provides a significant strategy to assist all nations and regions to cost-effectively sequester carbon, through improving organic recycling to help improve soil health while encouraging good farming practices and soil management.

2 The potential for Factor Five improvements in agricultural water productivity

Over the last half century worldwide fresh water demand has roughly tripled, while supplies are rapidly diminishing in quality and quantity.[49] With the vast amount of water being used for agriculture, significant water productivity improvements in the sector are a crucial component in ensuring sufficient future food and freshwater supplies.

The world is facing a serious water gap: some 20 percent more water is needed than is available to feed the more than 2 billion additional people who will be alive by 2025. Better farm management techniques, crops that are improved to flourish in low-water environments [form an important component of] an overall global water strategy.
Ismail Serageldin, Chairman of the World Commission on Water for the 21st Century and World Bank Vice President for Special Programs, 2000[50]

Crop production uses an estimated 7130km³ of water each year, corresponding to approximately 3000 litres to feed a single person for one day.[51] The United Nations Food and Agriculture Organization (FAO), and the International Fund for Agricultural Development (IFAD), estimate that to satisfy the growing demand for food between 2000 and 2030, production of food crops in developing countries needs to increase by 67 per cent, while restraining the increase in water use for agriculture to about 14 per cent.[52] However, the Worldwatch Institute reports that by 2025 numerous river basins and countries will face a situation in which 30 per cent or more of their irrigation demands cannot reliably be met because of water shortages.[53] Research by the Chinese Academy of Agricultural Sciences projects a fall in agricultural yields of 14 to 23 per cent by 2050 in China due to water shortages and other pressures.[54] As Lester Brown reflects, 'China's forays into the world market in early 2004 to buy 8 million tons of wheat could mark the beginning of the global shift from an era of grain surpluses to one of grain scarcity'.[55]

Water tables across the world are now falling at alarming rates from over-pumping of groundwater, freshwater wetlands have diminished in area by about half, and major rivers like the Amu Dar'ya, Colorado, Ganges, Indus, Rio Grande, Murray and Yellow now run dry for parts of the year.[56] In addition, freshwater availability does not match areas of population growth. Clearly there is a critical need to ensure the future integrity of fresh water supplies across the planet. Indeed, improving the 'productivity of water' (i.e. how much benefit is obtained from each unit of water consumed) will inevitably prove to be a high priority for many national and international government agencies in the not too distant future.

According to the United Nations, the major global uses of fresh water are for agriculture (mostly irrigation – 69 per cent), followed by industry (23 per cent), and domestic (household drinking water and sanitation – 8 per cent).[57] Although regional averages vary a great deal from these global figures, agriculture consistently comprises a significant proportion of the demand. In Africa for example 88 per cent of all water withdrawn is for agriculture, while domestic use accounts for 7 per cent, and industry for 5 per cent. In Europe, most water is used in industry (54 per cent), while agriculture uses 33 per cent, and domestic use accounts for 13 per cent. The reassuring news is that within the agricultural sector improved agricultural methods have the potential to play a key role in significantly reducing water demand, such as in increasing the efficiency of delivering and applying water to crops, and in increasing crop yields per litre of water consumed.

Here we demonstrate that the agricultural sector can achieve Factor Five improvements in water productivity, building on from the case study of 'subsurface drip irrigation' presented in *Factor Four*. In the following section we focus on the principles of an approach developed for the Californian agricultural sector by the Pacific Institute (an American independent non-profit water research and advocacy group headed by author of the biennial *World's Water*[58] and internationally renowned water expert Dr Peter Gleick), namely:[59]

- *Appropriate selection of crop species*: Selecting crops and variants of crops that are well suited to the intended bio-physical and climatic conditions can deliver in the order of 50 per cent water saving. We also consider the appropriate selection of livestock species as an extension of this strategy.
- *Efficient irrigation technologies*: As *Factor Four* showed in 1997, water efficiency savings through subsurface drip irrigation can be significant. It can also be made more affordable, especially for poorer agricultural regions in the under-developed and developing world.
- *Irrigation scheduling*: Using irrigation scheduling information that helps farmers more precisely meet crop water needs has been shown to reduce water usage by 17 per cent, and increase crop yields by as much as 8 per cent.
- *Advanced irrigation management*: Applying a range of emerging advanced irrigation management methods, such as regulated deficit irrigation, can deliver in the order of 30–50 per cent water savings.

- *Rainwater harvesting*: Using a range of techniques including micro-dams, channels and stream diversion, to divert rainfall over the flood plain ensures rainfall flows through the flood plain before it flows into rivers or out to sea, facilitating infiltration into the water tables and crop irrigation on the plains.
- *Treating and re-using urban wastewater for peri-urban agriculture*: Using treated and recycled water from cities as a source of irrigation water can deliver over 50 per cent reductions in water extraction levels from natural sources.

Depending on the geographical and cultural context, strategically investing in an appropriate combination of these strategies can provide the potential for farmers to reduce their demand for fresh water by Factor Five, or 80 per cent. Such improvements not only reduce the costs associated with accessing and distributing water, but also reduce susceptibility to climate change-related risks, such as increasingly frequent and severe droughts, reduced water availability, increasing water prices and growing competition for water from cities and industry. It is important to point out that such strategies, implemented effectively, minimize the energy needed to pump water through the irrigation systems, thus enabling the energy demand for irrigation to be more easily met with renewable energy sources onsite.

A whole system approach to Factor Five in agricultural water productivity

Although agriculture is responsible for 70 per cent of the fresh water consumed, water demand within this sector varies significantly, from cereals and grains, to meat and dairy, as indicated in Table 4.3, with even larger variability if drainage and losses in the delivery of water are included. Cereals and grains can consume anywhere between 0.4 and 5.0m³/kg, while meat production (poultry, pork, beef) ranges from about 2.0 to 32.2m³/kg. Table 4.3 also shows how water demand varies considerably around the planet, with China, America, India and Brazil being the major 'food bowls' in agricultural production.

By increasing the volumes of cereals, grains and livestock to meet growing produce demands, inefficient water practices are adding increasing pressure on already stretched water resources.[60] Countries can increase their water productivity but sustainable practices are crucial to being able to meet demand in the longer term. For example, China has both a significant shortage of arable land (9 per cent of the global total compared to 13 per cent in America), as well as ten persons to feed per hectare of arable land, which is more than twice the world average of 4.4 persons per hectare.[61] Yet China has remained largely self-sufficient in food production and is a major producer of many important commodities. The productivity of Chinese agriculture is higher than the global average, maintained by double- and triple-cropping and applying large quantities of fertilizer and labour to the limited land available. More than 40 per cent

Table 4.3 *Agricultural production: Indicative tonnage and*
on-farm water requirements

Product	Global produce (Mt)	Water use (m³/kg)	Major production locations (in decreasing order)
Cereals and grains			
Maize (corn)	800	0.5–2.1	US, China
Wheat	607	0.8–1.5	China, India, US, Russia, France
Rice	400	1.6–3.5	China, India, Indonesia, Bangladesh, Vietnam, Thailand, Myanmar, Philippines
Potatoes	322	0.9–1.0	China, Russian Federation, India, US
Soybean	216	1.7–2.2	US, Brazil, Argentina, China
Barley	136	1.3	Russia, Canada, Germany, France
Sorghum	65	2.8	US, Nigeria, India, Mexico
Millet	32	4.5–5.0	India, Nigeria
Oats	26	1.6–2.4	Russian Federation, Canada, US, Poland, Australia, Germany
Rye	16	0.9–1.2	Poland, Russian Federation, Germany
Meat and dairy			
Milk	560	1.3	US, India, Russia, Brazil, China
Pork	155	3.4	China, US
Poultry	87	2.0–4.6	US, China, Brazil, EU
Beef	62	16.7–32.2	Australia, US, Argentina, New Zealand, Brazil, EU, China
Lamb	9	7.0	China, EU, Australia, New Zealand, Iran, Turkey, India
Other – food			
Coffee	8	17.0	Brazil, Colombia, Indonesia, Vietnam, Mexico
Tea	4	24.5	India, China, Kenya, Sri Lanka
Other – non-food			
Cotton	23.6	5.3–17.0	China, India, US, Pakistan, Brazil, Uzbekistan
Tobacco	6.3	0.4–0.6	China, India, Brazil, US, EU
Hemp[a]	0.1	0.3	China, India, Russian Federation, Korea

Note: a These figures are from 2005 and include only hemp seed and hemp tow waste, due to the unavailability of other data.
Source: This table was compiled from a number of sources[62]

of the land is irrigated in comparison to the global average of 18 per cent, and American average of 13 per cent.[63] However, only about 30 per cent of the water used in Chinese agriculture reaches the crop root zone, due to conveyance losses and inefficient irrigation practices.[64] From these figures it is clear that a whole system approach to agricultural productivity is needed, to ensure that food production is managed by addressing water availability constraints.

In 2008, responding to a number of water availability challenges facing the Californian agricultural sector, including uncontrolled urbanization, global market pressures, and threats to the reliability and availability of fresh water, the Pacific Institute assessed the potential to improve agricultural water-use efficiency.[65] The study focused on the Sacramento–San Joaquin Delta, which supplies half of the water used for California's agriculture and water to the states residents, and developed recommendations for the public, growers and policy makers working to improve water use. The study shows that using strategies such as those discussed below, farmers could substantially reduce freshwater extraction, and save the equivalent of as much as 3–20 dams worth of water per annum in California. Furthermore, the report found that these savings could be achieved without adversely affecting the economic productivity of the agricultural sector. According to the researchers, farmers who shift away from water-intensive crops, invest in high-tech watering systems and irrigate only at precise times in the growing cycle could save as much as 3.4 million acre-feet (4194 million m^3) of water each year.[66] We now consider a range of water productivity strategies in more detail.

Appropriate selection of crop species and livestock choices
Crop shifting

Crop shifting involves shifting from low-income, high water-use crops to high-income, low water-use crops, and the movement of crops from dry regions of the country to regions with more water. In the first instance, where possible (if the land type and environment permits), low water-demanding and drought resistant crops should be cultivated, and preference given to those varieties that also have a higher biomass. Countries of rapid population growth, including India, Bangladesh and China, are promising areas for such a shift, with the potential for better return on investment.[67] Switching crops from, for example, cotton to vegetables or fruit could be highly profitable for the farmer as well as being good for water conservation, since despite the fact that a larger percentage of vegetables are irrigated, they use nearly half the amount of water that cotton uses per hectare.

Cereals have a central place in the human diet, with roughly half of the world's cropland devoted to their production.[68] In 2025 it is predicted that the world's farmers may be producing roughly three billion tons of cereals to feed a potential human population of eight billion,[69] compared with the 2008 yield of just over two billion tons.[70] Rice is the primary source of food for more than half the world's population,[71] consuming around 30 per cent of the fresh water used for crops worldwide.[72] Asian farmers produce about 90 per cent of the total global production of rice, and Asian countries consume 90 per cent of what is produced.[73] Corn, more generally known as maize, is native to the western hemisphere, but has become one of the most important crops in both the developed and developing world. Researchers are studying alternative crops that use less water (i.e. wheat instead of rice, and sorghum instead of corn) to increase the global cereal production capacity, as the following examples demonstrate:

- *Maize (corn)*: Maize grows in the temperate climates of North America and western Europe, producing an average of seven tons per hectare, compared with an average of just 2.5 tons per hectare for farmers in the developing world. One-half of the 60 million hectares (148 million acres) of corn planted in the developing world is subject to periodic droughts. Researchers at the International Maize and Wheat Improvement Center, known as CIMMYT, have created hardy new breeds of tropical corn, such as the drought-tolerant Tuxpeño corn that can produce 2.8 tons per hectare, increasing harvests by 40 per cent under drought conditions.

- *Wheat*: Wheat has relatively few natural insect enemies, but has histori- cally been restricted to temperate and subtropical zones. Researchers have been able to modify the grain through intensive plant breeding, to make it productive even in hot climates with strong built-in resistance to major diseases. The improved stability of yields facilitates better long-term water- use planning, and reduced pest management procedures minimize chemical use.[74]

- *Rice*: An international team of scientists has produced a new type of 'Hardy' rice that shows a significant increase in biomass under both drought and non-drought conditions. The research found that this variety grows better and uses water more efficiently than other rice crops, with its biomass increasing by around 50 per cent under conditions of water depri- vation (drought) compared to the unmodified version of the same type of rice.[75]

In addition, switching of major crops to species that are more drought and soil tolerant may also contribute to Factor Five-type reductions in water demand:

- *Barley*: Barley is more adaptable than other cereals, tolerating many diverse environments except for acidic and wet soils, with a wider ecologi- cal range than any other cereal. The grain can be grown on soils unsuitable for wheat, and at altitudes unsuitable for wheat or oats. Because of its salt and drought tolerance barley can also be grown near desert areas.[76]

- *Oats*: Oats are even more adaptable, having a lower summer heat require- ment and greater tolerance to rain than wheat, rye or barley. Thus, oats are particularly important in areas with cool, wet summers such as north-west Europe. However, although oats have many health benefits for human consumption, the main use for oats has historically been for animal feed, and global oat production has more than halved since 1960.[77]

- *Rye*: Rye is a hardy grain that is more tolerant to frost and drought than wheat, and is often grown under conditions where other cereals fail as its highly developed root system uses 20–30 per cent less water than wheat. Rye is used as a cover crop to reduce soil erosion, enhance soil water reten- tion, contribute a green manure and reduce weed growth (reducing the need for herbicides).[78] Rye can also be grown in a wider range of environ- mental conditions than any other small grain. Rye growing areas and harvest have diminished by more than half since the early 1960s, with modern harvest equipment not being built to manage the significant height of rye, which currently has a lack of dwarf varieties.[79]

Livestock choices and land management

According to the UN FAO, direct emissions from meat production account for about 18 per cent of the world's total greenhouse gas emissions.[80] The UN further predicts that the number of farmed animals will double in the next 50 years – for example global production of meat is projected to more than double from 229 million tons in 1999–2001 to 465 million tons in 2050, and milk production is projected to grow from 580 to 1043 million tons.[81] It is therefore crucial to address both consumption and water and energy requirements of animal products. This is a complex issue because net emissions from meat production vary considerably depending on whether or not the livestock are grazed over large expanses of land or through confined energy-intensive feed-lot farming. For instance, if livestock are grazed over large expanses of land, as they are in Mongolia, Australia, Africa and parts of North and South America, there is potential to significantly offset their emissions through applying strategies to improve soil carbon in rangelands. The FAO's 2006 report *Livestock's Long Shadow*, also found that the livestock sector's potential contribution to solving climate change and environmental problems is equally large[82] – from protecting native habitat and stopping land clearing, enriching their soils with carbon, grazing their cattle, or if in feed-lot, improving feed and feed additives, findings that have been supported by the Worldwatch Institute.[83]

There are also a number of significant process-based opportunities to improve water productivity in livestock agriculture. This is important because livestock production accounts for more than 8 per cent of global human water use, mainly through the irrigation of feed crops. The water productivity of livestock can be improved primarily through improving the process of producing feedstock – for both grains and grasses that are grown and fed to livestock, or that are grown and grazed upon directly. Soil and water conservation practices and conservation agriculture technologies can improve both yields and efficient use of available land and water, avoiding the felling of forests and additional irrigation to produce feedstock. Opportunities for consideration are summarized in Table 4.4.

Efficient irrigation technologies

In many countries more than 90 per cent of the irrigated land surface still receives water by flooding or through open channels which may or may not be sealed, leading to significant water loss from leakage, soil seepage and evaporation. Methods involving the use of efficient irrigation technology are focused on supplying just enough water to plants, where and when they need it. Typically, efficient irrigation technologies involve shifting from indiscriminate irrigation, for example through flooding or open channel irrigation, to targeted low-pressure sprinklers or drip (including subsurface) irrigation, particularly for multiple vintage crops such as grapes, fruits and nuts. Low-pressure sprinklers can reduce water use by up to 30 per cent,[85] while subsurface drip irrigation uses drip lines buried underground that release small amounts of water into the plant root zone, which can reduce water use by at least 50 per

Table 4.4 *Whole-system opportunities for improving livestock water productivity*

Opportunity	Consideration
Reducing water demand	– Rotating animals and crops to allow the pasture to replenish. – Increasing biodiversity on the land to increase ground cover and hence reduce erosion, as well as reducing weeds and pests.
Resource-enhancing technologies	– Managing the number and type of animals on the land, through, for example, 'managed intensive rotational grazing' (practised in the UK and New Zealand), 'deferred grazing' (traditionally practised in Middle Eastern countries), multispecies grazing, and three-strata agroforestry systems comprising grass, fodder shrubs and tree crops such as oil and coconut palms or cashew nuts. – Improving soil health through returning nutrient-rich wastewater and solids to the land in a way that replenishes the soil.
Resource sparing technologies	– Introducing multi-phase feeding and careful monitoring, whereby feed composition is better suited to the animals, resulting in less waste and less nitrogen and phosphate emissions to the environment. – Reducing the amount of cereals and grains forming part of the feedstock, and replacing with nutrient-rich grass and fodder.
Waste management technologies	– Including onsite wastewater treatment to address biological oxygen demand and nitrogen and phosphorus imbalances, before returning to the land. – Treating and recycling greywater (for cleaning etc.) onsite. – Using livestock waste as feed, energy or fertilizer.

Source: Adapted from Steinfield et al (1998)[84]

cent.[86] Hence there is significant potential to reduce water consumption as only a few countries – Cyprus, Israel and Jordan – use drip irrigation on a meaningful scale. Meanwhile India and China use such technology on just 1–3 per cent of irrigated land, while the US incorporates drip irrigation on only 4 per cent of its land.[87] Farmers in India, Israel, Jordan, Spain and the US have shown that drip irrigation systems that deliver water directly to crop roots can reduce water use by 30–70 per cent and raise crop yields by 20–90 per cent.

Oregon State University researchers have summarized a number of additional advantages in using subsurface drip irrigation processes that can help to ensure that return on investments for drip irrigation are reasonable, including the following:[88]

- Adaptability to fields with uneven topography or shape, as well as not contributing to subsequent effects of excessive infiltration and runoff, such as salinization from rising water tables or washing away of topsoil.
- Extreme efficiency with precise water application while preventing over-watering and subsequent runoff.
- Precision in the application of nutrients, leading to reduced requirement and hence reduced costs associated with fertilizer use.
- Ability to assist tractor operations and movement flexibility by avoiding the need for a grid of channels, or overhead sprinkler equipment.

- The system can also be automated and monitored by computer and does not require constant monitoring by farmers to gauge watering requirements. Such systems can also incorporate predicted weather patterns to avoid overwatering in times of predictable rainfall.

Case study: Affordable drip irrigation

Uptake in developing countries of drip irrigation has been historically slow due to lack of finance to be able to afford the upfront costs for piping, valves, installation and monitoring, and this is a significant issue, as some 95 per cent of the world's 1.1 billion farmers live in developing countries and the vast majority cultivate plots of less than 2ha (5 acres).[89] Previous initiatives have rarely succeeded because the drip irrigation technology has been directed at larger commercial farmers with the funds to invest in infrastructure, rather than poor smallholder farmers. In 2001, international water expert Sandra Postel and her colleagues compared the differences in markets for affordable drip irrigation and conventional (large-scale) drip irrigation and identified a number of criteria that need to be met for successful use in developing countries, including: affordability for farmers earning less than US$200–300 per year; rapid payback, divisibility and expandability for farms to grow as income increases; and water efficiency for stretching already scarce water supplies in arid and semi-arid lands and tropical areas with long dry seasons.[90]

In recent years, small-scale drip-irrigation system technology – virtually a bucket that relies on gravity to distribute the water through flexible plastic tubing as shown in Figure 4.1 – has been increasingly used to irrigate small vegetable gardens with roughly 100 plants (covering 25m^2), with somewhat larger drum systems irrigating 125m^2.[91] Cost-effective large-scale drip systems using plastic lines that can be moved easily are also becoming popular, with typical payback periods of less than a year.[92] By reducing water demand and improving crop yield, this form of irrigation can dramatically raise incomes of smallholders. Postel estimates that the combination of these drip technologies at various scales has the potential to profitably irrigate ten million hectares of India's cropland, or nearly one tenth of the total, and sees a similar potential for China, which is now also expanding its drip-irrigated area to save scarce water.[93] She and her colleagues report that studies in several countries show such methods can reduce water use by 30–70 per cent and raise yields by 20–90 per cent due to the steady supply of water that just meets crop needs.[94] This combination of reduced water use and higher yields can at least double water productivity.

Irrigation scheduling

Crop water requirements vary over time and are dependent on weather and soil conditions, hence the system can benefit from in-soil monitoring in order to save water and also to potentially improve yield. Smart irrigation scheduling provides a means to evaluate water needs in real time, then apply a specific amount of water at a specific time that is sufficient to meet crop

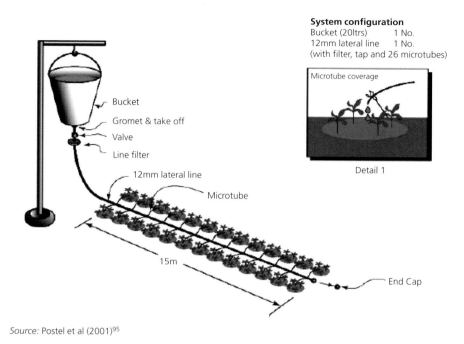

System configuration
Bucket (20ltrs)   1 No.
12mm lateral line   1 No.
(with filter, tap and 26 microtubes)

Microtube coverage

Detail 1

Bucket
Gromet & take off
Valve
Line filter
12mm lateral line
Microtube
15m
End Cap

Source: Postel et al (2001)[95]

Figure 4.1 *Schematic of a bucket kit system*

requirements. Despite the potential for irrigation scheduling to improve business, most farmers still primarily rely on visual inspection or previous experiences to determine when to irrigate. The California Irrigation Management Information System (CIMIS) is an example of an inexpensive system set up to provide timely information to growers and landscape irrigators about the water demands of their plants and the likely climatic conditions facing them. With this information, growers can make smart decisions about when, where and how much to irrigate, reducing overall irrigation water needs, increasing crop water productivity, and saving money. A recent independent assessment of the programme suggested that growers using CIMIS have reduced applied water use on their lands by an average of 13 per cent, and increased yields by 8 per cent. The cost to state and local agencies of operating the system is approximately US$850,000 per year, while estimated benefits exceed US$30 million per year.[96]

Advanced irrigation management (deficit drip irrigation)

The results achieved through efficient irrigation systems and irrigation scheduling are significant; however, they can be further enhanced to achieve in the order of 80 per cent reductions in water demand. The traditional irrigation strategy is to supply irrigated areas with sufficient water so that crops transpire at their maximum potential – meaning that water is provided to meet full crop evapotranspiration requirements throughout the season. However, a growing body of international work shows that water use can be reduced, particularly in orchards and vineyards without negative impacts on production. Called 'deficit irrigation', the innovation is based on the fact that when many plants are given less water (i.e. below the level of traditional, full crop evapotranspiration levels), this triggers the plant's ability to hold water and hence reduces water lost through transpiration.[97] A recent UN FAO report presents a number of deficit irrigation studies focused on various crops in semi-arid climates around the world, concluding that substantial water savings can be achieved with little impact on crop yield and quality.[98]

Case study: Partial root-zone drying

One exciting area of research and development in the field of deficit drip irrigation is that of the partial dry zone irrigation technique.[99] The technique is called 'partial root-zone drying' because at any one time only half the root-zone is in a drying state. The process, developed by Dr Peter Dry and Dr Brian Loveys in Australia, involves using two lines of drip-line irrigation for each row, one on each side, instead of the usual one, hence one side of the root system of the plant can be kept wet while the other side is deprived of water. The grower irrigates through one line at a time, two or three times a week for a couple of weeks (whatever local conditions dictate), then the same on the other line – that pattern continuing throughout the season. The switching of the wetting/drying from one side to the other may be as short as three days in midsummer in some situations. The drying roots send a message to the rest of the plant that it is deprived of water, so the leaf stomata close, preventing excess moisture loss and reducing excessive shoot growth. In other words the plant is 'tricked' into believing it is water stressed and the end result is a plant that uses the water it has far more efficiently than it otherwise would, as well as reducing unneeded shoot growth. This allows up to another 50 per cent reduction in the total amount of water needed to irrigate many crops on top of traditional drip irrigation. Further to the results from Australia, an international consortium has been formed and funded by the European Commission, comprising scientists from Cyprus, Turkey, Portugal and the UK. The partial root-zone drying irrigation system is now being tested on olives, citrus fruits, tomatoes, aubergines, raspberries and cotton, and according to the researchers, all crops tested to date have yielded similar results.[100]

Rainwater harvesting

An enormous variety of small-scale innovations are available that can catch and store rainfall for agriculture while also achieving erosion and flood control, as well as aquifer replenishment – collectively referred to as 'rainwater harvesting' technology.[101] In addition to storage containers (i.e. rainwater tanks and bladders), rainwater harvesting can include micro-dams and channels and stream diversions that direct rainfall and river flow out over flood plains – often restoring landscapes to their original hydrology (i.e. prior to human settlement). Contrary to large-scale public investments that often take 10–30 years to get from the drawing board to implementation, rainwater harvesting can be cheap and has the potential for high adoption rates in the developing world – in the order of several hundred thousand villages over several years in parts of India.[102]

Treating and re-using urban stormwater and wastewater in peri-urban agriculture

According to a 2005 FAO report, urban and peri-urban farms – those within or immediately adjacent to a city – currently supply food to 700 million urban residents worldwide, and the domestic wastewater from roughly a thousand households can sustain one farmer.[103] Yet in virtually all cities, most of the water that falls on that city and is not used by homes or industry, is running out to sea as stormwater or as treated wastewater. The FAO estimates that across 50 countries, 20 million hectares is already directly or indirectly irrigated with wastewater[104] – close to 10 per cent of the total irrigated area of the world.[105] Hence, precedents are already being set for wastewater to be re-used on peri-urban agriculture, turning several related problems into integrated solutions. As Table 4.5 shows, there is significant potential for wastewater to be treated to different levels suitable for use in a variety of applications, such as recharging groundwater aquifers, supplying industrial processes, irrigating certain crops or even augmenting potable supplies.

Such a strategy provides an opportunity for municipalities to shift from a focus on dealing with urban wastewater, to treating it as a resource to stimulate market gardens and farming in and around cities. In developing countries it also contributes to addressing the poverty and malnutrition challenge for those living in the peri-urban areas, which are often the slums of medium to large cities. As climate change worsens, and oil prices rise, addressing wastewater will help to conserve oil and reduce 'food miles' if governments encourage high-value crops like vegetables and fruit to be grown close to population

Table 4.5 *Estimated volumes of wastewater (million m³/year) in Asia*

Country	Sewage in urban areas	Industrial effluents	Total wastewater
China	37,290	22,672	59,962
Japan	Not available	Not available	17,100
Republic of Korea	5939	956	6895
Uzbekistan	1083	4580	5663
India (23 metropolitan cities only)	3250	140	3390
Islamic Republic of Iran	2000	600	2600
Malaysia	1400	3	1403
Turkmenistan	268	913	1181
Sri Lanka	350	225	950
Vietnam	540	350	890

Source: Adapted from Economic and Social Commission for Asia and the Pacific (2000)[106]

centres. Seventy per cent of Israeli municipal wastewater is treated and re-used, mainly for agricultural irrigation of non-food crops and further efforts to capture, treat and re-use more wastewater are under way in Jordan. By the mid 1990s, Californian residents relied on more than 2460 billion litres (160 billion gallons) of reclaimed water annually for irrigating landscapes, golf courses and crops, recharging groundwater aquifers, supplying industrial processes and even flushing toilets.[107] The Californian agriculture sector is now exploring innovative uses of recycled water in peri-urban agriculture such as secondary-treated wastewater re-use on fodder and fibre crops and tertiary-treated water for vegetable and fruit crops.[108]

To conclude, in order to provide the food required with the water available the agricultural sector will need to undertake significant improvements along the lines of those outlined above. The previous discussion has shown that there is a range of strategies to enable farmers to dramatically improve water productivity. Agricultural systems have the ability to source much of their energy needs from what are now often seen as waste steams – such as waste manure from cows and waste woody biomass. These opportunities, plus advances in wind and solar technologies, are opening up new ways for farmers to earn new income and power their irrigation systems more cost effectively with renewable energy. With today's technologies it is feasible for many farmers to not just achieve Factor Five but to exceed it.

Notes

1   United Nations Food and Agricultural Organization (2006).
2   Schnepf (2004) p2.
3   UK Carbon Trust (2006).
4   Hawken et al (1999) Chp 10.
5   Jaswal and Das Gupta (2006) cited in Kataria and Joshi (2006).
6   Ali (2006).
7   Cao et al (2008).
8   UK Carbon Trust (2006).
9   Gale et al (2002).
10   ibid.
11   Environmental Entrepreneurs (2007) 'Dairy Strategy October 2007',
        www.e2.org/ext/doc/E2C2DairyStrategyOct2007.pdf;jsessionid=
        392FAB9D56E0586F0AA093A4A37DC473, accessed 16 April 2009;
        Clemens and Ahlgrimm (2001).
12   Enviros Consulting Limited (2006); Subler (2009).
13   UK Carbon Trust (2006).
14   Black and Rogers (1993) p4.
15   Clemens and Ahlgrimm (2001); Clemens et al (2006).
16   UK Carbon Trust (2006).
17   Lovegrove and Dennis (2006).
18   UK Carbon Trust (2006).
19   ibid.
20   ibid.

21 USDA (undated) 'Save Money, Save Energy with Conservation Tillage', www.nm.nrcs.usda.gov/news/publications/conservation-tillage.pdf, accessed 23 April 2009.
22 IPCC (2007) see 'Agriculture'.
23 US Environmental Protection Agency (2009b).
24 Enviros Consulting Limited (2006).
25 The Bioenergy Site (2008).
26 Chitsomboon and Changplayngam (2007).
27 Ali (2006).
28 Marchaim (1992) Chp 11.
29 Enviros Consulting Limited (2006); Anaerobic Digestion (2009) 'Agricultural Biogas Production in China', www.anaerobic-digestion.com/html/ agricultural_biogas_production.php, accessed 23 April 2009.
30 Webber and Cuellar (2008) reported in *Science Daily* (2008).
31 Richter (2004).
32 CSIRO (2007).
33 IPCC (2007) Chapter 8 'Agriculture'; CSIRO (2007).
34 Hatfield-Dodds et al (2007).
35 Ali (2006).
36 Ashden Awards (2007) 'Centre for Rural Technology, Nepal: Upgraded water mills in the Himalayas', www.ashdenawards.org/winners/crt#, accessed 26 April 2009.
37 Ali (2006).
38 Wind Energy & Solar Power Australia (undated) 'Solar bore and surface water pumping', www.energymatters.com.au/renewable-energy/solar-power/pumping/, accessed 23 April 2009.
39 Schaeffer et al (1996).
40 Union of Concerned Scientists (undated) 'Farming the Wind: Wind power and agriculture', www.ucsusa.org/clean_energy/technology_and_impacts/impacts/ farming-the-wind-wind-power.html, accessed 23 April 2009.
41 Union of Concerned Scientists (undated) 'Farming the Wind: Wind power and agriculture', www.ucsusa.org/clean_energy/technology_and_impacts/impacts/ farming-the-wind-wind-power.html, accessed 23 April 2009.
42 The Ashden Awards for Sustainable Energy (2007) 'Centre for Rural Technology, Nepal: Upgraded water mills in the Himalayas', www.ashdenawards.org/files/ reports/CRT_Nepal_2007_Technical_report_.pdf, accessed 26 April 2009.
43 Hargroves et al (2005).
44 Lal (2003).
45 IPCC (2007) see 'Agriculture'.
46 Watson et al (2000) p204.
47 Earthbeat Radio National (2000).
48 IPCC (2007) see 'Agriculture'.
49 Worldwatch Institute (2009) 'Boosting water productivity', www.worldwatch.org/node/811, accessed 13 April 2009.
50 World Water Forum (2000) 'Scientists and Farmers Create Improved Crops for a Water-Scarce World', Press release from the Second World Water Forum, 21 March 2000.
51 Molden et al (2007).
52 FAO and IFAD (2006).
53 Worldwatch Institute (2009) 'Boosting water productivity', www.worldwatch.org/node/811, accessed 13 April 2009.

54   Watts (2009).

55   Dow Jones Newswires (2004); China National Grain and Oils Information Center (undated) 'China Grain Market Weekly Reports', cited in Brown (2000).

56   Worldwatch Institute (2009) 'Boosting water productivity', www.worldwatch.org/node/811, accessed 13 April 2009; Brown, L. (2008).

57   FAO and IFAD (2006).

58   Gleick (2008).

59   Cooley et al (2008).

60   Postel (2001).

61   Gale et al (2002) p41.

62   This table was compiled from a number of sources: Global production figures (rounded up) were drawn from the following: AWI (2007) *Wool Facts*, Australian Wool Innovation Limited, Australia; Cotton Incorporated (2009) 'US Cotton Market Monthly Economic Letter', www.cottoninc.com/MarketInformation/MonthlyEconomicLetter/; FAOSTAT (2008) 'Production Statistics', http://faostat.fao.org/site/567/ DesktopDefault.aspx?PageID=567#ancor; MLA (2006) 'Fast facts – Australia's sheepmeat industry', www.mla.com.au/NR/rdonlyres/51787F9C-9D3E-4FB2-A610-8CB5D17E0CC6/0/FastfactsSheepmeat2006.pdf. Water requirement figures (rounded up to one decimal point) were drawn from the following sources: Bellefontaine et al (2002); DEEDI and QPIF (2007); FAO (2008); Gale et al (2002); Gleick (2001); Gramene (2008) 'Comparative Maps: Rice, Sorghum, Barley (Hordeum), Millet, Oat, Rye', http://acorn.cshl.org/; Hoekstra and Chapagain (2008) Appendix XV; Kooistra and Termorshuizen (2006); Le Palais de Thes (2004) 'Tea producing countries: France', www.palaisdesthes.com/en/tea/tea-producing-countries.htm; Meyer (1997); Mississippi State University (2007); Mohanty (2009) slide 7; Molden (2007) p507; Moore (2003); McCorkle et al (2007); OTA (2009) 'Organic Cotton Facts', www.ota.com/organic/mt/organic_cotton.html; Water Footprint (undated) 'Product Gallery: Potatoes, Soybeans, Barley, Sorghum, Millet', www.waterfootprint.org/?page=files/productgallery&product=potato; USDA (2007); Workman (2007); Zimmer and Renault (2006).

63   Gale et al (2002) Table B-4, estimated from United Nations Food and Agricultural Organization, FAOSTAT database.

64   World Bank (1997).

65   Cooley et al (2008).

66   ibid.

67   Ali and Talukder (2008).

68   Dyson (1999).

69   Evans (1998).

70   IANS (2008).

71   Whyte (2007).

72   ibid.

73   Mohanty (2009) slides 5–6.

74   World Water Forum (2000) 'Scientists and Farmers Create Improved Crops for a Water-Scarce World', Press Release, 21 March 2000.

75   Karaba et al (2007) cited in Virginia Tech (2007).

76   Gramene (2005) 'Barley (Hordeum) Maps and Statistics', http://acorn.cshl.org/ species/hordeum/barley_maps_and_stats.html, accessed 21 April 2009.

77   Gramene (2005) 'Oats Maps and Statistics', http://acorn.cshl.org/species/ avena/oat_maps_and_stats.html, accessed 21 April 2009.

78   Gramene (2005) 'Rye Introduction', http://acorn.cshl.org/species/
      secale/rye_intro.html, accessed 21 April 2009.
79   Gramene (2005) 'Rye Maps and Statistics', http://acorn.cshl.org/species/
      secale/rye_maps_and_stats.html, accessed 21 April 2009.
80   Black (2008).
81   United Nations Food and Agricultural Organization (2006).
82   Sinha et al (2009).
83   Worldwatch Institute (2009).
84   Steinfield et al (1998).
85   Reich et al (2009); Lyden (undated).
86   von Weizsäcker et al (1997) pp80–81.
87   Brown, L. (2008) Chp 7.
88   Shock (2006).
89   Van Hofwegen and Svendsen (2000) cited in Postel et al (2001).
90   Postel et al (2001).
91   Shock (2006).
92   Brown, L. (2008) Chp 7.
93   ibid.
94   Postel et al (2001).
95   ibid.
96   Wong (1999).
97   Cooley et al (2008).
98   Goodwin and Boland (2002).
99   Smith and Hargroves (2008) 'Efficiency in irrigation', CL Creations,
      www.sustained.com.au/index.php?option=com_content&task=view&id=94&
      Itemid=29, accessed 21 February 2009.
100   Fifth Framework Programme (undated) 'FP5 Project Record',
      http://cordis.europa.eu/data/PROJ_FP5/ACTIONeqDndSESSIONeq
      112122005919ndDOCeq518ndTBLeqEN_PROJ.htm, accessed 2 May 2009.
101   Practical Action (undated) 'Rainwater Harvesting Technical Factsheets',
      http://practicalaction.org/?id=rainwater_harvesting, accessed 21 February 2009.
102   Rijsberman (2004).
103   Brown, L. (2008).
104   United Nations World Water Development Report (UNWWDR) (2003).
105   Ensink et al (2004).
106   Economic and Social Commission for Asia and the Pacific (2000) p15.
107   Gleick (2001).
108   The Pacific Institute (2007).

5

The Transport Sector

The Natural Edge Project

1 Introduction

The transportation sector accounts for 22 per cent of global energy use,[1] with passenger transport accounting for roughly two-thirds, and freight transport accounting roughly for the other third,[2] as Table 5.1 shows.

In OECD countries, virtually all energy for transportation comes from petroleum fuels.[3] According to the InterAcademy 2007 global sustainable energy study:

> *In the major energy-using industrialized countries nearly all (96 per cent) of transportation energy comes from non-renewable petroleum fuels, such as gasoline (47 per cent) and diesel (31 per cent). Road vehicles account for about three-quarters of all transportation energy use.*[4]

Table 5.1 *World transport energy use by mode*

Mode	Energy use (EJ[5])	Share (%)
Passenger transport		
Cars	34.20	44.5
Buses	4.76	6.2
Air	8.95	11.6
Other (motorbikes, rickshaws etc.)	1.20	1.6
Passenger and freight transport		
Rail	1.19	1.5
Freight transport		
Heavy freight trucks	12.48	16.2
Medium freight trucks	6.77	8.8
Shipping	7.32	9.5
Total	76.85	100.0

Source: WBCSD (2004)[6]

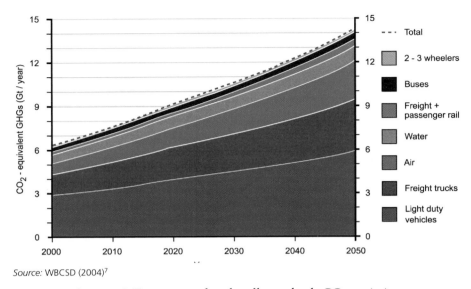

Source: WBCSD (2004)[7]

Figure 5.1 *Transport-related well-to-wheels CO_2 emissions*

Thus globally the transportation section makes a significant contribution to global greenhouse gas emissions. According to the IPCC in 2004, the global transportation sector was responsible for 23 per cent of world energy-related CO_2 emissions.[8] Figure 5.1 shows that road transport via cars (light duty vehicles) and freight trucks currently account for 74 per cent of total transport CO_2 emissions.[9]

The IPCC 4th Assessment Report makes the crucial point that the growth rate of energy usage and greenhouse gas emissions in the transportation sector is the highest among all the energy end-user sectors.[10] For instance, there has been exponential growth in private car ownership, with the 200 million cars in operation in 1970 expected to reach 1200 million by 2030.[11] Yet car usage is not the most rapidly growing transportation mode – that honour goes to air travel. Worldwide passenger air travel is growing 5 per cent annually, but in some regions like China[12] it has been growing at 12 per cent per annum.[13] Despite a range of efforts, current rates of energy efficiency improvement in transportation modes such as cars and aeroplanes[14] are not keeping pace with the exponential growth of these modes. Thus to achieve Factor Five improvements in energy productivity and 80 per cent reductions in greenhouse gas emissions over coming decades the following three strategies will need to be implemented:

- *Strategy One*: A significant improvement in energy efficiency through the improved design of all the major passenger and freight transportation modes (cars, air travel, trucking, rail and shipping).
- *Strategy Two*: A significant shift to more energy-efficient modes of transportation for both passenger and freight transport. Examples of such a

shift for passenger transport include increased use of public transport and cycling options, or using very fast trains and videoconferencing options instead of air travel. Examples of such a shift in freight transport include using rail and coastal shipping transport options instead of trucking wherever possible.

*   *Strategy Three*: A shift in transportation fuels over time, gradually sourcing higher percentages of energy for transportation from renewable electricity sources, second generation bio-fuels, and hydrogen, instead of fossil fuels.

This Sector Study focuses in detail on the first two strategies for both passenger and freight transport to show how Factor Five improvements in energy productivity can be achieved over the coming decades. Both strategies will enable significant cost-effective reductions in energy usage, greenhouse gas emissions, congestion and urban air pollution while also reducing each nation's oil dependency. The first strategy is also significant because the design changes and technologies needed to achieve Factor Five are also the design changes needed to enable more of the transportation sector to be powered by renewable energy. Ultra-efficient plug-in hybrid vehicles, buses and trucks, with lower power requirements, will enable transportation vehicles to be increasingly powered by electricity from renewable sources over the coming decades. Also the modal shifts in Strategy Two will lead, for instance, to more passenger and freight transportation on rail transport which is already powered by electricity. There are now studies that demonstrate that if Factor Five energy efficiency improvements and design changes are made, it is technically possible for transport to source approximately 50 per cent renewable energy by 2030 and 100 per cent renewable energy by 2050.[15]

As the previous Sector Studies have shown, Factor Five energy productivity improvements enable households and business to meet their energy needs through renewable energy. The same is true for the transportation sector. Factor Five energy efficiency improvements in transportation make it viable and cost effective for much higher percentages of the transportation sector's energy needs to be met with renewable energy. Thus all three strategies are mutually reinforcing and provide a multifaceted integrated approach to enable the achievement of Factor Five in this sector, significantly reducing oil dependency over the coming decades.

2 Cars and light vehicles

The potential for Factor Five improvements in fuel efficiency of cars and light vehicles

In 2005, OECD countries used 65 per cent of the world's transportation energy, with this energy use projected to grow by 15 per cent, from 62 to 73 terajoules (TJ) by 2030.[16] Of all transport modes and applications, cars and light vehicles (sport utility vehicles, pickups, minivans and full-size vans) account for the greatest energy use by far. In the US, for instance, cars and light

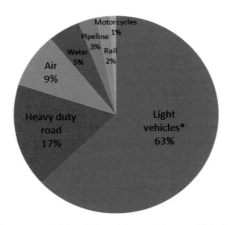

Note: * Light vehicles include cars, sport utility vehicles, pickups, minivans and full-size vans.
Source: Based on data from InterAcademy (2005)[17]

Figure 5.2 *US transportation energy consumption by mode, 2005*

vehicles account for 63 per cent of the total transportation energy use, as seen in Figure 5.2.[18] Meanwhile, in the UK, cars and light vehicles account for almost 70 per cent of the total transportation energy use.[19]

Non-OECD countries hence used 35 per cent of the world's transportation energy in 2005, with this energy use projected to grow by a staggering 55 per cent, from 33TJ to 70TJ by 2030,[20] and of all transport modes, as with OECD countries, road transport accounts for the greatest portion of this growth.[21] Vehicle sales in China and India are already growing rapidly – these two markets will be the largest for new cars and light vehicles over the period 2005–2030, with ownership projected to grow from 22 million to over 200 million in China, and from 11 million to 115 million in India.[22] The associated growth in fuel consumption is shown in Figure 5.3.

Given these significant trends, it is likely that the use of cars and light vehicles will be a dominant mode for at least the coming two decades, and thus it is important that efforts are made to reduce greenhouse gas emissions from this mode. Such efforts include increasing fuel efficiency, using alternative fuels and power sources, and reducing use – all of which will play a critical role in the transition to a sustainable transport future. Fortunately, it is technically possible to produce cars for the mainstream market that achieve in the order of 80 per cent greenhouse gas emissions reductions, with many automakers having produced concept vehicles and now investing heavily in R&D towards mass producing their key technologies. Even after 120 years of innovation in car design automakers are now finding numerous opportunities for fuel efficiency improvements. As Amory Lovins, internationally recognized leader in sustainable energy solutions, describes, there is significant opportunity for improvement:

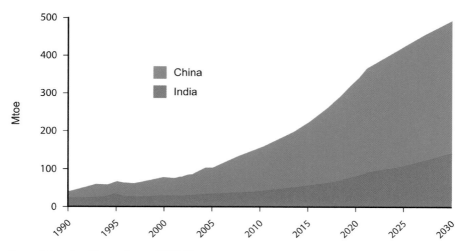

Source: International Energy Agency (2007b)[23]

Figure 5.3 *Road transport fuel consumption in China and India*

> *A modern car's engine, idling, driveline, and accessories dissipate seven-eighths of its fuel energy. Only one-eighth reaches the wheels. Of that, half heats the tires and road or heats the air that the car pushes aside. Only the last 6 percent accelerates the car (then heats the brakes when you stop). And since about 95 percent of the mass being accelerated is the car, not the driver, less than 1 percent of the fuel energy ultimately moves the driver.*
> Amory Lovins, Rocky Mountain Institute, 2007[24]

Currently, the largest car fleet is that of the US, where fuel economy standards are slightly above half that in the EU and Japan, as shown in Figure 5.4. According to Lovins, upgrading the US car fleet with the best conventional technologies already used in today's cars would improve the fleet's fuel efficiency by at least 25 per cent, with a less than one-year payback period.[25] A range of new design options are now being inspired by the performance of vehicles in the EU and Japan, resulting in small, lightweight cars, driven by low emissions engines. Further improvements, reaching 50 per cent overall, could arise from using a hybrid drive, as is the case with the Toyota Prius and Honda Civic, both of which are twice as fuel efficient as the average US car.[26] However, EU- and Japanese-style cars, suited to compact cities, are not the only option for US automakers.

By taking a whole system approach to the design of cars, fuel efficiency can be significantly improved, even of SUVs (sports utility vehicles), at lower costs than are achievable through conventional design. Rocky Mountain Institute (RMI) has shown that a strategic combination of reducing mass, drag and rolling resistance, together with using hybrid drives can reduce fuel

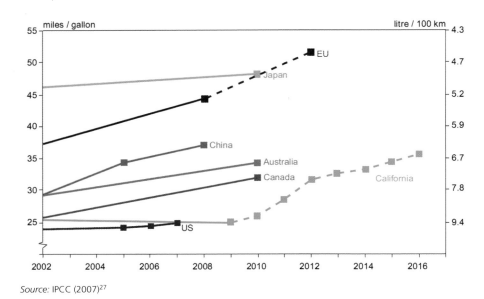

Source: IPCC (2007)[27]

Figure 5.4 *Comparison of auto fuel efficiency by auto fuel economy standards among countries, normalized to US test procedure*

consumption by 50 per cent at roughly no cost, and by more than 70 per cent with a two-year payback period (in the US).[28] Typically the various subsystems of a car are refined independently in order to improve their own efficiency, as shown in Figure 5.5; however, taking a whole system approach to the design[29] can deliver compounding efficiency gains, primarily by targeting mass reductions. By taking an approach as shown in Figure 5.6 the design first minimizes the mass of the structure, based on safety and performance standards, then reduces the required capacity of the propulsion system, the design load on the chassis, and potentially the need for additional trim. A smaller propulsion capacity means that a hybrid or electric drive can be used and thus the electrical system can be consolidated. A smaller propulsion system also requires a smaller volume of fluids, and using a hybrid or electric drive would almost eliminate the use of fluids. For example, applying such an approach to the design of the Hypercar Revolution, the team from RMI developed the design for a car with 57 per cent lighter structure and 34 per cent lighter chassis components, that then allowed a 38 per cent lighter propulsion system. Including reductions in the mass of the electrical system, trim and fluids, the overall vehicle was 52 per cent lighter.[30] Such a strategy for design is applicable to carmakers worldwide and can be further enhanced by using emerging advanced technology such as hybrid and electric drives and a range of options as outlined below.

Factor Five improvements in car fuel efficiency can be achieved through a whole system approach that recognizes the interaction between the various subsystems and focuses on the overall vehicle performance. A number of cars

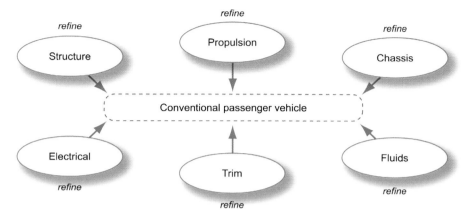

Source: The Natural Edge Project (2008)[31]

Figure 5.5 *The component design strategy of conventional vehicle design*

are now being designed using such a systems approach, and while there is some variation, the processes all incorporate the concept of a holistic approach, namely that rather than designing for specific individual component improvements (as in Figure 5.5), the design takes into account the whole system and captures opportunities for compounding reductions in energy requirements throughout the other subsystems (as in Figure 5.6). For example, reducing the mass of the vehicle body by using low-density, high-strength materials then reduces rolling resistance, and hence reduces the required power capacity,

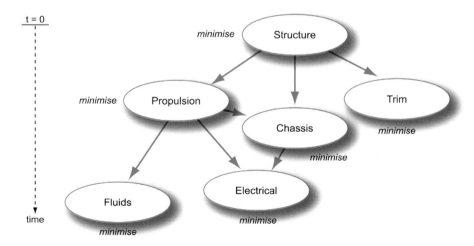

Source: The Natural Edge Project (2008)[32]

Figure 5.6 *The flow of compounding mass reduction in the system design strategy of whole system vehicle design*

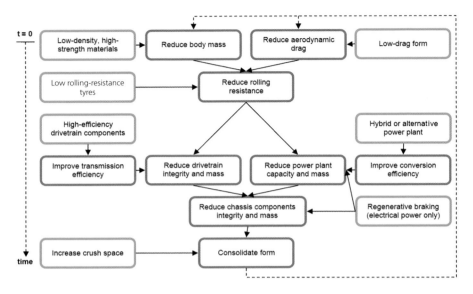

Source: Courtesy of Rocky Mountain Institute (Based on Brylawski and Lovins (1998)[33])

Figure 5.7 *Incorporating improvements into a passenger vehicle to reduce its fuel consumption*

along with reducing the design load on the drivetrain and chassis. Most of these additional impacts then lead to further mass reductions by using smaller subsystems and components. The design needs to be staged to allow for the fact that some individual improvements are actually better incorporated before other such improvements, making the order of the design very important.[34] In Figure 5.7 RMI expands on Figure 5.6, to show an advanced whole systems iterative sequence for incorporating improvements to minimize fuel consumption and to introduce other performance improvements.

Using such a whole system design process, RMI has shown that the fuel consumption of a typical, modern SUV can be reduced by 71 per cent, with Figure 5.8 showing the relative reductions achieved by each major innovation, when applied in the optimal order. Further to these significant advances, recent advances in electric propulsion and braking provide a very cost-effective option for developing Factor Five cars in the near future.

Next we briefly overview the key innovations that, when combined, can help achieve Factor Five improvements in fuel efficiency:

- *Materials*: New, low-density, high-strength metals, plastics and composite materials allow the mass of cars to be reduced, thus reducing the required propulsion power, and hence the total mass of heavy batteries required as part of a hybrid–electric or electric drive. Reducing the mass also reduces rolling resistance and thus further reduces the required propulsion power. RMI showed in their groundbreaking work, *Winning the Oil Endgame*,

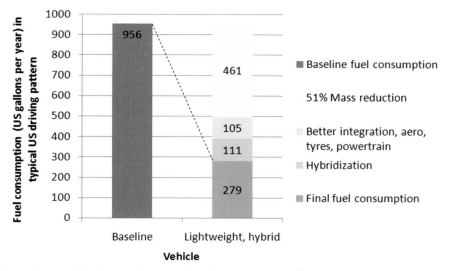

Source: Courtesy of Rocky Mountain Institute (Based on Lovins et al (2007)[35])

Figure 5.8 *The improvements to a sports utility vehicle (SUV) to reduce its fuel consumption*

that using advanced composites, such as carbon fibre, can improve fuel consumption by up to 50 per cent.[36] Also, light metals such as aluminium and magnesium can be used to substitute for steel and are currently being used to achieve weight reductions. For instance, as of 2000, all Audi A8 models were constructed with an aluminium body and suspension, which makes the car's mass 100kg less than that of an equivalent steel-constructed car.[37] The engines now also contain aluminium and magnesium components.[38] Further, in 2003, Jaguar released its XJ-X350 model with an all-aluminium body, which has a mass almost 30 per cent less than an equivalent steel-bodied car.[39]

- *Low-drag form*: A car's size and exterior shape are major influencing factors in the aerodynamic drag forces experienced. Accurate optimization and manufacturing of complex aerodynamic body features are now achievable through innovations in technologies such as computer-aided modelling, design and manufacturing. According to RMI, the largest opportunity for reducing drag is to make the car's under-body, which contributes about a quarter of the total drag, as smooth as the top side.[40]
- *Low rolling-resistance tyres*: Due to the properties of their material, conventional tyres suffer from a compromise between tread pattern detail, which affects the car's handling ability and safety, and the resulting rolling resistance. New 'fuel saver' tyres, resolve this compromise by replacing some of the tyre's tread compound with silica. These tyres can reduce fuel consumption by 3–8 per cent, and new generation tyres may reduce fuel consumption by an additional 2–9 per cent.[41]

- *Hybrids*: A hybrid electric drivetrain can power a vehicle using either its internal combustion engine, its batteries or a combination of both, depending on its configuration and operating mode. Most current hybrid electric cars use 'deep cycle', nickel-metal-hydride (NiMH) batteries, which can store about twice as much energy per unit mass as lead acid batteries (the type used in conventional vehicles).[42] Deep cycle batteries are charged by a combination of an electric generator driven by the internal combustion engine and the car's regenerative braking system, which harnesses the car's own inertia to generate electricity.[43] Hybrid electric drivetrains, together with some degree of the above innovations, have enabled automakers to improve the fuel consumption of current-model cars by at least 50 per cent.[44]

Once the vehicle is lightweight, aerodynamic and hybrid electric powered, plug-in technology can then be used to provide the option of charging the batteries via a typical electrical outlet, say at home or at work, or battery arrays can be swapped out, say at a service station, to allow greater flexibility and avoid issues with limited ranges. The ability to store energy in batteries to power the vehicle is cost effective because purchasing electricity directly from the grid is cheaper than generating electricity on board by burning fuel in an internal combustion engine. However, if the vehicle is not optimized for weight, drag and resistance, the size of the batteries required for a suitable driving range may be prohibitive. The automotive industry is now experimenting with lithium-ion (Li-ion) batteries, which can store roughly twice as much energy per unit mass as the nickel-metal-hydride (NiMH) batteries currently being used.[45] Hence the combination of plug-in technology and Li-ion batteries can enable a car to operate within the parameters for range and performance that car owners expect, and in doing so can deliver significant fuel savings over conventional designs.[46]

In December 2008, Chinese company, BYD, launched the world's first mass-produced plug-in hybrid electric vehicle (PHEV) at a competitive price of US$20,000, beating the major global automakers by 2–3 years.[47] The BYD hybrid, looking much like a luxury sedan town car, can run for 100 kilometres on one charge, a distance which is greater than almost all daily commutes to work. Toyota, General Motors, Ford, Volkswagen and California start-ups Fisker Automotive and Aptera Motors, have all now announced their intentions to introduce production PHEV automobiles in the next 2–5 years. The plug-in Toyota Prius will be sold to commercial fleets from later in 2009 with the other major car companies looking to bring out plug-in hybrids during 2010–2012.[48] Aftermarket conversion kits and services are available to convert production model hybrid vehicles to plug-ins at costs ranging from US$5000 for a lead-acid battery system to $35,000 for a Li-ion battery system.[49] Most PHEVs on the road in the US are conversions of 2004 or later Toyota Prius models, which have had plug-in charging added and their electric-only range extended.

Given this activity it will not be long before there are many PHEVs on the road, creating essentially a fleet of batteries on wheels. Since cars are often idle for much of the day, parked at home or at work, there is potential for plug-in vehicle owners to earn money while their cars are idle, by connecting them to the energy grid. However, the typical energy grid is not designed to capitalize on numerous small and dispersed energy sources and storage sites, and this, along with the need for many other upgrades to the grid, has called for a significant focus on what is being referred to as 'smart grids' – effectively using advances in technology and communications infrastructure to allow for the grid to be used more intelligently. Such improvements to the grid include: smart sensing to avoid power outages and system overloads; reducing interruptions, spikes and surges that affect electrical equipment; and regulating the use of centralized large-scale and dispersed small-scale energy storage. The latter improvement is of particular interest to the car industry, and research at Curtin University[50] has identified a range of studies that estimate that plug-in vehicle owners could be paid between US$3000 and US$5500 per annum for the multiple services their electric batteries can provide if connected to the grid.[51] However, it is important to note that such a system would need to be carefully managed to ensure that car owners who may need to use their car at an irregular time are not left with empty batteries, and that additional use of the battery does not reduce their life.

The most comprehensive study to date on vehicle-to-grid options was led by the University of Delaware[52] which demonstrated that a range of opportunities exist for vehicle-to-grid technologies, and that such opportunities have the potential to further drive the market for plug-in hybrids, electric vehicles and investment in smart grids, providing numerous benefits, with direct financial incentives outlined below:[53]

- *Spinning reserves*: A fleet of battery-powered vehicles connected to the electricity grid represents a significant energy storage resource that can act as a backup reserve, and a buffer, to help regulate variations across the grid, assuming proper controls are enacted to ensure that the batteries are not drawn down too far. This is of particular interest to energy utilities that have to ensure that electricity supply and demand are continually balanced. This is typically done through the use of ancillary services[54] which add stability and extra generating capacity to the grid. Utilities are often required to have access to reserves, referred to as 'spinning reserves', that can be called upon quickly (within minutes) to increase their output in case the demand is greater than anticipated, or if another generator experiences a sudden forced outage.[55] Hence, cars plugged into the grid at home or at work can be drawn on and could earn an estimated US$1500–2500 per year by selling electricity to utilities as 'spinning reserves'.[56]
- *Regulation services*: Electricity grids also need 'frequency control',[57] or regulation, which provides fine-tuned balancing (responding within seconds) of the supply and demand by keeping the frequency and voltage

on the grid to within acceptable limits by supplying small amounts of electricity to cover insufficient supply, as well as being able to absorb any excess electricity to prevent a potentially destructive overload.[58] Plug-in vehicles could instead be used to provide these services, as their batteries and power electronics enable them to provide a near instant response, synchronized with an existing AC signal from the grid. The capital costs to configure vehicles to participate in these services are estimated to be one to two orders of magnitude lower than building power plants.[59] Battery vehicles with telematics and power electronics are now being designed to allow vehicles to earn US$2000–3000 per year by selling 'regulation services' to utilities.[60]

- *Peak demand supply*: Energy utilities have to undertake significant investment to guarantee electricity during peak demand periods. It is often the case that in order to meet the demand in peak periods, at least 10 per cent 'spare' capacity is required, even though, for example in Australia, these reserves are only drawn on for an estimated 1 per cent of the year.[61] This 10 per cent of electricity supply capacity is then redundant during the predominant non-peak periods. Hence electricity utilities would be willing to pay a high price to plug-in vehicle owners for electricity from 10,000s of plug-in hybrids during those peak electricity demand periods. As Cameron Burns from RMI explains, 'By some estimates, a battery-electric vehicle, with about 40 kilowatt-hours of usable energy, could power an entire residential block for over an hour if necessary (during peak demand periods or blackouts)'.[62]
- *Balancing intermittent sources*: Not only do energy utilities and renewable energy companies need to invest in wind and solar farms and infrastructure but they also have to invest in energy storage to handle fluctuations in renewable energy output in order to guarantee a base load supply. Thus paying car owners to enable energy utilities/renewable energy suppliers to utilize their vehicle batteries as back up storage provides cost-effective way to add more renewable energy into the grid, without having to invest in anywhere near as much energy storage.[63] According to RMI this also creates a market for electricity from wind power and other 'around the clock' renewable energy options such as geothermal and tidal, pointing out that '"Night-charging" vehicles could be a lucrative twist on the business of selling electrons. That's good news for the U.S. wind industry. In many areas, wind tends to blow harder at night, creating more energy when the vehicles would be charging.'[64]

However, as with many new forms of technology, particularly ones that are strongly influenced by consumer behaviour, there is a range of concerns that need to be met in order to bring this opportunity to market on a meaningful scale. The following innovations will help address many community concerns about this technology:

- *Agreed use of batteries by utilities*: To allay concerns that plugging a car into the grid will leave it open to be used by utilities, there will need to be guarantees that utilities will not interact with cars without a formal and specific agreement with the owner. Governments will need to legislate significant penalties for any utility that steals electricity from batteries in these cars to assure the public that this won't happen. Utilities will also have to agree to only take electricity from the car at agreed times of the day, and allow for the user to both monitor the battery level (via the internet) and have the option to nominate times when the battery is to be recharged to 100 per cent.
- *Improved battery performance*: Concerns around the range of electric vehicles are driving significant investment in improving battery capacity, along with increasing the number of times batteries can be recharged, and partially charged. Plug-in hybrids also have the potential to switch over to petrol power when needed and the petrol engine can also be used to recharge the battery.
- *Ancillary batteries*: By ensuring plug-in hybrid vehicles have two batteries (one for starting the engine in addition to the main battery) they can always be started, irrespective of how much electricity has been withdrawn from the main battery, allowing the car to then run on petrol or diesel until the battery is recharged.
- *Battery switching stations*: Service stations can be set up to lease batteries to electric vehicle drivers so that they can exchange them if they need to on longer journeys. Plug-in hybrids need to be designed so that it is easy for batteries to be taken out and replaced in the car or space created to allow additional batteries to be fitted temporarily into the car.

Further to designing cars and light vehicles to reduce their energy requirement, and shifting to hybrid plug-in engines, alternative fuels, such as second generation bio-fuels, can be used to replace oil-based fuels and reduce greenhouse gas emissions. The issues associated with bio-fuels, such as competing with food production, have been briefly mentioned in the agricultural Sector Study. One promising bio-fuel is cellulosic ethanol,[65] which has the added benefit that it contains lignin, a material that is not used in the production of ethanol but can be burned to generate electricity. Using agricultural waste to produce both fuel and energy results in 90 per cent less greenhouse gas emissions compared to refining oil to produce petrol. In addition, the production of cellulosic ethanol may use a Factor of 10 less water, land and agricultural nutrients than the production of ethanol from corn.[66] Some automotive companies are now developing vehicles that can run on many fuels, thus ensuring that their vehicles are competitive no matter which fuel blends dominate the market in the future.

Given the above innovations, what fuel economy is technically possible? Combining these technical innovations could enable cars to be designed to achieve significant improvements in miles per gallon of petrol. This has been argued by RMI advisory board member and former Director of the Central Intelligence Agency, James Woolsey and former US Secretary of State George Schultz. As James Woolsey said in a US Senate Committee of Foreign Relations testimony in 2005:

> For example, a hybrid gasoline/electric vehicle, on the road today, if constructed from carbon composites would achieve around 100mpg. If it were to operate on 85 per cent cellulosic ethanol or a similar proportion of biodiesel or renewable diesel fuel, it would be achieving hundreds of miles per gallon of petroleum-derived fuel. If it were a plug-in version operating on either upgraded nickel-metal-hydride or newer lithium-ion batteries so that 30-mile trips or more could be undertaken on its overnight charge (from a renewable energy source) before it began utilizing liquid fuel at all, it could be obtaining in the range of 1000mpg (of petroleum).[67]

RMI is working hard to catalyse these sorts of step changes in the car industry through their Smart Garage[68] project, that builds on from and complements RMI's groundbreaking work in the 1990s to design the Hypercar, featured in *Factor Four*. Since *Factor Four* was published, RMI and the spin-off company Hypercar Inc. (now Fibreforge Inc.) have done much work to further improve the Hypercar design, considered next. The original Hypercar design has played a pivotal role in catalysing green car research globally, hence we now take a look at the Hypercar and then overview some of the more recent best practice 'greener' car models which combine at least some of the steps listed above.

Best practice case study – The Hypercar revolution

Factor Four featured the Hypercar concept for a passenger vehicle developed by RMI. Since then, RMI have elaborated on the concept, publishing the details of their own ideal passenger vehicle, the 'Hypercar Revolution', as shown in Figure 5.9 – a safe, well-performing, ultra-efficient SUV that is almost fully recyclable and competitively priced.

The key leverage points in improving the Revolution's fuel consumption are reducing the vehicle's mass, aerodynamic drag and rolling resistance:

- *Mass*: The Revolution achieves a mass about half that of a similar-sized conventional vehicle through the extensive use of advanced carbon fibre composite materials, plastics and low-density metals, as well as through designing structural components to serve multiple purposes, which results in the Revolution's primary structure having only 14 major components – about 65 per cent fewer than that of a conventional, stamped steel structure.[69] Most of these components are made of a composite material using a manufacturing process called 'Fibreforge', which requires very few sharp bends or deep draws, and thus has low tooling costs, high repeatability and

Source: Courtesy of RMI

Figure 5.9 *The 2000 Hypercar Revolution (114mpg)*

fewer processing steps than conventional car assembly.[70] Unlike steel, the composite materials have the benefits of being fatigue-resistant and rust proof.[71] RMI propose that the higher cost of the composite materials will be compensated by a reduction in replacement parts and assembly complexity.

- *Aerodynamic drag*: The Revolution experiences about half of the aerodynamic drag of a conventional vehicle, as a result of a smooth finish on its shell, and several aerodynamic features.[72] These features include: a smooth under-body that limits air flow out of the wheel wells; a tapered roofline; a clean trailing edge; a gutter along the roofline to trap cross-wind air flow; wheel arches designed to limit wheel-induced turbulence; and aerodynamic door handles.[73]
- *Rolling resistance*: The Revolution experiences about a third of the rolling resistance of a conventional vehicle[74] as a result of its low mass and the use of a run-flat tyre system, which exhibits 15 per cent less rolling resistance than a conventional tyre system.[75]

These innovations, see Figure 5.10, led to the Revolution requiring propulsion power of only 35kW for cruising and up to an additional 35kW for acceleration.[76] This low power requirement then makes a range of new propulsion options cost effective. These propulsion options are more efficient than internal combustion engines, but without first reducing mass, drag and rolling resistance would be too costly.

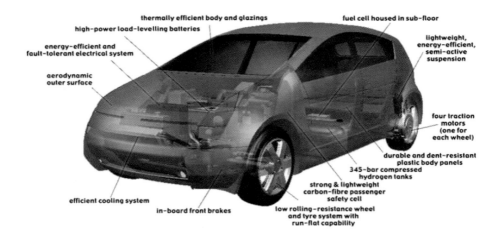

thermally efficient body and glazings

high-power load-levelling batteries

energy-efficient and
fault-tolerant electrical system

aerodynamic
outer surface

fuel cell housed in sub-floor

lightweight,
energy-efficient,
semi-active
suspension

four traction
motors
(one for
each wheel)

durable and dent-resistant
plastic body panels

345-bar compressed
hydrogen tanks

strong & lightweight
carbon-fibre passenger
safety cell

low rolling-resistance wheel
and tyre system with
run-flat capability

in-board front brakes

efficient cooling system

Source: Courtesy of RMI (Lovins and Cramer (2004)[77])

Figure 5.10 *Key design features of the Revolution*

The Revolution demonstrates the suitability of ambient pressure fuel cell technology combined with storage batteries, but RMI's earlier investigations also demonstrated the suitability of various hybrid technologies.[78] The fuel cell-based drivetrain resembles a modern-day hybrid drivetrain in that it uses the batteries to provide power for acceleration and incorporates small, high-efficiency motors to drive each wheel, coupled with a regenerative braking system to help recharge the battery.

Many automakers have now experimented with the key technological concepts demonstrated in the Revolution. These concepts, combined with innovations in Li-ion batteries and plug-in electric technology, are giving rise to mass-produced cars that achieve fuel economy up to Factor Five greater than conventional cars at a competitive cost, for instance:

- *BYD e6*: Chinese automaker BYD (Build Your Dream) has developed the e6,[79] the world's first mass-produced plug-in hybrid electric vehicle at a competitive price of US$20,000. The car uses BYD's iron-phosphate-based Li-ion batteries, which can be recharged more than 2000 times, and allows the car to travel 200,000 kilometres before needing to replace the batteries. When being recharged, the batteries reach 50 per cent charge in just ten minutes and 80 per cent charge just 15 minutes later. When parked, the battery can be recharged by a household electric plug or, when mobile, is recharged by electric generator driven by a one-litre petrol engine. In electric vehicle mode the e6 can travel as far as 100km on a single charge. The car, a five-seater sedan that looks similar to many of its competitors, accelerates from 0 to 100km/h in eight seconds and reaches a maximum speed of 160km/h.[80]

- *Toyota Prius*: Toyota have also experimented with plug-in technology and a Li-ion battery pack on the third-generation Prius, a combination that the company claims achieves a fuel economy of 3.6 litres per 100km in real world testing.[81] The third generation Prius also incorporates a number of other improvements on previous models. For instance, the inverter, electric motor and transaxle are all smaller and 20 per cent lighter overall. Toyota claims that the Prius has the cleanest aerodynamic profile of any mass-produced vehicle in the world through restyling the body shape, wheelhouse liner, wheel shape and especially the underfloor. There is an exhaust heat recirculation system, which reduces heat waste by warming the engine coolant during cold start-up and hence improves the car's performance. There is also an optional moon-roof packaged with solar panels that power a ventilation system. Light emitting diode (LED) lamps are used for low beams, tail lamps and stop lamps.
- *Loremo*: German automaker Loremo (LOw REsistance MObile)[82] has developed a small, lightweight car that achieves fuel economy of 1.5–2 litres per 100km, and looks like a small sports car. The 550kg car, which is powered by a two-cylinder 18kW turbo-diesel motor, accelerates from 0 to 100km/h in 20 seconds and reaches a maximum speed of 170km/h, and sells for €15,000. The car's impressive fuel consumption is a result of many innovations towards light-weighting and aerodynamic performance. The lightweight steel chassis has a mass of just 95kg but still performs well above average in crash simulations and provides excellent handling characteristics, while the thermoplastic body panels mould to the chassis. The unusual design has no doors – access to the front seats is by lifting the windshield, holding it as a door towards the front, and access to the rear seats is by vertically opening the tailgate – which allows for a large mass reduction while providing excellent safety performance (normal side doors are considerably heavier in order to withstand a sideward collision). Like the Prius, the Loremo achieves a low drag coefficient largely through a combination of its aerodynamic form, aerodynamic underside, intelligent chassis air-guiding system, lower tyre fins and the optimized air stream encasement, as well as through having an effective drag area of $0.25m^2$, which is about half that of the current most-aerodynamic cars, and positioning the rear seats backwards, which enables a much shorter car and improved aerodynamic streamlining. The company is also investigating the cost effectiveness of energy-efficient technology substitutions, such as carbon composite materials.
- *Chevy Volt*: The Chevy Volt,[83] due for market release in late 2010, will be General Motors' first plug-in extended-range electric vehicle. The Volt is expected to sell for about US$40,000.[84] On a full battery charge, the Volt is expected to achieve a range of 64km, which GM claims is far enough to transport 75 per cent of America's daily commuters without needing to recharge the battery pack. The Volt will be powered by a Li-ion battery that, when parked, can be recharged by a household electric plug or when

mobile can be recharged by an electric generator driven by a small engine that runs on any of a variety of on-board fuels, including gas or E85 ethanol.

Many of the innovations covered so far in this chapter, are also being used to improve the fuel consumption of other transportation vehicles – such as trucks, trains, ships and aircraft – by up to 65 per cent compared to their conventional counterparts. This will be discussed further in this chapter. Further improvements in fuel productivity in personal mobility arise from reducing car dependence through sustainable transport alternatives such as car sharing, using public transport, cycling and walking. There is much published about these alternatives and we now provide a succinct overview with extensive referencing to the key sources for interested readers.

Discouraging the use of cars

Transit-oriented cities

Private car ownership globally is expected to grow from 646 million cars in 2005 to 12 billion by 2030,[85] an increase of nearly 20 times. As the greenhouse gas emissions from cars has been estimated as being roughly 17 per cent of global emissions, a 20 times increase in car ownership without significant per vehicle reductions in emissions would be clearly dangerous. Apart from the options outlined above to reduce the energy consumption of cars and light vehicles, a range of actions can be taken to reduce the use of such vehicles. Many cities in the world are now investigating options for discouraging car use, particularly those cities with high population growth levels that experience excessive costs from congestion. Congestion costs were estimated to be as much as US$6.7 billion in Australia in 2005,[86] US$78 billion in the US as of 2007,[87] and are expected to be in the order of US$44 billion in the UK by 2010.[88] Such investigations include initiatives to increase public transport patronage and availability, promote and facilitate walking and cycling, and consider alternative transportation fuels for both cars and freight.[89] However, providing viable alternatives to car use will only succeed where contented car drivers perceive, and receive, the benefits or avoid the penalties or costs. Providing combinations of public transport, cycling and walking that allows for faster, cheaper and more convenient transport than driving a car is paramount. Achieving this can involve both increasing the cost and disruption of car ownership, (including carbon taxes, mandatory car-free days, inner-city congestion charges and reduced availability or increased cost of car parking in cities), and improving the viability of alternatives such as prioritizing public transport on roads, increasing the frequency and coverage of services, and providing transit hubs that allow rapid connections to various parts of the city, and which facilitate land-use concentrations around the hub.

Such an emphasis on interconnected public transport and development has led to what is now commonly referred to as transit-oriented design (TOD),

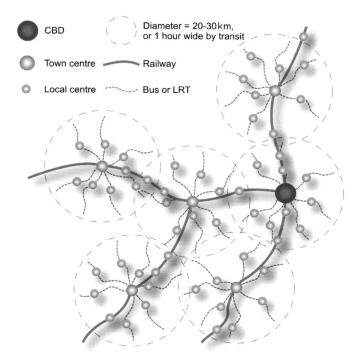

CBD

Town centre

Local centre

Diameter = 20-30km, or 1 hour wide by transit

Railway

Bus or LRT

Source: Courtesy of Peter Newman

Figure 5.11 *A conceptual plan for a transit-oriented city (based on Sydney, Australia)*

pioneered by experts such as Professor Peter Newman and others. The principles of TOD involve directing growth along transit-serviced corridors, where dense, mixed-use urban communities are concentrated around transit stations which link each community with the city as a whole.[90] Within each transit centre, bus feeder systems complement networks of cycle paths and walkways to ensure residents can quickly access the main transit corridor. Transit-oriented cities work on several fronts. First, they minimize cross-city trips with local, high-density centres of mixed residential, commercial, retail and civic spaces which are accessible to each other within a ten-minute walk. Second, they assist car-free movement between these nodes through easily accessed, high-speed transit corridors. The work of Richardson and Newman shown in Figure 5.11 illustrates how a transit-oriented city could be conceptualized, showing several dense, mixed-use urban areas connected through a web of high-speed transit corridors.[91] Residents in transit-oriented cities also spend less time and money on travelling, and enjoy a reduced sensitivity to fluctuating petrol prices. Newman concludes that healthier lifestyles result from walking and cycling, reduced congestion and pollution, while constraining car usage makes the streets safer.[92] Newman has also found that road-oriented cities have the highest costs, and rail-oriented cities the least, and that public transport creates twice as many jobs per dollar investment than road building.[93]

There are a number of additional benefits to pursuing a path of alternative transport. A car-reliant society leads not just to higher energy use and greenhouse gas emissions, but also greater urban pollution, congestion, health care costs, obesity and urban sprawl. Consideration of the costs and benefit of various transportation options must also take these traditionally external costs and benefits into account.[94] A car's convenience can make it the default or automatic mode of transport, even for short trips. For example, even in Australian cities with significant urban and suburban sprawl a study has shown that 25–37 per cent of trips are three kilometres or less, and 42–48 per cent of all trips are five kilometres or less.[95] The study showed that on average 40 per cent of trips could be made by bicycle, walking or public transport, or a combination of any two of these, and yet a further 40 per cent could be made by these same modes if the facilities, infrastructure and services were improved – showing that at least 80 per cent of car trips could be avoided.[96] Such a shift away from the car to more sustainable forms of transport yields significant health benefits as most alternatives to the automobile include some form of physical activity. The latest US research suggests that for every 60 minutes spent in the motor vehicle on average per day, the probability of a participant being obese increases by 6 per cent.[97] Physical inactivity is the second greatest preventable risk factor contributing to Australian's ill-health, and is known to contribute to obesity, hypertension, cardiovascular disease, stroke, diabetes, cancer and depression. Almost nine million Australian adults do not do enough daily physical activity,[98] resulting in half the population being overweight or obese, creating yearly costs estimated to be A\$58.2 billion to the nation.[99]

Sustainable transport can also benefit the economy. A 1997 study found cities that emphasize public transport, cycling and walking spend less on transportation. Particularly as public transport, walking and cycling need less land for infrastructure and associated requirements (parking etc.), with a single lane of railway able to carry up to 50,000 persons per hour (pph), a busway 7000pph, and a highway lane just 2500pph.[100] Further studies have shown that: more jobs result from building public transport systems per dollar invested than from constructing roads;[101] the use of private cars results in higher costs in traffic policing, accidents (including hospitalization and damage costs)[102] and air pollution effects on health and infrastructure. On average, the average OECD worker spends one day a week working to pay for the costs of their car,[103] and Newman found that in Australia the average household could save US\$536,000 over a lifetime by avoiding a second car.[104] A study of 84 cities undertaken by Kenworthy and Laube[105] confirms that cities with well-designed public transport systems have significantly less total transport costs, as a proportion of their city wealth, than those that rely on freeways and cars.[106] Kenworthy et al summarized and developed these arguments further in Chapter 19 of the TNEP book *The Natural Advantage of Nations*.[107]

Restricting car use and congestion charging[108]

The city of Bogotá is one of the most progressive cities in the world in directly discouraging car use by actively restricting the use of private cars in the city and increasing their gasoline tax by 20 per cent. Currently 40 per cent of all cars are restricted from the urban area during peak hours, and the city holds an internationally acclaimed car-free day each year.[109] This encourages the use of alternative modes of transport, discourages car use and significantly reduces congestion. The benefits recorded include: 43 per cent increase in trip velocity; 28 per cent decrease in accidents; and 29 per cent decrease in trip duration.[110] However, perhaps the most radical move in Bogotá's future will be the prohibition of private vehicles on the streets for six hours a day, during peak hours, taking effect from the 1 January 2015. Voted in by the citizens in a 2000 referendum, this was a conscious act to create a more liveable city where public transport is valued over private cars, pollution is minimized, and the streets are safer for walking and cycling.[111]

Other than directly restricting the use of cars, congestion pricing is now being recognized as a key mechanism to mitigating congestion and revitalizing inner city districts, with over 15 cities in OECD countries having successfully implemented a congestion tax.[112] Technology used in these cities includes displaying licences, stop and pay toll booths, radio tags at toll stations (e-tolls), and photographing the licence plates of cars. The goal of such systems is to allow the congestion charge to be applied without disruption to the flow of traffic. Common exemptions from the charging zone include residents, buses and taxis. Some schemes, such as in Milan, exempt fuel-efficient and lower-emission cars, while others such as those in Norway offer discounts to lighter vehicles. And Singapore, for example, charges different amounts depending on the time of day, and the road being used depending on levels of congestion. London is still a standout example, however,[113] having implemented a congestion pricing scheme in February 2003 to control congestion in the city centre. This bold action has been met with considerable success and public approval and has inspired many other cities around the world to implement similar schemes, including Stockholm (Sweden), Valletta (Malta) and Milan (Italy). Since the implementation of the charge in London, traffic entering the charging zone has decreased by 21 per cent, key traffic pollutants and accidents have decreased (with a 12 per cent drop in particulate matter and nitrous oxides, and a 20 per cent reduction in greenhouse gas emissions),[114] and £123 million was raised in the 2006/2007 financial year and spent on improving London's transport.[115]

Residents in other areas have also requested that the zone be extended, and businesses have overwhelmingly reported either neutral or positive impacts (69 per cent neutral impact, 22 per cent positive, and only a 9 per cent negative impact reported), with business finding that any associated costs were compensated by secondary effects such as reduced delivery times.[116] The success of the scheme then allowed the then Mayor, Ken Livingstone, in February 2008 to announce the increase of the congestion tax for cars and certain light vehicles with high carbon emissions to a £25 daily charge, up from £8. Hybrid cars have also been made exempt from the congestion tax.[117] Following Mayor Livingstone, Mayor Boris Johnson continued the congestion charges. However, he withdrew the increase for highly polluting cars of up to £25,[118] reduced the amount of the fine for non-payment, extended pay periods for charges,[119] and is planning to follow the Swedish lead to vary the price throughout the day based on congestion with drivers receiving a monthly bill.[120]

Following the early success of the London scheme, Stockholm introduced a congestion pricing scheme on a trial basis in 2005, while extending the public transport system to support the increased patronage, and then held a referendum to determine whether to introduce it permanently.[121] A system of automatic identification was utilized with the current fee displayed above the charging stations. The charge was varied at different times throughout the day, including peak periods (7:30–8:30am and 4:00–5:30pm), semi-peak periods (half an hour on either side of peak periods), and medium volume periods. Evenings, weekends and holidays were exempt from the charge, and there was a maximum daily charge. Some vehicle categories were exempt from the charge, including taxis, emergency vehicles, vehicles with disabled permits, foreign vehicles, motorcycles, buses over 14 tons and vehicles using alternative fuels.

The trial resulted in: an overall 22 per cent reduction in congestion; queuing times for the inbound city traffic in the morning fell by a third and were halved for outbound traffic in the evening; road use in the inner city, as measured by kilometres travelled, fell by 14 per cent;[122] and there was an average of 10 per cent reduction in air pollutants.[123] In a subsequent referendum, the public, which had initially had reservations about the scheme, voted for its continuation.[124] A cost–benefit analysis was undertaken as part of the trial period to assess its viability, and showed significant net benefits of 1048 million SEK per annum (approx US$124 million, April 2009) from an economic point of view; however, it is not confirmed that this revenue was invested in improving public transportation.[125]

Understandably, the introduction of such a charge carries with it considerable political risk. However, there are a growing number of international examples of successful systems beyond London and Stockholm, as well as a strong body of research to promote a congestion charge to the public with appropriate inclusions. Through good management and implementation and a strong educational campaign, congestion charging can be used to great effect.

Investing in public transport and other modes

Designing, or rather redesigning, cities for sustainable transport options rather than the car, is hardly new – until the 20th century all cities in the world were designed to be walkable and easy to get around without a car. Up until last century, trams and trains allowed growing populations to develop dense city centres and corridors where essential activities and services surrounded the stations. This form still predominates in most European and wealthy Asian cities. In Mumbai, over 84 per cent of daily trips are made by public transport, while in Chennai, Shanghai, Hong Kong and Dakar it is close to 70 per cent. In the US and Australia barely 10 per cent of all trips are currently being made on public transport, highlighting the great potential for improvement.[126] Switching to public transport and cycling using existing technology can achieve well over Factor Five reductions in fuel consumption and greenhouse gas emissions. For instance, one bus with 25 passengers reduces energy consumption and greenhouse gas emissions per capita by approximately 86 per cent per kilometre compared to 25 (single occupant) vehicles.[127] Hybrid engines, lightweight buses, and plug-in hybrid technology can enable even higher efficiency improvements.[128] Options for improving the quality of public transport and cycling infrastructure, service and accessibility are covered in great detail in a range of reports, studies and texts. In this part we outline some of the major opportunities for providing viable alternatives to cars in an attempt to reduce car usage, such as:

- *Walking*: Cities in which various activities and facilities are at most five kilometres away were the dominant urban form in towns and cities for 8000 years.[129] The city of Vancouver, as part of its 'EcoDensity' initiative, has invested in a range of measures to encourage and facilitate walking and cycling. Transport has been dramatically reprioritized to consider walking first, then cycling, transit, goods movement and finally private car use. In terms of encouraging walking, Vancouver has a policy of widening sidewalks, increasing landscaping (including street trees and benches) and requiring buildings to include awnings in their design. Pedestrian-controlled street crossings are being installed throughout the city, plus curb bulges to enhance visibility of oncoming traffic. As a result, trips made by walking have increased by 44 per cent and now account for 27 per cent of all trips to the city centre.[130]
- *Cycling*: Since its invention in the early 1800s, the humble bicycle has been a mainstay of private transportation, losing popularity only in the 1900s with the advent of the automobile. There are still cities in developed countries, however, where over 30 per cent of all commutes are made on bicycle, such as Amsterdam, Copenhagen and Freiburg. In Amsterdam every part of the city can be reached via an extensive network of bicycle routes, and over 75 per cent of all residents older than 12 own a bike, and half use it daily.[131] In Copenhagen bike riders have equal priority to car drivers and pedestrians, with 36 per cent of Copenhageners riding their bicycle to work.[132] In Freiburg 35 per cent of the residents have chosen to not own a car and a third of all trips are made on bicycles.[133]

  Bicycles are still the transportation mode of choice for commuting to work, school, shopping and general day-to-day activities throughout Asian countries. Not surprisingly, the region produces over 75 million bicycles each year[134] – three-quarters of the entire global production. In China, the 500 million bicycles in use far outnumber the 20 million cars. The Chinese bicycle manufacturing industry contributes significantly to their economy, employing over 150,000 people and generating in excess of US$1 billion worth of foreign exchange.[135] In fact bicycle manufacture globally exceeds car manufacture almost threefold.[136]

- *Rail*: Light rail can be between 2.5 and 5 times more energy efficient per capita than buses, and between 17.5 and 35 times more efficient than cars.[137] In fact, compared with the average efficiency of a car in the US, the Manila Light Rail Transit System in the Philippines is 59 times more energy efficient, and a similar efficiency is achieved in Beijing, China. In less dense cities in Europe, the average light rail system is seven times more efficient.[138] Light rail with overhead cables can also run on electricity without storage requirements, and hence the City of Calgary has built wind turbines to power their light rail trains, the C-Train. The 20,000 tons of greenhouse gases the C-Train emitted were already one tenth of those that would have resulted from its passengers driving their own cars; however, now its operational emissions are practically zero.[139] It is estimated that the switch to wind power carries increased riding costs of 0.5 per cent per passenger[140] – clearly not a disincentive as the C-Train, despite concerns it was oversized, is now attracting the highest ridership of any light rapid transit in North America.[141]

- *Car sharing*: Car sharing was featured in the original *Factor Four* publication.[142] The philosophy of car sharing is simple – individuals gain the benefits of private vehicle use without the costs and responsibilities of ownership. When *Factor Four* was written there were only a handful of car sharing schemes in the world. Now there are car sharing schemes in operation in some form in over 600 cities.[143] Vehicles are usually deployed in parking lots that can be easily accessed from homes, transit centres or major business centres and can be reserved online or by phone with up to a few minutes' notice. Smart cards or similar technologies provide access to members, who generally pay a small upfront fee to join the organization, and then a fee each time a car is used based on an hourly rate, and distance driven.[144] Additionally, one car sharing vehicle generally displaces 4–10 new privately owned cars in continental Europe, 7–10 vehicles in Australia, and 6–23 cars in North America.[145]

- *Combining options*: By combining walking or cycling with public transport, longer trips become feasible without a car. Bicycles can be transported on trains, ferries and buses – where purpose-built racks on the front of the bus can store and carry bikes, such as in Boulder, Colorado. Many cities are also providing 'park and ride' facilities for bike riders at public transport stops to enable bike riders to safely store their bike and continue their trip by bus, train or ferry.[146] Studies have shown that people's perception of how quickly they will arrive at their destination is a critical determinant in deciding whether to take public transport.[147] Peak hour public transport is often faster than driving, and as cycling to a train station can be at least four times faster than walking, a bike can greatly facilitate a switch in transportation modes. Even cycling alone can often beat a car. During peak hour, or at any time of the day, cycling avoids the time-consuming pitfalls of queuing at traffic lights, congestion and parking, and provides door-to-door transport. The average speed of an Australian car during peak hour is 19.7km/h,[148] and can be easily overtaken by the average cyclist riding at 20–25km/h.[149]

Improving the design of public transport vehicles: A focus on rail

Even though a shift to rail results in Factor Five energy productivity improvements per passenger compared to the car, trains can be better designed to further improve their energy productivity. The UK Carbon Trust argues that significant efficiencies could be achieved in this sector through energy efficiency, regenerative braking, lighter rolling stock, better traffic flow and load factor management, biodiesel and hybrid or fuel cell engines and renewable electricity.[150] Globally, passenger rail efficiencies have not improved much recently with the notable exception of Japan. This is due to a range of factors such as the fact that the global automobile R&D budget is 100 times greater than rail and it takes 30–40 years for existing rail stock to turn over.[151] The Swiss railways, which have an active R&D programme in this area, foresee up to 60 per cent improvements from energy efficiency, energy recovery from regenerative braking, light-weighting and reducing drag and friction. It is important to note that Swiss trains and railways are already more efficient than most other trains, and therefore 70–80 per cent efficiency improvements are technically possible in most countries for this sector.[152]

Japanese train manufacturer JR East Group[153] has been applying a range of strategies to improve the energy efficiency of passenger train design since 1993. Their latest trains, the E231 series, are 50 per cent more efficient than the 103 series, which has been the major metropolitan area commuter train. The E231 series achieves these savings mainly through lighter overall weight, effective use of braking energy, and greater motor efficiency. JR East Group's Niitsu Rolling Stock Manufacturing Factory has handled all aspects of the E231 manufacture since 1994, and they have designed the new models so that 90 per cent of the materials can be recycled. JR East Group believes that further efficiencies are possible through further improving the amount of energy re-used from regenerative braking. If these strategies are then combined with further improvements to aerodynamics, engines, logistics and sourcing of renewable energy, close to Factor Five could be achieved for the next generation of passenger trains.[154] JR East Group has also manufactured and is currently trialling the world first diesel hybrid electric passenger train. Diesel hybrid railcars operate efficiently by using electricity generated by a diesel engine to charge a battery, which reduces emissions, and by regenerative brakes, which charge the battery when braking. Efficiency in tests was approximately 20 per cent better than a standard diesel railcar. Also, since 2006, JR East has been proceeding with research and development of hybrid fuel cell systems for railway applications, as shown in Figure 5.12.

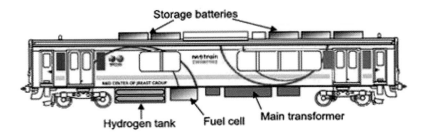

Storage batteries

Hydrogen tank   Fuel cell   Main transformer

Source: JR East (2006)[155]

Figure 5.12 *Schematic of hybrid fuel cell passenger train engine*

3 Heavy freight trucks

The potential for Factor Five improvements in fuel efficiency of heavy freight trucks

Globally, trucking is the principle carrier of freight over land and as such it is a large contributor to transportation-related fuel consumption and associated greenhouse gas emissions. According to the World Business Council for Sustainable Development, demand for trucking services is forecast to more than double over the next 50 years as demand for freight transport continues to rise, with the relative growth of emissions from various freight vehicles shown in Figure 5.13.[156] Of the forms of freight vehicles, trucks weighing 15,000kg (33,000lbs) or more ('heavy freight trucks', classified as 'Class 8'), represent a small proportion of the fleet, but a significant proportion of the fuel consumed. For example in the US, while Class 8 vehicles comprise about 2 million of the 45 million commercial trucks in use (i.e. under 5 per cent), they consume 68 per cent of the country's commercial truck fuel. Long-haul Class 8 trucks, which travel more than 160km (100 miles) per trip, account for almost 50 per cent of all commercial truck fuel used in the US.[157] Hence in this part we will focus on improving the energy productivity of heavy freight trucks.

The requirement for fuel in a truck is essentially to allow the engine to create enough kinetic energy to achieve speeds of up to at least 110km/h, while fully loaded. In order to do this enough power must be created to overcome both the aerodynamic drag losses from the air resistance of the truck (consuming up to 19 per cent of the energy), and the rolling resistance of the tyres caused by the weight of the truck (consuming 5–11 per cent), as shown in Figure 5.14. The remainder of the energy is lost in the engine as the fuel is converted into kinetic energy and transferred to the driveline of the vehicle. Hence any improvements to the shape of the truck that reduces aerodynamic drag, or reductions to the weight of the truck that reduces rolling resistance, can directly reduce the power output requirements for the engine and save fuel. However, it is important to note that aerodynamic performance and rolling

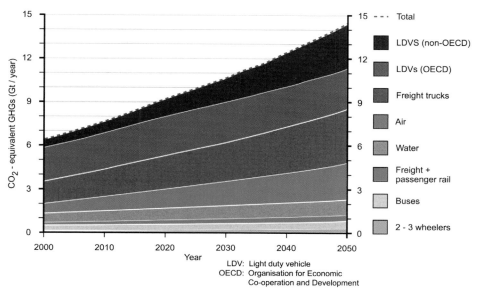

Source: WBCSD (2004)[158]

Figure 5.13 *Projections of transport related greenhouse gas emissions by transport mode, from 'well to wheel' (including extraction, production, distribution and use of the fuel)*

resistance are independent, meaning that improving one has very little effect on the other, but improvements in either will reduce the overall fuel consumption. As an approximate gauge, for trucks travelling at speeds greater than 80km/h, improvements in the aerodynamic performance will result in greater fuel savings, whereas for trucks travelling at speeds less than 80km/h, reductions in the rolling resistance will be more effective.[159]

In 2000, the US Department of Energy established the '21st Century Truck' programme, which set ambitious goals – including a 70 per cent improvement in energy efficiency for line-haul trucks and trailers (i.e. including Class 8 type heavy trucks).[160] This significant improvement was considered to be achievable with 'aggressive development and implementation of technologies currently being considered but not yet commercially viable'.[161] Investigating the potential for such improvements RMI, in 2005, found that reducing aerodynamic drag and rolling resistance by 50 per cent each, and reducing idling by 80 per cent (all very achievable), can save up to 50 per cent of fuel, increasing performance from around 2.5km/L to 5.0km/L (or 6.1 to 11.8mpg).[162] RMI points out that this assumes a combination of design innovations and current off-the-shelf technologies are used. According to RMI's 2007 *Winning the Oil Endgame* report,[163] improvements in the order of 70–80 per cent are well within reach in the trucking industry, by first reducing aerodynamic drag or rolling resistance (choosing the improvement with the greatest cost effective-

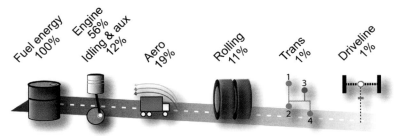

Source: Based on findings of RMI (2007)[164]

Figure 5.14 *Representation of estimated energy consumption at various stages of truck propulsion*

ness), and then by resizing and redesigning the engine to match the new required capacity. RMI suggests that the fuel economy can be further improved using a combination of existing and future controls and technologies (expected to be near market maturity by 2025), including operational improvements, such as reducing wasted kilometres through global positioning system (GPS) navigation, load-sensing cruise control, and improved driver behaviour by providing feedback though dashboard fuel economy indicators.[165]

The remainder of this section summarizes key opportunities identified by RMI and others for improving truck fuel economy, focusing on currently available technologies for vehicle, engine and operational/logistical improvements.[166]

Vehicle efficiencies – Reducing rolling resistance

As the rolling resistance is caused by the weight of the truck producing friction between the tyres and the road, friction can be reduced by reducing the weight of the vehicle.[167] Weight can be reduced by reducing the number of differentials, using lighter metals for differential housing, eliminating spacer blocks and using super singles tyres rather that pairs of tyres, as well as reducing the mass of the trailer through measures such as using alternative floor materials and eliminating excess steel in the frame.[168] Once the weight has been minimized a range of methods can then be used to further reduce the rolling resistance, including:[169]

1 *Tyre configuration*: Traditional twin-tyres optimized for fuel economy can save approximately 4 per cent fuel, and 'single-wide', 'wide base' or 'super singles' tyres can save 4–6 per cent fuel and 200lbs (90.7kg) per axle, meaning extra cargo and less 'dead weight' when empty.[170]

2 *Optimal tyre inflation*: Under-inflated tyres increase rolling resistance and also increase tyre wear, create irregular tread wear and reduce casing durability. Every 70kPa (10psi) of tyre under-inflation decreases fuel economy by 1 per cent. Under-inflation of trailer tyres also has a greater impact on fuel economy than under-inflation of prime mover tyres. Over-inflated tyres on the other hand, decrease rolling resistance and increase

fuel economy; however, they do increase tyre wear and a cost-effective balance needs to be reached in operation.

3   *Tyre and axle alignment*: The optimal alignment is 0 degrees, as a tyre that is misaligned by only one-quarter of a degree will try to travel 2–3m sideways per km travelled, which not only reduces truck fuel economy, but also increases tyre wear.

4   *Monitoring truck speed*: Decreasing the truck speed decreases tyre flexing and hence rolling resistance. Also higher speeds also cause tyre treads to wear 10–30 per cent faster with respect to distance travelled.[171]

Vehicle efficiencies – Improving aerodynamic performance

Aerodynamic drag is the result of forces acting on a truck due to pressure imbalances (i.e. including the prime mover and the trailer) as the truck moves through air.[172] The magnitude of aerodynamic drag depends on factors such as the truck's speed, external shape and particularly the frontal area of the truck.[173] The energy required to overcome aerodynamic drag increases with the cube of truck speed,[174] and hence this becomes the most significant contributor to power requirements in a typical truck at speeds faster than about 80km/h.[175] For heavy trucks travelling along interstate highways at over 100km/h the aerodynamic drag can contribute up to about half of the truck's power requirement.[176] The aerodynamic performance of heavy trucks has improved over the past few decades, with drag coefficients up to 40 per cent lower compared to what they were in the 1970s, mainly due to improvements in the leading surfaces of the truck, with RMI estimating that the theoretical limit of such improvements is up to 87 per cent, or about 0.13–0.19 compared to 1.0.[177] When travelling at 100km/h in a typical operating environment, modern trucks now experience about 30 per cent lower aerodynamic drag under steady wind tunnel conditions and 20 per cent in a typical operating environment, as well as operating at about 15 per cent and 10 per cent better fuel economy.[178] Such efficiencies can be achieved by improving the shape of prime movers and trailers to reduce turbulence, including:

- *Truck modifications*: full roof deflector (5–10 per cent reduction), chassis fairing (1–3 per cent reduction), sloped hood (2 per cent reduction), round corners, aero bumper (2 per cent reduction), air dam, flush headlights (0.5 per cent reduction), slanted windshield, curved windshield, side extenders (1–7 per cent reduction), skirts (plates which are mounted on the sides of trailers) and under-hood air cleaners (1–4 per cent reduction), concealed exhaust system, recessed door hinges, grab handles, aerodynamic mirrors (1–2 per cent reduction) and truck vision systems (3–4 per cent reduction) that can replace mirrors.[179]
- *Trailer modifications*: smooth-side van trailers with rounded leading corners, which induce the least aerodynamic drag. Contrast this to drop decks with irregular shaped loads, stock crates and car carriers which can induce 10–30 per cent more aerodynamic drag.[180]

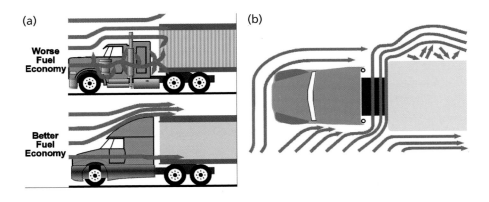

Source: Courtesy of Cummins

Figure 5.15 *Air turbulence around a moving truck as a result of
(a) various truck components, and (b) the truck–trailer gap*

The truck–trailer air gap can introduce aerodynamic drag in a cross-wind
environment, and is also a source of turbulence. According to Cummins, every
250mm increase in truck–trailer air gap beyond about 750mm, increases
aerodynamic drag by about 2 per cent.[181]

Turbulence can be further reduced through the use of 'aeroskirts', by
lowering the trailer floor and using low profile tyres. Although prime
mover–trailer combinations are limited to specific heights, widths and lengths
by state and federal regulations, their volumetric capacity can still be raised by
lowering the floor. Table 5.2 summarizes the indicative figures for prime mover
and trailer modifications, showing that although the aerodynamic improvements may add some weight to the vehicle, this can be more than compensated
by the weight reductions from one or more rolling resistance improvements.

Table 5.2 *Weight change for each truck modification*

Tractor–trailer modification	Weight change (kg)	
Engine downsize	− 454	(1000 lbs)
Rims/tyres	− 363	(800 lbs)
Tag axle	− 227	(500 lbs)
Lighter trailer	− 318	(700 lbs)
Subtotal of weight reductions	**− 1361 kg**	**(3000 lbs)**
Gap seal	+ 45	(100 lbs)
Sid skirts	+ 91	(200 lbs)
Rear drag device	+ 113	(250 lbs)
Turbo-compounding	+ 68	(150 lbs)
Subtotal of weight additions	**+ 318 kg**	**(700 lbs)**
Net Total	**− 1111 kg**	**(2300 lbs)**

Source: RMI (2008)[182]

Engine efficiencies – Reducing engine losses

Engine losses can account for 60–70 per cent of the fuel consumed, depending on operation conditions, and can be in the form of waste heat that passes through the exhaust system and the cooling system. These losses are associated with the thermodynamic engine cycle and reductions in this loss through engine design changes are possible.[183] Diesel engine efficiency is limited by the peak combustion temperatures and cylinder pressures that the engine materials can withstand. The typical, modern, heavy truck, diesel engine produces about 320kW at a brake thermal efficiency of about 40–44 per cent.[184] RMI describes a number of potential engine improvements that can improve fuel economy, as summarized in Table 5.3, in an attempt to address the aggressive target of the US Environmental Protection Agency and the diesel engine industry of 55 per cent by 2012.[185]

Table 5.3 *Potential engine improvements*

Engine component	Description
Oil-free engine turbomachinery	'Oil-Free turbomachinery is defined as high-speed rotating equipment, such as turbine engines, that operate without oil-lubricated rotor supports, that is, bearings, dampers and air/oil seals. We expect advances towards an oil-free turbomachinery to have some impact on the fuel economy gain in heavy trucks. By how much is uncertain, but it is known that relative to state-of-the-art oil lubricated systems, oil-free turbomachinery technology can offer significant system level benefits.'
Displacement on demand	'Displacement on demand technology deploys only the number of cylinders required to serve the current load, thus shifting the locus of engine operation to a region of higher thermal brake efficiency. The gain in a light-truck fuel economy can be very high, as much as 6 to 8 per cent.'
Variable intake valve timing	'Electronic control of the camshaft enables selection of optimum location for various engine operating conditions, maximizing torque and horsepower outputs, as well as significant emissions benefits from the engine's precise valve control.'
Variable intake lift, piezo-injectors, 42V electrical systems	'Variable intake lift, piezo-injectors, and increased voltage of electrical systems to 42V are at this point essentially part of standard modern system designs.'
Controllable electric pumps and drives	'Moving hydraulic and mechanical pump systems to controllable electric pumps and drives will have significant efficiency benefits.'
Homogeneous charge	'Homogeneous charge compression ignition (HCCI) is a new compression ignition combustion process that has the potential to be both highly efficient and produce very low emissions. HCCI is currently at the research stage. It is a lean combustion process and enables the combustion to take place spontaneously and homogeneously without flame propagation, eliminating heterogeneous air/fuel mixture regions, translating to a lower local flame temperature that reduces the amounts of nitric oxide (NO_x) and particulate matter emitted. HCCI can provide high, diesel-like efficiencies using gasoline, diesel fuel, and most alternative fuels. HCCI may incorporate the best features of both spark ignition (SI) engines and direct injection (DI) diesel engines. Like an SI engine the charge is well mixed which minimizes particulate emissions, and like a diesel engine it is compression ignited and has no throttling losses, which leads to high efficiency.'

Source: RMI (2008)[186]

Fuel economy can also be improved through internal engine braking, transitioning to better lubricants, improving engine cooling, the use of auxiliary power units and shifting to alternative fuels, as outlined in the following:[187]

- *Internal engine braking (transmission)*: Transmissions comprise a set of gears that transmit the engine output to the truck driveline. They are a major contributor to whether the engine operates at the optimum speed during the most common operating conditions. Using a non-optimal transmission can reduce fuel economy by up to 10–15 per cent. Optimizing the transmission includes selecting the gear ratios and number of gears to suit the most common truck load and travel terrain. Generally, operating fast gears and slow engines improves fuel economy. Automated transmissions are now available for trucks, which incorporate computer-controlled shift logic to determine the optimal gear changes for maximum fuel economy.[188] However, automated transmissions may not be as accurate at manual gear changes in some conditions, such as during frequent ascents and descents.

- *Engine lubricants*: Lubricants (usually lube oil) are used to reduce friction, and hence energy losses and wear between moving engine components in contact, and to transfer heat to the surrounding components. Temperatures that are too low mean that the lubricant is too viscous and more pumping energy is required to move it around the engine. If the temperature is too high the lubricant is too fluid to lubricate effectively, and using more lubricant than recommended can lead to excessive oil churning (or spin) losses, which can reduce fuel economy by 2 per cent. Using synthetic lubricants in engines reduces pumping energy losses and oil churning losses at low ambient temperatures, but performance is similar at normal operating temperatures. Synthetic lubricants are more cost effective in drivetrain components such as axles and transmissions, which frequently operate at extreme temperatures and rarely suffer from internal contaminants.

- *Engine cooling system*: Truck engines use a cooling system based on fluid moving throughout the engine block to remove heat, which is then removed by convective cooling by fan, and the trucks motion, in the radiator. In a typical, heavy, highway truck, the fan is active about 10 per cent of the travel time but can contribute tens of kilowatts to truck power requirements.[189] The fan automatically activates in response to high cooling system temperatures, high intake manifold (boost) air temperatures, and the air-conditioner compressor activating. Unnecessary fan activity can be minimized by ensuring that the fan clutch and thermostatic switch operate effectively, and by maintaining a clean charge air cooler and the appropriate coolant level. The air-conditioner compressor contributes about 50 per cent of fan activity. Excessive fan activity can be from an overcharged system, defective or incorrect head pressure switches, or poor condenser efficiency. Typical cooling system operating temperatures are above 80°C and every 15°C decrease in coolant temperature decreases fuel economy by 0.4 per cent.

- *Auxiliary power unit (APU)*: When a truck engine is idling, the engine idles higher than it needs to in order to provide power to other powered items (including air-conditioning, electronics, refrigeration, etc.). According to a study by Argonne National Laboratory, the average truck spends six hours idling each day, primarily to generate electricity for its auxiliary systems while parked.[190] APUs consist of a small generator that can supply heating, cooling and other accessory loads to the driver, without turning on the main engine, or allowing the engine to idle much lower. Drivers who sleep in their cabs overnight can engage the APU to stay warm instead of keeping the engine idling all night. Using an APU can cut main engine idling by 80–92 per cent and achieve in the order of 8 per cent fuel savings. Improving the efficiency of APUs can both further reduce the energy demand on the engine, and improve the average brake thermal efficiency. Improvements can be achieved by redesigning auxiliary pumping elements to make them more efficient, and by undertaking 'intelligent thermal management' – which includes considering areas ranging from optimizing the engineering of vehicle occupant thermal systems (i.e. air-conditioning) to the electrical decoupling of the now more efficient (but conventionally hydraulic or mechanical) pumps and cooling fans.[191]

- *Alternative fuel technologies*: There are now 'dual fuel' vehicles being designed and produced, with two parallel fuel systems feeding one engine. While the duplicated tanks cost space in some applications, the increased range and flexibility of operating on two fuels may be a significant incentive, for example where one of the fuels may be difficult to obtain in some locations. Alternatively, flexible-fuel or 'flex-fuel' vehicles are able to use a mixture of input fuels in the one tank to supplement petrol, typically ethanol, methanol or biobutanol.[192] Examples are: ethanol – an alcohol-based fuel made by fermenting and distilling starch crops such as corn, or 'cellulosic biomass' which includes trees and grasses, as mentioned previously; biodiesel – derived from vegetable oils and animal fats; natural gas (i.e. mostly methane); propane (liquefied petroleum gas); and hydrogen – which may be used in fuel cells to power electric motors or burned in internal combustion engines (ICEs). Scania is currently working on an ethanol-fuelled truck claiming fuel savings of up to 20 per cent, with Swedish buses having used this technology since the late 1980s. However, issues related to the sustainability of bio-fuel crops need to be addressed, such as competition for food crops, atmospheric emissions from burning biomass to create energy, and the shear quantity of biomass needed.

Engine efficiencies – Alternatives to ICEs

The most promising innovation is the 'hybrid electric truck'. In a conventional ICE-powered vehicle, the engine's energy is applied to the drive wheels through a 'transmission' and a 'differential'. The efficiency depends on its operating

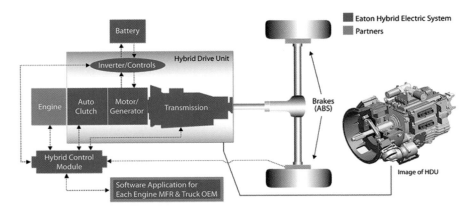

Source: Courtesy of Eaton Corporation, 2009

Figure 5.16 *Fedex/Eaton hybrid electric system*

rpm (revolutions per minute) and output torque, with generally low efficiency trends at low rpm. Much of the energy delivered to the drive wheels is used to accelerate the vehicle. Then, when the brakes are applied to slow the vehicle, the kinetic energy of the vehicle is primarily converted to heat in the brake pads, causing brake wear and tear and wasting energy. Depending upon the application, more than half of the energy delivered to the drive wheels is subsequently dissipated in the brake pads.[193] In contrast, hybrid electric technologies use multiple propulsion devices (i.e. a combustion engine and one or more electric motors) to propel a vehicle, with the potential to periodically charge the batteries from the electrical grid.[194] There are essentially two main technologies: 1) hybrid electric and 2) hybrid hydraulic – which may be utilized in vehicles 'in parallel', or 'in series', as we now discuss:

1 *Hybrid electric vehicle (HEV)*: In a HEV the diesel engine is coupled with electric motor/generator(s), such as a hybrid drive unit (HDU) and batteries (or other electrical storage devices) to create the hybrid system, as shown in Figure 5.16. In such systems some of the energy that is converted to heat in a conventional system during braking is recaptured through regenerative braking for use in accelerating the vehicle. If the electrical energy storage system in an electric hybrid has adequate capacity, the vehicle may be able to be connected to the electrical grid when it is not in use, charging the storage system. They can also provide power capability while the engine is off, for worksite hydraulic operations, and an auxiliary electric power source from the vehicle which can be used to operate other tools and equipment much like an auxiliary power unit (APU).

2 *Hybrid hydraulic vehicle (HHV)*: In a HHV the engine is coupled with hydraulic pumps or motors and hydraulic accumulators to create the hybrid system, as seen in Figure 5.17. Fluid power hybrid engines capture the vehicle's kinetic energy during braking by pumping hydraulic fluid from the

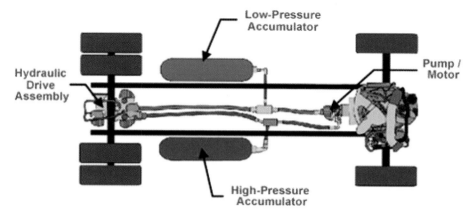

Source: Courtesy of Eaton Corporation, 2009

Figure 5.17 *Hybrid hydraulic vehicle*

low-pressure accumulator to the high-pressure accumulator.[195] The fluid compresses nitrogen gas in the high-pressure accumulator and pressurizes the system. This recovered energy is used to supplement or substitute the engine's power during acceleration. This system can even be installed on existing trucks, and in laboratory tests the technology achieved 60–70 per cent improvement in fuel economy with associated reductions in CO_2 emissions.[196] The energy recovery rate is higher and therefore the system is more efficient than battery-charged hybrids and is cheaper than gas-electric hybrids; however, the system requires more space than a battery.[197]

As hybrid vehicle design company Odyne explains, HEVs and HHVs can be designed with either series or parallel architectures:[198]

- *Parallel technology*: allows both energy sources to be used individually or together to power the vehicle. Parallel technologies are better suited where a larger percentage of travel may be highway driving. There are several configurations for this architecture, with fuel economy and emissions reductions of 20–30 per cent possible for parallel hybrid hydraulic systems.
- *Series technology*: has no direct connection between the internal combustion engine and the drive wheels – the electric traction motor is connected directly to the rear wheels through the differential without the use of a transmission. This technology is better suited to operate in an 'all electric-mode' or 'hybrid-mode' for vehicles travelling short distances, where there is frequent stopping and starting. The internal combustion engine drives a generator-charger system to keep the batteries charged to the appropriate levels, along with a regenerative braking system, and in the case of a plug-in hybrid, by an external electricity supply. Fuel economy and emissions reductions of 50–70 per cent or more are possible for series hybrid hydraulic systems.

There are a variety of hybrid options being developed for both parallel and series configurations for the trucking industry; however, as yet there are no 'mainstreamed' hybrid truck vehicles being mass-produced. Truck manufacturer Man is reported to have been working on a hybrid system for the last five years, saving up to 20 per cent on diesel consumption, with the hybrid electric system delivering a smooth acceleration.[199] According to the international truck and engine corporation Navistar, their Green Diesel Hybrid™ is up to 50 per cent more fuel efficient with 30–60 per cent lower emissions. Coca-Cola plans to use Eaton diesel electric hybrid trucks for delivery vehicles, which claim 30–60 per cent fuel efficiency improvements, with similar percentages in emission reductions, extended brake life and idle-time reductions of up to 87 per cent during worksite operations.[200] Hybrid system design company Odyne recently unveiled the first hybrid truck that uses compressed natural gas to power its engine, combined with plug-in technology, in a garbage truck which is expected to reduce fuel costs by 40 per cent.[201]

Operational/logistical improvements

While the engine and vehicle improvements outlined above offer significant opportunities for reducing fuel consumption and greenhouse gas emissions from trucks there are also several operational and logistical improvements that can further deliver reductions; for example:

- *GPS navigation*: Out-of-route distance contributes about 3–10 per cent of all distance travelled.[202] For a truck with a fuel economy of 2.6km/L and fuel at a cost of $1.30 per litre, every 100,000km of travel (about one year of travel) has $1500–5000 of out-of-route distance costs, which can be reduced by using technologies such as GPS navigation.
- *Fuel economy displays*: Dashboard indicators that assist drivers to monitor parameters related to fuel economy are in development.[203] For example, there are digital fuel economy displays that monitor instantaneous fuel consumption, trend graphs and average trip fuel economy. These displays may improve fuel economy by 1–5 per cent. There are also advanced tyre-pressure monitoring systems to optimize conditions to reduce rolling resistance.
- *Driver behaviour*: Driver behaviour can account for 20–30 per cent variation in fuel economy.[204] Behaviours include control of truck idle time, control of truck speed, acceleration and braking techniques, and gear shifting techniques. Some inefficient driving behaviour arises from low engine power and driveability challenges.
- *Loading configurations*: SC Johnson has found that truck loading and packing configurations can significantly affect fuel efficiency in the transportation of goods.[205] Research showed that the different weights and sizes of various products had a large effect on how their trucks should be packed for maximum efficiency. For example, a truckload full of wrapping products was significantly under the most efficient load weight, whereas a

smaller number of pallets of glass cleaner products reached the maximum weight target while leaving empty space in the trailer. The company now strategically packs multiple products on the same load, ensuring the most efficient weight capacity is reached, and thus uses fewer trucks. The company also revised its customer incentive plan from encouraging a minimum of two layers of every product with their shipments to allowing only one layer of product. This allowed more efficient combining of products in transportation and reduced the truck's weight and enabled more product to be loaded onto the trailer.

- *Day cabins*: SC Johnson also introduced the use of 'day cabs' into its fleet – trucks without a sleeping compartment – reducing the cab weight by 1360kg (3000lbs) and hence allowing more product to be transported.

Best practice case studies

Wal-Mart trucking fleet retrofit (US)

Further to the building energy efficiency measures covered previously, in 2005 Wal-Mart committed to doubling fuel efficiency in its trucking fleet of approximately 7200 semi-trailers by 2015 (i.e. a 50 per cent reduction in fuel use), including a 25 per cent reduction by 2010. The corporation estimated that this will save Wal-Mart nearly US$500 million by 2020. Wal-Mart has applied many of the design methodologies from RMI related to a systems approach to truck design in the redesign of their fleet for the long-haul trucks, such as those mentioned above. These trucks form the backbone of the Wal-Mart distribution network in the US, collectively travelling nearly 1500 million kilometres (900 million miles).[206] In typical driving conditions the trucks average about 2.6km/L (6mpg).

Changes made between 2005 and 2008 surpassed the 25 per cent goal by three years, and included the following features:[207]

- improving the aerodynamics of the prime mover and trailer, including the use of trailer side skirts;
- installing low rolling-resistance (wide-base) tyres, replacing the two wheels usually located on the rear axle with a wheel that is not quite as wide as the sum of the two wheels;
- reducing the weight of the vehicle by eliminating the internal drivetrain (making the rear axle lighter);
- installing APUs on all trucks that make overnight trips to cut down on engine idling, which eliminates the use of the vehicle's main engine to keep drivers warm or cool at night.

Wal-Mart has a number of trucks on which further fuel efficiency improvements are being trialled; these include:[209]

- 15 reclaimed-grease fuel trucks that will run on the cooking grease from Wal-Mart stores;
- 5 Peterbilt Model 386 heavy-duty hybrids (shown in Figure 5.18);

Source: Wal-Mart (2009)[208]

Figure 5.18 *Wal-Mart Eaton/Peterbilt diesel assist hybrid*

- 4 Peterbilt Model 386 trucks that will run on liquid natural gas (operating onsite);
- 1 full-propulsion Arivin Meritor hybrid operating in Detroit (the first of its kind).

UPS electric vehicle expansion

The profitability of package delivery companies like United Parcel Service (UPS), FedEx and DHL are significantly affected by fuel prices. As the world's largest package delivery company and a global provider of specialized transportation and logistics, UPS services more than 200 countries and territories. UPS also operates the largest alternative-energy fleet in the package-delivering industry, with approximately 20,000 low-emission and alternative-fuel vehicles out of approximately 88,000 ground vehicles. In 2008 UPS increased its commitment, including:[210]

- expanding its green fleets in the UK and Germany after nine months of successful trials, purchasing 12 custom-built electric vehicles;[211]
- expanding its US green fleet from 50 hybrid electric trucks to 250, the largest commercial order for such trucks by any company at the time;
- placing orders for seven hydraulic hybrid vehicles (HHV, as described previously), the first in the industry to do so;

- increasing its fleet of vehicles running on compressed natural gas from 800 to 1100;
- adding 167 CNG (compact natural gas) delivery vehicles to its fleets in Texas, Georgia and California.

Increasing industry supply of innovative trucks

With the increasing demand for energy-efficient vehicles, a number of trucking suppliers have announced innovations that improve fuel economy as part of their new vehicle stock; these include:[212]

- *Volvo Trucks – hybrid models (Sweden)*: Volvo Trucks is integrating hybrid truck technology into its vehicle specifications, supplying its first hybrid garbage truck in 2008. The trucks have a driveline which includes both a diesel engine and an electric motor, where each power source can be used separately or in combination with the other. Fuel consumption can be cut by up to 30 per cent by using the electric motor when the vehicle is idling and for acceleration (15–20 per cent), and adding an extra battery which features a plug-in recharging facility to power the ancillaries (10–14 per cent).
- *Navistar hybrid electrics (US)*: Navistar is expanding its offering of diesel electric hybrid trucks, stating that the new hybrid truck has proven fuel savings from 20–25 per cent on standard inner-city pickup and delivery applications. The company states that the new hybrids emit up to 33 per cent less carbon emissions, and 35 per cent less nitrogen oxide emissions when compared to standard diesel trucks.
- *Peterbilt Motors Co (US)*: Peterbilt Motors is offering new liquefied natural gas (LNG) configurations, where the LNG system is part of a joint agreement between Peterbilt and Westport Innovations Inc. to provide natural gas versions of select Peterbilt aerodynamic and vocational vehicles.
- *Freightliner Trucks (US)*: In 2008, Freightliner Trucks (a division of Mercedes-Benz) announced a 'Go for the Green' programme, offering US$5000 net incentive on orders for the Freightliner Business Class M2e Hybrid. This new truck advertises benefits including increased engine and brake life by over 100 per cent in urban delivery service, and mounted equipment such as buckets and lifts running from an 'electric power take-off' (ePTO), which minimizes idling.
- *US Environmental Protection Agency (US)*: The US EPA is now offering companies up to 25 per cent off the cost of a new hybrid truck, under the Diesel Emission Reduction Act (DERA), as long as they remove an existing diesel truck from service. It is estimated that the replacement trucks, if plug-in hybrids, can deliver up to 70 per cent better fuel economy than a conventionally powered truck.[213]

Alternatives to the use of trucks for freight

Comparing modes for freight transportation

Global freight transportation has grown faster than the global economy over the past two decades, expanding 3.6–5.9 per cent each year.[214] The Intergovernmental Panel on Climate Change (IPCC)[215] and World Business Council for Sustainable Development (WBCSD)[216] predict that the global average increase in rail and truck freight could be around 2.3 per cent per year by 2050.[217] Other US researchers have forecast growth of 4 per cent or more per year through to 2020.[218] Within this growth, the WBCSD has forecast that trucking is likely to experience the highest growth of all the freight modes over the next 50 years,[219] as shown in Figure 5.19, followed closely by rail. This poses a challenge as numerous studies have confirmed that road freight is responsible for a disproportionately large amount of the freight industry's greenhouse gas emissions.

Given such significant levels of expected future growth, nations focused on reducing energy consumption and greenhouse gas emissions need to ensure the most efficient modes of freight transportation. Indeed, the future role of trucking may be focused on short trips from rail and shipping yards to warehouses and vendors rather than doing the long-haul trips between destinations, with such a shift having the potential to reduce greenhouse gas emissions by as much as 85 per cent.[220] The global trends for modal distribution of freight are summarized in Figure 5.20 for America, Japan, France, the UK and Australia, and allowing for economic differences in these countries, it is clear that Australia and the US have the most energy-intensive freight system per GDP.[221]

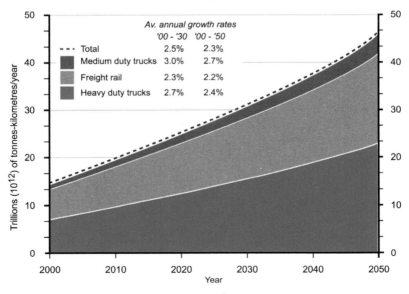

Source: WBCSD

Figure 5.19 *Forecast increase in freight transport*

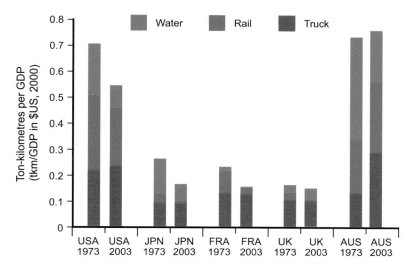

Source: Based on data from Kamakaté (2007)

Figure 5.20 *Energy intensity per GDP, in 1973 and 2003*

In Australia, despite a significant shift away from shipping to trucking between 1973 and 2003, a 2007 report by the Australia Institute concluded that shipping is well over 80 per cent more efficient than trucking freight (see Table 5.4). Companies moving their own freight by rail ('private' or 'ancillary' rail) are at least 80 per cent more efficient than companies trucking their freight, and third parties moving freight for other companies ('hire and reward rail') are still around 66 per cent more efficient than trucking.[222]

Currently, although Australian road freight transport accounts for only 38 per cent of domestic freight transported by volume, it is responsible for 84 per cent of the total freight transport emissions. Conversely, coastal shipping provided 22 per cent of freight movements by volume while only releasing 4 per cent of emissions, and rail moved 36 per cent of domestic freight and emitted only a marginally larger proportion of greenhouse gases.[223] In the US, where freight movements account for 9 per cent of the nation's total greenhouse gas emissions, shifting existing long-haul truck transport to rail could reduce total freight-related emissions by 85 per cent, a greater than Factor Five improvement, even taking into account truck transport at either end of the trip.[224]

There are also a number of other 'impacts' arising from road transport of freight which could be avoided by a shift to other modes of freight transportation, including externalities that carry significant costs to society but are currently not well documented or accounted for. These include road damage, an increase in likelihood and severity of road accidents, and health impacts from pollution and congestion – costs for which the industry is estimated to pay only between a half and two-thirds.[225]

Table 5.4 *Energy and emissions intensity for road, rail and shipping transport of freight in Australia*

Mode	Energy intensity (MJ-FFC/tkm) [a]	Emission intensity (g CO_2e/tkm) [b]
Road transport		
Light commercial vehicles	21.07	1532
Rigid trucks	2.95	209
Articulated trucks	0.98	71
Rail		
Ancillary	0.09	6.00
Coastal shipping	0.17	15.00

Notes: a Megajoule per ton km (MJ/tkm) on a full fuel cycle (FFC) basis. A 'full fuel cycle' includes feedstock production, extraction, fuel production, distribution, transport, storage, and vehicle operation, including refuelling, combustion, conversion, permeation, and evaporation.[226]
b Grams of carbon dioxide equivalent (g CO_2-e) per ton km
Source: Macintosh (2007)[227]

Unfortunately, the significant estimated growth in the global freight industry does not seem to be matched with any national strategies to reduce the resulting increase in greenhouse gas emissions. In 2008 a discussion paper prepared by the Australian National Transport Commission could not find a detailed national strategy for cutting freight transport emissions over the longer term anywhere in the world.[228] However, significant rail and shipping freight infrastructure already exists around the world, which can underpin a transition away from trucking. For example, in the US, rail is responsible for the same number of ton-kilometres (tkm) as road transport, each moving 40 per cent of the total domestic freight, and marine shipping already moves approximately 9 per cent of freight along the eastern and western coasts. In Europe, 45 per cent of freight is moved by trucks, whereas river and short sea transport are responsible for 40 to 44 per cent of the tkm.[229]

Increasing the portion of freight carried by rail and shipping involves development of 'multi-modal' systems, and is underpinned by the ability to move freight quickly and efficiently from one mode, such as rail, to another, such as trucks. However, currently the time and costs involved in moving freight between modes, and the trucks needed for door-to-door collection and delivery, are still higher than the cost savings achieved – although efficiencies are improving, with a gradual shift to 'containerization' of freight transport, aided by the creation of an ISO international standard for 'intermodal containers'.[230] More infrastructure is also needed, like additional rail lines and transfer stations (urban multi-modal hubs), but such infrastructure has large upfront costs and is likely to require government assistance.[231] One German company, Deutsche Bahn (DB), however, in the absence of such interventions, created intermodal opportunities within its own supply chain. As the largest provider of European surface freight, second largest provider worldwide of air freight, and third largest global maritime freight provider, DB decided to focus on integrating rail as an energy-efficient transportation mode.[232] Through the construction of 25 international rail-ports,[233] rail transportation has been integrated with truck and other transportation modes, and DB is able to remove 13,300 trucks from Europe's roads each day – the equivalent of three million loads, and close to 24 billion tkm per year.[234] And this has been achieved cost competitively.

These initiatives by the private sector are subsequently being reinforced through government policy, as the German 'Freight Transport and Logistics Masterplan'[235] now recognizes the synergistic benefits to German society from increasing the portion of freight carried by rail and inland waterways. Through both regulation and funding, the capacity of both rail and water transport will be increased – providing benefits to passenger traffic on both modes, as well as decreasing road congestion, pollution and wear and tear of roadways and infrastructure like bridges and culverts. However, the impact on the livelihood of truck drivers needs to be considered. A number of other countries are also currently investigating the potential for a large-scale switch to intermodal freight transport options, such as France, the UK and the US, as part of efforts to improve productivity and reduce greenhouse gas emissions from this sector.

Improving the energy productivity of rail

As discussed above, rail has many advantages over transporting freight by trucks on the road. Efficient hybrid diesel-electric motors now power freight trains, and steel wheels on steel tracks minimize friction compared to trucks. The ability to hook up multiple cars and carry more freight per locomotive than a truck also provides an energy advantage. The rail freight industry has worked hard to improve energy efficiency. As Figure 5.21 shows, the volume of rail freight in the US has nearly doubled while energy use has only marginally increased since 1980.[236] For example, American rail transport company CSX claims that it has improved the fuel efficiency of its standard locomotives by 80 per cent since 1980.[237]

While significant improvements have been made, still further energy productivity improvements could be made through improving the design of rail freight and through better logistics, informed by a range of recent studies.[238] As mentioned in the alternatives to automobiles section, Swiss railways are one of the most efficient in the world with a strong R&D programme that predicts further improvements, over their already leading performance, of up to 60 per cent are achievable through improved engine efficiency, energy recovery from dynamic braking, light-weighting and reducing drag and friction.[239] Additionally, the logistics of how existing railway systems for freight are used can also be improved to increase the amount of freight carried.[240] Rail infrastructure can also be improved, including improved tracks and additional freight yards so that more destinations have freight stops near them, and new switches and switching yards so that the lower cost per mile is not undone by indirect routes requiring more miles between start and destination. All together a range of strategies could be used to enable Factor Five improvements in energy productivity of rail for freight over the coming decades. The Center for

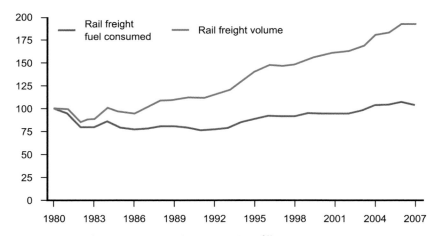

Source: Based on data from the Association of American Railroads[241]

Figure 5.21 *US rail freight volume versus rail freight fuel consumption, 1980–2007*

Transportation Research Argonne National Laboratory has published an extensive review of strategies to improve rail fuel efficiency. The major areas identified were engine efficiency (20 per cent), saving energy during idling (at least 10 per cent), using energy-efficient lighting (50 per cent) and reducing aerodynamic drag (5–10 per cent):[242]

1 *Engine efficiency*: The Center for Transportation Research has found that using advanced materials, the latest technologies, and advanced combustion concepts, a focused research and development programme could achieve thermal efficiencies for the diesel locomotive engine of 55 per cent, which would improve fuel efficiency by another 20 per cent.

2 *Reduced idling*: The Center also argues that 10 per cent improvements in fuel efficiency are achievable through minimizing the time that locomotives spend idling. In 2001, a detailed analysis of Class I locomotives showed that 6.3 per cent fuel efficiencies could be achieved through a focus on reducing idling through better design. US rail freight company CSX have introduced GenSet locomotives for use in switching yards to move carriages.[243] Rather than the usual one large diesel locomotive engine, a GenSet locomotive uses three 700 horsepower engines that can be shut down and started as quickly as a truck engine by the on-board computer, depending on power needs. The Genset locomotive's engine is 50 per cent more fuel efficient than that of traditional diesel locomotives and research is under way to improve power so they can then be used for all aspects of freight transport.[244]

3 *Energy-efficient lighting*: LED lighting can be used for locomotive headlights, and for lighting in the driver's cabin. LEDs use such little energy that they can be run all night using batteries rather than energy from the engine.

4   *Improving aerodynamics and reducing drag*:[245] While studies suggest there is minimal potential to improve aerodynamics of locomotive engines, studies do show that there is considerable potential to reduce aerodynamic-drag losses for certain car configurations, especially those that include empty cars and intermodal cars. Aerodynamic-drag losses of intermodal cars (two containers stacked on a flat car), can be as high as about 30 per cent.[246] Another study found that aerodynamic drag accounts for about 15 per cent of the round-trip fuel consumption for a coal train, largely due to air turbulence created by empty cars. A 25 per cent reduction in aerodynamic drag was achieved in an experiment using covers to direct the air flow over the empty cars, which also led to a 5 per cent fuel saving.

Further to these options, a number of additional strategies exist – such as energy and power recovery, optimizing speeds, improved logistics, materials efficiency and light-weighting, and nations investing in rail freight infrastructure:[247]

- *Energy and power recovery*: Although the first commercial applications of dynamic braking to recover energy have been used in hybrid cars, it is more effective to use dynamic braking in heavier vehicles like freight trains and trucks. Heavier vehicles need more power and energy to brake, which means there is greater potential energy which can be recaptured during braking or deceleration. Since the instantaneous energy produced by dynamic braking is high, locomotives can store this energy for later use. Many of the energy storage technologies being applied to cars to capture and store energy from dynamic braking are also relevant for freight trains, including batteries, fuel cells and capacitors.
- *Optimizing speeds*: The rail freight transport industry can also utilize IT systems to calculate the speed for trains to run at for optimal fuel efficiency. The on-board computer does this by taking into consideration the type of freight train, its weight, the gradient of the track and the GPS location to calculate the speed that will achieve a theoretical optimal fuel efficiency performance.[248]
- *Improved logistics*: Existing railway lines could be used more productively through improved logistics. The freight trains themselves can also be improved to carry higher loads of freight, further increasing the energy productivity of rail freight transport. The significance of this was highlighted in *Factor Four*, which even in 1997 showed that it was possible to increase the freight loads on existing rail tracks significantly without constructing any additional major infrastructure. In the case study, 'Quadrupling the capacity of existing railways', *Factor Four* outlined 'intelligent rail' strategies pioneered by Professor Rolk Kracke (University of Hanover), which are still, over a decade later, largely overlooked as a part of a strategy to improve energy productivity in freight by rail.

> *The main element of Kracke's proposal is safely increasing both the frequency and the load of freight trains on the lines. Kracke and his team are making proposals for new electronic control techniques for safely enabling freight trains to be able to run closer to each other, enabling more to be on the same tracks at one time. Being able to increase the amount of freight carried by rail does not only depend on the numbers of freight track lines and their length, nor the load which freight trains can carry, but also the speed at which they can be unloaded and re-loaded... Modern switching can be done by horizontally moving just containers across a platform, not entire railway cars. Twenty or more containers can simultaneously be switched from one train to the other or into a big warehouse. Using such simply sophisticated means, an entire goods train can be reconstituted in a mere 15 minutes.*
>
> von Weizsäcker et al, *Factor Four*, 1997[249]

- *Materials efficiency and light-weighting*: Steel cars have traditionally been used to make carriages for freight transport.[250] There is, in principle, potential this century to instead make the cars out of lighter components, such as light metals like aluminium or high-strength plastics. Reducing the weight of the cars which carry freight would then enable any particular locomotive to be able to pull greater freight loads without exceeding its load limits.

Several countries are moving to improve the efficiency of their transport sectors by making large investments in rail freight infrastructure, including improving the modal interfaces. For instance, China has invested US$292 billion to improve and extend its rail network from 78,000km in 2007, to over 120,000km by 2020, much of which will be dedicated to freight. This will extend their rail building capacity, which between 2003 and 2007 saw a per annum rail extension of on average 3.4 per cent.[251] India is also investing in rail, to the tune of US$4.3 billion, which will finance the building of two dedicated freight corridors, an eastern corridor that will run for 1279km, and a western corridor that will run for 1483km, most of which will be double tracked.[252] In Germany, investment in advanced rail transport has overturned long-standing trends, and currently the growth in rail transport of 12 per cent is outstripping that of road transport, at 8 per cent.[253]

Improving the energy productivity of shipping

As discussed above, shipping freight along coastlines and around the world is a relatively low-energy form of transportation, using 25–50 per cent as much fuel as a freight truck.[254] However, as 90 per cent of global cargos are carried aboard these vessels,[255] shipping still contributes an estimated 2.7[256] to 5[257] per cent of global greenhouse gas emissions at around 960 million tons of CO_2,

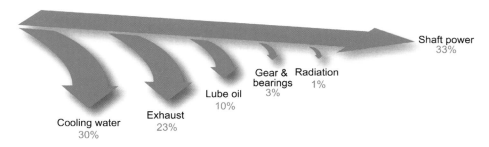

Gear & bearings 3%   Radiation 1%

Lube oil 10%

Exhaust 23%

Cooling water 30%

Shaft power 33%

Source: Based on data from King et al (2008)[258]

Figure 5.22 *Typical heat balance for a vessel with high-speed diesel engines for propulsion*

and consuming 300 million tons of fuel per year.[259] According to the International Maritime Organization (IMO), without corrective action or the introduction of new technologies, air emissions, due to increased fuel consumption by the world shipping fleet, could increase by 38–72 per cent by 2020.[260] Hence, there is a strong impetus to increase shipping efficiency. In shipping, most of the energy is lost as heat through the engine exhaust, or for engine cooling, as shown in Figure 5.22.

The good news is that by combining existing knowledge with emerging innovations Factor Five improvements are possible in shipping energy productivity, through options such as the use of fuel cells, anti-fouling coatings to reduce drag, improving hull design, air flotation, propeller design, harnessing wind for propulsion under favourable conditions, and by using renewable energy in ports. As ships have to be self-sufficient while travelling there are already a range of resource-saving initiatives used. For example, most plumbing fixtures are 'low-flow' to minimize the amount of on-board water storage, and the on-board energy use is minimized to reduce the amount of batteries that are needed to provide ongoing electricity.[261] However, a whole system approach to ship design can achieve further efficiencies, as summarized in Table 5.5.

4 Industry Sector Study: Air travel

Improving energy productivity of aircraft

In this era of globalization the demand for air travel is growing rapidly, with average growth in worldwide passenger air travel growing 5 per cent annually, but in some regions, like China,[262] it has been growing at 12 per cent.[263] Air travel uses 11.6 per cent of all energy used in the transport sector,[264] and is responsible for 2 per cent of global greenhouse gas emission, but these emissions could rise by as much as tenfold by 2050 given the growth in this sector.[265] The airline industry is now showing significant interest in

Table 5.5 *Efficiency innovations for shipping*

Innovation	Examples
Fuel cells – natural gas: while still a fossil fuel, a fuel cell using natural gas can result in 50 per cent less greenhouse gas emissions than a diesel engine. Current trials are under way to use fuel cells as auxiliary engines to drive an electric motor, and it is anticipated that they will eventually be able to be used to fully power a ship.[266]	The Oak Ridge National Laboratory and Berkeley cite two studies, one of the 'US Navy design study converting from gas turbine generator to PEM fuel cell with diesel reformer, yielding 30 percent fuel reduction', and another involving, 'replacing medium-speed diesels with molten carbonate fuel cells using natural gas, yielding 17 per cent decrease in fuel use; adding a steam turbine bottoming cycle to the fuel cells boosts system efficiency to 64 per cent.'[267]
Anti-fouling coatings: antifouling coatings can increase fuel efficiency by preventing organisms such as barnacles and weeds adding additional resistance to the ship's progress through the water.[268]	According to International Paint, 'Antifouling coatings provide the shipping industry with annual fuel savings of US$60 billion and reduced carbon dioxide emissions of 384 million tons per year'.[269]
Improving hull insulation: improving hull design can increase the energy efficiency of ships by, on average, 15 per cent.[270]	Increased hull and compartment insulation is another significant energy saver. HVAC requirements are typically the single largest electrical load on ships and are the primary driver for sizing service generators.[271] Installation of fresh air heat exchangers, in combination with tight construction to reduce other leak paths, can improve the efficiency of a ship's HVAC system by as much as 10–15 per cent.
Air flotation: by pumping air through cavities along the bottom of a ship, ships can effectively float on a thin bed of air, rather than water.	Dutch company DK Group is investigating ways in which to reduce the frictional drag of water on large ocean-faring vessels, estimating that fuel consumption can be cut by 15 per cent, while consuming only an additional 1 per cent of the ship's power. The first demonstration ship is being built, and it is predicted that this system would add approximately 2–3 per cent to the total cost.[272]
Advanced impellors: a new impellor design uses a spiral shape to channel water, increasing engine efficiency by 10 per cent.[273]	By attaching an electric motor, the same type of impellors can also generate electricity – for ships equipped with sails, when the wind is sufficient, the impellor may be trailed behind the ship such that its rotation in the water generates electricity which can be stored, or used to power other ship systems.[274]
Renewable energy for ships in port: renewable energy from onshore can be used for essential functions and services, such as lighting on ships while they are in port, potentially avoiding almost all emissions.	Usually ships use on-board power generation by auxiliary diesel engines. In Göteborg Port in Sweden, renewable wind energy is being used to run essential services on ships in port, cutting emissions by 94–97 per cent.

Table 5.5 *continued*

Innovation	Examples
Wind propulsion systems (up to 30 per cent in larger freighters): kites can act as parafoils and provide lift and propulsion to reduce fuel consumption by 10–30 per cent, with a return on the initial US$700,000 investment of 3–5 years.[275]	The *MV Beluga SkySails* is trialling a 320m^2 kite (to a theoretical maximum of 5000m^2). The carbon-fibre rope can be used to steer, permitting use even when sailing at steep angles into the wind.[276]
Wind propulsion systems (up to 70 per cent for small freighters): highly efficient designs are emerging, capable of powering cargo freighters. Wind propulsion systems have been available for more than two decades.	The *Maruta Jaya*, a 63m-long freighter is able to rely on its indosail rig to provide up to 70 per cent of its propulsion, in combination with a diesel-electric engine. The Greenpeace schooner *Rainbow Warrior II* uses an indosail rig, consuming 40 per cent less fuel.[277]

Source: Compiled by TNEP, sources as cited in the table text

developing solutions to reduce energy usage and greenhouse gas emissions. This is because fuel use contributes to around 20 per cent of operating costs,[278] plus the fact that aviation will be included in the EU Emissions Trading Scheme from 2012. Such inclusion will affect over 80 major airlines, of which 35 are headquartered outside the EU.[279] According to the IPCC, while airlines have already achieved significant energy productivity gains in the past decades, still many opportunities exist to further improve this. The IPCC, in 2007, stated that:

> *Passenger jet aircraft produced today are 70 per cent more fuel efficient than the equivalent aircraft produced 40 years ago and continued improvement is expected. A 20 per cent improvement over 1997 aircraft efficiency is likely by 2015 and possibly 40 to 50 per cent improvement is anticipated by 2050.[280] Still greater efficiency gains will depend on the potential of novel designs such as the blended wing body.[281]*

Thus with innovative designs, such as the blended wing body, shown in Figure 5.23, there is potential for aircraft to achieve over 50 per cent energy productivity improvements over the coming decades. A blended wing design approach integrates the engines, wings and the body into a single lifting surface thus improving the aerodynamics and fuel efficiency of aeroplanes. As the IPCC explains:

> *The blended wing body (flying wing) is not a new concept and in theory holds the prospect of significant fuel burn reductions: estimates suggest 20–30 per cent compared with an equivalent sized conventional aircraft carrying the same payload.[282]*

Figure 5.23 *Boeing testing X-48B blended wing body aircraft prototype (1/8th size)*

However, blended wing bodies also accommodate more passengers than conventional aircraft, which further reduces fuel burn per seat – approaching a 40 per cent reduction on a seat-kilometre per litre basis.[283] Figure 5.23 shows the Boeing X-48B prototype of the blended wind body concept, at 1/8th of full size, tested in 2007 at Edwards Air Force Base in California, during the aircraft's fifth flight.[284]

Other than redesigning the aircraft (as in the X-48B), significant progress towards efficiency improvements can be made across the existing fleet through the following whole-of-system approach:

- *Light-weighting through advanced composites*: Lightweight composite materials promise significant weight reductions and fuel efficiency. For instance, the use of advanced composites in the next generation Boeing 787 aircraft reduces fuel consumption by 20 per cent.[285] Light-weighting aircraft for long-haul flights makes their fuel consumption per passenger per kilometre comparable with car fuel efficiency per passenger per kilometre, for instance the Airbus A380 uses less than three litres per passenger per 100 kilometres.[286] This compares well with hybrid-car-level fuel efficiency per passenger per kilometre.
- *Ultra-efficient engine technology*: The ultra-efficient engines used in the blended wing aircraft are more fuel efficient than those traditionally used in aircraft and, as they are installed in a lightweight, blended wing body aircraft, can also be of smaller capacity. A study of various engines in such aircraft showed that using a particular General Electric engine can reduce

fuel consumption by 13 per cent; and that using a particular Pratt and Whitney engine can reduce fuel consumption by 16 per cent.[287] A later study by NASA showed that using the efficient engines can reduce fuel consumption by almost 24 per cent if various aerodynamic refinements were also incorporated.[288]

- *Distributed embedded wing propulsion*: Using boundary layer ingestion engine inlets allows the engines to be buried in the aircraft's fuselage, which can reduce drag and hence can reduce fuel consumption by almost 4 per cent.[289] However, embedded wing propulsion usually suffers from the challenge of the air flow nearest the fuselage being non-uniform and thus applying non-uniform and erratic pressure and velocity to the engine fan, which may then make engine performance unpredictable.[290] Fortunately, this challenge is also addressed by boundary layer ingestion engine inlets and active flow control.

- *Drag reduction*: Boundary layer ingestion engine inlets reduce fuel consumption by: a) reducing the mass and drag associated with having engine pylons; b) reducing the exposed surface area of the engine housing; and c) eliminating drag resulting from the engines and wings interfering with each other's air flow.[291] Overall drag reductions reduce fuel consumption by more than 5 per cent, but the use of the inlets attracts a large engine thrust penalty due to some air flow distortion on the inlet, so the overall reduction in fuel consumption is only 0.4 per cent.[292] This distortion can be overcome by using active flow control, which redistributes the flow near the inlet and also prevents flow separation by allowing a shorter diffuser to be used. The use of boundary layer ingestion engine inlets in combination with active flow control can reduce fuel consumption by 5.5 per cent,[293] although this value does not account for the resulting overall improvement in aircraft aerodynamic performance, and thus is likely to be higher.[294]

- *Air transportation and logistics*: Improvements in the air transportation systems and logistics, chiefly from information technology, are expected to save an additional 5–10 per cent of fuel, both in the air and on the ground.[295] For instance, the traditional aircraft approach towards a runway is done by 'stepping' down rather than a smooth steady descent. This meant that traditionally, at each step, the pilots changed the thrust of the engines. New technology means that airlines can work with air traffic control and airports to create a much smoother descent to the runway, improving fuel efficiency.

- *Alternative fuels (second generation bio-fuels)*: The airline industry is already researching and committing to targets regarding the use of bio-fuels. Newer aircraft like the Airbus are seeking to have a 50 per cent blend fuel approved for use by 2009, and a 100 per cent blend by 2013.[296] A Virgin Atlantic Boeing 747 flew from Heathrow to Amsterdam with one of its four engines using a 20 per cent blend mixed with jet fuel.[297] Emirates Airlines has tested flying from Dubai to San Francisco International Airport using bio-fuels.[298] Air New Zealand recently utilized a bio-fuel blend of 50:50 jatropha for a two hour flight. This is significant because jatropha plants are grown on arid and marginal land and hence do not need to compete for land resources with food production.[299]

When combined, the above aircraft features and improved logistics provide the airline industry with the potential to improve fuel efficiency and reduce greenhouse gas emissions. However, even though significant improvements are possible, the rate of growth of the industry and the risks of rebound effects necessitate that additional alternative strategies are encouraged as well. As the IPCC explains:

> *Introducing efficiencies hitherto not available to operators – efficiencies that result in lower fuel consumption and subsequently lower operating costs – may reduce fares and stimulate traffic and growth beyond that already anticipated based on the forecast demand for air travel. This eventuality cannot be overlooked because the net effect could be an increase in air traffic and consequently an increase in fuel burn and emissions. It is unclear to what extent any additional emissions caused by a rebound effect might offset anticipated reductions in emissions… No studies providing evidence on the existence or size of the rebound effect have been carried out.*[300]

Hence to ensure significant reductions in greenhouse gas emissions, alternatives to air travel are going to be needed, such as videoconferencing and very fast trains. We consider these briefly next.

Avoiding the need to travel by air through videoconferencing

In *Factor Four*, the authors showed that a six-hour videoconference can save some 99 per cent of energy and material resources that would be consumed by the transatlantic trips required to hold the same meeting in a single location.[301] Thus videoconferencing offers significant potential to reduce energy use and greenhouse gas emissions for governments, organizations and businesses for whom air travel is a significant component of their carbon footprint. Since *Factor Four* was published videoconferencing technologies have greatly improved. Video teleconference systems have rapidly evolved from highly expensive proprietary equipment, software and network requirements to standards-based technology that is readily available to the general public at a reasonable cost. Internet protocol-based videoconferencing was developed in the 1990s, and together with video compression technologies made it possible to conduct videoconferences from a personal computer. There is now a plethora of free videoconferencing services, web plug-ins and software available, such as Skype, MSN Messenger, Yahoo Messenger, NetMeeting and SightSpeed which have made this technology available to virtually anyone who owns a computer and has access to the internet. The cost effectiveness and quality of videoconferencing has improved along with broadband networks worldwide, with high-speed internet services making it possible to conduct national and international 'virtual meetings' without the environmental and financial costs of travel.[302]

The potential impact of using videoconferencing is already being realized by many companies and governments; for example:

- Air travel accounts for approximately 50 per cent of Pricewaterhouse Coopers' greenhouse gas emissions.[303] PricewaterhouseCoopers has brought in a comprehensive programme to encourage staff to reduce emissions from transport and where possible use videoconferencing and rail travel instead. From July 2008 to December 2009 PwC were able to show a reduction of over 2000 tons CO_2 from air travel, a financial saving in excess of £2 million.[304]
- The German company Deutsche Telekom and its subsidiary T-Mobile calculated that by conducting over 40,000 videoconferences between 2004 and 2007 they were able to reduce their CO_2 emissions by 7000 tons, mainly through reduced air travel, while also saving 200,000 hours of their employees' time.[305]
- Videoconference calls made in 2005 by the UK Department for International Development (DFID) between its two UK offices and its international field offices, as well as to partners, replaced an estimated 735 meetings, which would have emitted a net total of 303 tons of carbon emissions, with 4084 calls.[306]
- A collection of Swedish companies showed how conference calls enabled them to reduce the travel time for up to half of their employees, saving the companies 10 per cent of their travel budget.[307]
- Vodafone has developed a series of around 200 globally connected video-conferencing units, including six 'lounges', and all local operating companies are outfitted with videoconferencing facilities. Vodafone also has a pre-trip policy requiring travellers to consider videoconferencing as an alternative. As a result, the company saved 17,388 tons of CO_2 emissions in 2007/2008[308] through a 20 per cent reduction in air travel, while the video-conferencing lounges enabled employees to avoid making over 100 trips per month, per site. This provided savings to the company which resulted in a payback period on the investment of less than two months.

Following the success of these global efforts, the Australian government has committed to purchasing and deploying high-definition, large-screen videoconferencing systems at 20 locations throughout Australia. Given their A$280 million domestic airfare bill, the system is expected to provide not only significant reductions in the government's carbon emissions, but also large savings in their public-sector travel costs while increasing productivity. The system, which is the largest of its kind in the public sector worldwide, is expected to take less than a year to be fully installed and will replace a large variety of in-person meetings.[309]

Alternatives to air transport: Fast trains

Finally, there is significant promise for 'very-fast trains' to provide a realistic alternative to air travel, especially between cities that are no more than 500 miles apart.[310] This is important as the IPCC has shown that car and air travel between cities is one of the fastest growing areas of transport energy usage.[311] Paris and London, for instance, are 211 miles apart and the Eurostar fast train is roughly as fast, and slightly more reliable, than flying between the two cities. In the first half of 2008, 92.6 per cent of the Eurostar trips arrived on time or within 15 minutes, compared with just 62.3 per cent of competing short-haul flights. Hence, Eurostar has now captured over 70 per cent of the London–Paris transit market from the airlines.[312] However, Japan, with its high-speed bullet trains, has pioneered this mode of travel, with its bullet trains carrying almost a million passengers a day. According to Lester Brown:

> Japan's high-speed rail network now stretches for 1360 miles, linking nearly all its major cities. One of the most heavily travelled links is the original line between Tokyo and Osaka, where the bullet trains carry 117,000 passengers a day. The transit time of two hours and 30 minutes between the two cities compares with a driving time of eight hours... Although Japan's bullet trains have carried billions of passengers over 40 years at high speeds, there has not been a single casualty.[313]

Building on the experience gained by having the best fast train network in the world,[314] Japan is on the verge of releasing the next generation of fast trains, the 'Hayate' Shinkansen E5 Series, which is due to make its debut on the rail line between Tokyo and Aomori in mid-2011. These new trains are based on the Fastech 360 experimental trains and will be capable of speeds up to 340km/h, while providing greater comfort and safety due to improved car-tilting and new suspension mechanisms. In order to operate safely and efficiently at such speeds, the E5 series trains are designed to experience low drag, which is achieved largely through a combination of: a slender, 15m-long arrow-line shaped nose (a shape that reduces micro-pressure waves in tunnels) on the lead car; a smaller cross sectional area than the earlier series trains; covers over the wheels; and smooth covers between cars.[315] The trains' high operating efficiency is also aided by its lightweight aluminium-alloy-based body. The high amount of noise typically generated by a trains' pantograph (the arm extending from the train's roof that makes contact with the overhead powerlines) is reduced by: using one, rather than two, pantographs per train; a new shape; and by applying noise insulation.[316] This next generation fast train will feature an 18-seater super cabin, dubbed the 'Super Green Car', which will provide similar levels of comfort to that of business class on a plane.[317]

The innovations in fast trains, such as those in the E5 series, are particularly timely because President Obama and Vice President Biden announced on

16 April 2008 a plan for the US to invest significantly in fast trains. The plan includes initiatives to build a new high-speed passenger rail network in 100–600 mile corridors between major cities. It will be funded by the US$8 billion for rail from the economic-stimulus package, as well as another US$1 billion per year requested in the next budget over the next five years, and the administration has already identified ten potential corridors for high-speed rail.[318]

> *With high-speed rail system, we're going to be able to pull people off the road, lowering our dependence on foreign oil, lowering the bill for our gas in our gas tanks... We're going to loosen the congestion that also has great impact on productivity, I might add, the people sitting at stop lights right now in overcrowded streets and cities. We're also going to deal with the suffocation that's taking place in our major metropolitan areas as a consequence of that congestion. And we're going to significantly lessen the damage to our planet. This is a giant environmental down payment.*
>
> US Vice President Joe Biden, 2009[319]

To conclude, aeroplanes still can achieve significant energy efficiency improvements over the next few decades and reduce greenhouse gas emissions per passenger per kilometre. But efforts to reduce greenhouse gas emissions

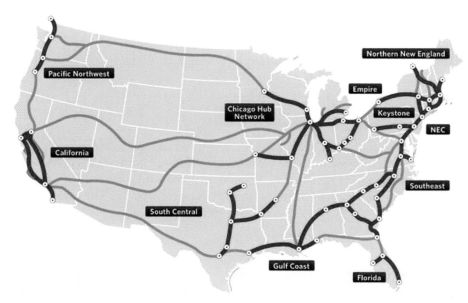

Source: US Department of Transport, Federal Railroad Administration

Figure 5.24 *Proposed high-speed rail corridor designations under the 2009 Obama–Biden High Speed Rail Plan*

through efficiency gains could be undermined by the forecast rapid growth of global air passenger transport. Hence efforts to improve aeroplane energy efficiency should be complemented wherever possible by videoconferencing and very fast trains over coming decades to achieve overall Factor Five energy reductions in this sector.

Notes

1 InterAcademy Council (2007) see 2.5 'Transportation Energy Efficiency'.
2 ibid.
3 InterAcademy Council (2007) see 2.5 'Transportation Energy Efficiency'.
4 ibid.
5 EJ = exaJoules. 1EJ is a million trillion joules.
6 World Business Council for Sustainable Development (2004).
7 World Business Council for Sustainable Development (2004).
8 IPCC (2007) see 'Transport and its Infrastructure'.
9 ibid.
10 IPCC (2007) see 'Transport and its Infrastructure'.
11 World Business Council for Sustainable Development (2004).
12 IPCC (2007) see 'Transport and its Infrastructure'.
13 World Business Council for Sustainable Development (2004).
14 Davidson (2005).
15 Lovins et al (2004); Mathiesen et al (2008).
16 Energy Information Administration (2008) Chp 6, Table 11.
17 InterAcademy Council (2007) see 2.5 'Transportation Energy Efficiency'.
18 InterAcademy Council (2007) see 2.5 'Transportation Energy Efficiency'.
19 Free Range Activism (2008) 'Sheet E10 – Energy and Transport: Re-Designing Our Need to Get Around', www.fraw.org.uk/download/ebo/e10/e10-energy_and_transport.html, accessed 6 April 2008.
20 Energy Information Administration (2008) Chp 6, Table 11.
21 International Energy Agency (IEA) (2007b) p121.
22 ibid, p122.
23 ibid, p122.
24 Lovins (2007b)
25 ibid.
26 Fuel Economy (undated) 'Fuel Economy: Compare Hybrids Side by Side', www.fueleconomy.gov/feg/hybrid_sbs.shtml, accessed 14 April 2009.
27 IPCC (2007) see 'Transport and its Infrastructure', p373.
28 Lovins (2007a)
29 Stasinopoulos et al (2008).
30 Lovins and Cramer (2004).
31 Stasinopoulos et al (2008).
32 ibid.
33 Brylawski and Lovins (1998) p6.
34 Stanisopoulos et al (2008).
35 Lovins et al (2004) p64.
36 ibid.
37 Autoweb (2000) 'Technical Data Audi A8 4.2 Quattro, Long-Wheelbase Version', autoweb.com.au/cms/title_Technical-Data-Audi-A8-42-quattro-longwheelbase-version/A_53168/newsarticle.html, accessed 21 May 2009.

38 Audi (undated) 'Audi A8: Performance', www.audi.com.au/audi/au/en2/
    new_cars/a8_new/a8_new/performance_features.html, accessed 21 May 2009.
39 Walton (2008).
40 Lovins et al (2004) p52.
41 Tyres-Online (2000) 'The Benefits of Silica in Tyre Design – A Revolution in
    Tyre Technology', www.tyres-online.co.uk/technology/silica.asp, accessed
    19 November 2008.
42 HybridCars (2008) 'The Hybrid Car Battery: A Definitive Guide',
    www.hybridcars.com/components.htm, accessed 14 April 2009.
43 HybridCars (2008) 'Regenerative Braking', www.hybridcars.com/components/
    regenerative-braking.html, accessed 14 April 2009.
44 Fuel Economy (undated) 'Fuel Economy: Compare Hybrids Side by Side',
    www.fueleconomy.gov/feg/hybrid_sbs.shtml, accessed 14 April 2009.
45 HybridCars (2008) 'The Hybrid Car Battery: A Definitive Guide',
    www.hybridcars.com/components.htm, accessed 14 April 2009.
46 HybridCars (2008) 'Plug-in Hybrid Batteries: Type Matters',
    www.hybridcars.com/plug-in-hybrids/phev-battery-types.html, accessed 14 April
    2009.
47 Evans (2008).
48 Ohnsman (2008).
49 Schwartzapfel (2008).
50 For further information see Went et al (2008).
51 Kempton et al (2001).
52 Kempton et al (2009).
53 ibid.
54 Went et al (2008).
55 Burns (2009).
56 Kempton et al (2001).
57 Went et al (2008).
58 Kempton and Tomic (2005a).
59 Kempton and Tomic (2005b).
60 Kempton et al (2001).
61 IPART (1999); IPART (2002).
62 Burns (2009).
63 Kempton and Tomic (2005a).
64 Burns (2009).
65 Iogen (undated) 'Lowers GHGs, Increases Energy Security, Helps Build Rural
    Economies', www.iogen.ca/key_messages/overview/m3_reduce_ghg.html,
    accessed 8 April 2009.
66 Stephen Chu cited in PBS (undated) 'e2: Energy – Growing Energy, Episode 4',
    www.pbs.org/e2/episodes/204_growing_energy_trailer.html, accessed 8 April
    2009.
67 Woolsey (2005).
68 RMI (2008).
69 Lovins and Cramer (2004).
70 RMI move (undated) 'Fiberforge®', http://move.rmi.org/markets-in-motion/
    case-studies/automotive/fiberforge-.html, accessed 4 March 2009.
71 Cramer and Brylawski (1996) p2.
72 Fox and Cramer (1997).
73 Lovins and Cramer (2004).
74 Fox and Cramer (1997).

75 Lovins and Cramer (2004).

76 ibid.

77 ibid.

78 Cramer and Brylawski (1996); Moore (1996); Fox and Cramer (1997).

79 Evans (2008) 'BYD Launch World's First Production Plug In Hybrid', *Gizmag*, www.gizmag.com/byd-launch-worlds-first-production-plug-in-hybrid/10573/, accessed 17 May 2009.

80 BYD Auto (undated) 'e6: Features', www.byd.com/showroom.php?car=e6, accessed 17 May 2009.

81 Korzeniewski (2009).

82 This case study is contributed courtesy of Andrea Schaller, Loremo, http://evolution.loremo.com/.

83 Chevrolet (undated) 'Chevy Volt: The Future is Electrifying', www.chevrolet.com/pages/open/default/future/volt.do, accessed 19 May 2009.

84 Strieber (2008).

85 Chamon et al (2008).

86 BTRE (2007).

87 Shrank and Lomaz (2007).

88 Goodwin (2004).

89 Lowe et al (2007) pp13–15.

90 Newman (2006).

91 Richardson and Newman (2008).

92 Newman (2006).

93 Newman (2001).

94 Trubka et al (2008).

95 Edwards and Magarey (2007).

96 Sloman (2006).

97 Frank et al (2004).

98 Medibank Private (2007) 'The cost of physical inactivity. What is the lack of participation in physical activity costing Australia?', www.medibank.com.au/Client/Documents/Pdfs/pyhsical_inactivity.pdf, accessed 15 September 2008.

99 Access Economics (2008) 'The growing cost of Obesity in 2008 – three years on', www.diabetesaustralia.com.au/PageFiles/7830/FULLREPORTGrowingCostOf Obesity2008.pdf, accessed 1 April 2009.

100 Kenworthy et al (1997).

101 Newman (2001).

102 Meyer and Cambridge Systematics Inc. (2008).

103 Australian Bureau of Statistics (2007) '2006 Census QuickStats: West Pennant Hills (State Suburb)', www.censusdata.abs.gov.au/, accessed 15 May 2008.

104 Newman (1998).

105 Kenworthy and Laube (2001).

106 Kenworthy and Laube (1999); Kenworthy and Hu (2002).

107 Hargroves and Smith (2005).

108 The authors wish to thank TNEP research officer Angie Reeves and Andrew Went for their assistance with this part.

109 Diaz (2001).

110 ibid.

111 ibid.

112 Roadpricing (undated) 'Cities', www.roadpricing.biz/, accessed 7 March 2008.

113 Taylor, M. (2008).

114 Environmental Defense Fund (2008) 'Transportation: Congestion Pricing', www.edf.org/page.cfm?tagID=6241, accessed 21 July 2008.

115 Mayor of London – Transport for London (undated) 'About the Congestion Charge: Benefits', www.tfl.gov.uk/roadusers/congestioncharging/6723.aspx, accessed 3 July 2008; Mayor of London – Transport for London (undated) 'About the Congestion Charge', www.tfl.gov.uk/roadusers/congestioncharging/6710.aspx, accessed 3 July 2008.

116 Litman (2006).

117 Mayor of London – Transport for London (undated) 'Congestion Charging', www.tfl.gov.uk/roadusers/congestioncharging/, accessed 7 March 2008.

118 BBC (2008b).

119 BBC (2008a).

120 *The Guardian* (2008).

121 Stockholmf?rsŒket (2006) 'About the Stockholm Trials', www.stockholmsforsoket.se/templates/page.aspx?id=2431, accessed 4 July 2008.

122 Stockholm STAD (2006) p9.

123 Transportation Alternatives (2008) 'Congestion Pricing: International Examples', www.transalt.org/campaigns/congestion/international, accessed 4 July 2008.

124 Stockholmförsöket (2006) 'Referendum on the implementation of congestion charges in the city of Stockholm', www.stockholmsforsoket.se/templates/page.aspx?id=10215, accessed 4 July 2008.

125 Transek (2006) p11.

126 Newman and Kenworthy (2007).

127 Northern Territory Government (2007) 'NT Greenhouse Gas Emissions: Transport', www.nt.gov.au/nreta/environment/greenhouse/emissions/transport.html, accessed 18 March 2009.

128 Union of Concerned Scientists (undated) 'Hybrid Transit Buses: Are They Really green?', www.hybridcenter.org/hybrid-transit-buses.html, accessed 3 April 2009.

129 Newman and Kenworthy (2007); City of Vancouver (COV) (2007).

130 City of Vancouver (COV) (2007).

131 Mygatt (2005); Gemeente Amsterdam (2008).

132 C40 Cities (2008).

133 ibid.

134 Car Free Asia (undated) 'Asia Today', www.carfreeasia.org/today.html, accessed 18 April 2009.

135 ibid.

136 Worldwatch Institute (2008).

137 Newman and Kenworthy (2007).

138 ibid.

139 Light Rail Now (2008) 'CTrain Light Rail growth continues with North East extension', www.lightrailnow.org/news/n_cal_2008-01a.htm, accessed 31 March 2009.

140 Calgary Transit (undated) 'Calgary Transit and The Environment', www.calgarytransit.com/environment/ride_d_wind.html, accessed 31 March 2009.

141 Light Rail Now (2008) 'CTrain Light Rail growth continues with North East extension', www.lightrailnow.org/news/n_cal_2008-01a.htm, accessed 31 March 2009.

142 von Weizsäcker et al (1997) pp128–129.

143 Shaheen and Cohen (2006) p5.

144 Shaheen and Meyn (2002) p12.

145 Shaheen and Cohen (2006) p3.
146 Bicycle Victoria (2009) 'Bike parking at train stations', www.bv.com.au/change-the-world/12251/, accessed 31 March 2009.
147 Newman and Kenworthy (2007).
148 Department of Sustainability and Environment (2006).
149 Bike for All (2006) 'Average speed of a car is just 7mph, says Citroen', www.bikeforall.net/news.php?articleshow=229, accessed 31 March 2009.
150 McAllister (2004).
151 ibid.
152 Lovins et al (2004).
153 JR East Group (2004) 'Development of Environmentally Friendly E231 Series', www.jreast.co.jp/e/environment/pdf_2004/report2004_p06-07.pdf, accessed 17 April 2008.
154 JR East Group (2006) 'Development of the World's First Fuel Cell Hybrid Railcar', JR East Group Press Release, www.jreast.co.jp/e/press/20060401/ accessed 17 April 2009.
155 ibid.
156 World Business Council for Sustainable Development (2004).
157 ibid, p89.
158 ibid, Figure 0.9, p19.
159 Cummins (2006) pp5–7.
160 US Department of Energy (USDOE/OSTI) (2000).
161 ibid, Table 4.1.
162 Bustnes (2005) p1.
163 Lovins et al (2004) Chp 6, p4.
164 Ogburn (2007).
165 ibid.
166 Smith et al (2007) Lecture 8.3.
167 Lovins et al (2004) Chp 6, p5.
168 Ogburn et al (2008).
169 Cummins (2006) pp4, 16, 17, 21, 22, 31.
170 Ogburn and Ramroth (2007).
171 Bridgestone cited in Kenworth Truck Company (2006) pp7–8.
172 Cummins (2006) p4.
173 Robert Bosch GmbH (2004).
174 ibid.
175 Cummins (2006) pp5–7.
176 ibid.
177 Lovins et al (2004) Chp 6, p6.
178 Wood and Bauer (2003) cited in Lovins et al (2004) Chp 6, p6.
179 Cummins (2006) p10; Kenworth Truck Company (2006) pp6,10.
180 Cummins (2006) p12.
181 ibid, pp10–11.
182 Ogburn et al (2008) p9.
183 US Department of Energy (USDOE/OSTI) (2000) pp4–3.
184 Lovins et al (2004) Chp 6, p11.
185 ibid, Chp 6, Figure 6.2, p11.
186 ibid, pp11–13.
187 ibid, p11.
188 Kenworth Truck Company (2006) p7.
189 Cummins (2006) p20.

190 Stodolsky (2002).

191 Lovins et al (2004) Chp 6, Figure 6.2, p11.

192 US Department of Energy (2009) 'Flex-fuel Vehicles', www.fueleconomy.gov/feg/flextech.shtml, accessed 18 April 2009.

193 US Department of Energy (2009) 'How Hybrids Work', www.fueleconomy.gov/feg/hybridtech.shtml, accessed 18 April 2009.

194 World Business Council for Sustainable Development (2004) p174.

195 US Environmental Protection Agency (2006) 'Hydraulic Hybrid – The Most Efficient Lowest Cost Hybrids', www.epa.gov/OMS/technology/420f06043.htm, accessed 5 May 2009.

196 Hybrid Truck.Net (2008) 'Hybrid Utility Truck Technology Update', www.hybridtruck.net/featured/hybrid-utility-truck-technology, accessed 18 April 2009; NextEnergy (2009) 'Developing the Next Generation for Hybrid Vehicles', www.nextenergy.org/successes/case000004.aspx, accessed 18 April 2009.

197 Eaton (undated) 'Series Hybrid Hydraulic', www.eaton.com/EatonCom/ ProductsServices/Hybrid/SystemsOverview/SeriesHydraulic/index.htm, accessed 3 May 2009.

198 Odyne (2009) 'Technology', www.odyne.com/technology.php, accessed 18 April 2009.

199 DW-World (2008) 'Hybrid Engines – The Green Truck Wave', www.blinkx.com/video/hybrid-engines-the-green-truck-wave/ ISFmRxTxkXLfq_aLEmjtjQ, accessed 18 April 2009.

200 Navistar (2008) 'Green Diesel Hybrid™ Demonstrated to California Government Officials', Navistar video, www.greendieseltechnology.com/, accessed 18 April 2009; Alles, D. (2009) 'President Obama Previews First Plug-In Hybrid Electric Utility Truck System Developed by Eaton and EPRI for Southern California Edison', Eaton Corporation Press Release, 19 March 2009.

201 Hybrid Truck.Net (2008) 'Hybrid Utility Truck Technology Update', www.hybridtruck.net/featured/hybrid-utility-truck-technology, accessed 18 April 2009; NextEnergy (2009) 'Developing the Next Generation for Hybrid Vehicles', www.nextenergy.org/successes/case000004.aspx, accessed 18 April 2009.

202 Lovins et al (2004) Chp 6, p14; Kenworth Truck Company (2006) p10.

203 ibid.

204 Cummins (2006) pp4, 24, 26, 28, 31.

205 SC Johnson (2007) 'SC Johnson Environment News', www.scjohnson.com/ Environment/news_detail.asp?art_id=311, accessed 28 March 2009.

206 RMI (undated) 'Wal-Mart's Truck Fleet', *Mobility and Vehicle Efficiency (MOVE) News*, Rocky Mountain Institute.

207 ibid.

208 Wal-Mart (2009) 'Trucking Fleet (image)', http://walmartstores.com/Sustainability/ 7674.aspx, accessed 29 March 2009.

209 *Environmental Leader* (2009c); Wal-Mart (undated) 'Climate and Energy: Trucking Fleet', http://walmartstores.com/Sustainability/7674.aspx, accessed 28 March 2009.

210 UPS (undated) 'UPS adds 50 hybrids to its "green fleet"', http://compass.ups.com/ features/article.aspx?id=968&srch_pos=1&srch_phr=green+fleet&WT.svl= SRCH, accessed 28 March 2008.

211 *Environmental Leader* (2008b).

212 Volvo Trucks, Europe Division (2008) 'Volvo's hybrids for France and England', www.volvo.com/group/usa/en-us/newsmedia/corpnews/NewsItemPage.htm? channelId=3090&ItemID=54372&sl=en-gb, accessed 27 March 2009.

213 *Environmental Leader* (2009b).
214 Corbett and Winebrake (2007).
215 IPCC (2007).
216 World Business Council for Sustainable Development (2004).
217 World Business Council for Sustainable Development (2004) Figure 2.5, p32.
218 Corbett and Winebrake (2007).
219 World Business Council for Sustainable Development (2004).
220 Freight on Rail (2009) 'Useful Facts and Figures', www.freightonrail.org.uk/
    FactsFigures.htm, accessed 9 April 2009; Frey and Kuo (2007a).
221 Kamakaté (2007).
222 Kamakaté (2007) Slides 16–17.
223 Macintosh (2007) pp19–20.
224 Frey and Kuo (2007b).
225 Freight on Rail (2008) 'Useful Facts and Figures', www.freightonrail.org.uk/
    FactsFigures.htm, accessed 2 April 2009; National Transport Commission and
    Rare Consulting (2008) Appendix F, pp51–53.
226 McKinney and Muench (2008) p2.
227 Macintosh (2007) pvii.
228 National Transport Commission and Rare Consulting (2008) p5.
229 Corbett and Winebrake (2007).
230 ISO (2000).
231 National Transport Commission and Rare Consulting (2008) Table 3, p21.
232 Deutsche Bahn (2008) 'Europe's No. 1 in inter-modal transport',
    www.deutschebahn.com/site/nachhaltigkeitsbericht__2007/en/our__products/
    sustainable__logistics/intermodal/intermodal.html, accessed 2 April 2009.
233 Deutsche Bahn (2008) 'Designing Sustainable Logistics',
    www.deutschebahn.com/site/nachhaltigkeitsbericht__2007/en/our__products/
    sustainable__logistics/logistics__strategy/logistics__strategy.html, accessed
    2 April 2009.
234 Deutsche Bahn (2008) 'The train as an alternative',
    www.deutschebahn.com/site/nachhaltigkeitsbericht__2007/en/our__products/
    sustainable__transportation/future/future.html, accessed 2 April 2009.
235 Federal Ministry of Transport, Building and Urban Affairs (2008).
236 Association of American Railroads Policy and Economics Department (2009).
237 CSX (2008) 'Public Private Partnership Brings New GenSet Ultra-Low Emission
    Locomotives to CSX Transportation', CSX Press Release, 27 May 2008.
238 Jochem (2004).
239 Lovins et al (2004).
240 von Weizsäcker et al (1997).
241 Association of American Railroads Policy and Economics Department (2009).
242 Stodolsky et al (2002).
243 Bean (2008).
244 ibid.
245 Jochem (2004).
246 Stodolsky et al (2002).
247 ibid.
248 Association of American Railroads Policy and Economics Department (2009).
249 von Weizsäcker et al (1997) pp121–123.
250 Denver and Rio Grande (undated) 'Freight Cars', http://ghostdepot.com/rg/
    rolling%20stock/freight/freight.htm, accessed 17 April 2009.
251 Xinhua News Agency (2008).

252 Dedicated Freight Corridor Corporation of India Ltd (undated) 'DFC Project', www.dfccil.org/wps/portal/DFCCILPortal, accessed 6 March 2009.
253 Deutsche Bahn (2008) 'Designing Sustainable Logistics', www.deutschebahn.com/site/nachhaltigkeitsbericht__2007/en/our__products/sustainable__logistics/logistics__strategy/logistics__strategy.html, accessed 2 April 2009.
254 Macintosh (2007).
255 Petz (2008).
256 Kleiner (2007).
257 Petz (2008).
258 King et al (2008) Figure 3, p11.
259 Pianoforte (2008).
260 ibid.
261 King et al (2008), pp7–12.
262 IPCC (2007) see 'Transport and its Infrastructure'.
263 World Business Council for Sustainable Development (2002).
264 IPCC (2007) see 'Transport and its Infrastructure'.
265 IPCC (1999) see 'Aviation and the Global Atmosphere'.
266 Kleiner (2007).
267 Interlaboratory Working Group (2000) Appendix C-3.
268 Pianoforte (2008).
269 Brown, J. (2008).
270 Kleiner (2007).
271 King et al (2008) pp7–12.
272 Kleiner (2007).
273 Terhark (2005).
274 Clift (2005).
275 ibid.
276 Kleiner (2007).
277 Petz (2008).
278 ICAO (2006).
279 Reuters (2008).
280 IPCC (1999) see 'Aviation and the Global Atmosphere'.
281 IPCC (2007) see 'Transport and its Infrastructure'.
282 Leifsson and Mason (2005) cited in IPCC (2007) see 'Transport and its Infrastructure'.
283 Lovins et al (2004) Chp 12, p16.
284 NASA (undated) 'Dryden Flight Research Centre: X-48B Blending Wing Body', www.nasa.gov/centers/dryden/research/X-48B/index.html, accessed 15 April 2009.
285 Lovins et al (2004).
286 Airbus (undated) '380 Navigator – Design', http://events.airbus.com/A380/Default2.aspx?ArtId=667, accessed 15 April 2009.
287 Daggett et al (2003a) pp43–44.
288 Daggett et al (2003b) p8.
289 ibid, Chp12, p16.
290 ibid, Chp 12, p17.
291 Lovins et al (2004) Chp 12, p16.
292 Daggett et al (2003b) p21.
293 ibid.
294 Lovins et al (2004) Chp 12, p18.

295 Lovins et al (2004).
296 Marsh (2008).
297 Biello (2008).
298 *Environmental Leader* (2008a).
299 *Environmental Leader* (2009a).
300 IPCC (1999) see 'Aviation and the Global Atmosphere'.
301 von Weizsäcker et al (1997) pp112–114.
302 World Wild Fund for Nature (2009)
303 Institute of Travel Management (2009).
304 ibid.
305 Zero Emission Meeting (undated) 'Examples and Figures', www.zero-emission-meetings.com/content/examples, accessed 15 April 2009.
306 James (2007).
307 Arnfalk (2002).
308 Vodafone (undated) 'Transport', www.vodafone.com/start/responsibility/environment/transport.html, accessed 15 April 2009.
309 ECOS (2009).
310 Brown, L. (2008).
311 IPCC (2007), see 'Transport and its Infrastructure'.
312 Seat 61 (undated) 'London to Paris by Eurostar', www.seat61.com/London-Paris-train.htm, accessed 15 April 2008.
313 Brown, L. (2008).
314 Demerjian (2009).
315 JR East Group (2008).
316 East Japan Railway Company (2005) 'FASTECH 360 High-Speed Shinkansen Test Train to Debut: Running Tests to Start with the Aim of the World's Best Shinkansen Service', East Japan Railway Company Press Release, 9 March 2005.
317 Demerjian (2009).
318 Department of Transportation (undated) 'Federal Railroad Administration: High-Speed Railroad Corridor Descriptions', www.fra.dot.gov/us/content/203, accessed 3 May 2009.
319 Sheppard (2009).

Part II
Making It Happen

Ernst von Weizsäcker

Introduction

Ernst von Weizsäcker

Part I of this book clearly contains the core of the Factor Five message – that 80 per cent improvements in resource productivity are possible and that some leaders are already demonstrating that it can be done. The Sector Studies describe lots of very exciting opportunities, mostly for entire branches of our economies, to become dramatically more resource efficient than is the case today. A somewhat similar message, albeit focused mostly on leading examples of isolated technologies, was also the core of *Factor Four*. There, we had offered 50 examples of a fourfold, or better, increase of energy or resource productivity. In *Factor Four*, we, meaning Ernst von Weizsäcker, Amory Lovins and Hunter Lovins, were hoping and expecting that all this was going to become broadly used and applied. Amory Lovins' ingenious innovation of a car capable of doing 150 miles on a gallon of petrol (about 1.5 litres per 100 kilometres) sounded like an automatic success story for a world wanting more motorization under conditions of dwindling oil resources, and increasing concerns with global warming. But what happened? In America it was the time of the avid expansion of that new fleet of Sport Utility Vehicles (SUVs) and Hummers needing much more fuel than their compact predecessors. Similarly, logistics of produce transport, as highlighted in *Factor Four* through the 'Strawberry Yoghurt' case study, was hoped to become less intensive by a factor of four; however, in reality, the mileage increased. Water-saving devices, the leasing instead of selling of solvents, and the re-use of package containers still remain insignificant niche businesses. And all in all, energy and resource consumption has relentlessly been on the rise during the last 15 years following the first publication of *Factor Four*.

What went wrong? Well, most people would say nothing went wrong, as the world enjoyed an almost unprecedented period of continued growth. China with its absolutely formidable economic expansion served as a power engine for the industrialized countries, helping to curb inflation worldwide by supplying goods and parts of goods at low prices. Energy prices too remained at seductively low levels encouraging not only the SUV fleet in the US, but also the expansion of innovations and habits around the world that consume ever growing amounts of energy. At the same time, a new form of globalized financial capitalism fascinated the world. All in all, there was neither a strong enough economic or emotional reason to put the environment and resource productivity high on the agenda. It was not until the new alarm about global warming, and the soaring prices for oil and many mineral resources, that resource productivity came back into the limelight. We do consider the time of neglect of resource productivity as a dangerous loss of time. Given the challenges outlined in the Introduction, and in line with the reasoning of Nicholas Stern,[1] we feel we cannot afford another period of 15 years of waiting or timid steps. For purely economic reasons, the countries of the world need to actively accelerate the transition to a sustainable society. We as authors therefore want to explore this time what can be done politically to *make sustainable development really happen*. Yet 'this time' is also the time of a major economic crisis during which not everybody is motivated to look ahead to unknown territory. Our exploration will therefore have to include some considerations persuading such hesitating people that the resource productivity road is actually also a great opportunity for overcoming the recession, as many are now realizing.

Chapters 6 and 7 offer an overview of instruments proven to be useful in environmental policy, as well as the increase of resource productivity. However, we cannot fail to observe in the end that economic growth and the 'rebound effect' (Chapter 8) have been much stronger than all steering instruments, and as a result energy consumption, greenhouse gas emissions, water and minerals extraction and land conversion has grown and grown despite laudable efforts to improve resource productivity. We see only very minor chances of reverting this deleterious trend by the use, however intensified, of the set of instruments outlined. If we want the transformative changes that appear to be necessary for stabilizing climate and stopping the destruction of biodiversity, we have to go a few major steps further. We shall be addressing this big challenge in Chapters 9, 10 and 11.

6

Regulation: The Visible Hand

Ernst von Weizsäcker

Pollution control: The success story of state intervention

During the 1960s and 1970s, environmental pollution rose to intolerable levels in most industrialized countries. Pollution was broadly seen as a failure of the market, or of the 'Invisible Hand' (an expression coined by Adam Smith, the arch-father of the market economy, to describe the action of the market acting without government intervention). This view led environmental activists to call for laws and other action by the 'Visible Hand' of the state. It was this 'critical of the markets' mindset that led to a large body of environmental legislation, essentially in all OECD countries. As it turned out, pollution control legislation and enforcement from that era became a spectacular success story. After 20 to 30 years, many of these initial environmental problems had largely disappeared. The air in Pittsburgh, in Osaka, in the Ruhr district got cleaner, and the same happened with the water of the Ohio, Thames and Rhine rivers and of lakes suffering from eutrophication and pollution not long ago.

Earlier analyses, for example by Edward Mishan[2] or the authors of *Limits to Growth*,[3] had suggested that environmental degradation could only be halted by a transition to a non-growth society. Hence, it was quite a pleasant surprise that pollution control regulation brought pollution levels down, and with hardly any noticeable reduction of economic growth. Japan was particularly successful in this regard. After the disasters of mercury and cadmium pollution, killing fish, fishermen and fish-eating communities, and severe air pollution in the industrial agglomerations of Tokyo and Kansai, strict regulation was introduced making polluting processes illegal or very expensive. The heavy metals calamities disappeared within a few years. For SO_2 and NO_x the process took some 15 years.[4] Similarly, waste laws in most industrialized countries ended the earlier anarchy of wild waste dumps and gradually introduced safe waste treatment, recycling and waste-avoiding technologies, although there are still some embarrassing exceptions to the rule.

Different countries had different legal approaches to pollution control. In the US, most of the basic legislation was enacted during the 1970s, among them the Clean Air Act, the Clean Water Act, the Resource Conservation and Recovery Act, the Toxic Substances Control Act, the Endangered Species Act and, perhaps most importantly, the National Environmental Policy Act (NEPA), which was signed into law on January 1, 1970. The Environmental Protection Agency (EPA) was also created in 1970, and was entrusted with powers to enforce legislation. In 1980, after the Love Canal chemical disaster, President Carter signed into law the Superfund legislation. These moves on the national level were accompanied by a considerable amount of state legislation, notably California's stricter air standards. Thousands of court cases helped give respect to the legislation but also created a growing frustration with industry about what was seen as 'red tape' harassment.

In the European Community, as it was then called, the approach was somewhat different. Except for some early legislation in France, the Netherlands and Germany, most environmental standards were defined by European Directives, which were often phased in over long periods, and which had to be translated into national laws by all member countries. The European Commission monitored the legislation and from time to time sued member countries for non-compliance at the European Court. Factories and other commercial operations had to apply for licence to operate. Once local authorities saw the relevant standards met by the applicant, installations were approved, and from then on companies had little to fear from litigation. Although the industry often complained about unreasonable standards, it was acknowledged that this system was easier to deal with than the American habit of shear endless litigation. Also, some early warning, notably in Japan, helped industry to anticipate future standards and adjust production accordingly. The command and control approach to pollution control was actually rational from the point of view of the state's mandate for public health and for protecting the environment. It was attractive both for environmental pressure groups and for politicians as it demonstrated determination to act and promised quick results. In the context of this book, it needs to be stated that such command and control legislation did little to increase energy and resource efficiency. As a matter of fact, Sumikura calls the late 1970s the 'years of optimism' because at that time the pollution nightmares had mostly disappeared, and Japan in 1976 proudly presented its success to the OECD.[5] Some disappointment set in when Japan, like other countries, realized that energy and material efficiency were much less susceptible to direct regulation than pollution control.

The success stories of pollution control by direct state intervention were essentially restricted to the industrialized countries. The developing countries

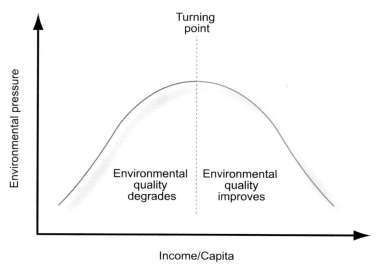

Source: Based on Grossman and Krueger (1991)[6]

Figure 6.1 *Stylized Kuznets environmental curve*

were generally of the view that they could not afford costly pollution control measures. When the rich countries succeeded in reducing pollution to low and manageable levels, the new paradigm of the environmental Kuznets curve was born (Figure 6.1) showing that typically countries start clean and poor, then industrialize and become prosperous but dirty, and then they can afford costly pollution control measures and within some 20 more years end up being rich and clean. Clearly this paradigm is extremely tempting for the developing countries – and for polluting industries – as it serves as a perfect excuse not to incur the cost of pollution control and the respective legislation unless and until enough wealth has been amassed to pay the bills.

The success stories of pollution control also supported the idea that the state should maintain the chief responsibility for the environment through direct regulation. Ideas of market instruments such as tradable permits for water and air pollutants entered the scene rather late. They became popular during the 1980s, as part of a general pro-market mindset. But their function remained that of an instrument to reach the state-defined goal just a bit more swiftly and perhaps at lower cost.

Energy efficiency regulation

Energy efficiency first became a public concern after the oil price shock of 1973. In response, several countries began addressing the wasteful use of energy in home heating systems. Sweden took the lead by introducing the Swedish Building Norm (Svensk Byggnorm) of 1975, which defined maximum U-values (heat losses in watts per square metre and degree Kelvin) for four different parts of houses, ranging from $0.2W/m^2K$ for the roof, to 2.0 for the windows (frame and glass). As a comparison, standard single-glazed windows have a U-value of 5.6, double-glazed windows of 2.8. The 1975 norm for windows therefore required considerably lower heat losses than were achievable by just double-glazed windows! In later years, restrictions on allowed U-values were lowered further, making for even more ambitious requirements. Elsewhere, European architects and physicists were able to cut energy losses ever further. The most widespread design method is perhaps the German Passivhaus (see Chapter 2), more or less equivalent to the Swiss Minergie house. Neither of these advances has as yet been made binding; but they served the purpose of encouraging lawmakers to step up mandatory requirements.

Indeed, the US, some EU countries, China, Japan and Australia have all gone down the path of better regulation for higher levels of energy efficiency in improved building standards to some degree.[7] In particular the UK government's *Code for Sustainable Homes* legislates binding regulations for energy reduction with staggered targets: 25 per cent more efficient by 2010, 44 per cent by 2013 and 100 per cent, or zero emissions, by 2016. Now passed into law, the code sets minimum standards for both energy and water efficiency. In addition, the UK government has agreed that any home achieving a Level 6 sustainability rating will be exempt from stamp duty.[8] In France, the government has committed to ensuring that all new buildings should 'produce more energy than they consume' by 2020.[9] In China, a new building construction statute was introduced in 2006 including requirements for mandatory energy efficiency for buildings. The Designing Standard for Energy Conservation in Civil Building requires construction contractors to use energy-efficient building materials and to adopt energy-saving technology in heating, air-conditioning, ventilation and lighting systems in civil buildings. Energy efficiency in building construction has also been written into China's 11th Five-Year Plan (2006–2010).[10]

In the US, much of the command and control legislation on energy efficiency is left to state and local governments, and overall has been quite ineffective. Renewable Portfolio Standards have been in place since the late 1970s, and some were later amended. In Massachusetts and California a 'least-cost best-fit' rule required utilities to pursue the cheapest alternative for providing additional supply that is possible at any given point in time – helping to encourage the provision of efficiency, or 'negawatts',[11] which is often the cheapest option by far.[12] To make profits less dependent on energy sales, a variety of states require a certain amount of demand to be met with efficiency, and California provides financial incentives to utilities allowing them to charge higher rates per kilowatt-hour, for meeting this goal, while fining them if they fail. Also electricity rates for private consumers follow a progressive path, discouraging households from overuse. In Connecticut, energy efficiency and demand-response measures are helping to provide two-thirds of the state's expected demand in the next couple of years. Maryland is now requiring a 15 per cent reduction in energy demand by 2015. Minnesota and Illinois have annual improvement requirements of 1.5 per cent and 2 per cent respectively. Connecticut's commitment to efficiency has been made clear with a 300 per cent increase in state investments in the sector. Around a third of US states are following California's lead in mandating reductions in greenhouse gas emissions, most of them incorporating funds for energy efficiency programmes to help them accomplish these goals. And it is price effective for them to be doing so, costing about 5 cents less a kWh to save that amount of electricity than to buy it from a pre-existing power plant, let alone build a new one.

These are somewhat haphazardly collected examples of legislators' activity. We don't claim anything like completeness, and in later chapters we argue that this kind of legislation is quite vulnerable to the rebound effect (Chapter 8). But it is worth knowing that politicians at different levels do have a chance of influencing technology and behaviour by direct legislation.

Command and control legislation also has a significant history in the automobile sector. In 1975, the US adopted the first CAFE standards (Corporate Average Fuel Economy). The measure was meant to increase fuel efficiency to a level of 27 miles per gallon (mpg) for passenger cars. Light trucks were not regulated in the beginning and enjoyed tax privileges over passenger cars. This was a critical weak point in the law. During the 1980s gasoline prices tumbled and this loophole was exploited to the fullest. It led to the development and wide adoption of sport utility vehicles (SUVs) which had higher gas consumption than many average pre-CAFE passenger cars. The next wave of energy efficiency cars came only when gas prices went up again, since 2005, with hybrid cars that could achieve 50mpg taking the lead.

A somewhat different approach to command and control legislation on energy efficiency was taken by Japan with its 'Top Runner Programme'. It was developed in 1999, on top of the existing Energy Conservation Law and applied to an increasing number of vehicles, appliances and other machinery. Instead of setting a minimum efficiency requirement for the year of adoption, the government first identified the most efficient model on the market and then stipulated that the efficiency of this 'top runner' model should become the standard within four to eight years. By the target year, each manufacturer must ensure that the weighted average of the efficiency of all its products in that particular category is at least equal to that of the top runner model. This approach eliminates the need to ban specific inefficient models from the market. At the same time, manufacturers are made accountable and, perhaps most importantly, they are stimulated to voluntarily develop products with an even higher efficiency than the top runner model. China made energy efficiency a state goal in 2006 with the adoption of the 11th Five-Year Plan that aims at increasing national energy productivity by 20 per cent during those five years, a bold commitment that will not be entirely fulfilled, in part because China increasingly exports energy-intensive supplies to countries that are trying to reduce their direct carbon footprints.

Banning or discouraging wasteful technologies

Another, even more direct command and control approach to increasing energy productivity is the banning of wasteful technologies, most widely known for the ban of incandescent light bulbs. Cuba was the first country to do this. In 2007 all incandescent light bulbs were exchanged, and further imports and sales were completely banned. In the US, the pace has been much slower. California will phase out the use of incandescent bulbs by 2018 as part of the bill of October, 2007. The federal Clean Energy Act of 2007 effectively bans incandescent light bulbs that produce 310–2600 lumens (roughly 40–150 watts), with some functional exceptions. Canada wants to phase out incandescent light bulbs by 2012 but goes a step beyond that by requiring the use of light emitting diode (LED) lamps in certain functions including traffic lights, meaning that even compact fluorescent lamps are not allowed for these purposes. The EU joined the trend by deciding in December 2008 to ban sales of incandescent light bulbs in four consecutive annual steps, beginning 1 September 2009 with bulbs of 100 watts and more, then down to 75, 60 and 25 watts, respectively. Similar moves exist in Australia and New Zealand. A next wave of bans may happen with plasma TV screens, which are much more energy intensive than ordinary screens.

Banning is the harshest measure. A softer approach is energy performance labelling and in some cases rules for public procurement to select the best performers only. A comprehensive system for energy performance in appliances has been introduced in the US under the name of the 'Energy Star'. It was and is voluntary but in times of high electricity cost has gained considerable traction. Moreover, efficiency-oriented public procurement (see below) will phase out low-efficiency office equipment and household appliances. The energy demand in residential buildings accounts for 25 per cent of the final energy needs in the EU, with electricity used for domestic appliances in households showing the sharpest increase. The EU is responding to this issue by requiring energy labelling of household appliances and to demand minimum efficiency requirements.[13] In the EU, industrial norms, which tend to be obligatory, often have components of energy performance. In Germany, it is the DIN Institute adopting DIN standards. The DIN EN 15.000 series is all about efficiency, notably in the building sector. Frequent updating serves to keep pace with technological progress, in line with the 'best available technology' principle developed for pollution control.

Responding to rising energy consumption from electronics and appliances, the Japanese government has set strict new energy-saving targets, focusing on 18 types of consumer and business electronics. Home and office air-conditioners, for instance, must be redesigned to use 63 per cent less power by 2008. The targets have sparked a frenzy among electronics makers, who are producing record numbers of energy-saving consumer products.[14] Since the late 1980s, China has developed a comprehensive programme of energy efficiency standards and labelling for household appliances.[15] Energy efficiency standards in China are currently below global best practice, suggesting that there is room for improvement. Where China is leading it is creating significant expert success stories. For instance, China is already the world's largest manufacturer of energy-efficient compact fluorescent lamps, accounting for an estimated 80 per cent of global output. The export industry is booming with sales around the two billion mark.

Water purification and re-use

In the case of water, pollution control and efficiency measures are mutually related and enjoy synergies. In the wake of the heavy river and lake pollution during the 1960s and 1970s, European countries introduced increasingly strict laws with respect to water pollution, mostly harmonized by EU directives. One of the strictest directives was the 1983 EU Drinking Water Directive 98/83/EC. To assure the safety of drinking water everywhere in the EU, the Drinking Water Directive (DWD) sets standards for the most common substances ('parameters') that can be found in drinking water. In the DWD a total of 48 microbiological and chemical parameters must be monitored and tested regularly. Strict drinking water standards define the water quality in the pipe system of populated areas. Drinking water suppliers, extracting their water from rivers, reservoirs, lakes and groundwater, served as a strong lobby for ever more ambitious water purification standards so that the water extracted was essentially unpolluted. In effect, wastewater treatment and water purification are now so effective that water has become a perfectly recyclable commodity. The water of the river Rhine, flowing from Switzerland through France and Germany and reaching the North Sea in the Netherlands, now travels through civilization an average of ten times, which may be interpreted as a tenfold increase of water *efficiency*.

In the urban water sector, most urban water utilities are simply required in their statutory requirements and by regulation to ensure supply of water and maximize the financial return from providing it. In other words water utilities, under current regulations, are required to maximize financial return and their main way of achieving this is by selling more water.[16] They therefore have no incentive to help their customers use water more efficiently. As is well known from Californian electric utilities, smart regulation can decouple profits from sales – they are rewarded for helping their customers use electricity more efficiently. The benefit lies in part in saving the capital cost of building new power plants. The analogy for water is the delay or abandoning of costly new reservoirs or other supply installations. So it should be the case that a least-cost strategy of water savings can be installed.

Public procurement

One way of influencing development towards sustainable development is public procurement. The public purchasing power can drive markets to a considerable extent. This can have a major impact on markets of buildings, goods and services. The most widespread programme using this purchasing power was developed in Japan, as the 'Green Purchasing Network', created during the year of adoption of the Kyoto Protocol, 1997. It includes a large number of public authorities but also private firms, all entering a commitment of green procurement whenever it can be done at tolerable costs. Later, an international Green Purchasing Network was created and is supported by catalogues, updated each year, of products that are recommended for green procurement. ICLEI, the International Council of Local Environmental Initiatives, with a membership of more than 1000 large and small cities, in 2004 launched 'Procura+' a sustainable procurement campaign with a systematic exchange of experience, sources of supplies and so on.[17] Also the European Union is strongly supporting public procurement and has issued a handbook.[18] Furthermore, the Obama administration and many other countries are supporting such efforts, although the effects so far on energy and resource efficiency are hard to assess.

Cyclical society: The modern form of waste legislation

For more than a hundred years, cities and agglomerations of the world have used waste disposal services to keep streets and cities clean. The waste was typically dumped somewhere in the wider vicinity of the cities. Since the rise of modern environmental policy, unregulated waste dumps were made illegal, and technologies were developed to burn or otherwise detoxify the waste. Sewage sludge was offered, often sold, to agriculture as fertilizer, until health authorities, farmers and consumers began to worry about heavy metals getting into the food chain and human kitchens. This led to mandatory sludge incineration in many countries. It was not until the late 1980s that some countries, notably Germany and Japan, began to redefine waste as secondary raw materials that should be recycled. In Germany, packaging wastes were used as a forerunner, demonstrating that a separate collection system (the 'Green Dot' system) was capable of recycling some 70 per cent of the raw materials used.

The legal basis, adopted in 1991, was the Packaging Regulation (Verpackungsverordnung). It was followed in 1996 by the Recycling and Waste Act (Kreislaufwirtschafts- und Abfallgesetz) establishing a hierarchy of 'avoiding – re-using – safe removal'. Safe removal outside industry was concretized by the Technical Instruction Municipal Waste (TA Siedlungsabfall) of 2005, obliging municipalities to burn all remaining waste in incinerators of highest available air pollution control. In Japan, similar legislation was adopted in 2001, the Law for the Promotion of the Effective Utilization of Resources (LPEUR). It is said to have been inspired by the German law and was accompanied by the Home Appliances Recycling Law (HARC) and other specific legislation. The whole set of laws stands under the general '3R' principle:

reduce – re-use – recycle. The ultimate if idealistic aim is to recycle everything, leaving nothing to waste dumping.

Based on German and Japanese experiences, China in late 2008 adopted the Circular Economy Promotion Law, the first in the world using the term 'circular economy' in its title. The Law quotes the Japanese terms of reduction, re-use and recycling[19] and applies them to activities in the processes of resources exploitation, production, distribution and consumption. The Law swiftly entered into force, in January 2009, symbolizing the government's determination to move the country to a new and greener stage of development. The circular economy is being implemented at three levels: 1) enterprises, 2) industrial parks, and 3) the regional level, involving all the sectors ranging from resource exploitation, production, distribution and consumption. The circular economy at the company level is referred to as 'small circulation'; at the level of ecological industrial parks (modelled after the Kalundborg industrial park in Denmark) it is called 'medium circulation', and at the regional level it is 'big circulation'. The latter includes resource and energy cascades and efficiency at company levels and eco-friendly, resource-efficient lifestyles at the consumer's end. Product labelling helps consumers to judge indirect resource consumption. Also, the Circular Economy Promotion Law was mandated in the mentioned 11th Five-Year Plan, and motivated by the steep increase since 2000 of world resource prices, which analysts linked to steeply rising demand from China.

The needed paradigm shift will require more than regulation

All examples of direct regulation, except the ones on water purification and re-use, fall far short of bringing countries close to a factor of five of resource productivity improvements. Japan, arguably the most advanced country on energy efficiency legislation with its long history since the mid 1970s of phasing out energy-intensive industries, and with its more recent Top Runner Programme, is still unhappy at not meeting its own commitments in the context of the Kyoto Protocol and is still struggling with its uncomfortable dependence on imports of oil and other raw materials. Command and control legislation, of which we featured only a very small sample, typically addresses efficiency of specified goods or services. It does nothing to reduce the quantity of use of such goods and services. Direct regulation of resource efficiency is particularly vulnerable to what shall be described in Chapter 8 as the rebound effect, or the 'Khazzoom-Brookes Postulate', which highlights that efficiency gains tend to encourage additional consumption of the respective goods, leaving little or nothing for the environment. For a detailed discussion see Chapter 8. Direct regulation, or the Visible Hand, may be able to enforce the phase-out of inefficient methods and tools. But if we also want to influence consumptive behaviour we had better consider instruments addressing the quantity of consumption of goods. 'Economic instruments' can help in this regard, making it reasonable both for industry and for consumers to save resources not only by more efficient products and procedures but also by reducing unnecessary consumption.

Notes

1   Stern (2007).
2   Mishan (1967).
3   Meadows et al (1972).
4   Sumikura (1998).
5   ibid, p246.
6   Grossman and Krueger (1991).
7   The Insulation Council of Australia and New Zealand (2006) 'ICANZ applauds ACT 5-Star decision', ICANZ Press Release, 20 February 2006.
8   BBC (2006).
9   Deutsche Well (2007).
10   IPCC (2007) see 'Policies, Instruments and Co-operative Arrangements'.
11   'Negawatts' is a term coined by Amory Lovins.
12   Lubber (2008).
13   European Commission (undated) 'Energy Efficiency', http://ec.europa.eu/energy/demand/legislation/domestic_en.htm, accessed 10 April 2008.
14   Faiola (2006).
15   Lin (2002).
16   Dovers (2008).
17   ICLEI (2009).
18   European Communities (2004).
19   In Chinese, the term of 'recycling' is translated into 'resourcization'. It means make wastes as new resources, which is based on old Chinese traditions.

7

Economic Instruments for the Environment, for Efficiency and for Renewable Energies

Ernst von Weizsäcker

Voluntary commitments

The main conclusion drawn in Chapter 6 was that although direct state regulation has been successful in achieving quick results in pollution control, it has largely failed to influence the growing levels of resource consumption, to date. There may be much scope for improved direct regulation on resource productivity, but there is also a need to enhance the role of indirect, elegant, sometimes voluntary, not so intrusive and yet effective, instruments – most of which are called 'economic instruments'. This chapter begins by summarizing some voluntary commitments, environmental auditing and environmental management systems. Responding mostly to public feelings, in some cases also to dissuade the state from adopting binding rules, private firms since the early 1970s have developed an impressive array of voluntary commitments for good environmental stewardship and socially proactive conduct. Such commitments commonly run under the name of corporate social responsibility, or CSR.[1] It is not surprising that firms that have faced public criticism over a range of issues, such as Shell, Nike, McDonald's or Wal-Mart, are now among the most visible proponents of CSR and environmental sustainability, as shown in the Sector Studies in Part I. Some say this is to divert attention from dirty business activities,[2] but if such efforts lead to measurable changes, the motive question becomes less important.

The challenge of extending the significant Factor Five improvements outlined in the Sector Studies in this book is that a focus on CSR, or 'do-goodery' as McKibben calls it, however sincerely motivated, has not automatically led to significant advances in resource productivity or overall reductions in resource consumption. CSR has been shown to be useful in identifying and eliminating damaging practices, in cultivating high levels of innovation and creativity around environmental and social challenges, and indeed to arrive at some additional resource efficiency both onsite and in the supply chain. Among the earliest to emphasize the importance of resource productivity was the World Business Council for Sustainable Development (WBCSD) when introducing the term 'eco-efficiency' as early as 1992,[3] and making it one of its prime goals. In the 1999 book *Natural Capitalism*, Paul Hawken, Amory Lovins and Hunter Lovins go many steps further and suggest that not only is a revolutionary increase of resource efficiency possible and profitable, but also that it essentially needs courageous business leaders to drive such a process in order for it to become a widespread reality.[4] However, for all the excellent research and formulations characterizing 'natural capitalism', in 2009, some ten years later, the worldwide reality unfortunately still speaks a different language. The resource intensity of GDP globally is only slowly receding (and even increasing in some of the rapidly developing countries), and absolute resource consumption keeps rising even in the rich countries (see Chapter 8). Looking at business practice across the world, it is clear that in the absence of external signals and incentives for a systematic and long-term strategy of resource productivity, CSR and commitments of individual companies will fall far short of the significant transformation needed.

More or less the same can be said about environmental auditing following well-defined rules, laid down in the EU in the EMAS Directive (EMAS for Environmental Management and Auditing Scheme), and internationally in the ISO 9011 Guidelines for quality and/or environmental management systems auditing. Such guidelines cannot do more than assess the organization's performance against criteria that have been set by the organization, with regard to complying with legislation regulations, and perhaps other 'beyond compliance' internal motivations. With a high variability in whether organizations just aim for legislative and regulatory compliance versus transformative improvements, it cannot be assumed that auditing will necessarily lead to anything like a doubling, let alone a fivefold increase of resource productivity. Rather, it is a tool that can help organizations meet such goals if they choose to. This leads us to environmental management systems (EMSs), which have become a popular management tool for companies to address the environmental impact of their activities, and a vehicle to drive company performance beyond regulatory compliance. Just theoretically, it is possible for individual firms to set and achieve internal goals towards Factor Five improvements; however, appropriate regulation, notably in terms of economic instruments, will be needed to increase the commercial viability of such noble management strategies. EMSs have evolved over the last two decades primarily in response to regulatory pressure for minimum environmental performance, including the voluntary ISO 14001 standard[5] released in 1996 and updated in 2004.[6] As a formal,

Table 7.1 *Observed benefits that are influencing the uptake of EMS worldwide*

Benefit	Description
Streamlined operations	Companies who adopt an EMS can streamline their business operations with regard to consumption of water, energy and resources, which may reduce their costs and improve their overall financial performance.
Self-regulation	Industry take-up of EMSs can pre-empt or dampen demand for new domestic regulations – a form of self-regulation grounded largely on business terms.[7]
Regulatory stability	Firms from countries with relatively high levels of adoption can promote the use of the standards in territories where they invest or set up factories, resulting in a global standardization of expectations.[8]
Reduced reporting	Companies may obtain exemption from otherwise applicable regulatory environmental monitoring requirements.
Improved reporting	Companies can use a common language to demonstrate their environmental performance to consumers and clients, potentially improving stakeholder satisfaction.
Tendering opportunities	Companies may be ineligible to tender for work as suppliers or contractors unless they are certified, or may receive preferential treatment if they do.
Improved public image	The presence of an EMS can assist an organization to demonstrate that it is responsible and considerate of environmental issues.
Brand development	Databases of certified organizations can be accessed online, and international entities promote the use of the standard within their member organizations.

Source: Compiled by The Natural Edge Project, sources as noted within the table text

procedural and process-based management system, ISO 14001's overarching principle of 'Plan, Do, Check, Act' is based on four assumptions:

1   Pollution is essentially a wasted resource.
2   Firms can self-regulate rather than just relying on government regulations to mitigate pollution.
3   Appropriate management systems can lead to desired outcomes such as improved environmental performance.
4   Third party auditing provides credibility and creates incentives for firms to follow through on their intentions.

The benefits from EMS may be summarized and categorized as described in Table 7.1. Of course, there are also many obstacles, barriers and limitations to using EMS for a dramatic increase of resource productivity, as outlined in Table 7.2.

Most global firms rely on a complex supply chain and have limited influence on its resource productivity. Transaction costs will invariably increase, at least in the short term, when significant changes to requirements for suppliers are planned. International competition from countries subsidizing or at least tolerating wasteful practices can make even very reasonable efficiency plans

Table 7.2 *Barriers to EMS being applied for transformational change*

Barrier	Description
Reactionary rather than proactive	An EMS may be reactionary, driven by external pressures rather than strategic planning by the organization itself, losing opportunities through low levels of investment of capital and attention paid to the system.
Avoiding more aggressive regulation	The underlying motivation for adopting firm-based global environmental standards may be to pre-empt more aggressive environmental regulation, and continue to deliver 'minimum practice'.
Resourcing aimed at just compliance	Resourcing may be specifically aimed, at best, at maintaining ISO 14000 compliance requirements, setting tokenistic objectives and targets leading to marginal changes.[9]
Lack of leveraging savings	Savings generated through implementation of the EMS may be used for investor dividends or in other company areas, rather than being invested in other, more capital-intensive operational improvements.
Lack of budget for implementation and review	Organizations may not provide sufficient human and financial resources to their EMS audit function for it to fulfil a role of evaluating and developing improvements in systems of environmental management and performance.[10]
Increasing number of stages models, tools, techniques, schemes, standards	Company resources may be taken up with assessing and choosing between the emerging models, tools, techniques, schemes and standards, restructuring and reporting, rather than focusing on operations and opportunities for improvement.[11]
Difficulty in measuring achievements	Some targets such as protecting specific species, or increased environmental awareness may be difficult to measure. Others may be time consuming and expensive to analyse, resulting in a reluctance to seek improvements.
EMS lock-in	An EMS may initially produce improvements in environmental performance, but may also constrain organizational focus to only looking for improvements within present production systems, rather than exploring for superior innovations that are more radical.[12]

Source: Compiled by The Natural Edge Project, sources as noted within the table text

futile or unprofitable.[13] Only a few examples exist, so far, of companies entering a major commitment towards enhanced resource productivity and renewable energy sourcing, such as those presented in Part I. Wal-Mart is an example because of its singularly high impact as one of the biggest players in the world. In 2005, Wal-Mart announced its business sustainability strategy to dramatically reduce the company's impact on the global environment and become, 'the most competitive and innovative company in the world'[14] – a transformational vision for a company with 1.6 million employees in more than 6000 stores worldwide and with 60,000 suppliers. In 2005, CEO Lee Scott committed Wal-Mart to three far-reaching goals:

1   To source 100 per cent of electricity from renewable energy.
2   To create zero waste.
3   To sell products that sustain natural resources and the environment.

The Vice President and Senior Director of Corporate Strategy and Business Strategy were chosen to lead the sustainability strategy, recognizing the need to keep environmental improvement tightly coupled with business value and profitability.[15] Understanding that a large part of the potential for environmental improvement exists within Wal-Mart's supply chain, Wal-Mart engaged in a 'Green Supply Chain Initiative', in cooperation with the US-based Environmental Defense Fund (EDF), a non-profit organization.[16] Led by EDF, the initiative is aimed at working with individual suppliers and manufacturers on energy saving and other issues in conjunction with China's trade and government leadership, in addition to other US and European retailers in future, covering another 20,000 factories. There are significant cost incentives for Wal-Mart to focus on its Chinese stores, as according to a forecast by Wal-Mart, just from its plan to reduce 5 per cent of packaging materials by 2013, the company would save about US$3.4 billion itself, and save over US$11 billion for its global supply chain. Wal-Mart's focus is also in line with goals already set by the Chinese government in water and air pollution as well as energy use.

Wal-Mart will gradually impose higher environmental and social standards on its 20,000 suppliers and sub-contractors in China (from which it imports US$15 billion annually)[17] to build up a more environmentally and socially responsible global supply chain. Under Wal-Mart's new supplier agreement, cooperating Chinese factories are asked to certify compliance with local laws and regulations on air emissions, wastewater discharges and its management of toxic substances and hazardous waste disposal. EDF and Wal-Mart have also announced a partnership to develop strategies and to monitor Wal-Mart's efforts to reduce plastic shopping bag waste by an average of one-third per store from 2008 levels by 2013, and in 2008 Wal-Mart announced that it would start tightening controls on its Chinese suppliers by requiring them to meet tougher quality standards or face losing the retailer's business.[18]

The pressures on Chinese and other suppliers have certainly helped to enhance the interest in EMS and ISO 14000 certification, and Wal-Mart is not alone. Otto Versand, Germany, Marks and Spencer, Britain, and Japanese retailers have added to the change of attitude among Chinese supply companies. Researchers in America found in 2007, that more than half of the 74 largest firms in eight retail and industrial sectors impose environmental requirements on their domestic and foreign suppliers.[19] In China, the number of environmentally certified enterprises has been growing exponentially. A study by Hong Kong and Shanghai researchers of 128 facilities in Beijing, Shanghai and Guangzhou concluded that the main drivers for certification were reported to be: 1) ensuring regulatory compliance, 2) enhancing the firm's reputation, and 3) improving environmental performance, in that order.[20] In the context of Factor Five, ordinary compliance, even excellence will not suffice. The strategy should be 'beyond compliance', which can be done, as Wal-Mart is showing. But as said before, regulatory perspectives and economic instruments favouring today's 'beyond compliance' environmental management will greatly help environmental pioneers to make money, not to lose it.

Economic instruments for the environment

Further to the use of regulations and management systems, much more dynamic responses can be expected from instruments actively raising the price of resource consumption or of pollution, known as the field of 'economic instruments for the environment'. In theory, it has been established since the 1970s, and many instruments have been trialled and implemented since. Table 7.3 presents a useful overview of the range of economic instruments for the environment.

In addition to Table 7.3, two important instruments that may also be considered 'economic' instruments exist, namely:

1 Demand-side regulation for electrical utilities with a view to decouple their business interest from the selling of kilowatt-hours.
2 Feed-in tariffs to promote renewable sources of energy, mostly electricity, by giving a long-term guarantee of cost-covering compensation.

Table 7.3 *Overview of economic instruments for the environment*

Topics	Description
Emissions/effluent trading	Allows regulated parties to trade emission responsibilities.
Resource allocation trading	Allows regulated parties to trade resource allocations.
Product fees and taxes	Sets levies on potentially harmful products to influence purchasing habits and can provide funds for recycling programmes.
Pollution fees and taxes	Requires regulated parties to pay for each unit of pollution emitted, discharged or disposed.
Resource-use fees and charges	Require resource users to pay for each unit of resources used.
Ecological fiscal reform	A government strategy that shifts fiscal policy from supporting undesired environmental outcomes to supporting positive environmental outcomes.
Deposit refund systems	Requires deposits on a product or packaging at time of sale, which are refunded on return.
Purchase of development rights	Provides a mechanism to financially compensate willing landowners to protect the natural heritage of their land versus undertaking a development project.
Transfer of development rights	Encourages high-density clusters of development on less-sensitive lands within a defined region, while minimizing development on ecologically sensitive lands.
Environmental subsidies	Provides grants, low-interest loans, loan guarantees or favourable tax treatment to promote specific activities and behaviour.
Legal liability	Requires parties causing environmental damage to compensate those harmed.
Financial security	Requires regulated parties to place financial assurance with a regulator to ensure performance.
Qualifying environmental trusts	One of several mechanisms to demonstrate, secure and assure appropriate finances are available for the reclamation of a site when operations cease.

Source: Environment Alberta, Canada[21]

Demand-side regulation has been applied particularly successfully in California since the 1970s, leading to the striking effect that the overall energy intensity of California is some 40 per cent lower than the US average. The system has been described elsewhere.[22] Feed-in tariffs or FITs, are much newer and will be briefly featured at the end of this chapter. Both utility policy and FITs, along with items in Table 7.3, have found useful applications in various industries and economies around the world. When considering a strategic approach to achieve Factor Five there is no reason to discard any of these options as ineffective. However, it is clear that a transformative change of course for the world's economies will require a strategic set of instruments, applied appropriately to each economy, that consistently makes the increase of energy and resource productivity highly attractive and profitable. Hence it is clear that over and above all other instruments, our societies have to introduce or strengthen two particular instruments that specifically affect prices of energy and resources, namely that of environmental taxes and tradable permits.

During the past 30 years or so, environmental economists dealing with these two instruments have shown a clear preference for tradable permits, and negotiated market solutions, as opposed to taxes. This preference was, of course, based on the pivotal work of Ronald Coase[23] and was associated with considerable suspicion about the state and its competence or willingness to deal with economic matters. Taxes were often decried as annoying symbols of state dominance and arrogance. This period of a pro-market bias, however, has come to an end as markets have proven to be dangerously fallible (as shown by the sub-prime mortgage crisis in 2008), making it easier to arrive at a balanced assessment and perhaps at a suitable combination of the two instruments. In a 2008 paper Stephen Smith[24] discusses pros and cons of green taxes and tradable permits. Most importantly, perhaps, he comes to the conclusion that, 'In principle, taxes and emissions trading have very similar properties. Indeed, under certainty and with a competitive allowance market, the economic and environmental effects of emissions taxes and auctioned tradable permits would be identical.'[25] He then goes on, however, to say that differences in the effects are expected under uncertainty of abatement cost, market imperfections, and administrative and measuring cost. As a matter of fact, also earlier authors, such as John Pezzey[26] or McKibbin and Wilcoxen[27] have come to similar conclusions. McKibbin and Wilcoxen suggested to combine both instruments, for example by a tradable permits regime with the upward uncertainties of permit prices being capped by governments selling unlimited permits as some ceiling price is reached. One particularly attractive combination (explored further in Chapter 9) is an *international* trading regime supported by *national* taxes attached to industry performance, leaving the nations some room to manoeuvre to attenuate price fluctuations, as it is typically the wild fluctuations of markets that cause capital destruction and social hardship.

In order to understand the best way to underpin Factor Five improvements let us now look into both emissions trading and environmental taxes and their respective histories in more detail. Both taxes and permits have a long history within the ambit of classical environmental policy, but have not in the past moved into the range of ambition characterizing a 'Factor Five' agenda. Also, for the promotion of renewable energies neither of the two instruments has been remotely as successful as the FITs, a rather new instrument that was never favoured by economists and has received very little interest until its success became common knowledge. The early design of emission trading systems was based on the Coase Theorem[28] saying that problems involving social costs (such as environmental nuisances) should preferably be solved by negotiated agreements between all parties involved. Ronald Coase says that negotiated or traded solutions are more cost effective than Pigovian taxes[29] (see 'Ecological taxes focused on energy' below) – in the absence of transaction cost, that is. In the case of tradable permits, markets can be established directly, under two conditions: 1) the overall 'cap' of emissions has to be fixed politically, and 2) the initial allocation of permits has to be defined either by free distribution – the 'grandfathering' model – or by auctioning, or combinations of the two. Hundreds of tradable emission permit schemes have been introduced over the past 30 years, beginning with an offset mechanism under the US Clean Air Act in 1977. The most important example so far for classical pollutants is the Acid Rain Program (Title IV of the 1990 Clean Air Act) introducing tradable permits for SO_2 emissions in the US.[30] Beyond CO_2 and SO_2, tradable permits were introduced for a range of pollution sources, such as landfills in the UK through the Landfill Allowance Trading Scheme (LATS),[31] chlorofluorocarbons (CFCs) after the Montreal Protocol on protecting the ozone layer,[32] fishing rights (New Zealand, Canada, Netherlands), salinity of discharges into rivers (Hunter River and Murray-Darling Basin in Australia), nutrient discharges (Belgium, US: Chesapeake Bay and Tar Pamlico Basin), nitrous oxides (Netherlands), volatile organic compounds (VOCs) (Canada, Poland, Switzerland), water policies in general[33] and many other fields.

Assessment of such experiences show a rather broad consensus on both effectiveness and efficiency, if compared with command and control measures, for instance: the effectiveness may have benefitted from a broadened interest in monitoring, as all honest players want to be sure that everybody is playing by the rules; and the efficiency may have been improved by identifying and capturing the 'low hanging fruits' (opportunities for improving resource productivity and reducing pollution with short payback periods) at an early stage, while giving the more systemic opportunities, or 'high hanging fruits', some convenient advance warning and allowing preparation for their capture.

Carbon trading: The EU-ETS

By far the most important theme for tradable permits has become the trade with greenhouse gas emissions, notably CO_2 emissions. The EU has boldly taken the initiative after the Kyoto Protocol came into force, to establish an Emissions Trading Scheme (ETS) for carbon dioxide; however, non-CO_2 greenhouse gas emissions, estimated by the IPCC in 2004 as being 20 per cent of overall greenhouse gas emissions,[34] are currently not included, other than indirectly through the Clean Development Mechanism, although nitrous oxide and perfluorocarbons have been identified as being included in the third trading period post-2012. Companies and entities bound by the EU-ETS (referred to as installations) are estimated to represent nearly 40 per cent of the EU's total greenhouse gas emissions, including non-CO_2 emissions.[35]

As part of the requirements of the ETS, installations must provide yearly reports of emissions and compare this with the allocations granted under the scheme. If the installation's emissions levels exceeded that of the allowance it would then be required to purchase allowances from other installations. In the case that the emissions were less than the allocation, installations are then free to sell them to installations that exceeded their emissions, hence promoting a reduction in emissions. In this process a high-emitting installation needs to decide to either act to reduce its emissions, or to pay for its competitors to innovate to improve their reductions in emissions further by buying their excess allowance. Shortly after the initiation of the ETS the European Climate Exchange (ECX) was created to provide a futures market to allow installations to hedge their bets on the price of carbon in the EU. With 'European Climate Exchange Carbon Financial Instruments' (ECX CFI) listed on the International Petroleum Exchange, installations can agree to futures contracts that allow them to lock-in prices for CFIs to be delivered at set dates in the future, independent of the future price and providing a risk management tool for exposure to price volatility. The establishment of such carbon-trading systems and CFIs has created diverse opportunities for sector leaders to become carbon-credit producers and profit from supplying the sector's laggards.

Criticism of the initial method of allocating allowances in the ETS – that of nations freely distributing them to their installations – highlighted that this method provided little incentive for installations to take a serious approach to emissions reductions. This has led to changes being recommended for the third trading period (post-2012), including a combination of central allocation by the EU, and a mechanism for auctioning up to 60 per cent of allocations. Also it can be expected that agricultural monocultures, nuclear energy and new dreams of 'geo-engineering', such as ocean fertilization to enhance algae growth and thus CO_2 absorption, will enter the game and ask for remuneration in terms of carbon reduction equivalents. The *ecological* prices to be paid for monocultures, nuclear energy and geo-engineering can be expected to be high, potentially much higher than the gains in terms of global warming reduction.

One aspect of the ETS is of worldwide significance and has turned out quite controversial; that is, the linking of European emissions to greenhouse gas reductions elsewhere. European industry was very sharp on the 'linking directive', opening a market of inexpensive measures abroad, which was actually foreseen in the Kyoto Protocol. Three 'flexible mechanisms' are outlined in the Protocol, giving industrialized countries options for fulfilling their commitments abroad and, thereby, creating an incentive also in developing countries to reduce emissions. The three mechanisms are:

1   Joint Implementation projects (JI) defined by Article 6 of the Kyoto Protocol;
2   the Clean Development Mechanism (CDM) defined by Article 12;
3   International Emissions Trading (IET) defined by Article 17.

By these mechanisms some incentives are created worldwide to reduce greenhouse gas emissions because European money is flowing into developing countries under the condition that reductions are achieved and certified as 'certified emission reductions' (CER). However, exactly these flexible mechanisms have come under heavy critique not only because they proved a cheap way out of obligations at home for some but also because of some unforeseen misuse abroad. One example may illustrate the problems that occurred, the nexus between ETS and the Montreal Protocol.

The Montreal Protocol, enacted in 1989, focused on the reduction in the use of ozone-depleting chemicals such as chlorofluorocarbons (CFCs), and the transition to alternatives such as hydrochlorofluorocarbons (HCFCs). However, the issue arose when HCFC-22 was identified as an appropriate alternative, and its production and use spiked, particularly in developing countries. HCFC-22 is not (yet) prohibited by the Protocol; however, in its production an insidious by-product appears, trifluoromethane, or HFC-23, which like many HFCs, is a 'super-greenhouse gas', with a global warming potential some 11,700 times stronger per molecule than that of CO_2. Hence the destruction of this compound in developing countries attracted CO_2 credits (through the CDM) and this incentivized new plans for the production of the HCFC alternatives. Kainaru et al[36] write:

> *Given the relatively low cost of HFC-23 destruction compared to the value of Certified Emission Reduction on the global carbon market, the CDM is inadvertently creating a 'perverse incentive' that has created windfall profits for HCFC-22 producers – effectively acting as a subsidy that is driving the expanded production of HCFC-22.*

As a result Kainaru points out that HFC-23 destruction projects have dominated the CDM market, accounting for 52 per cent of all projected carbon volumes transacted in 2006 and 64 per cent in 2005. In addition to the financial bonanza for producing ever more HCFC-22,[37] the low price of HFC-23 removal has had wider impacts in that it has substantially reduced CO_2-emission prices in Europe.

Other criticisms of the flexible mechanisms include the CDM support for large-scale pig farming in Mexico, from which the 2009 swine flu appears to have originated, and dubious afforestation projects at places where virgin forests were removed in the first place. Better monitoring and control in the CER process appears to be the minimum requirement for an extension of the flexible mechanisms.

Beyond the ETS: Global equity

Such shortcomings of the ETS don't diminish the need to establish a regime that makes it more profitable and reasonable worldwide, and especially in the developing countries, to significantly reduce CO_2 and other greenhouse gas emissions. The political challenge is twofold:

1 To set an appropriate cap on global emissions based on the scientific understanding of the resulting temperature increase above pre-industrial temperatures.
2 To distribute allowances for each country to contribute to meeting the global cap in a transparent and equitable way.

A potentially effective proposal answering both challenges is a system based on per capita equal emission rights, originally proposed in 1991 by Anil Agarwal and Sunita Narain[38] and later elaborated on by Aubrey Meyer and his Global Commons Institute, under the name of 'Contraction and Convergence'. In 2007 the *Australian Garnaut Review Interim Report* again presented the need to develop country-specific per capita emissions curves to achieve the overall global stabilization goals, as shown in Figure 7.1, and pointed out that 'Broad international agreement will require acceptance of global limits on emissions, sharing of rights to emissions across countries within these limits, and international collaboration to help achieve the national restrictions.'[39]

When Agarwal and Narain wrote their paper, a rather generous emission cap could be expected to be allowed. Meanwhile, given the constraints of stabilizing CO_2 concentrations, the per capita equal emission rights method would imply the need for dramatic reductions of greenhouse gas emissions in the North (shown in Figure 7.1), or else exorbitant payments to the South, both of which would require significant political support. In this situation, Paul Baer et al[40] suggest to acknowledge and promote a 'right to development in a carbon restrained world' by, for example, gaining access to technologies allowing the developing countries to achieve their goals of prosperity without much carbon burning. However, this emphasis on technology transfer is complicated by the fact that whatever technologies are owned by someone in the North, they are typically owned by private companies that would fight for retaining that property. As favourable as per capita equal rights may seem to the South, they still contain a bias in favour of the North. As we mentioned in the Introduction to the book, cumulative emissions are evidently much higher in the old industrialized countries than in the emerging economies. Dividing those figures by today's population leads to per capita accumulated emissions of the US of about 1000 metric tons, and of Germany nearly 800, while in China and India they would be as low as 60 and 25 metric tons, respectively.[41] China is actually proposing a regime of 'per capita accumulative emissions', although not realistically expecting this to materialize any time soon.

The huge advantage of per capita equal emission rights over the 'flexible mechanisms' of the Kyoto Protocol is that it would instantaneously become

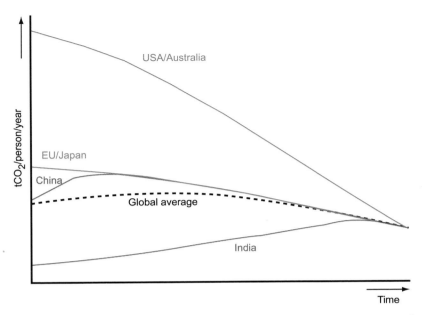

Source: Garnaut Interim Report (2008) Copyright Commonwealth of Australia, reproduced by permission[42]

Figure 7.1 *Contraction and convergence for different countries with 'head room' for the rapidly developing economies: a stylized, illustrative scenario*

highly profitable in the developing countries to slow down the construction of new coal power plants. Investors, including states, would weigh selling emission rights on the world market against the economic benefits of more coal-based electricity, and would soon discover the big potentials of saving energy and increasing energy productivity. Although the Copenhagen climate conference in December 2009 will hardly enter any serious discussion on per capita equal emission rights (accumulated or annual), some delegations will at least mention that no other model is conceivable of bringing developing countries on board quickly and in a massive way. And some delegations will hopefully be bold enough to demand a progressive global cap in CO_2e to be reached in the near future. But in the real world of countries preoccupied with economic recovery and economic development, one should not expect anything of this kind becoming the new 'Copenhagen Consensus'.[43]

In conclusion, trading may be the most efficient way of allocating greenhouse gas emissions, particularly when assuming that international emissions markets are the only realistic mechanism of finding, negotiating and swiftly adjusting appropriate levels of national carbon emissions and their reduction. On the other hand, it seems nearly inconceivable in the real world of today to arrive at a global cap and associated stabilization trajectory, that will really slow down, let alone halt, global warming, or arrive at a distribution scheme that makes it profitable and plausible in the developing countries to seriously consider scrapping plans for new emissions-intensive developments, such as coal power plants. It should be noted again that carbon markets can hardly avoid major and mostly unpredictable fluctuations, which can be extremely frustrating for investors supporting energy efficiency and renewable energies projects. Upward fluctuations can also cause major social hardship. Given such shortcomings, the hope of a regional or global regime of trading greenhouse gas emissions may not be reasonable, however necessary it is.

Thomas Friedman, in an April 2009 commentary,[44] paraphrases the attacks from the right wing towards the Obama administration's plans to implement a cap-and-trade scheme, as follows:

> *Cap-and-trade is a tax. Obama is going to raise your taxes and sacrifice U.S. jobs to combat this global-warming charade, which scientists think is nonsense. Worse, cap-and-trade will be managed by Wall Street. If you liked credit-default swaps, you're going to love carbon-offset swaps.*

That's caricature language but clearly indicates some of the vulnerability of a dogmatic cap-and-trade regime handled by clever speculators. But as Tom Friedman then concludes, it may in the end make a 'simple, transparent, economy-wide carbon tax' look much better than the adventures of carbon trading.

Ecological taxes focused on energy

This leads us to the other important instrument of putting a price tag on energy, CO_2 emissions or other environmentally problematic factors, namely ecologically motivated taxation; in short, 'green taxes'. As a matter of fact, green taxes have been widely used in OECD countries. The history of green taxes initially covered mostly classical pollutants such as SO_2, water effluents, sulphur in fuels, or waste. Some countries have raw materials taxes, water abstraction charges or a tax on incandescent light bulbs. These are meant to incentivize prudent use of resources, including energy. Water charges are also meant to finance the provision of clean water. Petrol taxes are a category of their own. Originally they were introduced as luxury taxes, at a time when motor vehicles were a luxury. In some countries they are understood as a means of financing road construction and maintenance, but in most places they have become just an important source of revenue for the state. Environmental motivations for petrol taxes came up only during the 1990s.

According to the OECD, the total amounts of revenues from environmentally related taxes range between 1 per cent of the GDP (US, Canada, Mexico and New Zealand), to 3–4 per cent (Scandinavian countries, the Netherlands and, recently, Turkey), and just under 5 per cent in Denmark.[45] These facts indicate that green taxation and charges (to finance certain tasks such as remediation of pollution) are well-known entities in environmental policies in

Europe. Some charges have been particularly successful, such as the German wastewater charges. The notable feature about them was that they were announced to be introduced five years before the first charges were made. But it was during this announcement phase, from 1976 to 1980, that most of the investments were made by the polluters to avoid the charge. The revenues were used to build wastewater treatment installations. As was announced at the outset, charges were reduced to marginal levels as pollution discharges went down. Similar charges were successfully applied in Sweden and the Netherlands, and within a decade or so of the charge, rivers and lakes were essentially restored to a healthy state. Despite the success stories, mostly in the domain of water, green charges and taxes have remained a rather modest factor of environmental policies. In no country have they been used systematically to reduce energy intensity, with the exception of the tax on incandescent light bulbs in Denmark, Latvia, Lithuania and Slovakia.

The Scandinavian countries, the Netherlands and Germany were the first to initiate an ecological tax reform (ETR), shifting the burden from taxes on labour, to taxes on energy or greenhouse gas emissions. Tax revenues in these countries added up to some €25 billion annually. As shown in Figure 7.2, in the UK, a petrol tax, or fuel duty, 'escalator' was introduced in 1993, but not with any important environmental motive. Nevertheless, the UK and Germany were among the few countries in the world that saw a reduction of total annual CO_2 emissions from the transport sector. Figure 7.2 shows the development, in comparison with the US and Canada. The figure shows how fuel price escalators in Britain and Germany have reduced CO_2 emissions from road traffic during a time of comfortable economic growth, with the US and Canada having no such tax, and consequently their emissions continued rising.

Some other European countries experienced at least a relative decoupling of fuel consumption from GDP growth. In Finland, it was estimated that, in the absence of energy/CO_2 taxation, carbon emissions would have been 7 per cent higher in 1998, if taxes had remained at the 1990 level. In Norway, taxes lowered CO_2 emissions of stationary combustion plants by some 21 per cent. The reductions in greenhouse gases closely follow the results for total fuel consumption, with the largest reductions (up to 5.9 per cent in 2004) occurring in regions with the highest tax rates, for example, Finland. In contrast, the German ETR was not particularly efficient in reducing total emissions because it did not initially include coal. However, overall the ETR alone resulted in a reduction of 2–3 per cent of CO_2 emissions – and in the transport sector clearly larger effects were noted. In reaction to the world oil price increase, transport fuel sales in Germany dropped by 17 per cent between 1999 and 2007 – after steady increases over several decades. In addition, the number of jobs created increased substantially – for example, by up to 0.5 per cent or up to 250,000 additional people employed between 1999 and 2003 (see Chapter 9). The overall finding is that European countries that implemented ETR have not experienced a negative impact on economic growth following the world oil price increase, and in some cases it was even slightly positive.

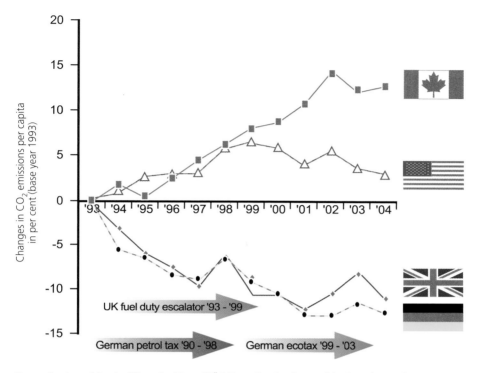

Source: Courtesy of Anselm Görres, President of FÖS (Green Taxation Germany) (Redrawn by TNEP)

Figure 7.2 *Changes of per capita CO_2 emissions from transport, in per cent, compared with base year 1993*

Although ETR is meant to be revenue neutral, it can have an inflationary effect. This is because energy and fuels weigh strongly in the consumer price index (CPI). Still only in Sweden, among the six countries introducing an ETR, was a tax-induced rise in the CPI measured. Energy-intensive industries don't like the ETR, because the compensation they receive via the reduction in social security contributions does not fully match their additional energy costs. They may have a small labour stock, while they consume large amounts of energy. However, due to significant energy savings (see Part I) the effective tax burden can be kept low. Some minor tax exemptions can also be considered and have been given in most ETR countries, mostly under the condition that companies showed they had taken strong measures to optimize their energy efficiency. In Denmark, industry improved energy intensity by close to 30 per cent in the decade from 1990 to 2000, whereas the Netherlands obtained improvements in the range of 10–15 per cent. A particular aspect of Denmark's programme of carbon/energy taxation, believed to have been significant for the marked impacts on energy productivity, was the earmarking of 20 per cent of the revenues to co-finance energy efficiency measures and upgrade production technology.

The EU came under pressure by countries like Sweden, Denmark and Germany to introduce a harmonized scheme for energy taxation. It was blocked for a long time by a rare coalition between Britain, saying that taxation was none of the EU's business, and Spain fearing disadvantages for their coal-based power plants. Ultimately, a compromise was found in a rather timid directive (2003/96/EC, OJ L283, 31 October 2003) obliging member countries to tax energy – albeit at a very low level, lower certainly than the UK's energy taxation so that Britain did not feel dragooned by the EU, and lower than the Spanish industry was fearing. In the typical language used in the EU, the reason given for the energy tax directive was to 'reduce distortions of competition', but hopefully a second motive might also be for increasing incentives to use energy more efficiently. In 2009, the Commission circulated an amendment to the directive, now making environmental reasons explicit, but at the time of writing this book, no results have been made available.

Consistency and predictability of price signal is what makes investors and industry move in the direction of better energy efficiency. Thomas Friedman in his book, *Hot, Flat and Crowded*, quotes General Electric's CEO Jeffrey Immelt, stating that:

> *We will take the technical risk, we will fund the technology breakthroughs, but I have to know that if I make it work, there is a $20 billion market I can step into.*

Jeff Immelt, while not understanding the details of the regulatory method applied in Denmark, Spain and Germany (see 'Feed-in tariffs for renewable energies' below), is obviously right in the assessment that predictability is of the essence for long-term investments and the related technological courage. This important aspect will be further developed in Chapter 9.

Water pricing

Water pricing is the norm not the exception in the industrialized countries. Attempts at modernizing and expanding water supply systems in the developing countries also invariably lead to the demand for water pricing on the part of the investors, be they private or public. As Andreas Kraemer et al say, 'the instrument of water pricing has the primary goal of financing water supply infrastructure.'[46] It is clear that this is the opposite of reducing water consumption through a hefty price signal. Nonetheless, water pricing can also become an important instrument for reducing the wasteful use of water. According to the findings of an OECD investigation, water consumed by agriculture in the late 1990s, mostly for irrigation, was essentially given away free in most countries, except the Netherlands (US$3.10/m^3), France (US$3/m^3), the UK (US$2.5/m^3) and to a lesser extent in Australia (US$1.6/m^3).[47] We follow the OECD reasoning saying that anything scarce and in demand should command a price. Water is scarce in some contexts (drought, degraded quality), so water pricing is increasingly seen as an acceptable instrument of public policy. Water-use charges, pollution charges, tradable permits for water withdrawals or release of specific pollutants, and fines, are all market-based approaches that can contribute to providing the funds needed to make water more accessible, healthier and more sustainable. The OECD countries are working toward the goal of 'internalizing' the full marginal costs (including environment costs) into water prices.

One particular area of water policy that has become increasingly subject to pricing principles is that of public water supply and wastewater services. Efficient and effective water-pricing systems provide incentives for efficient water use and for water quality protection. Obviously, the metering of water consumption is a prerequisite for the application of efficient water-pricing policies. About two-thirds of OECD member countries already meter more than 90 per cent of single-family houses, although universal metering remains a controversial issue in some contexts. In terms of the structure of prices for public water services, there is a clear trend in OECD countries away from fixed charges and towards volumetric charging; in other words, the more you use, the more you pay. Even where fixed charges still exist, in the tradition of communist rule, the policy of allowing large free allowances is in decline. Hungary, Poland and the Czech Republic, for example, already use pricing systems based solely on volumetric pricing, with no fixed charge element at all. Also, earlier tariffs giving discounts to large consumers are phased out and turned into the opposite of higher charges for high consumption. Here we see strong signals for water efficiency coming in.

Industrial effluent charges can also be set by pollution content. In France, for example, a charge is levied on the eight types of pollutant deemed most dangerous and difficult to treat (heavy metals, phosphorus, soluble salts, etc.). The charge is calculated as a function of pollution produced during the period of maximum activity on a normal day. In other cases, the charging formula involved can reflect the costs of treating a particular effluent, or the environmental sensitivity of the receiving waters. Service providers generally receive the proceeds of any industrial effluent charges. This revenue is sometimes channelled into an investment fund that can either allocate the money to water service providers, or to commission wastewater treatment investments directly. As the OECD results above show, the sector that has so far largely escaped any serious water charge is agriculture. Of course, it can be argued that rain is falling on agricultural land and later runs into the rivers and municipal water works, so that farmers can see themselves also as providers of water. However, in many dry parts of the world, this is simply not true. Here all the water collection, building of dams, and distribution networks allowing irrigation in arid and semi-arid areas is done by the state or by water companies that have to recover their cost from households and industry while the supplies to agriculture remain a financial liability of enormous dimensions. Given the considerable scope for the agricultural sector to increase water efficiency (see Chapter 4) it seems reasonable that a trajectory should be found to introduce realistic water prices also to agriculture, possibly in proportion with measured average efficiency gains in the sector (in accordance with the philosophy developed in Chapter 9).

Feed-in tariffs for renewable energies

As pointed out at the beginning of this chapter, feed-in tariffs (FITs) for renewable energies are a new and successful approach that has been all but popular among economists. However, after a bold initiative by Hermann Scheer, MP in the German Bundestag (Parliament), Germany just went ahead with this idea and adopted a scheme, effective 1999, to guarantee cost-covering compensations to providers of electricity from wind, biomass, small-scale hydropower, photovoltaics (PVs) and geothermal energy. Scandalous to economist's iron law of cost efficiency, the more expensive sources, notably PVs, got higher compensations than the cheaper ones. The guarantee was given for a timespan of 20 years, which is enough for writing off all initial investments and retaining some profits on the part of the provider.[48] The portfolio standards mentioned by Jeffrey Immelt above mostly came only on top of the FITs and were a much weaker incentive than to build new windmills and other devices providing renewable electricity. As a matter of fact, when a new government in Denmark in 2003 decided to scrap FITs and to move to portfolio standards alone, the demand for new installations almost collapsed.

In 2005, 10 per cent of electricity in Germany came from renewable sources and 70 per cent of this was supported with FITs. (The remaining 30 per cent represent essentially old hydropower exceeding the size limits stipulated in the law). The Federal Environment Ministry estimates that renewable energies will save 52 million tons of CO_2 by 2010. FITs have to be paid by the electrical utilities. Obviously, they did not like the idea at all but ultimately accepted because it was the law. They are allowed to pass the cost on to their customers, so that the average electricity price is rising. The average level of this rise was €0.0056 per kWh in 2005, corresponding roughly to a 3 per cent increase. This resulted from average prices of renewable energy fed into the grid of €0.0953 per kWh, which is roughly twice as expensive as the average cost of the displaced energy of €0.047 per kWh. The total of the difference amounted to €2.4 billion nationwide for one year.[49] The FITs are lowered every year to encourage more economically efficient production of renewable energy. As of 2008, the annual reductions are 1.5 per cent for electricity from wind, 5 per cent for electricity from PVs (enjoying the highest subsidy) and 1 per cent for electricity from biomass.

The FIT system has been copied in about 50 countries worldwide, most prominently perhaps Spain, which like Germany saw an explosive growth of wind power and some other renewables during the last few years. Under pressures of the fiscal crisis, Spain retreated from the FIT system in 2008, leading to an additional increase of unemployment. Most recently also, the UK decided to join, after many years of trying a 'renewables obligation' system (a portfolio standard), with some trading flexibility, which forces electrical generators to source a growing share of their power from renewables. Though it had some success promoting offshore wind power, it had little impact on microgeneration, solar power in particular. Germany claims that the law had created about 214,000 relatively stable jobs in the renewable energy sector.[50] In Spain, before the 2008 retreat, at least half that number would be realistic. And the Apollo Alliance in the US even thinks of three million jobs to be expected. How many of these jobs will remain in countries with high wages is a different question of course. China has created a strong industrial base for all relevant renewable energies and may attract investors from all over the world to create the respective jobs there.

Assuming that economists were right calling the system economically 'inefficient', what has been the reason for the overwhelming success of FITs? Remembering what Jeffrey Immelt said, we can assume that the main reason was the reliable expectation given to investors that the cost for every new windmill and every solar roof will be recovered in a foreseeable period of time, typically in the order of ten years, and thereafter the installation would essentially be a licence to print money, even after the FITs are phased out. This only holds, of course, if the windmills etc. are robust and well placed and that the grid connection is reliable, as well as ensuring the conditions that can be granted in countries like Denmark or Germany. If the future sees much stricter demand for carbon reduction, the price of carbon emission permits can further bolster the industry of renewable energies. Hence it is not surprising that this industry is moving out of the recession somewhat faster than other branches of industry.

Outlook

Economic instruments for energy efficiency and the environment do exist and can be both efficient and effective. The escalator idea of taxes slowly increasing end-consumer prices appears to be particularly effective. It does not hurt too much, and yet sends a strong signal to private and industrial consumers of energy and water that it will be increasingly important for them to become more efficient. Chapter 9 builds on from this important experience for a strategic and transformative idea of a long-term escalator for energy and water prices. It can be seen that green taxes have not as yet been used systematically for increasing energy and resource productivity; however, there is definitely scope for doing exactly that.

Notes

1   For an overview also emphasizing differences between a (Continental) European and an Anglo-Saxon understanding of CSR, see Williams and Aguilera (2008).
2   McKibben (2006).
3   Schmidheiny and the Business Council for Sustainable Development (1992); DeSimone and Popoff (2000).
4   Hawken et al (1999).

5   ISO (2004).
6   ISO is a non-governmental organization the 148 members of which are private sector national bodies (such as the American National Standards Institute), which then administer their own systems for accrediting auditors and certifying organizations to the standard.
7   Delmas (2002); Prakash and Potoski (2006a); Xia et al (2008).
8   Prakash and Potoski (2006a).
9   Taylor et al (2001).
10 Taylor et al (2001); Angel et al (2007).
11 Orsato (2006).
12 Konnola and Unruh (2007).
13 Prakash and Potoski (2006b).
14 Plambeck and Denend (2007); *China Daily* (2008).
15 Plambeck and Denend (2007).
16 *China Daily* (2008).
17 Hoovers (undated) 'Wal-Mart Stores, Inc. Basic Financial Information', cited in Vandenbergh (2007) p13.
18 *Environmental Leader* (2009d).
19 Vandenbergh (2007).
20 Fryxell et al (2004).
21 Government of Alberta (undated) 'Market Based Instruments and Fiscal Mechanisms', http://environment.alberta.ca/1996.html, accessed 3 May 2009.
22 Lovins et al (2002) pp333–334; Smith et al (2007) see Module B.
23 Coase (1960).
24 Smith (2008).
25 Smith (2008) para 200.
26 Pezzey (2003).
27 McKibbin and Wilcoxen (1997); Pizer (2002).
28 Coase (1960); Baumol and Oates (1988).
29 Pigou (1920) see Chp 10.
30 Stavins (1998).
31 Barrow (2006).
32 Anderson (1999) Chp 3.2.2.
33 Kraemer et al (2007).
34 IPCC (2007).
35 Europa (2008) 'Questions and Answers on the Commission's proposal to revise the EU Emissions Trading System', Europa Press Release, 23 January 2008.
36 Kaniaru et al (2007).
37 Wara (2007).
38 Agarwal and Narain (1991).
39 Garnaut (2008a) p27.
40 Baer et al (2008).
41 World Resources Institute (undated) 'Earth Trends Portal: Cumulative CO_2 emissions 1900–2004', http://earthtrends.wri.org/searchable_db/index.php?theme=3&variable_ID=779&action=select_countries, accessed 14 May 2009.
42 Garnaut (2008a).
43 The term refers to a conference mostly of renegades of mainstream environmental policy convened in 2005 by Björn Lomborg essentially arguing that money invested in combating tropical diseases would save more lives than money thrown at global warming mitigation (odd alternative, isn't it?).
44 Friedman (2009).

45 OECD/EEA (undated) 'Database on Instruments used for Environmental Policy and Natural Resources Management', www2.oecd.org/ecoinst/queries/index.htm, accessed 14 May 2009.
46 Kraemer et al (2007).
47 Jones (2003).
48 World Future Council (2008); Mendonca (2008).
49 World Future Council (2008); Mendonca (2008).
50 World Future Council (2008); Mendonca (2008) p5.

8

Addressing the Rebound Dilemma

Ernst von Weizsäcker

Introduction

Fundamentally the most pressing issue of the 21st century is that of managing 'growth'. The problem is that for the last three centuries the levels of growth in the consumption of resources (particularly oil, coal, water and timber) have steadily increased, in line with levels of economic growth. This has of course resulted in associated increases in the level of a range of environmental pressures, to the point that the environment's response to such pressures may actually impact on economic growth, now and for the foreseeable future. This is particularly the case for human-induced climate change. In the summary of the conclusions from the *Stern Review* it states that:

> *Our actions now and over the coming decades could create risks of major disruption to economic and social activity, on a scale similar to those associated with the great wars and the economic depression of the first half of the 20th century. And it will be difficult or impossible to reverse these changes. So prompt and strong action is clearly warranted.*[1]

However, delivering such prompt and strong action in practice is incredibly complicated, and even though the previous Sector Studies show what is possible, broad implementation involves a range of inter-related factors, each having varying effects on the outcome.

A particular complication, being the focus of this chapter, is that the increase of resource productivity does not always lead to reduced resource consumption. It can even lead to an overall increase in consumption levels. This phenomenon is commonly referred to as the 'rebound effect'. It means that improving resource productivity alone is not sufficient to address overall consumption levels. Complementary efforts need to be made to adjust policy mechanisms, affect resource prices, educate communities and account for increased population or affluence levels. Improving resource productivity may buy some time but eventually without a systemic approach the overall levels of consumption will continue to rise, along with the associated environmental pressures.

Factors affecting total resource consumption include:

- background levels of population growth (productivity may double but if population does also then the overall impact may be negligible);
- social norms and cultural practices (these may impact on choices for particular activities such as preferences for particular food types, along with social trends for the latest and greatest technologies);
- levels of affluence (with different levels of affluence leading to different behaviours).

The level of affluence is a particularly sensitive issue. Those living in poverty will find it unfair if environmental reasons are used to stop growth just before they benefit from it. But then resource productivity may serve as an unexpectedly simple way out of this social tension by allowing the poor to have better lives with stagnant resource consumption while inducing the rich to stabilize their economic well-being and reducing their resource consumption. Hence what was at first a technical issue is now a social and political issue, and will require a sophisticated and holistic approach.

The Khazzoom-Brookes Postulate

In short, we are talking about growth. Resource consumption has always grown with economic growth, or nearly. Jeff Rubin writes in his introductory leader to the more detailed paper by Rubin and Tal:[2] 'To date, there has only been one sure-fire way of reducing energy consumption – shrink the economy.' He continues: 'reducing energy consumption per unit of GDP has not been a viable policy option. From gasoline demand to the energy requirements of an average American home, the legacy of energy-efficiency improvements is ever-greater energy consumption.' Rubin does not say the policy option of reducing energy consumption per unit of GDP is not available, but he does say it has not prevented energy consumption from growing. Here we are. This is the 'rebound effect'. Unless and until we overcome this rebound effect, we will not reach any of the ecological goals that we and the community of climate experts consider necessary. This is the reason why we devote one full chapter to the phenomenon of the rebound effect. The phenomenon has been well known since the 1980s, chiefly through empirical work by Daniel Khazzoom in the US and Leonard Brookes in Britain, and it got a name, the Khazzoom-Brookes Postulate.[3] Independently the two researchers found that after the dramatic increase of oil and gas prices during the 1970s considerable efficiency gains

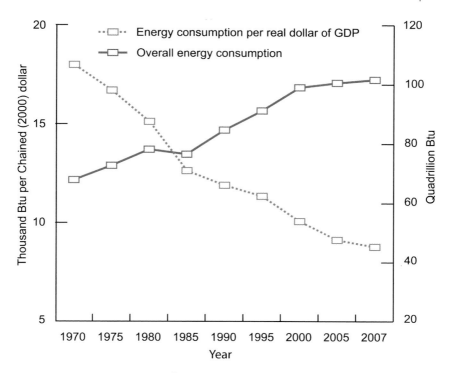

Figure 8.1 *A comparison of the overall energy consumption and the energy consumption per GDP for the US between 1949 and 2007*

were made, but that these efficiency gains were reducing the monthly cost of energy consumption and had the effect of more money being available for economic growth and indeed for energy consumption.

What was rather a visionary observation at that early time (1979 and 1980, respectively), became a very conspicuous and massive reality since the late 1980s until quite recently – when the 2008 economic crisis began to hit. Rubin and Tal present a number of striking trends from the US, including the trend seen in Figure 8.1 – which shows that following the 1974 OPEC oil crisis and up to 2007, US energy productivity doubled, but the overall energy consumption rose by 37 per cent.

The most commonly known story about the rebound effect is that of the CAFE (Corporate Average Fuel Economy) standards adopted in the US in 1975 and introduced in 1978. They brought average fuel efficiency of ordinary automobiles up to roughly 27 miles per gallon from the earlier 18mpg. This happened within some 20 years, more or less the lifetime of an automobile in the US. However, this improvement in fuel economy, combined with one of the lowest prices for oil in December 1986, led to a marked overall increase in driving miles that continued through to the mid 1990s. Rubin and Tal also point out that there was a significant shift away from the CAFE-regulated passenger cars to unregulated sport utility vehicles, or SUVs – which also enjoyed a tax advantage over passenger cars. The US government, notably under Ronald Reagan (1981–1989), refused the introduction of gasoline taxes, which are commonplace in most other industrialized countries, and even accepted a generous tax advantage for the new SUV fleet. The housing and automobile industries boomed no end, which was, of course, very welcome after the uncomfortable 'stagflation' of the previous period. Also, electricity use by household appliances rose between 1990 and 2005 while their efficiency increased, such as the refrigerators (with efficiency improving 10 per cent and use increasing 22 per cent) and air-conditioners (with efficiency improving 17 per cent and use increasing 35 per cent).[5]

There are, of course, assertions that the rebound effect does not hit as hard as Khazzoom and Brookes believe. For example, John 'Skip' Laitner[6] from the US Environmental Protection Agency (EPA) offers extremely optimistic figures, saying that:

> *the rebound effect might reduce overall savings by about 2–3% compared to a pure engineering analysis. In other words, an economy-wide, cost-effective engineering savings of 30% might turn out to be only a 29% savings from a macroeconomic perspective.*

Such assertions make it necessary to go a bit deeper than Rubin and Tal into the partly contentious issues of the rebound effect. One of the best modern analyses of the issues came from Horace Herring, a visiting research fellow at the Open University with over 25 years of investigating energy efficiency and the rebound effect.[7] He reviewed the controversies between Daniel Khazzoom and Amory Lovins in the US, and between Len Brookes and Michael Grubb in the UK, with Lovins and Grubb assuming that efficiency will lead to less energy consumption due to, as Grubb[8] puts it, 'saturation rates', resulting in limited levels of energy demand. Saturation means that additional consumption yields negligible marginal benefits. In line with Len Brookes' concerns, Hilliard Huntingdon's review of Grubbs work led to his conclusion that:

> *While saturation of individual appliances can be expected, rapid economy-wide saturation need not occur as new energy services and energy-using appliances are constantly emerging. The volume offers no evidence, historical or otherwise, for its assumptions about saturation rates.*[9]

In the American debate, Amory Lovins[10] has maintained that the 'rebound' effect by consumers of energy efficiency gains is small, whereas Khazzoom[11] argues that Lovins' analysis does not take into account macroeconomic responses to implicit changes in energy price caused by efficiency improve-

Table 8.1 *Summary of empirical evidence for direct rebound effects in the US residential sector*

Device	Potential size of rebound (percentage)	Number of studies
Space heating	10–30	26
Space cooling	0–50	9
Water heating	<10–40	5
Residential lighting	5–12	4
Appliance	0	2
Automotive transport	10–30	22

Source: Greening et al (2000)[12]

ments. This answer perhaps, also defeats Skip Laitner's proposition of a mere 2–3 per cent rebounding, as this also does not take macroeconomic responses into account. Laitner, Lovins and Grubb also have a point though. The empirical economists confronting them are in danger of inducing cynical conclusions on the part of business or politics, such as, 'All those noble efforts lead nowhere! The human nature is unchangeable. Let's just go ahead with more production and consumption until – well, we don't know.' This type of cynical rhetoric is quite widespread and is influential and often lumps all types of efforts into one broad assumption. However, the reality is that rebound effects are different for different types of efficiency improvements. For example the direct rebound effects in the residential sector have been studied extensively in the past two decades and the results from over 65 empirical studies are summarized in Table 8.1, showing considerable variation in the scale of the effect.

On the other hand, if we want to make progress on climate and other environmental challenges, we cannot ignore the trends presented above, for example in Figure 8.1. These trends clearly indicate that for all the merits of efficiency, energy and resource consumption has been rising, not falling – and in one of the richest country of the world! One factor, which has hardly been touched by Khazzoom, Brookes and their followers is the influence resource prices may have on consumption. Figure 8.1 shows that the period of steeply rising energy consumption were the years from about 1982 to 1999, which have been the years of cheap oil and gas. Although Khazzoom's and Brookes' first observations were published earlier, the big evidence in support of their papers, oddly, arrived a few years later when significant reductions in the price of oil occurred. The signal of low energy prices, particularly after oil prices were lowered in 1986 by Saudi Arabia, has greatly contributed to the propensity of Americans and others to consume more energy.

Seemingly contradictory findings by Sam Schurr, then Deputy Director of the Energy Study Center at the Electric Power Research Institute, that energy efficiency increased more rapidly at times of *low* energy prices can be explained by the double fact that, 1) much of the efficiency innovation was motivated by and developed during the previous oil price crisis, and 2) the spreading of the inventions was helped by the optimistic mindset that emerged after the nightmare of those extremely high oil prices had disappeared.[13] And Schurr did *not* say that energy consumption dropped when oil got cheap.

Moreover, this chapter is based on the same understanding as that George Monbiot communicated in his recent book, saying:

> *I wish to try to make my proposals as watertight as possible, so I will assume that Khazzoom and Brookes got it right. If they are wrong, it does my proposals no harm. But if they are right and we ignore them, we are in danger of devising a scheme for reducing carbon emissions which does not work.*[14]

So far, much of the rebound discussion has been restricted to energy. However, this is an incomplete picture, and once alert to the phenomenon, it can be found in many instances, including the following:

- Water efficiency gains in dry areas in the US, which we applauded in *Factor Four*, were strategically used to allow for additional housing, leading eventually to more water demand and consumption. Here you can even say the rebound effect was made on purpose.
- Innovation in the use of fibre optics, in an attempt to make telecommunications more materials efficient, saw the use of copper dramatically decrease, resulting in a decreasing market price. However, with this lower price came thousands of new copper applications, as copper consumption rapidly spread to the newly industrialized countries, temporarily leading to soaring copper prices.
- Agricultural land-use efficiency increased dramatically since the 1950s to supply the rapidly growing economies of the world, leading to the notorious overproduction in the EU. The EU set-aside payments for retiring farmland, until population growth – more meat consumption, more urban land-use and more bio-fuels – led to new land shortages, rising land prices and a new food crisis.
- The first mobile phones weighed several kilograms and were installed in police and managers' cars. Within 25 years they got fabulously light using less than 5 per cent of the material the pioneer machines needed. But the newly won smallness and low price made them more useful and attractive so that hundreds of millions were sold, instead of the few thousands of the first generation. The material flows from mobile phones are likely to have increased a millionfold over the past 25 years.

Hence, the evidence is clearly on the side of the rebound effect, in that efforts to improve efficiency have been fraught with increasing overall levels of consumption. It is important to understand that efforts to reduce the effect need to be considered through a systems approach. This means that a range of influences needs to be considered – such as the impact of population increases, technology trends, social movements and levels of affluence – when trying to understand the impacts on overall consumption from specific efficiency and productivity improvements. For instance, the rebound effect fundamentally cautions that if something is more efficient, meaning that it is cheaper to run, then the user will use more. However, this issue is also an issue of sociology. Those who are not using something as often as they would like to (because they cannot afford to), are of course likely to use it more if it's cheaper, but those that can afford to use it as often as they like, or have chosen not to use it for various reasons, are less likely to increase use. Hence, this 'rebound dilemma' makes policies addressing global warming, and other global challenges, quite a bit more difficult. But there is scope for such policies and this will be discussed in the second half of this chapter, and in subsequent chapters.

The Industrial and the Neolithic Revolutions

The modern rebound effect and the Khazzoom-Brookes Postulate are much in discussion in our days. Sometimes the impression is created as if the effect was a new phenomenon. The opposite is true and Khazzoom and Brookes have always acknowledged that. They refer to and quote William Stanley Jevons, whose lucid and famous book *The Coal Question*[15] clearly described a similar phenomenon for the first half of the 19th century. For instance, Jevons showed that improvements to iron production that reduced coal consumption by two-thirds led to a tenfold increase in total consumption in Scotland between the years 1830 and 1863. Jevons further discusses the long-term effects of James Watt's steam engine, certainly one of the greatest inventions in human history, and a device making far more efficient use of coal energy than Thomas Newcomen's archaic machines,[16] which were in use before. It was its elegance and efficiency that made James Watt's invention such a breakthrough for the use of coal-fired engines. They could be made considerably smaller than the Newcomen pumps and thus could be used to power ships and rail locomotives, not to mention dozens of new industrial applications. Watt's steam engine, through its energy efficiency, opened up a range of new applications and hence created enormous additional demand for coal to power the rapid growth.

This is what Jevons described some 80 years after James Watt's invention. He showed that Britain's impressive new wealth was closely associated with the rise of coal burning. Electricity was not yet in the picture during his time. He noticed that the steam engine, after a very short period of reduced demand for coal, enabled Britain to accelerate its development and led to steeply rising use of the fuel. Between 1830 and 1860 alone, coal use increased tenfold in Britain. Jevons is fully aware of the mechanism behind this 'paradox' – that is, industrial power became much more affordable through the efficient machines, which in turn allowed ever more industrial activity and innovation. Discussing measures to curb what he diagnoses as unsustainable consumption of coal, he clearly discards a coal tax, quoting other authors who paint horror pictures of the effects of such a tax. (We do not follow this logic of horror!) Instead, he positively considers a ban on coal exports, saying that Britain should not support her competitors with the fuel on which her entire wealth seemed to be resting. The most philosophical and perhaps most interesting chapter in Jevons' book is Chapter IX, 'Of the Natural Law of Social Growth', where he sees the growth of prosperity as a natural law, or nearly, and associates it with ever increasing coal consumption. But he also sees the limits of this expansion and predicts a gloomy end, saying:

> *We are growing rich and numerous upon a source of wealth of which the fertility does not yet apparently decrease with our demands upon it. Hence the uniform and extraordinary rate of growth which this country presents. We are like settlers spreading in a rich new country of which the boundaries are yet unknown and unfelt. But then I must point out the painful fact that such a rate of growth will before long render our consumption of coal comparable with the total supply. In the increasing depth and difficulty of coal mining we shall meet that vague, but inevitable boundary that will stop our progress.*[17]

To Jevons, efficiency gains are available but will be overwhelmed by the 'natural law' of expansion. Quoting Malthus, who was one of the most influential celebrities of his time, Jevons expresses fear about population growth while recognizing the fact that coal will for a long time to come allow further population growth.

Industrialization has meanwhile occurred in all continents and in all sectors, including agriculture, and made it possible to feed and house more than six billion people, an unimaginable feat at the time of Malthus and Jevons. But unless something quite extraordinary happens regarding our ability to deal with limited resources, humanity will end up meeting 'that vague, but inevitable boundary that will stop our progress', and as unforeseen by Jevons, this impact on our progress is more likely to be the reaction of the global environment to the associated pollution, than the exhaustion of the fuels that we rely on.

This leads us to a more general remark about the rebound effect. The effect appears to be a characteristic feature of human civilizations since time immemorial. Industrial rebound effects of Jevons' kind are the latecomers in a long history of humankind that has expanded based on the innovations of its predecessors. Humans learned to use and exploit nature, and if the resource efficiency of doing so increased, the result was additional population growth. Humans emerged from pre-human creatures as hunters and gatherers. At this time, the human population could grow to just a few million, an impressive number for a species on the top of the nutrition pyramid. But the carrying capacity of the Earth was more or less exhausted at this population size. Further population growth beyond the ecological limits did happen here and there, such as in the now famous case of Easter Island, but invariably led to severe effects caused by the eradication of game animals or other overuse of resources. It was not until the Neolithic Revolution, that is, the invention of farming and the corresponding intensification of land use, that more humans could inhabit the Earth. Farming made land use at least ten times, eventually a hundred times, more efficient in terms of output per hectare. And what was the effect? Human population grew at least tenfold, later a hundredfold, and the efficiency revolution resulted in the dire need for more land, not less, to support the booming population. Sedentary cultures (villages, cities, states) also allowed for elaborate social hierarchies with some privileged on the top being allowed to consume more food, employ slaves or servants, own more land, and organize progress towards harnessing natural resources such as water or minerals more efficiently, with a view of allowing additional consumption, or luxury. This can be also seen as the basis of social envy, one of the strongest forces of non-ending consumption increase.

Overcoming the rebound effect

At first glance, such considerations seem to render it impossible to use efficiency as a key part of efforts to combat environmental threats from overuse of resources. The success story of pollution control (see the Introduction to the book) does not come as a big relief because pollution control and resource consumption are two very different issues. The concept of 'cleaner' production has rather encouraged societies to go on consuming ever increasing amounts of resources. While most of the rebound effect literature debates the extent to which negative rebound effects exist, and what can be done to reduce them, Alan Pears makes the key point that there is in principle just as much potential for money saved from energy-efficient initiatives to be invested in new positive sustainable initiatives.[18] This could include investments in the home such as solar hot water systems, solar PV systems, purchasing accredited green power, investing in third party certified carbon-offsetting schemes, water efficiency and onsite rainwater harvesting, storage and treatment options, all leading to a positive amplification effect rather than a negative rebound effect. Hence, as such efforts require upfront investments, energy efficiency savings can help the average citizen, who may have many other important costs (mortgage repayments or rent, expenses on children, childcare etc.) to be able to save money to afford the upfront costs of these sustainability initiatives. Almost all of the best practice case studies featured in the Sector Studies of this book are of companies who have first invested in significant energy efficiency improvements and then used the financial savings from these to enable them to also invest in renewable energy and additional water-saving initiatives.

In order to achieve Factor Five we have to invent and introduce new mechanisms specifically addressing the negative sides of the rebound effect in order instead to encourage the use of energy efficiency as a strategy to enable positive amplification effects. Essentially, we see three quite different, but not mutually exclusive, approaches that are available, namely:

1   *Reducing or removing the damages done by resource consumption*: This is
    an agenda closely related to pollution control and has been dealt with in
    Chapter 6. Wind and solar energy, properly incentivized, replacing coal is
    surely part of the answer. Carbon capture and storage (CCS) is another
    option, although less attractive than renewable energies because it does not
    by itself create added value and its reliability is largely unproven. For
    materials, there is the concept of the 'cyclical economy', emerging from
    Japan with the Basic Law for Establishing a Cyclical Society (Cyclical
    Society Law) enacted in 2000,[19] imposing quite restrictive regulation
    regarding the use of materials and processes to ensure that materials can be
    easily and cost-effectively re-used. As a more far-reaching concept, there is
    also the 'cradle to cradle' approach by William McDonough and Michael
    Braungart,[20] which is actually quite generous in terms of efficiency but
    suggests very clear restrictions on materials that may be used in manufac-
    turing. Its ultimate goal is also the cyclical society.

2   *Investing in capital funds for future prosperity*: That is, the establishment
    of funds to provide capital stock for posterity after resources may have
    been depleted. This approach is not targeted at avoiding resource depletion
    but at compensating losses caused by depletion. Norway, conscious of the
    limited reach of its North Sea oil, decided to create a Petroleum Fund in
    1990, out of the proceeds from oil, later renamed 'Norway's Government
    Pension Fund'.[21] It currently has assets of about €160 billion invested in
    3000 publicly traded companies in over 30 countries.[22] This approach is
    not without its problems external to the country, as well as some internal
    problems for its politicians and citizens. Externally, the presence of one
    large fund could be seen to unduly influence or manipulate world or
    regional markets to its own benefit, thus requiring transparency and
    linkages to key international bodies.[23] Internally and among citizens, the
    fund can generate a 'resource curse' where 'abundance of natural resources
    stimulates dysfunctional economic policy choices ... and creates conflicts
    over the distribution of wealth'.[24] This 'resource curse' was found to be
    mild in the Norwegian case. Nevertheless, it increased citizen's political
    distrust, with voters critical of tight economic policy and wanting more of
    the fund spent immediately on health, education and aged care.

3   *Making resource consumption ever more expensive*: Ultimately, resource
    consumption should be so expensive that total resource consumption rests
    in a perfect balance with sustainable supplies of renewable (or recycled)
    resources, and the resulting ability of the biosphere to assimilate the associ-
    ated pollution and by-products. Chapter 9 will take this challenge up.

Notes

1   Stern (2007).
2   Rubin (2007); Rubin and Tal (2007).
3   Brookes (1979); Khazzoom (1980); Brookes (1990); The term 'Khazzoom-
    Brookes postulate' was introduced by Harry D. Saunders in Saunders (1992).

4   EIA (2007).
5   Rubin (2007) p1; Rubin and Tal (2007).
6   Laitner (2000).
7   Herring (1998).
8   Grubb (1990).
9   Huntingdon (1992).
10   Lovins (1988).
11   Khazzoom (1989).
12   Greening et al (2000).
13   Schurr (1985).
14   Monbiot (2007).
15   Jevons (1865).
16   From the Internet information available to us, we see no clear evidence that
     Newcomen's steam engine needed coal at all. If that is the case, Jevons' argument
     about coal-related efficiency gains sounds somewhat dubious. But for the flow of
     the argument in this subchapter, this point is of lesser importance.
17   Jevons (1865).
18   Pears (2004a).
19   Fumikazu (2007).
20   McDonough and Braungart (2002). Based on these ideas, a trade fair was
     organized in Frankfurt, Germany, in November 2008, featuring dozens of
     commercial success stories of cradle to cradle: Braungart and McDonough
     (2008).
21   Norges Bank (2006) 'Government Pension Fund', www.norges-bank.no/nbim/
     pension_fund/, accessed 14 May 2008.
22   International Monetary Fund (2003) 'IMF concludes 2002 article IV consultation
     with Norway', IMF Public Information Notice, 18 March 2003.
23   Austvik (1999).
24   Listhaug (2005).

9

A Long-term Ecological Tax Reform

Ernst von Weizsäcker

Introduction

Part I of this book focused on presenting a whole system approach to resource productivity based on best practices across a range of industries to demonstrate that Factor Five improvements were not only possible, but often being achieved. The chapters adhere closely to an academic style, with comprehensive referencing and notes, to ensure a rigorous presentation. The innovation over that of the work presented in *Factor Four* lies in this whole system design[1] approach to resource productivity gains – a transition that may be called 'transformational' – but it's still based on facts and figures. Chapters 6–8 then described a range of existing policies and instruments that are being used to underpin efforts to improve productivity. Chapter 8 ended with the observation, grim as it may be from an environmental point of view, that improvements in efficiency in the past were almost always overwhelmed by additional overall consumption, be it by an increase of population, higher standards of living or just by consumer behaviour; moreover, that in the real world, many of the exciting opportunities lying in the efficiency revolution remained mostly unrealized.

Amory Lovins' revolutionary 'Hypercar' has been around as a promising concept for over 15 years, but despite this the real revolution taking place in Detroit during that time went in the opposite direction – with the mass manufacturing of gas-guzzling sports utility vehicles (SUVs). Retrofitting homes and commercial buildings to the 'Passive House' standard is being driven by either research or progressive regulation in just a few European countries, with the odd standout around the world. On the whole the rapid uptake of plasma TV screens in OECD countries is offsetting many of the energy efficiency gains achieved. Construction of '6-star buildings' is happening only in signature buildings in cities around the world. Practical applications of light emitting diodes (LEDs) are still rare, present for the most part in speciality markets such as traffic lights and car brake lights. The cement industry is still indulging in the high energy-intensity limestone-based Portland cement and shows little intention of moving to alternatives such as 'geopolymers'. Water efficiency has remained a dream for most of the world's farmers with underground water reservoirs around the world being depleted at a mind-boggling rate. And the idea of a 'cyclical society' is only slowly moving from its conceptual stage to reality in Japan and a few other Asian countries. Hence, such efforts are being overwhelmed by the shear increase in consumption. The rebound effect, described in Chapter 8, is the dominant reality worldwide, attenuated a bit since 2008 by the unwelcome advent of the economic crisis.

On the other hand, as presented in the Introduction to the book, the ecological crisis is real and extremely dangerous. The world simply cannot afford to ignore it. The innocent phrase 'sustainable development' taken seriously implies truly transformational changes in all countries. To fill this postulate with substance, we suggest that a fivefold increase of resource productivity (at least) becomes a full-size reality in most of the world's countries, and that the rich countries finally learn to live with a degree of modesty. Two matters of course characterize reality everywhere in the world: 1) consumers consume what is affordable to them, and 2) producers produce what is profitable to them. Neither should be blamed for that. If we want the transition to a sustainable society, we must respect these matters of course and make use of them. It could look like this:

- Resource productivity should become ever more profitable for producers.
- Resource-saving goods and services should be more affordable to consumers than resource-wasting ones.
- While life-supporting goods and services should remain affordable, high consumption of natural goods should become increasingly more expensive.

Conventional environmental policies have hardly touched these dimensions of sustainable development. This has to change, and it is going to be a transformational change. But it will be unavoidable if this world is to maintain its beauty and the support systems for human life. This last part of our book is devoted to the political and cultural dimensions of such transformational changes. One additional and contentious topic on the agenda of sustainable development is population increase. It lies outside resource productivity and we cannot deal with it in the context of this book, but we recognize its crucial importance and emphasize that political and religious leaders should acknowledge population as one of the central problems of our days.

How can we make resource productivity ever more profitable for producers and resource-saving goods and services more affordable to consumers than resource-wasting ones? The evident answer, in a market-based global economy, lies in the price of resources. This chapter advocates a strategy of focusing on resource pricing through tax reform in a consistent and highly predictable way over the medium to long term.

Two different methods have been identified in Chapter 7 for pricing the relevant resources, notably carbon, energy and water. The two methods, which have been described as almost equivalent, are tradable permits and resource or emission taxes. Tradable permits in theory allow fixing the target levels of consumption and letting prices adjust to supply and demand changes. A trading regime in theory would be very efficient. On the other hand, taxes allow fixing prices (within limits) and leave the reaching of the target more or less undecided. This comparison seems to speak for tradable permits as the preferred instrument. However, at the end of Chapter 7, we realized that carbon markets as they are discussed in the real world of climate negotiations are far from leading to the reductions needed to stabilize climate. Such reductions would require very low caps and worldwide equitable commitments, both of which are far from the current reality in 2009. The previous chapters also mentioned that price fluctuations that may serve to adjust to oversupply or undersupply of permits are in danger of inviting speculation and causing major problems to investors and to socially vulnerable people. Nevertheless, carbon markets could well be the only feasible instrument at the international level, allowing countries a continuous exchange of permits. Also it was pointed out that environmental taxes can have a strong steering effect and can be designed such that capital destruction and social hardship are avoided. Revenue neutral green taxes reducing the fiscal load on human labour have been proven even to have net positive effects on employment and the economy. It may be that a long-term, revenue neutral ecological tax reform is most likely to instigate both producers and consumers to make strategic and permanent efforts towards energy efficiency.

This chapter elaborates on this idea and discusses some of the questions that are expected to be asked by critics. Before going into detail, the chapter investigates what effect markets have had on primary resource prices over the last two centuries. The chapter focuses its attention on resource prices for two reasons, namely that they are one of the crucial factors determining the profitability of resource productivity, and secondly that they are the main target of a long-term ecological tax reform.

Two centuries of falling resource prices

Surprisingly, primary resource prices (which also include primary energy) have had a tendency to fall over the last 200 years, as can be seen in Figure 9.1. Knowing that prices are the strongest and most pervasive language in a market economy, this period of falling resource prices has induced industry and consumers to become ever more negligent about resource efficiency. Exceptional phases such as the world wars and the energy price hikes of

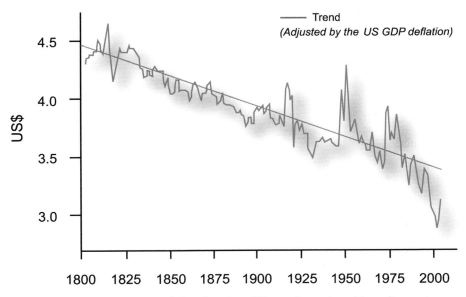

Note: Industrial raw industrials prices, inflation adjusted over 200 years. Prospecting, mining and transport technologies and related industries were the main drivers of bringing prices down.
Source: Based on data from The Bank Credit Analyst

Figure 9.1 *Real raw industrial commodity prices (in US terms) 1800–2004*

1973–1982 and 2000–2008 have sent signals of scarcity into the economies of the world, but the basic assumption remained that mineral and energy resources are simply 'available'.

The price hikes between 2000 and 2004 are indicated as an upward movement at the far right end of the curve. Some additional price increases occurred between 2004 and 2008. That recent trend brought prices back into the lower confidence interval of a secular downward trend. But when the economic crisis hit in late 2008, commodity prices tumbled back to essentially the lowest levels ever measured.

Before continuing the discussion of which instrument to apply and how to tailor it, let us look at the political landscape that has allowed resource prices to fall. It has been the explicit objective of business leaders and politicians for centuries to make natural resources available at ever lower prices. For business, lower resource prices simply improve the bottom line, and no one can afford paying a higher price than competitors do. And for politicians, it is extremely convenient, making people and businesses enjoy 'free lunches'. This political intention found its extreme expression in the Soviet Union, which put no price on environmental resources such as air and water, promulgating that all natural resources belonged to the public. A national policy that supported the use of free resources did not encourage conservation by individuals or firms.[2] The logical result in the Soviet Union, aside from creating a sense of communist justice among the poor, was an extremely wasteful kind of industry. Soviet citizens wasted energy, water and minerals to an extreme degree, certainly contributing to the ultimate collapse of the Soviet economies.

Of course, political preferences alone don't reduce resource prices. The long-term downward trend of resource prices was also supported by technological progress in exploration, mining and processing. And market competition served to reward low-cost suppliers. The Earth's geology has not so far shown any serious signs of depletion, except for the limited fossil fuels. Prospecting and mining was always systematically stepped up whenever commodity prices went up. Also, countries, companies and consumers became more modest or more energy efficient during these periods. This was the case during and after the two World Wars and after the two more recent oil price shocks of the 1970s and since 2000. Reduced energy intensity, trained during the 1970s and after, actually served as a key factor in stabilizing industrialized economies some 15 years later, when another quadrupling took place from US$9/barrel in 1998 to US$35/barrel in 2000.[3] The recent price hikes after 2000 are usually explained by soaring petrol imports to China and India. This was indeed the reason for an imbalance between supplies and demand and justified prices rising to roughly US$100 a barrel.

However, the last upwards push between 2005 and early 2008 sending prices through the roof was actually triggered mostly by quite reasonable considerations on the part of institutional investors. Noticing that commodities were playing an increasing role in financial markets they thought they should perhaps diversify their assets and include holdings of raw commodities. But then, even a modest 1 per cent of their assets allocated to commodities meant a huge and unprecedented additional inflow of funds into oil and other resources markets. Some speculators, realizing the mechanics of this new development, joined the booming market driving oil prices near the staggering level of US$150 a barrel. It was not until then that some very oil-dependent economies, most visibly the US, were pushed into a recession. Houses financed with sub-prime mortgages lost much of their value after commuting became a financial nightmare to the new homeowners, and that was the beginning of the sub-prime mortgage crisis and the financial meltdown. When the economies of the world began to shrink, oil and other commodity prices also collapsed from their speculative heights, reverting back to the long-term trend shown in Figure 9.1.

This description is surely at variance with the mainstream of the 'peak oil' discussion that started in 1956 with M. King Hubbert's anticipation of oil production to peak around 1970. After the discovery since the mid 1970s of major additional oil reserves, the peak oil discussion faded off until the first years of this century.[4] Also some other mineral resources such as copper, indium (used in transparent electrodes), rhodium (used in car catalytic converters) or phosphates (used in agriculture) were now included, as they are in high industrial demand that cannot be met with sufficient supply at present prices. Annual discovery rates of these resources have been falling behind annual consumption rates for some time. The peak oil discussion has certainly helped oil producers and traders defend rising oil prices. It was also important for alerting the broad public to certain real limits to resource consumption. However, aside from the lower demand and lower prices during times of sluggish economies, we don't expect peak oil and gas to be as dramatic in the early parts of the 21st century as it has been predicted by some authors, including Richard Heinberg.[5] The reason is simple – coal supplies have a geological reach of some additional 200 years, and coal liquefaction, using classical Fischer-Tropsch technology, would allow mass production of oil at prices of US$60–80 per barrel, assuming even high coal prices at US$100 per short ton.

The conclusion in this section is that markets driven by supply and demand are very unlikely to tell the full story of long-term scarcity. And when scarcity becomes apparent or when the public can be made to believe that the end is near, prices have a tendency to skyrocket. Both low prices and skyrocketing prices send wrong signals. The former invites squandering, the latter causes social and financial disruptions. We suggest that an enlightened leadership can do a lot to smooth out such fluctuations and can elegantly steer technology and behaviour into a high-price world and highest efficiency.

The concept of a long-term ecological tax reform

The last remarks above lead directly to the core of our proposal. We propose a long-term policy decision of actively increasing resource prices. Our central idea is to create a broad political consensus on a trajectory of steadily progressing energy and commodity prices (inflation corrected). The main criteria for such active price policy should be:

- simplicity, also in terms of administration and control;
- predictability and reliability;
- social and economic acceptability.

In effect, based on these criteria, a trajectory of energy and other primary resource prices rising in proportion with resource productivity increases is evident. Then, by definition, there would be no social hardship on average, and hardly any capital destruction, as those who achieve the average increase will feel no impact, those who exceed it will benefit, with only those who fall behind the average efficiency improvement feeling the economic pressure. The socio-economic effect of this strategy can be expected to be positive for economies such as China, Bangladesh, the US, Japan, Germany and Egypt – all being countries importing energy and raw materials. They will be gently induced to become less dependent on such imports, leaving more domestic capital and wealth for distribution. Some of the commodity-exporting countries and companies will conversely suffer export losses. But they represent a minority of countries, and a predictable and smooth transition will allow them to adjust and to move themselves into an economy of high added value and low carbon consumption.

Which is the best method of making raw material and energy prices rise predictably and in steps corresponding to their respective productivity gains? A cap-and-trade regime may qualify, while gradually reducing cap levels. On the international scale, as said before, cap and trade may be the only regime that is working. This is because it is very difficult to imagine countries agreeing on a common tax level for carbon emissions or fuels as well as on the distribution of revenues. As also said before, cap-and-trade regimes, with their unavoidable fluctuations, have a tendency of frustrating investors and hitting the poorest strata of society more than the affluent.

A political decision of fixing prices many years in advance sounds like a much more attractive method. In countries such as China, energy prices have been fixed by the state for decades. These countries can theoretically decide on the suggested price trajectory without much debate or a need to justify their decision against the fiction of a 'free market'. Other countries have the option of taxing energy and other primary raw materials. Our proposal is that this is done by adopting legislation requiring annual adjustments in response to measured resource productivity gains. To avoid too many debates each year, the adjustments can be foreseen every five years only, which coincides with China's regular Five-Year Plans. As different sectors develop their efficiencies differently, a political preference is possible for different price trajectories for those different sectors. However, in macroeconomic terms the best strategy would be to have the price signal uniform, thereby letting some sectors grow and others (slowly) shrink.

The idea of linking energy and other resource prices to gains in resource productivity has two different roots. One is the social and economic policy consideration that resource prices rising in proportion with resource productivity will not on average cause any social hardship or unbearable cost increases for industry. The other is the observation outlined below (subchapter on 'The paradigm of a twentyfold increase of labour productivity') of gross wages having increased in parallel with labour productivity gains over more than a hundred years. This parallel development of labour productivity and gross wages has been the backbone of the Industrial Revolution and has surely benefitted essentially all people, in some way. Recognizing the logic behind this parallel development, investors have always exploited any given opportunity of increasing labour productivity, knowing there was hardly any safer bet for the future. However, at a time of high unemployment and scarce natural resources, progress by increasing labour productivity has become less rational from a macroeconomic point of view. Moving investors to give a higher priority to resource productivity would make today's societies more prosperous and more competitive.

Clearly the best way of moving investors in the new direction of steeply rising resource productivity would be a long-term and predictable trajectory of rising resource prices.

History of energy taxes[6]

The idea of energy and resource taxes is actually not a new one, as has been said in Chapter 7. It dates back to the British economist Arthur Cecil Pigou,[7] who proposed taxes reflecting and penalizing negative, what we now call 'external effects'. He thought of activities such as trains producing thick smoke and sparks that have negative impacts on the landscape they are crossing, such as cornfields. Dry cornfields could catch fire from the sparks, and the smoke badly polluted the farmland. Such damages were 'external effects' on farmers or others affected from the train. As a matter of fairness in regards to taxation, Pigou suggested taxes to make up for such external costs and to induce train operators to avoid the damage. Later, K. William Kapp,[8] William Baumol and Wallace Oates,[9] and Hans-Christoph Binswanger[10] developed the idea further. Binswanger, in particular, proposed the idea to raise energy taxes and use the fiscal revenues for reducing indirect labour costs, particularly contributions to pension funds. He proposed that it was good for the economy if the scarcer factors were taxed, while the less scarce factors (human labour) were freed from some of their fiscal burden. Binswanger's ideas were instrumental in shaping the Ecological Tax Reform (ETR) in Germany that was introduced in 1999. It consisted of a scheme of annually increasing taxes on transport fuels, electricity and heating fuels, while reducing social security contributions by companies, offset by the increased taxes. This increased energy use and decreased the cost of human labour.

According to studies by the German Institute for Economic Research, the ETR created up to 250,000 additional jobs in Germany by 2003 (only four years after its adoption), mainly by reducing indirect labour costs, but to some extent also by creating demand for energy efficiency. Apart from this, the rising demand for renewable sources of energy has created many jobs, though the main reason for this was the Renewable Energy Sources Act with its generous feed-in tariffs (FITs) (Chapter 7). Many other countries have introduced green tax schemes[11] with frequent success in slowing down the increase in energy consumption or creating additional jobs. Increasingly, the US debate is also moving towards green taxes. Thomas Friedman[12] (the influential commentator and author), Professor Gregory Mankiw (Harvard Professor and Chairman of the Council of Economic Advisers (2003–2006) of the Bush White House) and Professor Lawrence Summers[13] (now a leading member of the Obama economic team) have joined in promoting the basic idea of taxing greenhouse gas emissions, energy or other factors seen as problematic for the environment.

Overcoming the dilemma of short-term instruments

Most of these old and new approaches of pricing energy and the environment have one problem in common – they tend to be measures that are introduced at once. Hence they are subject to the debate over whether the thing being taxed is well defined, and if the size of the tax is adequate for the intended purpose. It is essentially the question asked already by Arthur Pigou. These questions lead to the typical dilemma of short-term (tax) instruments – either the tax is high and will hit polluters and consumers hard, creating problems for the poor and capital destruction for industry, or it is low and has very limited effects. There have been some good examples of overcoming this dilemma. The German wastewater charges, mentioned in Chapter 7, were announced a few years before being actually collected and had their strongest steering effect during the announcement period when the charge was still zero.

Another success story for an ecological tax was the Swedish NO_x charge of roughly US$4 per kilogram nitrous oxides emitted from power plants, with all revenues redistributed to the electric power sector. The redistribution system made sure that the sector as a whole did not suffer, but a strong incentive was maintained to stop polluting. As pointed out in Chapter 8, even in Sweden, which is arguably the country with the broadest experience and the strongest emphasis on green taxation, only 5 per cent of total tax revenues were green taxes. This may indicate that there is some room for a higher percentage.

Two other European schemes were introduced in small steps: 1) the British 'escalator' on transport fuels, introduced in 1993, and 2) the German ETR, introduced in 1999 (see Figure 7.2). Both schemes were progressive, meaning that year by year the duty increased by small amounts. But the announcement of further steps had a major effect on customer behaviour, not surprising for psychologists. One of the major effects was that families would buy a more fuel-efficient car when the old one was taken out of duty. Railways and other public transport enjoyed a renaissance, and unnecessary trips were reduced. After decades of ever increasing fuel consumption, the ETR, together with the increasing world oil prices, made an unexpected turn around in the transport policy and the respective CO_2 emissions of these countries. The 'escalator' idea seems to show a way out of the dilemma of short-term pricing instruments. Figure 7.2 in Chapter 7 compared the British and German experiences with Canada and the US. In these two countries, the increasing efficiency of compact cars was more than compensated (in the absence of a price signal), by the introduction of tax-privileged SUVs and by added miles driven. No signs of recovery can be seen in the mostly outdated and inefficient railway system. This is the type of consumer and policy rebound to efficiency that we must try to avoid through the use of such instruments as the ETR.

The poor, the blue-collar workers, the investors and the fiscal conservatives

Objections against ETR or energy-related taxes tend to come from both the left and the right – from advocates of the poor and blue-collar workers, as well as from the investor community and fiscal conservatives.[14] Advocates of the poor talk of the relatively high importance of energy costs for the poor in terms of total purchasing power, with energy and water taxes said to be 'regressive', hitting the poor more than the rich.[15] This assertion is based on the fact that taxing negative externalities usually entails exerting a burden on consumption, and since the poor spend a higher percentage of their income on consumption than the rich, any shift towards consumption taxes can be regressive. However, conventional regulatory approaches can affect prices in much the same way, while lacking the revenue-recycling potential of ecological taxes. Hence, one of the strengths of the ecological tax approach is precisely that, unlike regulations, it provides revenue for ensuring low-income groups are not worse off. This can be done by reductions in (regressive) consumption taxes, or increasing welfare payments such as providing additional payment to the unemployed, pensioners and the disabled.

This regressive effect is almost universally observed for water charges and taxes, and the removal of subsidies for drinking water (although generous water subsidies for rich farmers abound and tell a different story). For energy, the statement is true only for the wealthy countries because in the poor countries the rich tend to have more energy-intensive lifestyles than the poor; however, a high energy tax can surely work against poor households' aspirations to reach more convenient and prosperous lifestyles. Hence, these statements about regressive effects of taxes can be countered simply by granting a tax free minimum tableau of, say, one gigajoule of energy per person per week, or 200 litres of water per person per week. Then the really poor would actually benefit, while the burden would shift towards the middle income and rich strata of the society. This has been effectively applied in the water tariff system in Setubal, Portugal.

Blue-collar workers, too, have a tendency of disliking ecological taxes as they associate environmental regulation and taxes with job losses. They typically use similar lines of arguments with the additional apprehension that energy taxes would destroy industrial jobs. There is surely some truth in this fear – if industry is unable or not willing to change technologies and practices to reduce energy and water intensity. Part I of this book is taking much of the legitimacy out these fears, arguing that exciting technological options exist to make a range of sectors significantly more energy and water efficient, and thereby much less vulnerable to resource taxation, even to the point that it can become a lucrative ongoing competitive advantage, especially with slow-moving competitors.

Nevertheless fears of job losses from environmental taxes or regulations are common. A nationwide poll, conducted in the US found that 33 per cent of those polled felt themselves 'likely' or 'somewhat likely' to lose their job as a consequence of environmental regulation.[16] However, a study undertaken as part of this poll found that virtually all economists who have studied the jobs–environment debate over the last 30 years agree that these fears are unfounded. In reality, at the economy-wide level, the study concludes that there has simply been no trade off between jobs and the environment, stating:

> *at the local level, in sharp contrast to the conventional wisdom, layoffs from environmental protection have been very, very small. Even in the most extreme cases, such as protection of forests, or closing down fisheries, or steps to address acid rain, job losses from environmental protection have been minute compared to more garden-variety layoff events.*[17]

In practice the real economy-wide effects of much of the environmental regulation enacted has been to shift jobs without increasing the overall level of unemployment. Globally there are now significant numbers of people who work in the 'environmental industry sector' as a result of these regulatory changes. In fact, regulation-induced plant closings and layoffs are very rare, with the study showing that in the US, about 1,000,000 workers are laid off each year due to factors such as import competition, shifts in demand or corporate downsizing, compared to annual layoffs in manufacturing due to environmental regulation in the order of 100 to 3000 per year. Further, there is significant evidence to suggest that applying ecological taxes while reducing payroll tax can help create significantly higher employment. In 1994, DRI and other consultancies commissioned by the European Commission modelled a scenario where all the revenues from pollution taxes were used to reduce employer's non-wage labour costs, such as social security payments, superfund payments and payroll tax. The study showed that employment in the UK would be increased by 2.2 million through such tax shifting.[18]

Aside from such reassurances regarding jobs, there are also those that take a more radical view saying that the classical model of heavy industry and mass manufacturing is part of the ecological problem of our days and should be overcome by less consumption and a move to the service sector. Even the unions are becoming remarkably open minded about the need for structural change, as is documented in the European Trade Union Confederation's joint statement with the European Environmental Bureau, EEB.[19] To smooth the transition, certain temporary exemptions for the manufacturing sector can be granted, as in Germany, to avoid the destruction of invested capital. Or the Swedish NO_x model can be applied, recycling all revenues into the sector so that the sector as such is not losing out.

Investors have a tendency to indiscriminately despise taxes. However, they need not fear a revenue neutral energy tax escalator. On the contrary, what they should fear is unpredictability and unfair national rates creating competitive disadvantages. If it is possible politically to reach a consensus about a long-term trajectory for green taxes, that could result in a 'heaven on Earth' for many investors. It would mean that they can confidently move into ambitious technological and infrastructural projects with very limited risks, thanks to predictability of one of the most important factors, plus efficiency gains and the prospects of new markets. This will eventually lead to major advantages over competitors currently working under conditions of substantially lower resource prices, and therefore giving too little attention to the actual scarcity of these unrealistically priced resources. Just imagine a new oil price shock or a crisis of water availability, you would expect the companies and countries weathering the storm easily to be those that have developed a highly efficient way of using those scarce resources.

This leaves the camp of fiscal conservatives as adversaries of an ecological tax reform. Their views may be ideologically fixed, but they should acknowledge that green taxes have a tendency of falling over time, as energy or water consumption fall. The opposite is the case with income taxes, which have a tendency of increasing over time. For energy and other resource taxes, you would indeed need an escalator to avoid dwindling fiscal revenue.

The paradigm of a twentyfold increase of labour productivity

Let us now move on and draw a bold analogy between the history of technological progress and its increase of labour productivity on one side, and the prospects of a new chapter of technological progress through increasing resource productivity on the other. The Industrial Revolution, which is still going on, has been a revolution indeed. Labour productivity grew at least twentyfold over time. During the 19th century, the increase in what came to be the industrialized countries was less than 1 per cent per year, which is not all that spectacular. The rate increased to 1.5 per cent, notably in the US during the first half of the 20th century, and from 3 up to 7 per cent from 1950 to 1973

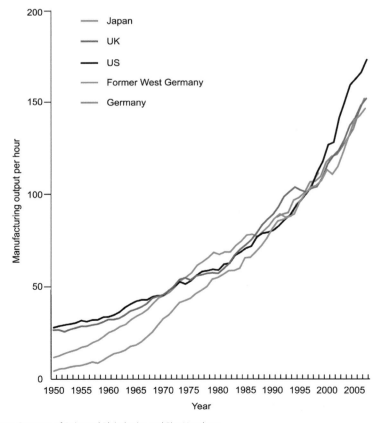

Source: Courtesy of Raimund Bleischwitz and Piet Hausberg

Figure 9.2 *The increase of labour productivity in different countries*

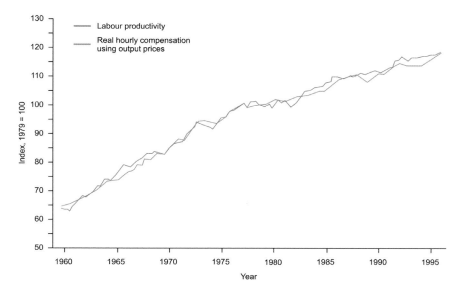

Note: Gross wages (real hourly compensation), and labour productivity rise mostly in parallel
Source: Based on data from the Department of Commerce, Department of Labor, and Council of Economic Advisers

Figure 9.3 *Real compensation and labour productivity for the non-farm business sector*

and just a little less thereafter. For a graphical representation see Figure 9.2. The figure shows the total increase of labour productivity from 1950 to 2005, growing many fold in the US, Germany, Britain and Japan.[20] The near-exponential increase of all curves indicates that rates of increase remained relatively stable over the decades, although there were shorter periods of higher rates, for example in Japan and West Germany during the 1950s and 1960s, characterized in Japan by absorbing or copying technologies from abroad, and in both countries by rebuilding their economies after the destructions of the war.

Freer trade has certainly helped speed up the race to higher labour productivity. One fact, well known by organized labour and by employers, is that negotiations for higher wages and other benefits have taken the rise in labour productivity as their yardstick for wage increases. It was only during the recent neoliberal and neoconservative phase since the early 1980s, that wages began to lag behind productivity gains, due mostly, as the employers saw it, to competition from low-wage countries.

What is not so well known is that productivity gains also went up in parallel with gross labour cost. Empirically, it is not easy to distinguish this effect from the former, because what you observe is simply that wages and productivity go up in parallel (Figure 9.3).

However, employers know that the race for competitiveness and for increasing labour productivity is always spurred by wage increases. The wave of acquisitions and mergers and the rise of the business consultancy industry over the last 20 years were essentially built on that race to stay competitive through labour rationalization (another term for productivity gains). This latter trend of labour costs spurring labour productivity is an exciting indication of the potential for resource costs to spur energy and resource productivity improvements. As a matter of fact, the 'oil crisis' of the 1970s served as an unwelcome experiment for this hypothesis. As energy prices went up across the board, a new mentality set in that focused on energy efficiency, as mentioned in the previous chapter. Figure 9.4 shows how during the years from 1973 to 1982, when energy prices were high, the energy intensity of OECD countries went down dramatically, although the process levelled off when prices went down again after the early 1980s.

Given the potential demonstrated in Part I of our book of increasing resource productivity by a factor of five or so, it becomes quite plausible to assume that energy and resource productivity can be economically induced to increase by a very substantial factor, provided price signals reward those investing in the productivity increase. We even count on some acceleration of the process because once engineers, investors, managers and consumers become accustomed to the dynamic process, they are likely to trust it and anticipate more to come, which could easily speed things up. This was surely the experience with labour productivity, as was documented in Figure 9.2.

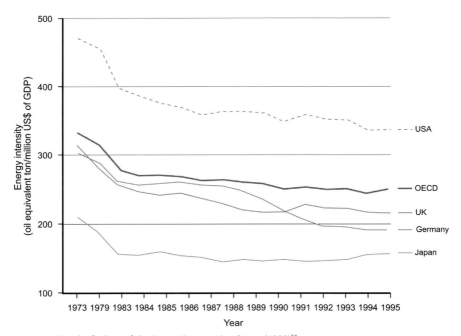

Source: Based on the findings of the Energy Conservation Center (1998)[21]

Figure 9.4 *Energy intensity per GDP by major countries*

How could it work in market economies?

Let us come back to the central proposal of this chapter. We have suggested increasing the prices of energy and of other primary resources by as many percentage points as the energy and resource productivity has increased in the previous year. Adjustments may be made using taxes and should begin one month after the statistical data of energy and materials productivity gains in the previous year is available. It was also stated that practical reasons or political customs, such as a four-year election cycle or the Chinese Five-Year Plans, could speak for a longer period of reference, such as four or five years. To avoid abrupt changes, annual steps could still be agreed on. The system should be essentially revenue neutral, meaning that revenue generated for the government is used transparently, such as reducing the fiscal or parafiscal load on human labour (e.g. superannuation contributions). Revenue could also be used to provide incentives/rebates/subsidies to encourage companies and households to further invest in resource-saving activities. Some may be used to subsidize a small amount of resource consumption by the poorest communities.

This system of increase should preferably be made binding for 50 years or more, with fairly tough clauses for exemptions or deviations from the rule. For practical reasons, a certain corridor should be defined allowing small deviations from the exact increase. See Figure 9.5, symbolizing a corridor within which small fluctuations are allowed. As the upper or lower boundary is approached, a state intervention could move prices back to the middle.

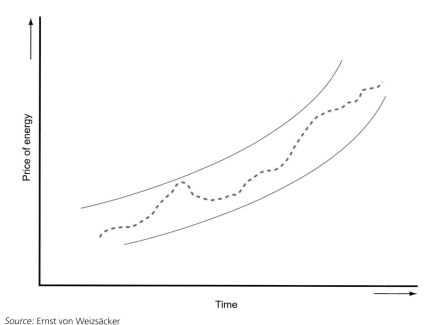

Source: Ernst von Weizsäcker

Figure 9.5 *A corridor of increasing energy price fluctuations*

Different sectors such as transportation fuels, electricity and so forth may be treated differently. Even smaller sectors of the economy could be granted a closed revenue neutral 'pool' – as Sweden did for the electricity industry. However, such exemptions should preferably be time-limited and should not prevent the structural change from energy-intensive to energy-efficient production. For materials the target price refers to primary raw materials. Thereby, the commercial value of secondary raw materials would continuously rise. The Japanese and Chinese concepts of a 'cyclical society' would greatly benefit from taxes on primary raw materials. It is assumed here that the administrative costs of such a tax would be dramatically lower than the costs of detailed recycling laws. In the case of water, the tax base would be water extraction, leading to an increasing incentive for water purification. In Chapter 7 the water extraction taxes already in use in a number of EU countries were mentioned.

Strong reasons may turn up for acceleration of the trajectory or for somewhat broader corridors. If a manifest crisis of oil availability or climate risks plagues the countries, they should feel free to let prices rise faster, and a somewhat flatter increase may be considered in case of major political objections. The history of wages and labour productivity has also had phases where wages rose faster than productivity, and others where their rise was slower. Many such aberrations were corrected later.

The economist's justification for the proposed scheme is internalization of external cost. While it is possible to fully appreciate the strength of the argument, there is no need to become very exact in 'calculating' externalities. The calculations of the cost of global warming or of biodiversity losses invariably are based on informed guesses and difficult-to-assess assumptions. For the political justification of the mid- and long-term ETR, there is no need for exactitude of the calculations. It will perfectly suffice to prove that externalities of energy use and resource extraction are higher than those of human labour. In this case, the tax shift from labour to resources would lead to better internalization than the present fiscal systems are able to provide. More positive 'externalities' (macroeconomic gains) would accrue if countries pioneering the efficiency technologies are rewarded by successful competition on international technology markets.

The idea of a long-term ETR can serve as an idealized model for moving technology, infrastructure and consumer behaviour and investors' decisions in the direction of sustainable development. This bold and effective policy instrument has the advantage of addressing both efficiency and sufficiency at the same time. In the next chapter, we argue that the mindset dominating between the early 1980s and 2008, which states we should step back and leave all major developments to the markets, would make it next to impossible to agree on a state-defined trajectory of rising energy prices. As a matter of fact, we are arguing in Chapter 10 that the change of this mindset was a pre-condition for a serious discussion of any such long-term policy.

Why do price signals (resource prices) matter so much to whether or not Factor Five innovations are taken up in the marketplace? Thomas Friedman in *Hot, Flat and Crowded* sums it up brilliantly on pages 250–260, explaining that some innovations, like the mobile phone, are taken up by the market rapidly, with no changes to pricing, because they offer a new service not offered by existing technologies – in this case the landline phone. Similarly, ipods enable purchasing, storing and listening to music in a whole new way unlike any previous technology. Like mobile phones and ipods, the upfront investment costs of solar-powered LED lighting, solar hot water systems, super-windows and wind farms are higher than existing and traditional technologies. But these Factor Five technologies, unlike mobile phones and ipods, simply provide the same service as existing less-efficient lighting, electric hot water systems and coal fired power stations. Thus, even though these Factor Five technologies are financially more sensible in the long run, most consumers are unlikely to pay more upfront for Factor Five innovations when cheaper versions exist which provide the same service. Nate Lewis, a US energy expert, uses jolly language to illustrate this point:

> Today, we already have cheap energy from coal, gas and oil. So getting people to pay more to shift to clean fuels (and more energy efficient products) is like trying to get funding for NASA to build a new spaceship to the moon, when Southwest Airlines already flies there and gives away free peanuts! I already have a cheap ride to the moon, and a ride is a ride. For most people, electricity is electricity, no matter how it is generated. Making [cleaner] energy doesn't provide them with something new. So you are asking them to pay for something they already have that does the exact same thing. Nobody would be buying ipods in the numbers they have if their cell phones could already download music.[22]

Therefore, to facilitate the uptake of Factor Five innovations on the scale and timeframe needed, we need government to level the playing field by not subsidizing transport and traditional industry, and instead provide price signals to internalize the negative environmental externalities. That is what will create the market demand to drive the changes needed to avoid dangerous climate change and ecosystem collapse over the coming decades. As Friedman explains:

> There is only one way to change that outlook. The Government needs to come in and tell you, that from now on you are going to pay the full cost of all the CO_2 and pollution from your incandescent, coal powered light fixture, and therefore it is going to cost you $125 more a month to turn on that light. Then my solar powered light for only $100 more a month looks like a bargain, and you'll take ten and so will all the other readers of this book,

and six months later, guess what? I will be back with the same solar lighting system for only $75 more a month. I will be down the cost–volume learning curve and, innovation being what it is, I will eventually get a solar light cost below that of the coal-powered one. I will have taken my new innovation to scale.[23]

In 2000, the International Energy Agency (OECD's energy arm), published *Experience Curves for Energy Technology Policy* which described how, if government raises resource prices, it moves new Factor Five technologies and design solutions faster down the learning curve, achieving much larger uptake in the marketplace at significantly lower costs much more quickly. The IEA study stated that:

> *With historical annual growth rates of 15 per cent, photovoltaic modules will reach break-even point around the year 2025. Doubling the rate of growth will move the break-even point 10 years ahead to 2015... If we want cost efficient, CO_2 mitigation technologies available the first decades of the new century, these technologies must be given the opportunity to learn in the current marketplace.*[24]

A policy to raise resource prices in line with resource productivity gains is also essential to provide certainty for business to enable them to invest in Factor Five improvements with confidence. Many people have hoped that the recent high oil prices would be sufficient to start a global drive to Factor Five innovation. But the reality is that while major corporations were interested in opportunities from a high oil price, they were also very cautious as they knew the high oil price could plunge just as quickly as it soared, if global demand – especially China and India – were to fall. In the marketplace CEOs base their long-term 40–50 year investments on the historic floor price of commodities, not their temporary peaks. Thus it is only a policy that ratchets up the floor price of resource commodities over time that will ensure a global shift to Factor Five resource productivity investments.

General Electric's CEO Jeffrey Immelt, whose company is one of the leading companies investing in eco-innovation, makes this point in Friedman's *Hot, Flat and Crowded*, stating that:

> *The big [manufacturing] and energy players are not going to make a multi-billion dollar, forty year bet on a 15 minute market signal. That just doesn't work... GE is now into a third generation of innovation in wind turbines thanks to the European Union. Countries like Denmark, Spain, and Germany imposed portfolio standards for wind power on their utilities – requiring them to produce a certain amount each year – and offered long term subsidies. This created a big market for wind. What scares*

us is making these big R&D investments and not knowing if we will ever get an order.[25]

Chad Holliday, CEO of DuPont also argues publicly for the need for a carbon price to provide a credible floor price for energy that reflects the currently externalized costs. Chad Holliday in conversation with Thomas Friedman stated that:

> *We used to own an oil company [Conoco]... I paid the three best consulting companies in the world to tell me what the price of crude oil was going to be. They assured me that it could not go over $24 a barrel... [Today] the market is not sure where the oil price is going to go. Just like it is way up there now, no one can assure it will not go back down. That is why Jeff Immelt and I are arguing that there has to be a cost of carbon, no matter how you create it. There has to be a simple price signal.*[26]

Notes

1   Stasinopoulos et al (2008).
2   Henry and Douhovnikoff (2008) p440.
3   Mankiw (2007) 'Where have all the oil shocks gone?', Greg Mankiw's Blog, 28 October 2007.
4   Greene and Hopson (2003); Hirsch et al (2005).
5   Heinberg (2007).
6   See also Chapter 8 of this book.
7   Pigou (1920).
8   Kapp (1971).
9   Baumol and Oates (1988).
10 Binswanger et al (1983).
11 See Chapter 7 of this book, and Schlegelmilch (1999).
12 Friedman (2008) pp259–266.
13 Summers (2007).
14 For a more complete treatment of the objections against an ecological tax reform see von Weizsäcker and Jesinghaus (1992).
15 Smith (1995).
16 Goldstein (1999) p5.
17 Goldstein (1999) p15.
18 European Communities (1994).
19 ETUC (2005) 'Make Lisbon Work for Sustainable Development', www.etuc.org/a/982, accessed 4 May 2009.
20 Updated from Bleischwitz (1998).
21 Energy Conservation Center (1998) see 'Energy Situation in Major Countries'.
22 Friedman (2008) p252.
23 Friedman (2008) pp251–252.
24 International Energy Agency (2000).
25 Friedman (2008) pp255–256.
26 Friedman (2008) p257.

10
Balancing Public with Private Goods

Ernst von Weizsäcker

Factor Five needs a strong state

Many of the suggestions made in this book are not politically feasible in a market that leaves almost no role for the state. For 25 years, beginning in the early 1980s and culminating in the late 1990s, we have seen a phase of rejection of a strong state and of almost total belief in the powers of the markets. Liberalization, deregulation and privatization were the characterizing features of the era. State interventions met with utmost suspicion, and each and every environmental measure taken on national levels was in danger of being rejected as trade distorting by the World Trade Organization (WTO) or by the Commissioner for the Internal Market (in the EU). While it would be foolish to ignore the legitimate reasons lying behind the mindset of market dominance, we see equal legitimacy in maintaining that the state has an indispensable role to play in moving the economy from wasteful to efficient. The reason is simple, and now well known. Markets reflect production and distribution costs and customer's willingness to pay. They don't reflect long-term scarcities and environmental 'externalities'. This failure, together with ever more efficient mining and transportation techniques, made resource prices decline over the last 200 years, as shown in Figure 9.1.

It cannot be denied that markets can eventually lead to rising resource prices, as limits of mineral resources and, more importantly, of land availability, come close. However, the timing of such price increases are unlikely to reflect the reality of the pressures on the environment, and would in fact occur through non-linear jumps or wild fluctuations, influenced by cartels, protectionist responses and speculation, and periodically attenuated by social policy measures trying to beat and overcome the physical realities. Such 'jump and stop and go' developments are very unlikely to produce a reliable, rational and early signal inducing the kind of strategic and dramatic increase of resource productivity that the world needs, as previously discussed. Given this state of affairs, we cannot but observe with satisfaction that the era or mindset of a 'minimal state' has come to an end, through the 2008 global financial crisis. Like others, we would have preferred the transition to be much smoother and not triggered by absurdities of suspect credit default swaps handled by arrogant and greedy analysts and investors. But who was there to steer the chain of events? Surely the political clout of the public sector was far too weak at the time to prevent the disaster from occurring.

Now that the world is in a painful recession, people, including politicians, business leaders and academic economists are rediscovering the need for public institutions. The most urgent task appears to have been bailing out the ailing banks and insurance companies, second to restore the trust and reliability that the private sector has so badly damaged, and third to incur huge public debts for 'stimulus packages', that is, reinventing Keynesianism, which had fallen into disgrace during the 1980s. Beyond these immediate concerns, the state is needed at all times for setting a reliable and enforceable legal frame, for an atmosphere of trust far beyond lending operations, for justice, law and order, for infrastructure and education, and indeed for a healthy environment. Adam Smith would not disagree with this assessment.

Markets are good at optimizing resource allocation and technical innovation within an agreed frame and set of broad objectives. But they are poor at defining that frame. The previous chapter proposed a long-term trajectory of steadily rising energy and resource prices, presented as the most efficient, the most effective and the most socially benign mechanism to drive a Factor Five agenda. But it is perfectly clear that such a trajectory requires a strong state, for a very long time. As the previous chapter pointed out, predictable increases of energy and resource prices would give strong and long-term signals to producers, traders and consumers to move in a direction of resource productivity. The signal is also meant to reach habits and daily decisions at the level of families and individuals. Markets, by contrast, are subject to unpredictable fluctuations, often leading to the frustration of investors, both private and public, into technologies and operations that won't pay off in less than five years.

The public sector and public interests have the better part of their tradition and success stories at the levels of villages, townships, perhaps provinces and nation states. However, in times of a globalized economy some important public issues require international cooperation and coordination. Some legal rules and financial instruments would even benefit from substantive harmonization, so as to discourage the migration of industries to states allowing very low standards. The environment is not alone as a public good benefitting from international cooperation and coordination. Other concerns include human rights, the sciences, infrastructure, corporate law and many others matters belonging to the realm of public goods require international coordination. In case of conflicts of interests between the private sector and public goods, the latter are just too weak if they are only protected and defended at national levels, because mobile capital can search for places where the respective public goods enjoy little to no protection, and even active exploitation.

We could leave it at that, stating that we need a healthy balance between markets and the state. But we want more. To achieve the goal of Factor Five, we shall need a long-term balance, with a reliable state capable of providing a high degree of certainty for innovators and investors. We feel that a deep look back into the history of the last century will help us understand what happened and what could be done to avoid a repetition of such exaggeration. As we look back, we shall learn how the collapse of communism had an unexpected effect on the West. If the Reagan–Thatcher movement started as a perfectly understandable and in many regards legitimate conservative response to 70 years of state dominance and some specific 'liberal' mistakes of the 1970s, market dominance after 1990 turned into a nightmare of arrogance on the part of rent-maximizing investors and speculators.

Why communism collapsed

Let us begin our historical description with a watershed event that occurred quite recently – the collapse of communism, just before 1990. When it happened, it was greeted as a long-awaited liberation by hundreds of millions of people. It also came as an immeasurable relief worldwide from the fears of a Third World War, fears that were felt throughout the 40 years of the Cold War. As unanimous as the celebrations were when the Cold War ended, there were a number of interpretations as to why it happened. Essentially two different views persist – the Anglo-Saxon and the continental European one.

In the US and much of the Anglo-Saxon world, the explanation is fairly simple. After many years of American and Western weakness, self-doubts and even ingratiation with communism, President Ronald Reagan showed strong leadership in the West and engaged in a crystal clear confrontation between the free West and the authoritarian regimes of the East. This confrontation was successful. The better and stronger system, according to Reagan's firm belief, defeated the weaker one, for moral, economic, political and military reasons.[1] The very idea that there was a good principle and an evil one competing for dominance in the world and that the good empire defeated the evil one is in a sense related to the philosophy of allowing markets (the good principle) to dominate over the state (which was depicted as greedy, inefficient, full of 'red tape', and harassing to free citizens).

In much of Europe, however, the explanation of why communism collapsed is quite different and starts much earlier, namely in the 1960s – the heyday of decolonization, the civil rights movement in America, the Beatles, unrest at universities, and the rise of environmentalism and civil society. These new movements resonated extremely well with people living oppressed lives in the East demanding Western music and Western freedoms, and ogling at

Western prosperity. When the Soviet Union and her allies in 1968 crushed the 'Prague Spring' (an uprising for a Third Way between socialism and free markets) and when a little later German Chancellor Willy Brandt began the détente policy (i.e. the opposite of crystal clear confrontation), it became clear to the world and to the young generation in the East that communism had lost its legitimacy and attraction. Détente also refuted the notorious communist propaganda of capitalism being inherently militaristic and aggressive. To put it in simplified terms – communism lost the competition not to capitalism but to civil society, and that some 15 years before the fall of the Berlin Wall.

The late Reagan years, according to the prevalent European interpretation, have been rather the Gorbachev years. USSR Party Chairman Michail Gorbachev himself was impressed with the ideas of the peace movement, the Prague Spring and a social market economy. He definitely knew that he could not possibly run the risk of an all-out war. He was surely very unhappy about Ronald Reagan's confrontation but resisted internal pressures from the Red Army for a continued rearmament. Instead, he artfully steered events domestically and internationally towards a non-violent transition.[2] Continental Europeans never during this period felt motivated to give markets dominance over the state. Yet, they worked on the completion of the Internal Market, which transferred considerable authorities from nation states to the European Community, later the European Union. This process did strengthen markets, but the understanding was always that the state or the EU authorities remained fully in charge of securing public goods and social equity and cohesion.

Later historians will probably find some truth in both the American and the European interpretation of the fall of communism. But there is also some communality between the two views. Both interpretations agreed that communism, based on W. I. Lenin's ideology, was bad economics for anything like an advanced technological society. In an age of electronic communication, an authoritarian, central planning system was miserably inefficient. Significantly, in the context of this book, Lenin's and Stalin's[3] concept of communism also included the ideology that energy, water and bread should be provided at very low cost. Economists both in Europe and the US are not surprised that a system that would not allow prices to reflect the true cost of production would run into deep troubles. In short, aside from all military and political factors, you could say that communism collapsed because it would not let prices tell the economic truth. But if that was so, capitalism could collapse if it wasn't allowing prices to tell the 'ecological truth'.

Let us from here dig a bit deeper into history. The collapse of communism in 1989 was the end point of a 70-year phase of state dominance, starting with World War I in 1914. During this period, first militaristic nationalism, most gruesome during the German Nazi time, and later state-centred economic planning saw the private sector rather as a subordinate part of nation states. Indeed, in the US and a few other countries, the private sector always enjoyed a stronger and more independent role – as President Calvin Coolidge proclaimed in the 1920s, 'The business of America is business.' Most other countries, however, such as Japan, India, Mexico, the West European countries, or China before and after the communist revolution, followed an entirely state-driven path of development.

After World War II, the ideological difference between a market-oriented model of development, embraced by the US, and Soviet communism became the main line of controversy worldwide. State dominance was now more associated with the Nazi terror and with Stalin's communism. Against these very unattractive models of governance, the ideal of the 'free world' (civil liberties, free markets and democracy) was created, as the core of 'Western' identity. Yet communism was aggressively spreading at the time, conquering Czechoslovakia, turning China upside down, intruding in South Korea, and threatening further expansion in Latin America, Asia, Europe and European colonies in Africa. The best answer to this communist 'bacillus', as it was called, was the creation of an economically successful market economy with a social face. US Secretary of State George C. Marshall, the former top military general of the US Army, launched the European Recovery Program, and European states established a highly inclusive model of a social market economy with a view to refute the communist monopoly claim over social justice. The social market economy was still very much based on state dominance, as education, social security, postal services, railways and airlines as well as most utilities remained in public hands, and some governments, such as Clement Attlee's Labour government in Britain, even renationalized certain businesses that were seen as crucial for the economy.

Twenty years later terrible pollution problems plagued the Western countries, and nobody doubted that it was a new task for the state to set the rules to reduce pollution to tolerable levels. Similarly, when the Club of Rome in 1972 published *Limits to Growth*, the state was called to action to reduce resource consumption by industry and to re-educate people to more modest lifestyles. The newly decolonized countries saw themselves as the 'Third World', conceivably representing a 'Third Way' between capitalism and communism. Their vision was also absolutely state centred, and it resonated well with intellectuals both in the communist bloc and in Western democracies. On the side of economic theory, the dominant creed became Keynesianism, implying massive state interventions ('deficit spending') to stimulate the economy in times of recession or stagnation, assuming that states could pay the bills later, when a recovering economy would let revenues gush.

What brought this phase of state dominance to its end? It was almost certainly the extremely uncomfortable situation called 'stagflation' that developed during the 1970s nearly worldwide.[4] The oil price shocks of 1973 and 1978 pushed nearly all countries, except the oil-exporting countries, into recession and steeply rising unemployment. When Keynesian deficit spending was applied to remedy the situation, things only got worse, and a rampant inflation set in, caused mainly by public overspending. The sum of unemployment and inflation percentages was called the 'misery index', or the 'stagflation index', as shown in Figure 10.1.

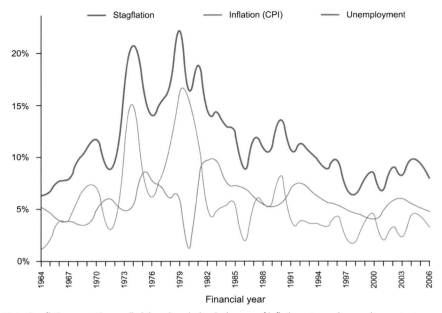

Note: Stagflation, sometimes called the misery index, is the sum of inflation rates and unemployment rates.
Source: Courtesy of Brady Postma, based on data from US Bureau of Labor Statistics

Figure 10.1 *Inflation, unemployment and stagflation in the US*

Stagflation was the signal for Prime Minister Margret Thatcher in the UK and for President Ronald Reagan in the US to fundamentally challenge the mindset of deficit spending and of the state-dominated societies. Based on the philosophy of Milton Friedman and the Chicago School of Economics, they reverted economic policies to 'supply-side economics', assuming that economic growth can be stimulated by offering incentives for industry to supply goods and services. Tax reduction and deregulation were seen as such incentives. The role of the state, according to the new philosophy, should be drastically reduced and all functions that could conceivably be done by private business should be taken away from the state. The new pro-market strategy was very successful not only in the UK and the US but also in Chile, where it was introduced with US support a few years earlier by dictator Augusto Pinochet. Later success stories were New Zealand under the Labour Prime Minister David Lange and the Netherlands, where a broad societal consensus was orchestrated by Prime Minister Ruud Lubbers. Gradually the idea of a state reduced to core functions became the mainstream position among academic economists and enjoyed growing political support in many countries. Contrasting stagflation (associated with Keynesianism) and some encouraging growth rates in the neo-conservative countries made it plausible even for some earlier progressive thinkers to take sides with the conservative trend, which certainly played a major role in de-legitimizing all forms of state dominance, including the earlier dreams of a 'Third Way'.

While it is not the intention of this chapter to deny the merits of conservative governments reducing inflation, bureaucratic regulations and excessive fiscal loads, the economic upswing celebrated by Britain, the US or New Zealand since the mid 1980s also had reasons completely outside the conservative ideology. Most importantly, oil and other commodity prices were conveniently falling, reflecting rising supplies due to additional discoveries, and slowing demand from sluggish economies. Moreover, the successes of the US and other countries came at a high price abroad. Falling commodity prices, in combination with the high interest rates the Federal Reserve Bank had imposed on the US dollar sent many developing countries into a deep debt crisis. In effect, the 1980s saw a massive transfer of economic wealth from the poor countries to the rich, in particular to the US.

Another victim of the conservative policy reversal was the environment. Market fundamentalists and some of their political patrons showed an open contempt for environmental concerns. President Reagan's first Secretary of the Interior, James Watt, in charge of the environment portfolio, said about environmentalists, 'A left-wing cult dedicated to bringing down the type of government I believe in'[5]; and on his agenda he said, 'We will mine more, drill more, cut more timber.'[6] Environmental 'optimism' (meaning that the environment was in a healthy state and perfectly capable of restoring itself) was a standard element in their rhetoric, aggressively opposing the language of the Club of Rome and of environmentalists of earlier times. The Reagan administration declared it as its duty to reverse much of the strict environmental legislation adopted in the US during the 1970s.

Market triumphalism

Reagan and Thatcher were successful leaders in their own countries and were recognized abroad for their economic success, but remained controversial political figures. The risky confrontation with the Soviet empire, the tough stance on indebted developing countries, and the negligence concerning the environment were among the most important issues of critics of the neo-conservative leaders. The 'Washington Consensus', strongly backed by Reagan and Thatcher, subjected indebted developing countries to painful structural adjustments. In much of Latin America, the 1980s are often referred to as the 'lost decade' during which much of the middle class were driven into poverty while just a few moved up to the financial elite.[7] This mostly negative perception changed after the collapse of the Soviet Union. Reagan's skilful handling of the Reykjavik Summit with Gorbachev was acknowledged on the international stage. An increasing number of people worldwide, including people of developing countries, saw the downsides of bureaucratic government and the benefits of a free exchange of goods and services. The Uruguay Round of the General Agreement on Tariffs and Trade (GATT), which started in 1986 but had stagnated until 1990, got a new lease of life. By 1993 it became the most far-reaching free trade round in history, leading to the creation in 1994 of the World Trade Organization (WTO).

But then, also after 1990, something happened that was neither planned nor predicted by anybody – capitalism, fully conscious of its complete victory, became more and more one-sided and arrogant. The earlier practice of social inclusion crumbled and was replaced by the philosophy of maximization of returns on investment. Publicly traded companies were relentlessly forced into increasing their shareholder value lest they be taken over by competitors or by private equity companies that might come in, slash staff, chop up the company, remove all that was not highly profitable, and finally leave taking huge profits with them. This method earned them admiration on the financial markets but also the questionable title of 'locusts' in circles of globalization critics. They surely were major players if not trendsetters in what soon was called the 'global casino'.[8] Countries were pushed into a mutual competition of pleasing investors. Deregulation, tax cuts for corporations (see Figure 10.2), reduced social benefits for workers, and business-friendly planning procedures were the currency of this intensified wooing of potential investors. Almost no space was left for the environment and for long-term thinking. For many years, the gap between the rich and the poor was widening in nearly all countries, as is documented in the International Labour Organization's (ILO) 2008 *World of Work* Report.[9]

Markets triumphed over states and forced politicians worldwide to adopt policies that pleased investors. As long as economic expansion continued and stock prices kept rising, the public in most countries welcomed, or at least toler-

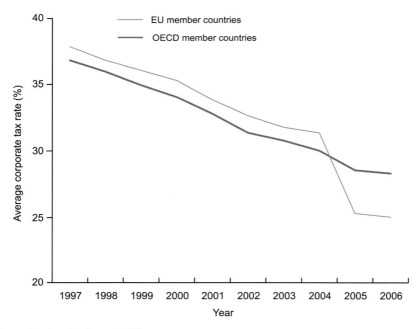

Source: Based on data from KPMG[10]

Figure 10.2 *OECD and EU average corporate tax rates (1997–2006)*

ated, the new doctrine, assuming that economic growth would eventually benefit all. Support was strongest in the winning countries such as China, Singapore, the US, Australia, Ireland or Estonia. Ireland and Estonia were the leaders in the EU in reducing corporate taxes, thereby inducing companies from all over Europe to move their operations, or headquarters into these tax havens. All told, however, this was a zero sum game; what (temporarily) Ireland won was lost by Sweden, France or Germany, while the real winners were companies and their shareholders, and the losers were the public goods and the people depending on them. At the same time a new movement of globalization critics emerged pinpointing growing inequality, environmental degradation and warning of dangerous market instabilities, as were observed during the Asian, Mexican and Russian currency crises of the late 1990s.[11] Also, in academic circles, the monopoly position of pure market economics was challenged by more balanced voices. Herman Daly and his school of ecological economists opposed the myopic growth paradigm and environmental cynicism of the Chicago school and its political supporters.[12] Nicholas Stern in his famous review of the economics of climate change,[13] called global warming the biggest market failure ever, adding substance to the spreading recognition that markets can't be left alone in tackling the problems of the world.[14]

Market dominance went hand in hand with deregulation, liberalization and privatization of earlier public functions. The motive was increasing economic efficiency, innovation and growth through open competition. The promise to the public was also to bring prices down. This worked for airlines, telecommunication and a few other sectors. In the case of water, health services, education, local public transport and other state-subsidized functions, predictably the effect was the opposite, as the private operators were not willing to work at prices and fees below cost coverage. In electricity, gas, waste management and a few other cases, the price effect was mixed.[15] Regarding resource efficiency, reduced prices such as in the airlines sector were absolutely the wrong signal. Cheap flights fuelled fabulous growth rates for the sector with the largest greenhouse gas footprints per hour. Competition in the power sector also encouraged additional consumption, unless very strict regulation, like in California, moved the utilities and the appliance industry toward electrical efficiency.

Clearly there has been a lot to say about misgivings of market triumphalism long before the economic collapse of 2008. It will be important not to forget this as people begin to work on remedies to the collapse. It won't be enough to work on a re-regulation of the financial sector and to remove those perverse incentives for corporate managers that were part of the problem. Equally destructive, were the competitive battles for highest returns on investment, the ignorance and cynicism about resources and the environment, and the general contempt for the state.

Much of the economic crisis, as is well known, resulted from the fouling of millions of sub-prime mortgages on private homes in the US. They accumulated in good faith during a phase of fallacious and cynical environmental optimism since the Reagan years. Ridiculously low fuel prices encouraged millions of American families to build homes up to 50 miles away from potential jobs and many services. Real estate value in the US was seen as an absolutely safe bet for investors and lenders. And mortgage companies gave bonuses to their agents and leaders in proportion to the number of new contracts. A bubble of secondary mortgages grew to gigantic dimensions and rested on the assumption of steadily rising real estate values. And this assumption was based on the illusion that daily long-distance commuting even with gas-guzzling SUVs would remain affordable to the average commuter for a very long time. All this gigantic edifice of illusions and instruments to conceal the illusion collapsed when finally oil prices began to tell a story of real scarcity. America and the world, we are suggesting, would have been spared the financial crisis if prices for commuting and housing had been much closer to the ecological truth in the first place. Of course, financial deregulation and excessive profit expectations also played a role in the saga of the financial meltdown.

Global rules and civil society can help defend public interest

Since the second half of 2008, the dominance of markets over the public sector imbalance has come into disrepute and has de facto ended. What is still missing is a newly established and stable balance between private and public interests, between markets and the state. The new balance should restore long-term thinking, social equity and environmental sustainability, accompanied by a technological transition toward the significant levels of resource productivity described in this book. Defending the rights of the weaker parts of society and setting incentives for an ecologically sustainable development is something markets and the private sector cannot provide. On the other hand, we see and to a large extent accept, the neoliberal logic of markets being indispensable for overcoming certain notorious state inefficiencies. So there is no point, in an era of global competition, in resurrecting the old powers of nation states. Protectionism that is a temptation in times of crisis has never truly worked and impedes the creation of new wealth. What we have called a 'strong state' is surely not an arrogant, protectionist and bureaucratic state. Are there other ways and means of re-establishing a healthy balance between public goods and private interests? The answer will have two quite different components, with one being 'global governance' and the other 'civil society'.

Global governance means that rules and institutions must be further developed and adopted, and they have to be respected by private businesses from all countries. Climate policy clearly needs a global regime with no major geographical loopholes. Similarly, the ILO's 'Core Labour Standards' should be respected and enforced in some way everywhere. So far among the specialized agencies and bodies of the United Nations system, only the WTO has muscles to enforce its rules. The WTO rules, however, are intrinsically pro-market and against government stipulations, which usually are seen as 'trade barriers'. The ILO, the United Nations Educational, Scientific and Cultural Organization (UNESCO) and the UN Environment Programme (UNEP) have essentially no sanctions at their hands to enforce restrictions to business operations for the sake of labour rights, culture or the environment. Global governance is a long-term agenda also requiring a reform of the United Nations including its Security Council, and the international financial institutions. This book cannot even begin to outline the political steps that will be needed on this agenda. But some steps have already been made in the right direction – for example, measures against tax evasion, tax havens and related problems that were discussed and partly adopted at the London G20 Summit in April 2009.

The other essential agenda is the strengthening of civil society. During the restless late 1960s and early 1970s, when the state was criticized by millions of mostly young intellectuals, while the private sector enjoyed even less sympathies, a 'third force' emerged and found its themes in environmental activism, pacifism, justice, feminism and many other themes. When the first United Nations Conference on the Human Environment (UNCHE) was held in Stockholm in 1972, civil society organizations (CSOs), less stringently also called non-governmental organizations (NGOs), turned up by the hundreds and greatly influenced media reporting about the conference, and thereby many delegates. This event and many others afterwards created a new understanding of a global movement standing for public goods that were not sufficiently represented by states, let alone private companies.[16] CSOs are usually well connected and tend to be able to launch campaigns locally, nationally and internationally. They can influence international negotiations, for instance on climate or on biodiversity. They can name and shame and help boycott private firms as well as states violating or neglecting important principles related to public goods. During the time of market triumphalism, many CSOs, suffering from lack of funds, were lured into the orbit of private companies, often for no other purpose than green-washing, or for very limited tasks not conflicting with the business interests of the corporate sector. Now is the time, we feel, that CSOs can emancipate themselves from such limited roles and help create a worldwide consciousness and legal frame for environmental sustainability.

What we can imagine is a movement bringing global governance and the civil society together in a new and very worthy undertaking, the 'Global Green New Deal' proclaimed by UNEP's Executive Director, Achim Steiner, and meanwhile by others, as a promising way of overcoming the economic downturn. If civil society stands together asking for all stimulus packages to be greened and if consumer organizations – perhaps the most influential CSOs – launch a worldwide trend of green purchasing, there is a good chance for the Green New Deal becoming a reality.

Notes

1   Wilentz (2008).
2   Gorbachev (2003).
3   Fiehn and Corin (2002).
4   Bruno and Sachs (1985).
5   Yahoo geocities (undated) 'The Reagan Years: Environment', www.geocities.com/thereaganyears/environment.htm, accessed 3 May 2009.
6   ibid.
7   Carrasco (2007).
8   Midleton (2003); Henderson (2008).
9   ILO (2008).
10 KPMG (2004) Table 2.
11 Klein (2007).
12 Daly (1999).
13 Stern (2007).
14 For further reading on limits to globalized markets see Stiglitz (2002, 2006).
15 For further evidence in various sectors see von Weizsäcker et al (2005).
16 Princen and Finger (1994).

11
Sufficiency in a Civilized World

Ernst von Weizsäcker

The World has enough to fulfil all our needs but not our greed.
Mahatma Gandhi

Introduction

The recent economic downturn since 2008 has thrown many families into poverty, homelessness, even bitter hunger, a fate hundreds of millions of people worldwide have experienced for a very long time. The challenge surely remains to allow and reinstitute a decent living for all those hundreds of millions, leading almost inevitably to more resource consumption again. All the more urgent will it be for the well-to-do to learn to live with less resource consumption and not to demand ever more material consumption.

This leads us to question why it is so difficult to depart from material dreams towards sufficiency. Well, for many people, if not most, is not the typical dream to be able to secure the means for a decent living? That could mean a nice family home or at least a comfortable apartment, one car, if not two, healthy food, good-quality clothing and some cosmetics, reliable medical care, access to global culture and entertainment, and enjoyable sports and holidays. And when the neighbours move up the ladder to having additional rooms for a nanny or a visitor, a high-end cuisine, perhaps a golf club membership, fancy communications technology, and long-distance tourism, people will feel the temptation of going for similar attributes of wealth. Individuals and families shouldn't be blamed for such widespread attitudes. They are subject to the respective conditioning from marketing, the media and politics, all wanting more growth, with little regard to its environmental impact. Growth is widely seen as the basis for jobs at least in the consumer goods, touristic and construction industries. However, in its current form it is a significant driver for a deteriorating climate, destruction of more and more natural habitats, and resource depletion. It is exactly what is not sustainable for a world of seven or more billion humans. Even with significant productivity gains the world cannot fulfil all such dreams of consumption and pleasures for an ever growing world population. Our civilizations worldwide have to face *sufficiency*, or *some* limits to greed, growth and consumption. The political art will be to make this process satisfying for most sides. We assume that high-quality life and satisfaction based on the two pillars of efficiency and sufficiency can be achieved even for a world of seven or more billion people.

The insight is not all that new. It was at the core of the growth concerns of the early 1970s. One of the first attempts at putting the concerns into a formula was made by Paul Ehrlich and John Holdren,[1] with the famous 'IPAT' formula, namely:

$I = P \times A \times T$, *suggesting that the environmental Impact (I) could be estimated by Population (P) times Affluence per capita (A) times a technology factor (T).*

At the time of publication, technology mostly referred to pollution control. As pollution control succeeded, T was shrinking, meaning a reduction of the (negative) environmental impact even at times of growing population and affluence. In the context of this book, T would shrink fivefold as resource productivity grows fivefold. It is clear that the potential of resource productivity increases, on which we have presented an optimistic but technically realistic outlook, will eventually be exhausted. A factor of five improvement may just not be enough under conditions of rapid growth of population and affluence to prevent a dangerous deterioration of climate or other worldwide environmental conditions. Hence it will be reasonable also to look at the other factors of IPAT, population and affluence. Population is not a factor we are addressing to any significant extent in this book; however, we feel we can say something about reducing 'affluence'.

When talking about curbing affluence, we refer to consumption above the requirements of a decent living, such as food, shelter and reasonable amenities including mobility. For the provision of those, Part I of this book has offered ample evidence on the scope of increasing resource productivity, which should indeed be exploited to the fullest. But we suggest that in addition to this a movement towards sufficiency – that is, shifting lifestyles closer to the level of requirement for a decent living – will be needed. Note that also the term of 'sustainable consumption' as it was outlined in 2002 by the UNEP *Sustainable Consumption and Production* report,[2] refers essentially to the same matter of reducing affluence, referring to the concept of 'Low Impact Affluence'.[3]

Research by a team at the Commonwealth Scientific and Industrial Research Organisation (CSIRO) and Sydney University, Australia, demonstrated the importance of sustainable consumption by showing that households' purchasing decisions of consumer items have a far greater negative

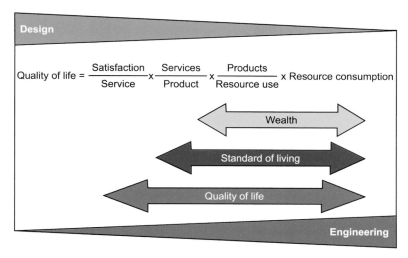

Source: Courtesy of Joachim Spangenberg

Figure 11.1 *Quality of life seen as the product of four variables*

environmental impact indirectly than many of the changes they made to their energy and water usage at home.[4] They concluded that a household's consumption footprint to a large degree defines its ecological footprint. Consumer choices in favour of the efficiency improvements outlined in Part I of this book will play an important part in reducing the ecological footprints. In addition to efficiency-oriented purchasing, it could also involve lifestyle changes that could fall under the lower affluence category, such as: drinking filtered water from the tap instead of bottled water; avoiding plasma TV screens and creating consumer demand for LED TV screens; growing some vegetables, fruit and herbs locally and avoiding transport energy; and using bicycles and public transport for commuting instead of automobiles.

Ecological concerns using the IPAT formula by its definition seeks a *reduction*, in the case of 'I'. Related formulae have been developed seeking an *increase*, for example of 'quality of life'. Joachim Spangenberg[5] has proposed the relations shown in Figure 11.1. The Factor Five story comprises the second and third variables, services per product and products per resource use. A Factor Five improvement in resource productivity would provide twice the quality of life per unit of resource consumption than a factor of 2.5, assuming the same satisfaction per service unit.

'Sufficiency' is embedded in the first variable called 'satisfaction per service'. As people enjoy more satisfaction from the same service, their felt quality of life is increasing without added resource consumption and even without added efficiency. The resource-productivity-focused considerations in Spangenberg's picture are mostly related to engineering, while the movement from (technical) services to felt satisfaction and quality of life relates to what he calls 'design'. By the flat and continuous triangles in his picture, symbolizing design on the upper side and engineering on the lower, Spangenberg indicates a close vicinity, even overlap, between resource productivity and sufficiency, which was also the case with the results of the CSIRO study. Figure 11.1 indicates that there are mutual synergies between resource productivity and sufficiency. It will be important also to note that reducing 'A' in the IPAT formula does not always mean a reduction of consumption-based affluence but can just as well mean a redefinition of affluence into pleasures of a less resource-consuming nature, which would increase the first variable in Spangenberg's equation, 'satisfaction per service', which again is a measure of sufficiency.

Measuring happiness

The IPAT equation, as well as Spangenberg's multiplication shown in Figure 11.1, cannot claim to be quantitative, unless and until the respective factors are quantifiable, which is not the case for I and A. Attempts have been made to quantify 'I', for example in the case of climate with the *Stern Review* establishing itself as a well-respected reference on the matter. Other topics have found other measures, such as the Ecological Footprint, the loss of biodiversity, the degree of eutrophication, and MIPS (material input per service), according to leading thinkers in the field such as Friedrich Schmidt-Bleek. What has caused rather more difficulty is a measure for the quality of life (e.g. for Spangenberg's formula), or affluence in the IPAT formula.

What is it that makes people happy? Rather than the material goods listed earlier as components for a decent living, it may be having a successful marriage, meaningful work, friends, being a part of a community. A shift to sustainable consumption can be a part of society's improving overall happiness, well-being and quality of life, rather than a sacrifice.[6] Factor Five products and system improvements can hugely help societies in this transition to sustainable consumption. All this is hardly taken care of in the gross domestic product (GDP), which is essentially a measure of turnover, not of happiness. There is a host of literature[7] about the inconsistencies, incompleteness and even dangers lying in the usual GDP yardstick. For instance, typical traffic accidents increase the GDP because they trigger car repair or replacement, rescue services, medical treatment, sometimes legal proceedings, rehabilitation, enhanced insurance premiums and so on, and yet nobody would therefore wish more accidents to happen. Also environmental damages can be sources of huge GDP growth. Imagine the effect on the construction industry worldwide of a one-metre rise of the sea level.

Herman Daly was one of the pioneers of establishing alternative measures of well-being. He once said that, 'Current economic growth has uncoupled itself from the world and has become irrelevant. Worse, it has become a blind guide.'[8] In his pivotal book[9] he developed the Index for Sustainable Economic Welfare (ISEW), estimating the amount and quality of essential services and taking into account that a deteriorating environment means a loss of the

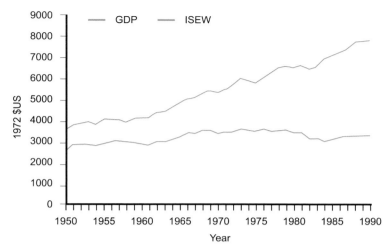

Source: Based on data from Cobb and Cobb (1994)[10]

Figure 11.2 *The Index of Sustainable Economic Welfare (ISEW)
compared to US GDP from 1950 to 1990*

quality of life. He then compared the rise and development of the ISEW with
that of the GDP, and observed that in all industrialized countries the ISEW and
GDP went together until the early 1970s – after which the GDP kept growing,
while the ISEW lagged behind, as Figure 11.2 indicates for the US.

Other measures of satisfaction, human needs or happiness have been developed. The most widely used one is the Human Development Index (HDI), a
standardised measurement used by the United Nations Development
Programme (UNDP) in their annual Human Development Reports. HDI = 1
means 'perfect' human development services. The HDI also correlates with
GDP and also with the Ecological Footprints but not strictly. Figure 11.3, from
the Global Footprint Network, shows sub-Saharan African countries rather
systematically with low HDI and small footprints, and the rich OECD
countries with large footprints and highest HDI, but it also shows that there is
scope among the small footprint countries to achieve a higher HDI, and scope
for high HDI countries to reduce their footprints. To quantify this statement in
the context of Factor Five: a fivefold increase of resource productivity – that is,
reduced specific ecological footprints – could move all countries, or nearly all,
into what is depicted as the 'sustainability quadrant' – the rich reducing their
resource consumption without losing any HDI, and the poor moving up the
HDI without enlarging their footprints.

The fact that per capita 'permitted' footprints were twice as large in 1961
than in 2005 (the horizontal dotted lines) results, of course, from the fact that
world population was about half as large in 1961 compared with 2005.

Yet another approach has been taken by Richard Heinberg[11] saying that,
past a certain point, increased consumption does not translate to an increase in

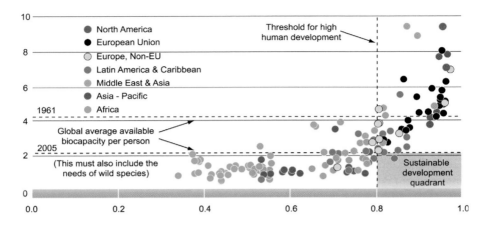

Note: The 'sustainable development quadrant' of HDI, above 0.8 and footprints below two hectares per person is underpopulated (Cuba just made it into the quadrant), meaning that we live in an unsustainable world. A factor of five of efficiency improvement theoretically could move nearly all countries into the quadrant.
Source: Global Footprint Network (2008)[12]

Figure 11.3 *The Human Development Index and Ecological Footprint of Nations*

happiness. He presents data collected from BP, World Values Survey and the UN, showing Mexico's and Venezuela's self-reported happiness to be close to 20 per cent higher than the US while simultaneously using 25–35 per cent of US energy consumption per capita. This and many other similar findings suggest that once human beings have crossed a threshold of consumption, there may be a decline down the other side of a happiness curve.

The message of this subchapter is that once a certain degree of wealth is reached and is distributed with a degree of fairness, politicians and the broader public need not be afraid if growth and consumption are flattening out, provided other factors supporting happiness are strong. One big concern remains, though – employment. Under the present conditions, employment hinges on turnover (GDP) not on happiness, and this will be investigated at the end of this chapter. But it may be noted already here, that the shift of emphasis advocated in Chapter 9 from increasing labour productivity to resource productivity through a reduction of the fiscal load on labour, and the increase of the fiscal load on resources can reduce unemployment.

Satisfaction in strong communities

There is a large body of experience and empirical literature about satisfaction and happiness outside material growth. It is assumed that the increasing of resource productivity, or elegance of production and consumption, will satisfy many people beyond the goods and services they enjoy. Knowing that the damaging ecological footprints are reduced can make people proud and happy. The systems improvements shown in many examples of Part I of this book also involve teamwork and community development. Think of the teamwork for greening of restaurants, agriculture or transport systems. They all involve a transition from isolated, competition-dominated work to honouring team results. As Mary Clark observes:[13] 'the survival of our species from earliest times to the present required co-operation and human bonding rather than competing'. Her anthropology may contradict the commonly held view in the tradition of Thomas Hobbes of selfish, materialistic and mutually competing humans, but Clark's rich historical and empirical evidence is very strong, and the idea that seven billion mutually competing individuals steered essentially by the Invisible Hand will solve the huge environmental problems outlined in the Introduction is outright absurd. Humans need communities almost as much as honeybees and ants do.

Mary Clark on satisfaction

Human 'satisfaction' in life arises from the fulfilment of three genetically inscribed psychological needs that seem obvious, yet often conflict with each other in our day-to-day experiences. The first to manifest itself is our need for 'attachment', that biologically powerful bond that exists between a helpless newborn infant and its mother. Indeed, human infants attract positive attention from most everyone around them. This is a universal, inborn human trait that insures our species' continued existence. Moreover, this 'need' to feel accepted by others, to be valued for one's self, continues throughout human life. Obituaries often recount how people's lives 'mattered' to those around them.

At the same time that we are forming strong attachments, however, we each increasingly assert our own independence of action, our personal 'autonomy'. No one likes being ordered about – told how, when, where and why – to live their life. Without the freedom to explore, we never become problem-solvers. From learning the skill of walking, to learning to pilot a jet plane, or to conduct an orchestra, or most important of all, to create solutions to novel problems – all are accomplished by our own independent self-motivation. We need to discover for ourselves how to solve a task, and when we do discover the answer to a 'puzzle' there is a giant wave of satisfaction – our psychological reward – a feeling of 'triumph', of being 'in control' of our world. Undue restriction of personal freedom is universally distasteful and deeply resented. We are not programmable robots – yet our overly organized, super-efficient modern societies increasingly impose robot-like skills on upcoming generations.

Our third, and by far most complex human need is for 'meaning'. Culture is, in fact, the subject matter that dominates library shelves and our daily lives. What is the 'tapestry of meaning' that results in a group of emotionally needy and yet freedom-loving human beings to function as an effective social unit? Each human society satisfies this collective necessity via its past long history of experiences – engraved in the expected behavioural rules that constitute 'the way we live'. Codes of behaviour, relationships, duties – all are enfolded into the traditional institutions that accumulate and slowly (often imperceptibly) evolve over time. These codes have strong emotional power, as well, for they define 'who' each individual is within the group – thus framing his or her 'existential identity'.

Each human culture has tackled the inevitable tensions between our need for attachment (belonging/being accepted) and our need for autonomy (acting independently) in its own unique ways. These give rise to the 'cultural story' or the 'social brain' – what I like to call, a 'tapestry of meaning', that is transmitted into the brains of each new generation.

Not surprisingly, few cultural tapestries (or world views) are uniformly accepted by all members of a society, particularly in our modern era of global-wide multicultural awareness. There are tensions between the autonomous desires of some people to loosen old restrictions, and the powerful emotional attachment to familiar customs by others. 'Sacred' social histories or religious arguments often block simple modifications of the tapestry of meaning, leading to deep emotional rifts within a society. Furthermore, many societies have in recent decades experienced increasing immigrations of peoples from other cultures who want to 'assimilate', further muddying the 'meaning' of the original collective story. Spreading dissatisfaction, for whatever reason, often results in an imposition of greater social controls and a loss of individual autonomy within modern societies.

This sequence of events can all too easily snowball into a 'police state', with extreme forms of ideological 'justification' added to the cultural tapestry. Widespread dissatisfaction – from anger to outright fear – may spread through such a society. Even when the stress on a culture is less severe, the process of adaptive change of its 'sacred institutions' in order to meet new external circumstances, is likely to arouse deep-seated unease – significant emotional dissatisfaction – unless the people, themselves, are able autonomously to express their preferences and feel a sense of ownership in the process. At a minimum, this requires some sort of outlet for the peoples' voices – the intended role of a democracy.

Simply 'voting' however, is only minimally satisfying to the human psyche. In very large societies, it is perhaps the only 'efficient' method of introducing acceptable changes in social patterns and institutions. Far more powerful, albeit much slower *and costly in terms of individual social commitment, would be much longer-lasting social dialogues regarding possible changes – nationwide discussions, held at many local places and recurring over a long period of time (at least a year) for major changes in the shared tapestry of meaning. This would allow psychological 'ownership' of the changes being introduced, and a higher likelihood of widespread satisfaction with the outcome. (What is being suggested here is a much more active, participatory form of social decision-making than currently exists in the world's democracies.)*

A model for this already exists, albeit in informal ways, in most large societies. I am speaking of the spontaneous grassroots activities that already occur, not at national levels, but locally. Within most large modern societies, there are small groups organized to redress – or at least ameliorate – the neglected consequences of local social inadequacies.

One small example encapsulates the situation I am trying to describe. It comes from my niece, and it explains what social compassion means far better than all the social scientists' piles of research data. After celebrating at home on Christmas Eve, her family group of seven went 'off to San Francisco Christmas morning to prepare meals in the 'tenderloin' (poorest district in San Francisco) for some 3700 people. It took most of the day, and we were exhausted by the time we got off BART (the Bay Area Rapid Transport), but it was such a great experience. We'll definitely do it again.

This sort of fully autonomous, grassroots activity yields enormous satisfaction to all concerned – the givers and receivers. It offers a model for achieving social change, of whatever sort, by using the power of positive emotional rewards, that increase human satisfaction, in order to initiate needed institutional change, rather than coercive threats and punishments that subtract from a society's reservoir of satisfaction.

Several authors also describe new forms of community building, often motivated by concerns about destruction of the environment and leading to high degrees of satisfaction among participants. Richard Heinberg was already mentioned in a related context. Others include Thomas Homer-Dixon,[14] Julian Darley, Bill McKibben, Rob Hopkins,[15] Howard Odum and David Holmgren, to name those best known in the Anglo-Saxon world. They all in different ways suggest that a more mature civilization will be a lot more elegant and efficient than ours is today and will also acknowledge the virtues of culture, human friendship, intergenerational solidarity and indeed sufficiency. Many speak about the value of prosperity with less material inputs, as well as being outside or beyond our efficiency agenda. Odum called it the 'prosperous road down' and some are using the term 'transition culture' – an exploration into the value of a life lived with less available energy input. In different, if related, ways, all authors argue that reduced material inputs need not be a negative thing at all.

Indeed, it can have quite positive effects, such as the reconnection to land, community, and an appreciation for the resources and character of immediate surroundings. Efforts are afoot to create 'transition towns' – in Totnes, UK, Kinsale, Ireland and Eudlo, Australia. These are places committed to pursuing a higher quality of living without a higher level of consumption. Kinsale, for example, is a town of approximately 3000 people, which adopted a plan in 2005. Without losing appreciation for all that they have been given by industrialized society, this re-localized and empowered community is trying to rediscover the value in growing its own food, building its own energy-efficient homes, generating its own electricity (within a ten-mile radius), supporting its local artists, designing user-friendly transportation systems for bicycles and electric vehicles, and even developing its own local aquaculture. Aside from the social impetus holding the community together, it can be assumed that Kinsale achieves more than Factor Five improvements in resource consumption – and much of that not by high-tech efficiency but rather by low-tech sufficiency.

Coming back closer to the productivity of land and harvesting, produce from low-input plant cultivation is not an experience restricted to rural communities. The concept of 'permaculture' developed by David Holmgren in the 1970s and evolving over 30 years is also applicable in cities with some garden space. According to the Permaworld Foundation, permaculture is defined as, 'consciously designed landscapes which mimic the patterns and relationships found in nature, while yielding abundance of food, fibre and energy for provision of local needs'.[16] It became a lifeline reality in Cuba after the Soviet collapse in 1989/1990, when Cuba was suddenly cut off from previously steady supplies of energy and some food. Within a short time, using permaculture or similar techniques, many Cuban towns learned to produce 80–100 per cent of the food its citizens needed. While we look at transformation towns, permaculture and similar experiments with a degree of sympathy, we feel they are far from serving as realistic models for seven billion people. Historical experience with similar movements during the 1970s, or even during the 19th century, seems to suggest that they are not really stable, and if they are, can become museum pieces such as the Amish culture in Pennsylvania.

Time, jobs and growth reconsidered

Sustainable consumption is closely related to having enough time to enjoy. The OECD's 2009 study, *Society at a Glance*,[17] showed that the French and the Japanese use considerably more time than Mexicans or US Americans for eating and for sleeping. And yet, you find much less obesity in France or Japan than in the US. And the French use much less energy, live longer, and seemingly have developed a superior *savoir vivre*. Having time for the pleasures of life has been a priority concern in France for a long time. As early as 1979, a group of authors writing under the pseudonym Adret published a book[18] suggesting reduction of the average daily work time to two hours, and the book became extremely popular in France. It never worked out that way, but chiefly, as the advocates of the book say, international competition forced France into the relentless race for highest economic output, regardless of the quality of life lost in the process. Also in Germany, time plays an increasing role in discussions about the quality of life. A recent study on consumer policy to sustainable development puts consumer sovereignty over time at the top of concerns.[19] The idea is that scarce time almost invariably leads to indiscriminate overconsumption while comfortable time availability induces consumers to select more carefully, to take the time also for repairing things and to find pleasure relaxing at home, or with friends, without the felt need for crazy weekend tours to some distant islands.

Such rather anecdotal evidence can nevertheless lead to a new consideration of the role of jobs and of economic growth. If more time allows people to live happier, with less consumption, and typically with less money, it may be suggestive to think of a scenario where people work less whenever labour productivity grows. That would mean that the economy need not grow to keep the same workforce employed. The price paid for this is, of course, stagnant monthly incomes. But if in parallel resource productivity goes up, the purchasing power of the income does increase. And if the climate gets stabilized, jobs become more secure, and more free time becomes available, many people, probably the majority would find this a perfectly reasonable option. The downside is likely to be international competition again. If other countries don't follow suit, they may be able to throw goods and services on the market beating the products of the country doing the experiment.

This book can in no way answer all questions relating to the transformations a climate-friendly and resource-efficient society will have to go through. This last chapter in particular is more a set of questions than of answers. It is meant to encourage readers and politicians to reflect on the challenges with a fresh mind and with the courage to explore new avenues. It is hardly imaginable to find avenues allowing for unchanged further economic growth. The time is now also to think of avenues of high satisfaction with low economic turnover (GDP) and yet with lower rates of unemployment.

Notes

1   Ehrlich and Holdren (1971). The paper contains the basic idea, but the final formulation of IPAT originated from Paul Ehrlich.
2   UNEP (2002).
3   Hargroves and Smith (2005).
4   *Sydney Morning Herald* (2007).
5   Spangenberg (2009).
6   Daly (1996).
7   Daly and Cobb (1989).
8   Daly (2003).

9   Daly and Cobb (1989).

10   Cobb and Cobb (1994).

11   Heinberg (2004, 2007).

12   Global Footprint Network (undated) 'Our Human Development Initiative', www.footprintnetwork.org/en/index.php/GFN/page/fighting_poverty_our_human_development_initiative/, accessed 18 May 2009.

13   Clark (2002).

14   Homer-Dixon (2006).

15   Hopkins (2005).

16   Holmgren Design Services (undated) 'Permaculture: Peak Oil – The Source of Permaculture Vision and Innovation', www.holmgren.com.au/, accessed 12 May 2009.

17   OECD (2009). For country data see www.oecd.org/els/social/indicators/SAG, accessed 18 May 2009.

18   Adret (1979).

19   Eckert et al (2006).

Reference List

60 Minutes (2009) 'Could "Buy American" rule spark trade war?', *CBS News*, 13 February 2009

Abraham, L. E. (1996) 'Daylighting', in Public Technology Inc. and US Green Building Council (eds) *Sustainable Building Technical Manual*, Public Technology Inc., ppiv.7–iv.20.

ACTU/ACF (2008) *Green Gold Rush: How Ambitious Environmental Policy can Make Australia a Leader in the Global Race for Green Jobs*, Australian Council of Trade Unions and the Australian Conservation Foundation

Adret (1979) *Travailler deux heures par jour*, Le Seuil, Paris

Agarwal, A. and Narain, S. (1991) *Global Warming in an Unequal World: A Case of Environmental Colonialism*, Centre for Science and Environment, New Delhi

Alaoui, A., Feraille, A., Dimassi, A. and Nguyen, V. H. (2007) 'Experimental study of sulfoaluminate concrete based materials', CONSEC'07 Tours, France

Ali, M. and Talukder, M. (2008) 'Increasing water productivity in crop production – A synthesis', *Agricultural Water Management*, vol 95, no11, pp1201–1213

Ali, N. (2006) 'Energy management in agriculture: Status, issues and the strategy', presentation to 'Balancing Energy, Development and Climate Priorities in India', New Delhi, 30 November to 1 December 2006

American Council for an Energy-Efficient Economy (2004) 'Testimony of William R. Prindle', 7 October 2004, ACEEE Joint Economic Committee

American Iron and Steel Institute (2005) *Saving One Barrel of Oil per Ton (SOBOT): A New Roadmap for Transformation of Steelmaking Process*, American Iron and Steel Institute

American Iron and Steel Institute (2008) 'American steel committed to a sustainable future', News Releases, American Iron and Steel Institute, 21 April

Anderson, R. C. (1999) *Economic Savings from Using Economic Incentives for Environmental Pollution Control*, Report prepared for the US Environmental Protection Agency

Angel, D., Hamilton, T. and Huber, M. (2007) 'Global environmental standards for industry', *Annual Review of Environmental Resources*, vol 32, pp295–316

Architectural Energy Corporation (2003) *Design Brief: Integrated Design for Small Commercial HVAC*, Energy Design Resources

Arnfalk, P. (2002) 'Virtual mobility and pollution prevention: The emerging role of ICT based communication in organisations and its impact on travel', Dissertation, Lund University, Lund, Sweden

ASHRAE (1997) *ASHRAE Handbook: Fundamentals*, ASHRAE, Atlanta, GA

Aspen Publishers (2004) 'An Illinois Passivhaus', *Energy Design Update*, vol 24, no 5, Aspen Publishers

The Associated Press (2007) 'Europe to unplug from common light bulbs. In warming stand, bulb makers agree to eliminate least efficient lighting', *The Associated Press*, 7 March

Association of American Railroads Policy and Economics Department (2009) *Railroads: Green from the Start*, Association of American Railroads

Astle, P. (2008) 'The barriers to a greater use of reclaimed steel in the UK construction industry', MPhil thesis, Department of Engineering, University of Cambridge, UK

Atherton, J. (2007) 'Declaration of the metals industry on recycling principles', *International Journal of Life Cycle Analysis*, vol 12, no 1, pp59–60

Atif, M. R. and Galasiu, A. D. (2003) 'Energy performance of daylight-linked automatic lighting control systems in large atrium spaces: Report on two field-monitored case studies', *Energy and Buildings*, vol 35, pp441–461

Australia Food and Grocery Council (2003) *Environment Report 2003*, Department of Environment and Water, Australia

Australian Conservation Foundation (2005) 'Peter Garrett opening the new 60L building', *ACF Feature Articles*, May 2005

Australian Dairy Farmers (2004) *National Water Initiative*, Submission to COAG Senior Officials Group on Water, Australian Dairy Farmers

Australian Greenhouse Office (1999) *Australian Commercial Building Sector Greenhouse Gas Emissions 1990–2010*, Department of the Environment and Heritage, Commonwealth of Australia

Australian Greenhouse Office (2005a) *Energy Audit Tool: Lighting Control*, Department of the Environment and Heritage, Commonwealth of Australia

Australian Greenhouse Office (2005b) *Working Energy Program: Heating, Ventilation and Air-Conditioning (HVAC)*, Department of the Environment and Heritage, Commonwealth of Australia

Australian Greenhouse Office (2005c) *Energy Audit Tool: Boilers*, Department of the Environment and Heritage, Commonwealth of Australia

Australian Institute of Refrigeration, Air-Conditioning and Heating (2003) 'Case Study: Award winner makes its mark', *EcoLibrium*, August 2003, AIRAH

Australian Institute of Refrigeration, Air-Conditioning and Heating (2005) *Last Days of the Cooling Tower?*, AIRAH

Austvik, O. G. (1999) 'Norway's dependence on the oil and gas markets', *Internasjonal Politkk*, vol 57, no 3, p379

AWI (2007) *Wool Facts*, Australian Wool Innovation Limited, Australia

Baer, P., Athanasiou, T., Kartha, S. and Benedict, E. (2008) *The Greenhouse Development Rights Framework*, Heinrich Böll Foundation, Berlin

Barrow, M. (2006) *Initial Effects of the Landfill Allowance Trading Scheme*, Mimeo, University of Sussex

Bates, B. C., Kundzewicz, Z. W., Wu, S. and Palutikof, J. P. (eds) (2008) *Climate Change and Water*, Technical Paper of the Intergovernmental Panel on Climate Change, IPCC Secretariat, Geneva

Baumol, W. J. and Oates, W. E. (1988) *The Theory of Environmental Policy*, Cambridge University Press, Cambridge, UK

BBC (2006) 'Zero carbon homes plan unveiled', *BBC News*, London, 13 December 2006

BBC (2008a) 'Cut congestion zone, says Johnson', *BBC News*, 14 January 2008

BBC (2008b) 'Mayor quashes £25 C-charge hike', *BBC News*, 8 July 2008

Bean, P. (2008) 'Genset Locomotives blaze a trail down the low-emissions path', *Ecollo*, 14 October 2008

Bellefontaine, R., Petit. S., Pain-Orcet, M., Deleporte, P. and Bertault, J. G. (2002) *Trees Outside Forests and Production Systems*, Food and Agriculture Organization of the United Nations

Bennett-Woods, D. (2008) *Nanotechnology: Ethics and Society*, CRC Press, London and Boca Raton

Bertoldi, P. and Atanasiu, B. (2007) *Status Report 2006: Electricity Consumption and Efficiency Trends in the Enlarged European Union*, Institute for Environment and Sustainability

Biello, D. (2008) 'Jumbo jet no longer biofuel virgin after palm oil fuels flight', *Scientific American*, 25 February 2008

Binswanger, H. C., Frisch, H. and Nutzingeru, H. (1983) *Arbeit ohne Umweltzerstörung*, Fischer, Frankfurt

The Bioenergy Site (2008) 'China fires up first chicken manure-biogas plant', *The Bioenergy Site Latest News*, 6 August

Black, R. (2008) 'Shun meat, says UN climate chief', *BBC News*, 7 September 2008

Black, R. D., and Rogers, D. H. (1993) *Evaluating Pumping Plant Efficiency Using On-Farm Fuel Bills*, Kansas State University Cooperative Extension Service, Manhattan, Kansas, p4

Blanch, D. (2004) 'Waste plastic fuels Australian steelmaking's new hope', Transcript, *ABC Radio Australia*, 8 August 2004

Bleischwitz, R. (1998) *Ressourcenproduktivität. Innovationen für Umwelt und Beschäftigung*, Springer, Berlin and Heidelberg

Bodart, M. and Herde, A. D. (2002) 'Global energy savings in office buildings by the use of daylighting', *Energy and Buildings*, vol 34, pp421–429

Bowmer, K. (2004) *Water Innovation: A New Era for Australia*, Cl Creations, Lane Cove, NSW

Boyd, B. K. and Gove, S. (2000) 'Nucor Corporation and the U.S. steel industry', in Hitt, M. A., Ireland, R. D. and Hoskisson, R. E. (eds) *Strategic Management: Competitiveness and Globalization*, 4th Edition, Southwestern Publishing, Santa Fe, Oklahoma

Braungart, M. and McDonough, W. (eds) (2008) *Die nächste industrielle Revolution*, EVA, Hamburg

Brookes, L. (1979) 'A low energy strategy for the UK by G Leach et al: A review and reply', *Atom*, no 269, pp3–8

Brookes, L. (1990) 'Energy efficiency and economic fallacies', *Energy Policy*, vol 18, no 2, pp199–201

Brown, J. (2008) 'Coatings show their worth', *Ship Repair & Conversion Technology*, The Royal Institution of Naval Architects, 2nd Quarter

Brown, L. (2000) *Pushing Beyond the Earth's Limits*, Earth Policy Institute, Washington DC

Brown, L. (2008) *Plan B 3.0: Mobilizing to Save Civilization*, W.W. Norton & Company, New York

Bruno, M. and Sachs, J. (1985) *Economics of Worldwide Stagflation*, Harvard University Press, Cambridge, MA

Brylawski, M. M. and Lovins, A. B. (1998) *Advanced Composites: The Car is at the Cross Roads*, Rocky Mountain Institute, Snowmass, CO

BTRE (2007) *Estimating Urban Traffic and Congestion Cost Trends for Australian Cities*, Bureau of Transport and Regional Economics, Australian Government

Burke, W. (1996) 'Building envelope', in Public Technology Inc. and US Green Building Council (eds) *Sustainable Building Technical Manual*, Public Technology Inc., ppiv.21-iv.26

Burns, C. (2009) *The Smart Garage (Vehicle to Grid): Guiding the Next Big Energy Solution*, Rocky Mountain Institute, Snowmass, CO

Business Wire (2006) 'Americans eat out nearly one out of every four meals and snacks, spending almost half their food', *Business Wire*, 14 June

Bustnes, O. E. (2005) *Taking on the Leadership Challenge in Class 8 Trucking: How to Double Class 8 Truck Efficiency – Profitably*, Rocky Mountain Institute, Snowmass, CO

C40 Cities (2008) *Transport: Copenhagen, Denmark*, Climate Leadership Group, Clinton Foundation

California Energy Commission (2003) *Distributed Energy Resource Guide: Fuel Cells*, State of California Government

Cao, S., Xie, G. and Zhen, L. (2008) 'Total embodied energy requirements and its decomposition in China's agricultural sector', *Ecological Economics*, 16 September

Carbon Trust (2006) *Heating, Ventilation and Air Conditioning (HVAC): Saving Energy without Compromising Comfort*, Queen's Printer and Controller of HMSO

Carrasco, E. R. (2007) 'The 1980s: The debt crisis & the lost decade', Part V, *The E-Book on International Finance and Development*, The University of Iowa Center for International Finance and Development

Cemex (2006) *2006 Sustainable Development Report*, Cemex

Central Institute of Information & Techno-Economic Research for Steel Industry (undated) *Russian Steel Industry Against the Background of World Raw Materials Problems*, Central institute of Information & Techno-Economic Research for Steel Industry, Russia

Chamon, M., Mauro, P. and Okawa, Y. (2008) 'Mass car ownership in the emerging market giants', *Economic Policy*, vol 23, no 54, pp243–296

China Daily (2008) 'Eco-shopping helps Beijing improve its environment', *China Daily*, 10 November

Chitsomboon, P. and Changplayngam, P. (2007) 'Pig manure sweet money for Thai farmer', Reuters, 9 October

Chiu, A. (2009) *One Twelfth of Global Electricity Comes from Combined Heat and Power Systems*, Worldwatch Institute, Washington, DC

Cho, J. M. and Giannini-Spohn, S. (2007) 'A China environmental health research brief: Environmental and health threats from cement production in China', paper prepared for the China Environment Forum, Washington, DC

City of Melbourne (2007) 'Eco-building cuts CO_2 87%, Electricity 82%, Gas 87% and Water 72%: Eco-building – Council House 2 (CH2) New Municipal Office Building', case study presented at C40 Large Cities Climate Summit, 14–17 May 2007, New York City

City of Vancouver (COV) (2007) *Transportation Plan Update – A Decade of Progress*, The City of Vancouver, Canada

Clark, M. (2002) *In Search of Human Nature*, Routledge, Abingdon

Clemens, J. and Ahlgrimm, H. J. (2001) 'Greenhouse gases from animal husbandry: Mitigation options', *Nutrient Cycling in Agroecosystems*, vol 60, pp287–300

Clemens, J., Trimborn, M., Weiland, P. and Amon, B. (2006) 'Mitigation of greenhouse gas emissions by anaerobic digestion of cattle slurry', *Agriculture, Ecosystems and Environment*, vol 112, pp171–177

Clift, W. (2005) 'The good ship *Ethereal*', *RMI Solutions*, Spring, pp5–9

Coase, R. (1960) 'The problem of social cost', *The Journal of Law and Economics*, vol 3, pp1–44

Cobb, C. and Cobb, J. (1994) *The Green National Product*, University Press of America, Lanham MD

Collier, R. (2008) 'Can China go green?', *China Digital Times*, 16 December

Communities and Local Government (2008) 'New proposals to make the 2016 zero carbon homes target a reality', News Release, 17 December, COI News Distribution Service

Cooley, H., Christian-Smith, J. and Gleick, P. H. (2008) *More with Less: Agricultural Water Conservation and Efficiency in California – A Special Focus on the Delta*, The Pacific Institute, Seattle, WA

Corbett, J. and Winebrake, J. (2007) 'Sustainable goods movement – Environmental implications of trucks, trains, ships and planes', *Environmental Magazine*, Air and Waste Management Association, November

Cramer, D. R. and Brylawski, M. M. (1996) *Ultralight-Hybrid Vehicle Design: Implications for the Recycling Industry*, Rocky Mountain Institute, Snowmass, CO

CSIRO (2007) *Biofuels in Australia: An Overview of Issues and Prospects*, Rural Industries Research and Development Corporation

Cui, Y. and Wang, X. (2006) 'The state of the Chinese cement industry in 2005 and its future prospects', *Cement International*, vol 4, pp36–43

Cummins (2006) *Every Drop: Secrets of Better Fuel Economy*, Cummins, USA

Daggett, D. L., Brown, S. T. and Kawai, R. T. (2003a) *Ultra-Efficient Engine Diameter Study*, NASA CR-2003-212309, National Aeronautics and Space Administration, Washington, DC

Daggett, D. L., Kawai, R. and Friedman, D. (2003b) *Blended Wing Body Systems Studies: Boundary Layer Ingestion Inlets with Active Flow Control*, NASA/CR-2003-212670, National Aeronautics and Space Administration, Washington, DC, p8

Dairy Australia (2007) *Dairy 2007 Situation and Outlook*, Dairy Australia

Daly, H. (1996) *Beyond Growth: The Economics of Sustainable Development*, Beacon Press, Boston, MA

Daly, H. (1999) *Ecological Economics and the Ecology of Economics*, Edward Elgar, Cheltenham

Daly, H. (2003) 'Selected growth fallacies', *Social Contract Journal*, vol 13, no 3

Daly, H. and Cobb, J. B. (1989) *For the Common Good: Redirecting the Economy toward Community, the Environment and Sustainable Future*, Beacon Press, Boston, MA

Davidovits, J. (1991) 'Geopolymers – Inorganic polymeric new materials', *Journal of Thermal Analysis*, vol 37, no 8, pp1633–1656

Davidovits, J. (2002) '30 years of successes and failures in geopolymer applications – Market trends and potential breakthroughs', Geopolymer 2002 Conference, 28–29 October, Melbourne, Australia

Davidson, S. (2005) 'Air transport impacts take off', *ECOS: Towards A Sustainable Future*, no 123, Commonwealth Scientific and Industrial Research Organisation, Clayton, South Victoria, Australia

De Beer, J. G., Worrell, E. and Blok, K. (1998) 'Future technologies for energy efficient iron and steelmaking', *Annual Review of Energy and Environment*, vol 23, pp123–205

DEEDI and QPIF (2007) *Information Paper on Industrial Hemp*, Department of Employment, Economic Development and Innovation & Queensland Primary Industries and Fisheries, Queensland Government

Del Percio, S. (2009) 'Barton Group Headquarters: LEED Platinum 105 in Glens Falls', *GreenBuildingsNYC*

Delmas, M. (2002) 'The diffusion of environmental management standards in Europe and the United States: An institutional perspective', *Policy and Science*, vol 35, pp91–119

Demerjian, D. (2009) 'This ride makes bullet trains look slow', *Wired*, 1 April

Demos, T. and Tkaczyk, C. (2009) 'Global 500: The top 25', *CNN Global Edition*.
Department of Environment and Water Resources (DEWR) (2007) *ESD Design Guide: Office and Public Buildings*, 3rd edition, DEWR, Australia
Department of Environment, Water, Heritage and the Arts (DEWHA) (2007) *Water Efficiency Guide: Office and Public Buildings*, DEWHA, Australia
Department of Environment, Water, Heritage and the Arts (DEWHA) (2009) *Your Home Technical Manual: Australia's Guide to Environmentally Sustainable Homes – Water Use*, DEWHA, Australia
Department of Sustainability and Environment (2006) *2006 Melbourne Atlas*, Victorian Government
Desha, C. and Hargroves, K (2010) *Engineering Education for Sustainable Development: A Guide to Rapid Curriculum Renewal*, The Natural Edge Project, Earthscan, London
DeSimone, L. D. and Popoff, F. (2000) *Eco-Efficiency – The Business Link to Sustainable Development*, MIT Press, Cambridge MA
Deutsche Well (2007) 'Sarkozy promises green revolution for France', *Deutsche Well*, 25 October
Diaz, O. E. (2001) 'Car free Bogotá: The response to the transportation challenge', *The New Colonist*, Duncansville, PA
Dickson, M. H. and Fanelli, M. (2004) *What is Geothermal Energy?* Istituto di Geoscienze e Georisorse, CNR, Pisa, Italy
Ditze, A. and Scharf, C. (2008) *Recycling of Magnesium*, Papierflieger Verlag, Clausthal-Zellerfeld, Germany
Dovers, S. (2008) 'Urban water: Policy, institutions and government', in Troy, P. (ed) *Troubled Waters*, Australian National University Epress, Australia
Dow Jones Newswires (2004) 'China delegation bought more than 500,000 MT US wheat', *Traders*, 19 February
Drechsler, M. and Graham, A. (2005) 'Innovative materials technologies: Bringing resource sustainability to construction and mining industries', presented at the 48th Institute of Quarrying Conference, 12–15 October, Adelaide SA
Duxson, P. (2008) 'Low carbon cement: Are we making any progress?', *BEDP Environment Design Guide*, Royal Australian Institute of Architects
Duxson, P. (2009a) Personal communication with Peter Duxson, Zeobond Director, 31 March
Duxson, P. (2009b) Personal communications with Peter Duxson, Zeobond Director, 2 April
Duxson, P., Provis, J., Lukey, G. and van Deventer, J. (2007) 'The role of inorganic polymer technology in the development of green concrete', *Cement and Concrete Research*, vol 37, pp1590–1597
Dymond, J. (2006) 'Brussels' hi-tech eco house', *BBC News*, 23 March 2006
Dyson, T. (1999) 'World food trends and prospects to 2025', proceedings of the National Academy of Sciences colloquium, 'Plants and Population: Is There Time?', 5–6 December 1998, Arnold and Mabel Beckman Center, Irvine, CA
Earthbeat Radio National (2000) 'Can soils soak up greenhouse gases?', Interview: Rattan Lal, *ABC Earthbeat Radio*, 16 December
East Japan Railway Company (2005) 'FASTECH 360 high-speed Shinkansen test train to debut: Running tests to start with the aim of the world's best Shinkansen service', East Japan Railway Company Press Release, 9 March
East, R. (2006) 'Sifting myths from mountains: On the long green march', in Green Futures (ed) *Greening the Dragon – China's Search for a Sustainable Future*, Green Futures Special Supplement, Forum for the Future, September

Eckert, S., Karg, G. and Zängler, T. (2006) *Leitbilder nachhaltigen Konsums im Rahmen einer aktivierenden Verbraucherpolitik*, TU München, Munich

Ecological Homes (2002) *Wastewater Systems*, Ecological Homes, Australia

Economic and Social Commission for Asia and the Pacific (2000) *Water Resources Series No. 79*, United Nations, New York

ECOS (2009) 'Videoconferencing to cut public sector airfares and emission', *ECOS Magazine*, no 148, Commonwealth Scientific and Industrial Research Organisation, Clayton, South Victoria, Australia

Educogen (2001) *The European Education Tool on Cogeneration*, 2nd edition, The European Association for the Promotion of Cogeneration, Belgium

Edwards, S. and Magarey, P. (2007) 'Cycling fact sheet: Environmental benefits of cycling', Cycling Promotion Fund and Bicycling Federation of Australia, Australia

Ehrlich, P. R. and Holdren, J. P. (1971) 'Impact of population growth', *Science*, vol 171, pp1212–17

Eichholtz, P., Kok, N. and Quigley, J. (2008) *Doing Well by Doing Good? Green Office Buildings*, Maastricht University, Netherlands, and University of California, Berkeley

Elliott, R. and Spurr, M. (1999) *Combined Heat and Power: Capturing Wasted Energy*, American Council for an Energy-Efficient Economy, Washington, DC

Energy Conservation Center (1998) *Energy Conservation Databook 1998*, ECCJ, Japan

Energy Information Administration (EIA) (1998) *Form EIA-846: Manufacturing Energy Consumption Survey, and Form EIA-810, Monthly Refinery Report*, EIA, Washington, DC

Energy Information Administration (EIA) (2006) *Annual Energy Outlook*, EIA, Washington, DC

Energy Information Administration (EIA) (2007) *Annual Energy Review 2007*, Report No. DOE/EIA-0384, EIA, Washington, DC

Energy Information Administration (EIA) (2008) *International Energy Outlook 2008*, EIA, Washington, DC

Energy Resource (2006) 'Wal-Mart turns to energy-saving LED lighting in 500-store retrofit', *Energy Resource*, 16 November

Engineers Australia (2001) *Sustainable Energy Innovation in the Commercial Building Sector: The Challenge of a New Culture*, Sustainable Energy Building and Construction Taskforce Report, Engineers Australia

Ensink, J., Mahmood, T., van de Hoek, W., Raschid-Sally, L. and Amerasinghe, F. (2004) 'A nation-wide assessment of wastewater use in Pakistan: An obscure activity or a vitally important one?' *Water Policy*, vol 6, pp1–10

Environment News Service (2006) 'Cutting energy waste in China, India, Brazil could avert climate change', *Environment News Service*, 30 May

Environmental Leader (2008a) 'Continental airlines touts green efforts', *Environmental Leader*, 29 December

Environmental Leader (2008b) 'UPS expands electric vehicle fleets', *Environmental Leader*, 12 November

Environmental Leader (2009a) 'Air New Zealand completes flight powered by jatropha biofuel', *Environmental Leader*, 5 January

Environmental Leader (2009b) 'Options abound for low-emission big trucks', *Environmental Leader*, 20 March

Environmental Leader (2009c) 'Wal-Mart tests new trucks, surpasses fuel efficiency goals', *Environmental Leader*, 3 February

Environmental Leader (2009d) 'Wal-Mart unveils largest PV installation in Latin America', *Environmental Leader*, 20 January

Enviros Consulting Limited (2006) *Anaerobic Digestion in Agriculture: Policies and Markets for Growth*, Department of Environment, Food and Rural Affairs, London

ESource (1999) 'Prospectus: Multi-client study – Delivering energy and energy services to the restaurant sector', *ESource*, Boulder, CO

European Association of Plastics Recycling and Recovery Organisations (2008) *The Compelling Facts about Plastics: An Analysis of Plastics Production, Demand and Recovery for 2007 in Europe*, European Association of Plastics Recycling and Recovery Organisations, Brussels

European Communities (1994) *Potential Benefits of Integration of Environmental and Economic Policies: An Incentive-based Approach to Policy Integration*, European Communities Environmental Policy Series, Brussels, pp336–337

European Communities (2004) *Buying Green! A Handbook on Environmental Public Procurement*, Office for Official Publications of the European Communities, Luxembourg

Evans, L. T. (1998) 'Greater crop production: Whence and whither?', in Waterlow, J. C., Armstrong, D. G., Fowden, L. and Riley, R. (eds) *Feeding a World Population of More than Eight Billion People*, Oxford University Press, New York, pp89–97

Evans, P (2008) 'BYD launch world's first production plug-in hybrid', *Gizmag*, 15 December

Faiola, A. (2006) 'Turn off the heat – How Japan made energy saving an art form', *The Guardian*, 17 February

FAO (2008) 'World potato production 1991–2007', *Potato World*, Food and Agriculture Organization of the United Nations, Rome

FAO and IFAD (2006) 'Water for food, agriculture and sustainable livelihoods', in United Nations (eds) *The 2nd UN World Water Development Report*, United Nations World Water Assessment Programme

Faramarzi, R., Coburn, B. and Sarhadian, R. (2002) 'Performance and energy impact of installing glass doors on an open vertical deli/dairy display case', *ASHRAE Transactions: Symposia.*

Federal Ministry of Transport, Building and Urban Affairs (2008) *Freight Transport and Logistics Masterplan*, Federal Government, Germany

Feist, W. (1996) *The Passive House in Darmstadt-Kranichstein Planning, Construction, Results*, Passive House Institute, Darmstadt

Fenton, M. (1998) *Iron and Steel Recycling in the United States in 1998*, US Department of Interior and US Geological Survey

Ferret (2005) *Salt into Steel*, Ferret, Chatswood, Australia

Fiehn, T. and Corin, C. (2002) *Communist Russia under Lenin and Stalin*, Hodder Murray Publications, London

FLSMidth (2006) 'Cement plant pyro-technology', presentation to the IEA-WBCSD Workshop 'Energy Efficiency and CO_2 Emission Reduction Potentials and Policies in the Cement Industry', IEA, Paris, 4–5 September

Food and Water Watch (2007) *Fuels and Emissions from Industrial Agriculture*, Food and Water Watch, Washington, DC

Fortmeyer, R. (2008) 'The Council House 2 (CH2) building', *Grandbuild.com (Technology)*, 14 August

Fox, J. W. and Cramer, D. R. (1997) *Hypercars: A Market-Oriented Approach to Meeting Lifecycle Environmental Goals*, Rocky Mountain Institute, Snowmass, CO

Francisco, P. W., Davis, B., Baylon, D. and Palmiter, L. (2004) 'Heat pumps system performance in northern climates', *ASHRAE Transactions*, vol 110, part 1, pp442–451

Frank, L., Andersen, M. and Schmid, T. (2004) 'Obesity relationships with community design, physical activity, and time spent in cars', *American Journal of Preventive Medicine*, vol 27, no 2, pp87–96

Fraunhofer Institute for Solar Energy Systems (2000) *The Solar House in Freiburg: From a Self-Sufficient Solar House, to a Research Platform*, Fraunhofer Institute for Solar Energy Systems (ISE), Freiburg, Germany

Frechette, R. and Gilchrist, R. (2008) *Towards Zero Energy: A Case Study of the Pearl River Tower, Guangzhou, China*, Council on Tall Buildings and Urban Habitat, Illinois Institute of Technology, Chicago, IL

Frechette, R., and Gilchrist, R. (2009) 'Seeking zero energy', *Civil Engineering*, American Society of Civil Engineering, vol 79, no 1, January

Freedonia Group Inc. (2008) *World Cement*, Freedonia Group Inc., Cleveland, OH

Frey, C. and Kuo, P. (2007a) 'Assessment of potential reduction in greenhouse gas (GHG) emissions in freight transportation', Proceedings, International Emission Inventory Conference, US Environmental Protection Agency, Raleigh, NC, 15–17 May

Frey, C. and Kuo, P. (2007b) *Assessment of Potential Reduction in Greenhouse Gas (GHG) Emissions in Freight Transportation*, North Carolina State University, Raleigh, NC

Friedman, T. (2008) *Hot, Flat and Crowded: Why the World Needs a Green Revolution – And How We Can Renew our Global Future*, Allen Lane, London

Friedman, T. (2009) 'Show us the ball', *The New York Times*, 9 April

Fryxell, G., Wing-Hung Lo, C. and Chung, S. (2004) 'Influence of motivations for seeking ISO 14001 certification on perceptions of EMS effectiveness in China', *Environmental Management*, vol 33, no 2, pp239–251, Springer-Verlag, New York

Fuji Xerox Australia (2008) *Fuji Xerox Australia Sustainability Report*, Fuji Xerox Australia

Fumikazu, Y. (2007) *The Cyclical Economy of Japan*, Hokkaido University, Sapporo, Japan

Gale, F., Tuan, F., Lohmar, B., Hsu, H. and Gilmour, B. (2002) 'China's food and agriculture: Issues for the 21st century', *Agricultural Information Bulletin*, no AIB775, April 2002, US Department of Agriculture, Economic Research Service

Gans, W., Shipley, A. M. and Elliot, R. N. (2007) *Survey of Emissions Models for Combined Heat and Power Systems*, American Council for an Energy-Efficient Economy, Washington, DC

Garg, V. and Bansal, N. K. (2000) 'Smart occupancy sensors to reduce energy consumption', *Energy and Buildings*, vol 32, pp81–87

Garnaut, R. (2008a) *Garnaut Interim Report*, Commonwealth of Australia, Australia

Garnaut, R. (2008b) *The Garnaut Climate Change Review Final Report*, Garnaut Climate Change Review, Cambridge University Press, Port Melbourne

Gauna, K. and Page, E. (2005) *Lighting Research Program: Project 2.1 Hybrid Outdoor Lighting Systems – Final Report*, California Lighting Technology Center, Davis, CA

Gemeente Amsterdam (2008) *Amsterdam Paves the Way for Cyclists*, Gemeente Amsterdam, Netherlands

Geyer, R. (2004) 'Environmental and economic evaluation of supply loops and their constraints', PhD thesis, Centre for Environmental Strategy, University of Surrey, Guildford

Gleick, P (2001) 'Making every drop count', *Scientific American*, February, pp28–33

Gleick, P. (2008) *The World's Water 2008–2009: The Biennial Report on Freshwater Resources*, Island Press, Chicago, IL

Gleick, P. and Cooley, H. (2009) 'Energy implications of bottled water', *Environmental Research Letters*, vol 4

Glukhovsky, V. D. (1994) 'Ancient, modern and future concretes', Proceedings of the First International Conference on Alkaline Cements and Concretes, Kiev, Ukraine, pp1–9

Goldstein, E. (1999) *The Trade Off Myth: Fact & Fiction About Jobs and the Environment*, Island Press, Washington DC

Goodwin, I. and Boland, A. M. (2002) *Scheduling Deficit Irrigation of Fruit Trees for Optimizing Water Use Efficiency in Deficit Irrigation Practices*, FAO Technical Papers, Water Report No. 22

Goodwin, P. (2004) 'The economic costs of road traffic congestion', Discussion paper, The Rail Freight Group, London

Goorskey, S., Smith, A. and Wang, K. (2004) '#8 kitchen appliances', *RMI Home Energy Briefs*, Rocky Mountain Institute, Snowmass, CO

Gorbachev, M. (2003) *Conversations with Gorbachev: On Perestroika, the Prague Spring, and the Crossroads of Socialism*, Columbia University Press, New York

Gordon, K. L., Sullivan, G. P., Armstrong, P. R., Richman, E. E. and Matzke, B. D. (2006) *Spectrally Enhanced Lighting Program Implementation for Energy Savings: Field Evaluation*, Pacific Northwest National Laboratory, Richland, WA

Gore, A. (2006) *An Inconvenient Truth: The Planetary Emergency of Global Warming and What We Can Do About It*, Rodale Press, Emmaus, PA

Grant, B. (2007) 'Can labs go green?', *The Scientist*, vol 21, no 6, p270

Green Growth (2008) 'Confederation of Indian Industry Sohrabji Godrej Green Business Center Building India', United Nations Economic and Social Commission for Asia and the Pacific, Bangkok

Green News (2008) 'Wal-Mart Canada opens first environmental demonstration store', *Green News*, Friday 16 January 2009

GreenBuilding (2006) *GreenBuilding: Enhanced Energy Efficiency for Non-Residential Buildings*, German Energy Agency, Berlin

Greene, D. L. and Hopson, J. L. (2003) *Running Out of and Into Oil: Analyzing Global Depletion and Transition Through 2050*, Oak Ridge National Laboratory, Oak Ridge, TN

Greening, L. A., Greene, D. and Difiglio, C. (2000) 'Energy efficiency and consumption: The rebound effect – A survey', *Energy Policy*, vol 28, pp389–401

Griffith, B., Long, N., Torcellini, P. and Judkoff, R. (2007) *Assessment of the Technical Potential for Achieving Net Zero-Energy Buildings in the Commercial Sector*, National Renewable Energy Laboratory, Boulder, CO

Groscurth, H.M., Bräuer, W., Hohmeyer, O., Kühn, I. and Weinreich, S (1998) *Long-Term Integration of Renewable Energy Sources into the European Energy System*, Physica Verlag, Heidelberg

Grossman, G. and Krueger, A. (1991) 'Environmental impacts of a North American free trade agreement', National Bureau of Economic Research Working Paper 3914, NBER, Cambridge, MA.

Grubb, M. (1990) *Energy Policies and the Greenhouse Effect*, Royal Institute of International Affairs, London

Grunwald, M. (2008) 'America's untapped energy resource: Boosting efficiency', *Time Magazine*, 31 December

The Guardian (2008) 'Johnson promises "less stick, more carrot" for London commuters', *The Guardian*, 3 March

Gumbel, P. (2008) 'Lighting: Bright idea', *Time Magazine*, 4 December

Gupta, S. (2003) 'Barefoot, female and a solar engineer', *infochange, Women's Feature Service*, January

Gupta, S. (2009) 'Barefoot, female and a solar engineer', *Boloji.com*, 28 April

Hamilton, C., Turton, H., Saddler, H. and Jinlong, M. (2002) 'Long-term greenhouse gas scenarios: A pilot study of how Australia can achieve deep cuts in emissions', Discussion Paper Number 48, The Australia Institute, Manuka, ACT

Harfst, W. (2008) 'Enhanced cooling tower maintenance saves water', *Maintenance Technology*, October

Hargroves, K. and Smith, M. (2005) *The Natural Advantage of Nations: Business Opportunities, Innovation and Governance in the 21st Century*, Earthscan, London, The Natural Edge Project, Australia

Hargroves, K., Smith, M. and Lovins, L. H. (2005) *Prospering in a Carbon Constrained World: Profitable Opportunities for Greenhouse Gas Emissions Reduction*, Chicago and European Climate Exchange (CCX/EUX) Opportunities Executive Report

Harrington, L. and Holt, S. (2006) *Matching World's Best Regulated Efficiency Standards: Australia's Success in Adopting New Refrigerator MEPS Energy Efficient Strategies*, Australian Greenhouse Office, Department of the Environment and Heritage, Australia.

Harris, S. (2007) 'The potential role of industrial symbiosis in combating global warming', International Conference on Climate Change, 29–31 May, Hong Kong

Harvey, L. (2006) *A Handbook on Low-energy Buildings and District Energy Systems: Fundamentals, Techniques and Examples*, James and James, London

Hatfield-Dodds, S., Carwardine, J., Dunlop, M., Graham, P. and Klein, C. (2007) 'Rural Australia providing climate solutions', *Preliminary Report to the Agricultural Alliance on Climate Change*, Commonwealth Scientific and Industrial Research Organisation, Clayton, South Victoria, Australia

Hawken, P., Lovins, A. and Lovins, H. (1999) *Natural Capitalism: Creating the Next Industrial Revolution*, Earthscan, London

Heinberg, R. (2004) *Powerdown: Options and Actions for a Post-Carbon World*, New Society Publishers, Gabriola Island, BC

Heinberg, R. (2007) *Peak Everything: Waking Up to the Century of Declines*, New Society Publishers, Gabriola Island, BC

Henderson, H. (2008) 'Changing games in the global casino', *IPS Columns*, 6 August

Hendriks, C., Worrell, E., de Jager, D., Blok, K. and Riemer, P. (2004) 'Emission Reduction of Greenhouse Gases from the Cement Industry', paper presented to the Greenhouse Gas Control Technologies Conference

Henry, L. A. and Douhovnikoff, V. (2008) 'Environmental issues in Russia', *Annual Review of Environmental Resources*, vol 33, pp437–460

Herring, H. (1998) *Does Improving Energy Efficiency Save Energy: The Economist Debate?*, The Open University, Energy and Environment Research Unit, Report No. 74

Heschong Mahone Group (1999) *Daylighting in Schools: An Investigation into the Relationship Between Daylighting and Human Performance*, Pacific Gas and Electric Company, San Francisco, CA

Hewlett-Packard Development Company (2007a) 'Global citizenship', presentation, personal communication with HP Australia

Hewlett-Packard Development Company (2007b) *Energy Efficiency Setup Guide*, HP Development Company, Palo Alto, CA

Hird, W. (2005) 'Recycled water – case study: BlueScope Steel, Port Kembla Steelworks', presented at the International Conference on Integrated Concepts on Water Recycling, Wollongong, NSW, Australia, 14–17 February

Hirsch, R. L. (2005) 'The inevitable peaking of world oil production', *The Atlantic Council of the US Bulletin*, vol XVI, no 3

Hirsch, R. L., Bezdek, R. and Wendling, R. (2005) *Peaking of World Oil Production: Impacts, Mitigation, and Risk Management*, US Department of Energy/National Energy Technology Laboratory

Hoekstra, A. Y. and Chapagain, A. K. (2008) *Globalization of Water: Sharing the Planet's Freshwater Resources*, Blackwell Publishing, Oxford

Homer-Dixon, T. (2006) *The Upside of Down: Catastrophe, Creativity, and the Renewal of Civilization*, Knopf, Island Press

Hopkins, R. (2005) *2021: An Energy Descent Action Plan*, Kinsale Further Education College, Kinsale, Co. Cork

Houghton, R. (2005) 'The contemporary carbon cycle' in Schlesinger, W. (ed) *Biogeochemistry*, Elsevier Science, Amsterdam, pp473–513

Humphreys, K. and Mahasenan, M. (2002) *Towards a Sustainable Cement Industry*, World Business Council for Sustainable Development (WBCSD), Geneva, Switzerland

Huntingdon, H. (1992) 'Review of Grubb et al, Energy Policies and the Greenhouse Effect', *Energy Journal*, vol 13, no 4, pp220–224

IAI (2006) *Aluminium for Future Generations: Sustainability Update 2005*, International Aluminium Institute, London

IANS (2008) 'Surge in cereal production to bring food market relief', *Thaindian News*, 19 July

ICAO (2006) *Form A – ICAO Reporting Form for Air Carrier Traffic*, International Civil Aviation Organization, Montreal, Canada

ICLEI (2009) 'If climate change is the problem, sustainable procurement is the solution', *ICLEI Newsletter*, no 33, Winter 2008/2009

ILO (2008) *World of Work 2008: Global Income Equality Gap is Vast and Growing*, International Labour Organization Report, Geneva

IMF (2009) 'World economic outlook: Global economy contracts, with slow recovery next year', *IMF Survey Magazine*, 22 April

Institute of Materials, Minerals and Mining (2002) 'The HIsmelt Iron-Making Process', *Materials World*, vol 10, no 11, pp28–30

Institute of Travel Management (2009) *Case Study 5 PricewaterhouseCoopers*, Institute of Travel Management Project Icarus, Macclesfield, Cheshire

InterAcademy Council (2007) *Lighting the Way: Toward a Sustainable Energy*, InterAcademy Council, Amsterdam, the Netherlands

Interlaboratory Working Group (2000) *Scenarios for a Clean Energy Future*, Oak Ridge National Laboratory and Berkeley, California

International Energy Agency (2000) *Experience Curves for Energy Technology Policy*, OECD/IEA, Paris

International Energy Agency (2002) *Renewables in Global Energy Supply: An IEA Fact Sheet*, IEA, Paris

International Energy Agency (2003) *Cool Appliances: Policy Strategies for Energy Efficiency Homes*, IEA, Paris

International Energy Agency (2004) *30 Years of Energy Use in IEA Countries*, IEA, Paris

International Energy Agency (2006a) *Light's Labour's Lost: Policies for Energy-Efficient Lighting*, IEA, Paris

International Energy Agency (2006b) *World Energy Outlook 2006*, IEA, Paris

International Energy Agency (2006c) 'Energy efficiency and CO_2 emission reduction potentials and policies in the cement industry', IEA and WBCSD Workshop, Paris, 4–5 September

International Energy Agency (2006d) *Energy Technology Perspectives 2006: Scenarios and Strategies to 2050*, IEA, Paris

International Energy Agency (IEA) (2007a) *Tracking Industrial Energy Efficiency and CO$_2$ Emissions – Energy Indicators*, IEA, Paris

International Energy Agency (2007b) *World Energy Outlook 2007: China and India Insights*, Organisation for Economic Co-operation and Development and IEA, Paris

International Energy Agency (2008) *World Energy Outlook 2008*, IEA, Paris

International Iron and Steel Institute (1998) *Energy Use in the Steel Industry*, IISI, Brussels

International Iron and Steel Institute (2005) *Steel: The Foundation of a Sustainable Future Sustainability*, Report of the World Steel Industry 2005, IISI, Brussels

International Iron and Steel Institute (2008) *Sustainability Report 2008: The Measure of Our Sustainability*, Report of the World Steel Industry, IISI, Brussels

IPART (1999) 'Regulation of network service providers', Discussion Paper DP-34, Independent Pricing and Regulatory Tribunal, Sydney

IPART (2002) 'Inquiry into the role of demand management and other options in the provision of energy services', Interim Report, Review Report No. 02-1, Independent Pricing and Regulatory Tribunal, Sydney

IPCC (1999) *Special report of the Intergovernmental Panel on Climate Change (IPCC)*, Contribution of Working Groups I and III, Cambridge University Press, Cambridge

IPCC (2001) *Climate Change 2001: The Scientific Basis*, Contribution of Working Group I to the 3rd Assessment Report of the Intergovernmental Panel of Climate Change, Cambridge University Press, Cambridge

IPCC (2007) *Climate Change 2007: Mitigation of Climate Change*, Contribution of Working Group III to the 4th Assessment Report of the Intergovernmental Panel on Climate Change, Cambridge University Press, Cambridge

ISO (2000) *Business Plan: ISO/TC 104 Freight Containers*, International Organization for Standardization, Geneva

ISO (2004) *ISO 14001: 2004 Environmental Management Systems – Specification with Guidance for Use*, International Organization for Standardization, Geneva

Ivanhoe Cambridge (2007) *Case Study – Commercial Building: Metrotower Office Complex*, Ivanhoe Cambridge, Montreal, Canada

Jacobs, P. (2003) *Small HVAC System Design Guide: Design Guidelines*, California Energy Commission, Sacramento, CA

Jafri, S. A. (2004) 'Kalam to open world's greenest building' *Rediff.com*, 13 July

James, P. (2007) *Conferencing at DFID – The Economic, Environmental and Social Impacts*, SustainIT, Peterborough

Janssen, R. (2004) *Final Report: Towards Energy Efficient Buildings in Europe*, The European Alliance of Companies for Energy Efficiency in Buildings (EuroACE), Brussels

Japan Cement Association (JCA) (2006) 'Cement industry's status and activities for GHG emissions reduction in Japan', IEA–WBCSD Workshop on Energy Efficiency and CO$_2$ Emission Reduction Potentials and Policies in the Cement Industry, 4–5 September, Paris

Jaswal, P. and Das Gupta, M. (2006) 'Energy demands and sustaining growth in South and East Asia', Topic Paper, Session 2: 'Challenges and Risks to Development in Asia Parallel Group 2A', Asia 2015 Conference, www.asia2015conference.org.

Jennings, J. D., Rubinstein, F. M., DiBartolomeo, D. and Blanc, S. L. (2000) *Comparison of Control Options in Private Offices in an Advanced Lighting Controls Testbed*, Lawrence Berkeley National Laboratory, University of California, Berkeley

Jevons, W. S. (1865) *The Coal Question*, Macmillan, London

Jochem, E. (ed) (2004) *Steps Towards a Sustainable Development: A White Book for R&D of Energy-Efficient Technologies*, Novatlantis, Villigen, Switzerland

Jones, T. (2003) 'Pricing water: Water pricing is becoming more widespread, with the dual aim of expanding supply and encouraging more responsible use', *OECD Observer*, no 236

Josa, A., Aguado, A., Heino, A., Byars, E. and Cardin, A. (2004) 'Comparative analysis of available life-cycle inventories of cement in the EU', *Cement and Concrete Research*, vol 34, pp1313–1320

JR East Group (2008) *Super Green Car*, East Japan Railway Company, Tokyo, Japan

Kamakaté, F. (2007) 'Understanding current and future trends in energy intensity from heavy-duty trucks', presentation by the International Council on Clean Transportation to the International Workshop on Fuel Efficiency Policies for Heavy-Duty Vehicles, International Energy Agency, 22 June

Kaniaru, D., Shende, R., Stone, S. and Zaelke, D. (2007) 'Strengthening the Montreal Protocol: Insurance against abrupt climate change', *Sustainable Development Law and Policy Publication*, March

Kapp, K. W. (1971) *The Social Costs of Private Enterprise*, Schocken Books, New York

Karaba, A., Dixit, S., Greco, R., Aharoni, A., Trijatmiko, K., Marsch-Martinez, N., Krishnan, A., Nataraja, K., Udayakumar, M., and Pereira, A. (2007) 'Improvement of water use efficiency in rice by expression of HARDY an Arabidopsis drought and salt tolerance gene', *Proceedings of the National Academy of Sciences*, vol 104, no 39, pp15270–15275

Kataria, P. and Joshi, A. (2006) *Energy Use in Indian Agriculture*, Punjab Agricultural University, India

Kats, G. (2003) *The Costs and Financial Benefits of Green Buildings*, a report to California's Sustainable Building Task Force

Kavanagh, L. (2007) Personal communication with Larry Kavanagh, American Iron & Steel Institute (AISI), 29 January

Kempton, W. and Tomic, J. (2005a) 'Vehicle to grid fundamentals: Calculating capacity and net revenue', *Journal of Power Sources*, vol 144, no 1, pp268–279

Kempton, W. and Tomic, J. (2005b) 'Vehicle to grid implementation: From stabilizing the grid to supporting large-scale renewable energy', *Journal of Power Sources*, vol 144, no 1, pp280–294

Kempton, W., Tomic, J., Letendre, S., Brooks, A. and Lipman, T. (2001) *Vehicle-to-Grid Power: Battery, Hybrid, and Fuel Cell Vehicles as Resources for Distributed Electric Power in California*, report prepared for California Air and Resources Board, California EPA, and LA Department of Air and Water

Kempton, W., Udo, V., Huber, K., Komara, K., Letendre, S., Baker, S., Brunner, D. and Pearre, N. (2009) *A Test of Vehicle-to-Grid (V2G) for Energy Storage and Frequency Regulation in the PJM System*, University of Delaware, Pepco Holdings Inc., PJM Interconnect, and Green Mountain College

Kennett, S. (2009) 'BREEAM and LEED to work together on new global standard', *Building Sustainability*, 3 March

Kenway, S. J., Priestley, A., Cook, S., Seo, S., Inman, M., Gregory, A. and Hall, M. (2008) *Energy Use in the Provision and Consumption of Urban Water in Australia and New Zealand*, Commonwealth Scientific and Industrial Research Organisation Water For A Healthy Country Flagship, Australia

Kenworth Truck Company (2006) *White Paper on Fuel Economy*, Kenworth Truck Company, Kirkland, WA

Kenworthy, J. and Laube, F. (1999) *An International Sourcebook of Automobile Dependence in Cities, 1960–1990*, University Press of Colorado, Boulder, CO

Kenworthy, J. and Laube, F. (2001) *The Millennium Cities Database for Sustainable Transport*, International Union of Public Transport (UITP) and Institute for Sustainability and Technology Policy (ISTP), Brussels

Kenworthy, J. and Hu, G. (2002) 'Transport and urban form in Chinese cities: An international comparative and policy perspective with implications for sustainable urban transport in China', *DISP* [Zurich], vol 151, pp4–14

Kenworthy, J., Laube, F., Newman, P. and Barter, P. (1997) *Indicators of Transport Efficiency in 37 Cities*, Report to World Bank, ISTP, Murdoch University, Western Australia

Khazzoom, D. J. (1980) 'Economic implications of mandated efficiency standards for household appliances', *The Energy Journal*, vol 1, pp21–40

Khazzoom, D. J. (1989) 'Energy savings from more efficient appliances: A rejoinder', *Energy Journal*, vol 10, no 1, pp157–166

Kim, Y. and Worrell, E. (2002) 'CO_2 emission trends in the cement industry: An international comparison', *Mitigation and Adaptation Strategies for Global Change*, vol 7, no 2, pp115–133

King, B., Payne, J. and Villiott, C. (2008) *Green Vessel Design: Guiding Principles for Environmental Best-Practices through Design*, Elliott Bay Design Group, Seattle, WA

Klein, N. (2007) *The Shock Doctrine: The Rise of Disaster Capitalism*, Metropolitan Books, New York

Kleiner, K. (2007) 'The Shipping Forecast', *Nature*, 20 September, vol 449, pp272–273

Koerner, P. (2008) 'LEED Platinum home of the future reduces energy costs by 80%', *Jetson Green* (on-line magazine)

Kondratiev, N. D. (1984) *The Long Wave Cycle*, Richardson & Snyder, New York

Kondratiev, N. D., Wilson, S. and Makasheva, N. (1998) *The Works of Nikolai D. Kondratiev*, 4 volume set, Pickering and Chatto, London

Kong, P. (undated) 'Reducing your carbon footprint in the client environment', presentation, HP and Intel, personal communication with HP Australia

Konnola, T. and Unruh, G. (2007) 'Really changing the course: The limitations of environmental management systems for innovation', *Business Strategy and the Environment*, vol 16, Wiley InterScience, John Wiley & Sons Inc., Malden, MA

Kooistra, K. and Termorshuizen, A. (2006) *The Sustainability of Cotton: Consequences for Man and Environment*, Goede Waar & Co., Amsterdam

Kornevall, C. (2008) 'Building boom in Brazil needs a green plan', World Business Council for Sustainable Development (WBCSD) Energy Efficient Buildings (EEB) Blog

Korzeniewski, J. (2009) 'Toyota: Plug-in Prius returning 65 MPG in testing', *Autobloggreen*, 2 February

KPMG (2004) *KPMG's Corporate Tax Rates Survey – January 2004*, KPMG International

Kraemer, R. A., Kampa, E. and Interwies, E. (2007) *The Role of Tradable Permits in Water Pollution Control*, Contract paper for the Inter-American Development Bank, Washington, DC

Krivenko, P. V. (1999) 'Alkaline cements: Structure, properties, aspects of durability', Proceedings of the Second International Conference on Alkaline Cements and Concretes, May 1999, Kiev, Ukraine, pp3–43.

Kruska, M., Ichiro, D., Ohbayashi, M., Takase, K., Tetsunari, I., Evans, G., Herbergs, S., Lehmann, H., Mallon, K., Peter, S. and Aßman, D. (2003) *Energy Rich Japan*, Greenpeace International and Greenpeace Japan

Laitner, J. A. (2000) *Energy Efficiency: Rebounding to a Sound Analytical Perspective*, Elsevier, Amsterdam

Lal, R. (2003) 'Global potential of soil carbon sequestration to mitigate the greenhouse effect', *Critical Reviews in Plant Sciences*, vol 22, pp151–184

Lamprinidi, S. and Ringland, L. (2008) *A Snapshot of Sustainability Reporting in the Construction and Real Estate Sector*, Global Reporting Initiative Research and Development Series

Lawrence Berkeley National Laboratory (2004) *China Energy Databook*, Version 6.0, China Energy Group

Lee, E. S., DiBartolomeo, D. L. and Selkowitz, S. E. (1998) 'Thermal and daylighting performance of an automated Venetian blind and lighting system in a full-scale private office', *Energy and Buildings*, vol 29, pp47–63

Leifsson, L. T., and Mason, W. H. (2005) 'The blended wing body aircraft', *Velabrogd* (Student Magazine of the Department of Mechanical and Industrial Engineering), University of Iceland, Reykjavik, Iceland, April, pp8–10

Li, D. H. W. and Lam, J. C. (2003) 'An investigation of daylighting performance and energy saving in a daylight corridor', *Energy and Buildings*, vol 35, pp365–373

Lidderdale, J., Day, T. and Jones, P. (2006) 'Fuel cell CHP for buildings', presented at the Chartered Institution of Building Services Engineers (CIBSE) Annual Conference, 21 November

Liedtke, C. and Merten, T. (1994) 'MIPS: Resource management and sustainable development', Proceedings of the Second International Conference on 'The Recycling of Metal', 19–21 October, Amsterdam, pp163–173

Lin, J. (2002) 'Appliance efficiency standards and labelling programs in China', *Annual Review of Energy and the Environment*, vol 27, pp349–367

Lister, M. (2009) Personal communications with Mark Lister, Szencorp's Group Manager of Corporate Affairs, 9 April

Listhaug, O. (2005) 'Oil wealth dissatisfaction and political trust in Norway: A resource curse', *West European Politics*, vol 28, no 4, pp834–851

Litman, T. (2006) *London Congestion Pricing, Implications for Other Cities*, Victoria Transport Policy Institute, Canada

Lovegrove, K. and Dennis, M. (2006) 'Solar thermal energy systems in Australia', *International Journal of Environmental Studies*, vol 63, no 6, pp791–802

Lovins, A. (1988) 'Energy savings resulting from the adoption of more efficient appliances: Another view', *Energy Journal*, vol 9, no 2, pp155–162

Lovins, A. (2004) 'Energy efficiency, taxonomic overview for earth's energy balance', in Cleveland, C. J. (ed) *Encyclopaedia of Energy*, volume 1, Elsevier, Amsterdam

Lovins, A. B. (2005) 'More profit with less carbon', *Scientific American*, September

Lovins, A. B. (2007a) 'Class lectures in advanced energy efficiency: 3 – Transportation', Stanford University, Stanford, CA

Lovins, A. B. (2007b) 'Reinventing the wheels: The automotive efficiency revolution', *Economic Perspectives*, vol 1, no 2, pp 9–12

Lovins, A. B. and Cramer, D. R. (2004) 'Hypercars, hydrogen, and the automotive transition', *International Journal of Vehicle Design*, vol 35, no 1/2, pp50–85

Lovins, A. B., Datta, K., Feiler, T., Rabago, K., Swisher, J., Lehmann, A. and Wicker, K. (2002) *Small is Profitable: The Hidden Economic Benefits of Making Electrical Resources the Right Size*, Rocky Mountain Institute, Snowmass, CO

Lovins, A. B., Datta, E. K., Bustnes, O. E., Koomey, J. G. and Glasgow, N. J. (2004) *Winning the Oil Endgame: Innovation for Profits, Jobs and Security*, Rocky Mountain Institute, Snowmass, CO

Lowe, I., McEvoy, J., McKnoulty, J., Derrington, P. and Losee, S. (2007) *Brisbane's Plan for Action on Climate Change and Energy*, Brisbane City Council, Australia

Lubber, M. S. (2008) 'Capturing energy efficiency in Mass', *Contributors/projo.com/ The Providence Journal*, 20 July

Lyden, N. M. (undated) 'Micro-sprinkler irrigation improves orchard production', *Southwest Farm Press*

Macintosh, A. (2007) *Climate Change and Australian Coastal Shipping*, Discussion Paper Number 97 to The Australia Institute, Manuka, ACT

MacMillan, G. (2009) Personal communication with Glenn MacMillan, Genesis Now engineer, 20 March

Madew, R. (2006) *Dollars and Sense of Green Buildings*, Green Building Council of Australia

Mailer, A. (2007) Personal communication with Alistair Mailer, Project Manager, The Green Building Partnership, 11 October

Mailer, A. (2009) Personal communication with Alistair Mailer, Project Manager, The Green Building Partnership, 27 April

Marchaim, U. (1992) *Biogas Process for Sustainable Development*, Food and Agricultural Organization of the United Nations

Marquand, R. (2006) 'A "green" building arises amid Beijing smog', *The Christian Science Monitor*, 3 April

Marsh, G. (2008) 'Biofuels: Aviation alternative?', *Renewable Energy Focus*, vol 9, no 4, July–August, pp48–51

Martcheck, K. (2006) 'Modelling more sustainable aluminium: Case study', *International Journal of LCA*, vol 11, pp34–37

Martin, K. (2008) 'Obama to "repower America"', *EDIE News*, 16 December

Martin, N., Worrell, E. and Price, L. (1999a) *Energy Efficiency and Carbon Dioxide Emissions Reduction Opportunities in the US Iron and Steel Sector*, Environmental Energy Technologies Division, Ernest Orlando Lawrence Berkeley National Laboratory, Berkeley, CA

Martin, N., Worrell, E. and Price, L. (1999b) *Energy Efficiency and Carbon Dioxide Emissions Reduction Opportunities in the US Cement Industry: Environmental Energy Technologies*, Ernest Orlando Lawrence Berkeley National Laboratory, Berkeley, CA

Martin, N., Worrell, E., Ruth, M., Price, L., Elliott, R., Shipley, Q. and Thorne, J. (2000) *Emerging Energy-Efficient Industrial Technologies*, Lawrence Berkeley National Laboratory/American Council for an Energy-Efficient Economy, Berkeley, CA/Washington, DC

Mathiesen, B., Lund, H. and Norgaard, P. (2008) 'Integrated transport and renewable energy systems', *Utilities Policy*, vol 16, pp107–116

Mathur, A. (2007) 'Energy efficiency in buildings in India: An overview', presentation by the Director General of the Bureau of Energy Efficiency, Ministry of Power, Government of India, at the 2nd meeting of the Indo-German Energy Forum, 20 December

McAllister, I. (2004) 'Moving to a low carbon economy', The Railway Forum Seminar, The Carbon Trust

McCorkle, D., Hanselka, D., Bean, B., McCollum, T., Amosson, S., Klose, S. and Waller, M. (2007) *The Economic Benefits of Forage Sorghum Silage as an Alternative Food Crop*, Texas Cooperative Extension – The Texas A&M University System

McCowan, B., Coughlin, T., Bergeron, P. and Epstein, G. (2002) 'High performance lighting options for school facilities', in American Council for Energy-Efficient Economy, *2002 ACEEE Summer Study on Energy Efficiency in Buildings*, American Council for an Energy Efficient-Economy, Washington, DC, pp253–268

McDonough, W. and Braungart, M. (2002) *Cradle To Cradle: Remaking the Way We Make Things*, North Point Press, San Francisco

McKibben, B. (2006) 'Hype or hope: Is corporate do-goodery for real?', *Mother Jones*, November–December

McKibbin, W. J. and Wilcoxen, P. (1997) 'A better way to slow global climate change', *Brookings Policy Brief*, no 17, Brookings Institution, Washington, DC

McKinney, J. and Muench, T. (2008) 'Regulation scoping paper: Alternative and renewable fuel and vehicle technology program', Draft staff paper – California Energy Commission, July

McKinsey & Company (2007) *Curbing Global Energy Demand Growth: The Energy Productivity Opportunity*, McKinsey & Company

McKinsey & Company (2008) 'Revolutionizing data centre efficiency', presentation, Green Enterprise Computing: Capitalizing on Current Opportunities and Exploring Future Trends in Energy Efficiency, 27–30 April, Orlando, CA

McKinsey Global Institute (2007) *Curbing Global Energy Demand Growth: The Energy Productivity Opportunity – Residential Sector*, McKinsey Global Institute

McKinsey Global Institute (2008) *Fuelling Sustainable Development: The Energy Productivity Solution*, McKinsey Global Institute

Meadows, D., Meadows, D., Randers, J. and Behrens, W. (1972) *The Limits to Growth: A Report to the Club of Rome*, Universe Books, New York

Mendonca, M. (2008) *Feed-in Tariffs: Accelerating the Development of Renewable Energy*, Earthscan, London

Merritt, F. S. and Ricketts, J. T. (2001) *Building Design and Construction Handbook*, 6th edition, McGraw-Hill, Maidenhead, Berkshire

Meyer, M. and Cambridge Systematics Inc. (2008) *Crashes vs Congestion – What's the Cost to Society?*, prepared for AAA, Cambridge Systematics Inc., Cambridge, MA

Meyer, W. (1997) *Water for Food*, Commonwealth Scientific and Industrial Research Organisation, Australia

Midleton, N. (2003) *The Global Casino: An Introduction to Global Issues*, Oxford University Press, Oxford

Mills, E. (2000) *Global Lighting Energy Use and Greenhouse Gas Emissions*, Lawrence Berkeley Laboratories, Berkeley, CA

Mills, E. (2005) 'The specter of fuel-based lighting', *Science*, vol 308, pp1263–1264

Mills, E. (2009) 'Sustainable scientists', *Environmental Science & Technology*, vol 43, no 4, pp979–985

Mills, E., Shamshoian, G., Blazek, M., Naughton, P., Seese, R., Tschudi, W. and Sartor, D. (2007) 'The business case for energy management in high-tech industries', *Energy Efficiency*, vol 1, no 1, pp5–20

Minerals Council of Australia (2007) *Climate Change: A Global Challenge Requiring a Global Solution*, Minerals Council of Australia, Kingston, ACT

Ministerial Council on Energy (2003) *National Appliance and Equipment Energy Efficiency Program: A Study of Office Equipment Operational Energy Use Issues*, Commonwealth of Australia

Miranda, J. M., Fernández-Jiménez, A., González, J. A. and Palomo, A. (2005) 'Corrosion resistance in activated fly ash mortars', *Cement and Concrete Research*, vol 35, no 6, pp1210–1217

Mishan, E. J. (1967) *The Costs of Economic Growth*, Staples Press, London

Mississippi State University (2007) 'Major poultry-producing countries', in *Economic Impact of the Mississippi Poultry Industry – 2007*, Mississippi State University, Cullis Wade Depot, MS

Mobbs, M. (1999) *Sustainable House: Living for Our Future*, Choice Books, Sydney

Mohanty, S. (2009) 'Food security and rural livelihood: What role for trade agreements?', proceedings of 'Rice Science for a Better World'.

Molden, D. (2007) *Water for Food, Water for Life: A Comprehensive Assessment of Water Management in Agriculture*, Earthscan, London

Molden, D., Frenken, K., Barker, R., de Fraiture, C., Mati, B., Svendsen, M., Sadoff, C. and Finlayson, C. M. (2007) 'Trends in water and agricultural development', in Molden, D. (ed) *Water for Food, Water for Life*, International Water Management Institute, Earthscan, London

Monbiot, G. (2007) *Heat: How to Stop the Planet Burning*, South End Press, Cambridge, MA

Moore, J. R. (2003) 'Swine production: A global perspective', Alltech UK – Proceedings of Alltech's 19th Annual Symposium, Lexington, Kentucky, 11–14 May 2003, USA

Moore, T. C. (1996) 'Ultralight hybrid vehicles: Principles and design', 13th International Electric Vehicle Symposium, October 1996, Osaka, Japan

MSNBC (2009) 'Is Wal-Mart going green? CEO vows to be "good steward for the environment" in announcing goals', *MSNBC.com. News*, 25 October

Müller, N. and Harnisch, J. (2008) *A Blueprint for a Climate Friendly Cement Industry: How to Turn Around the Trend of Cement Related Emissions in the Developing World*, report prepared for the World Wild Fund for Nature – Lafarge Conservation Partnership, Ecofys Germany GmbH, Germany

Muntingh, Y. (2006) 'Durability and diffusive behaviour evaluation of geopolymeric material', MSc Thesis, University of Stellenbosch, South Africa

Mygatt, E. (2005) *Bicycle Production Remains Strong Worldwide*, The Earth Policy Institute, Washington, DC

Nakicenovic, N. and Swart, R. (eds) (2000) *IPCC Special Report on Emissions Scenarios*, Cambridge University Press, Cambridge

National Bureau of Statistics of China (2007) *2007 China Statistical Yearbook*, National Bureau of Statistics of China, Beijing

National Ready Mixed Concrete Association (2008) *Concrete CO_2 Factsheet*, National Ready Mixed Concrete Association, Silver Spring, MD

National Transport Commission and Rare Consulting (2008) *Freight Transport in a Carbon Constrained Economy*, Discussion Paper, National Transport Commission, Melbourne, Australia

Net Balance Foundation (2007) *Zeobond Carbon Emission Life Cycle Assessment of Geopolymer Concrete*, Net Balance Foundation, Melbourne, Australia

Netherlands Environmental Assessment Agency (2007) *Global CO_2 Emissions*, Netherlands Environmental Assessment Agency, Bilthoven

Newman, P. (1998) 'Transport', Interview transcript from *Radio National Earthbeat*, 12 September

Newman, P. (2001) 'Transportation energy in global cities: Sustainable transportation comes in from the cold?', *Natural Resources Forum*, vol 25, no 2, pp91–107

Newman, P. (2006) 'Sustainable transport for sustainable cities', *Issues*, no 76, September, pp6–10

Newman, P. and Kenworthy, J. (1999) *Sustainability and Cities: Overcoming Automobile Dependence*, Island Press, Washington, DC

Newman, P. and Kenworthy, J. (2007) 'Transportation energy in global cities: Sustainability comes in from the cold', *Natural Resouces Forum*, vol 25, no 2, pp91–107

Nowak, R. (2008) 'Hopes build for eco-concrete', *New Scientist*, 26 January

NSW Health Department (2001) *Septic Tank and Collection Well Accreditation Guideline*, New South Wales State Government, Australia

Nucor Corporation (2007) 'Nucor start up Trinidad DRI production', *Steelonthenet.com*, 16 January

OECD (2003a) *Environmental Policy in the Steel Industry: Using Economic Instruments*, Organisation for Economic Co-operation and Development, Paris

OECD (2003b) *Environmentally Sustainable Buildings: Challenges and Policies*, Organisation for Economic Co-operation and Development, Paris

OECD (2008) *OECD Environmental Outlook to 2030*, Organisation for Economic Co-operation and Development, Paris

OECD (2009) *Society at a Glance 2009*, Organisation for Economic Co-operation and Development, Paris

Ogburn, M. (2007) 'Profitable GHG reduction through fuel economy: Off-the-shelf technologies that bring savings to your bottom line', presentation to Rocky Mountain Institute, Snowmass, CO

Ogburn, M. and Ramroth, L. (2007) *Truck Efficiency and GHG Reduction Opportunities in the Canadian Truck Fleet*, Executive Summary, Rocky Mountain Institute, Snowmass, CO

Ogburn, M., Ramroth, L. and Lovins, A. (2008) *Transformational Trucks: Determining the Energy Efficiency Limits of a Class-8 Tractor-Trailer*, Rocky Mountain Institute, Snowmass, CO

Ohnsman, A. (2008) 'Toyota plans electric car, earlier Plug-In Prius test', *Bloomberg*, 28 August

Okazaki, T., Nakamura, M. and Kotani, K. (2004) 'Voluntary initiatives of Japan's steel industry against global warming', paper presented at IPCC Industrial Expert Meeting (ITDT) in Tokyo, 21–23 September.

Okuwaki, A. (2004) 'Feedstock recycling of plastics in Japan', *Polymer Degradation and Stabilization*, vol 85, pp981–988

O'Neal, D. L., Rodriguez, A., Davis, M. and Kondepudi, S. (2002) 'Return air leakage impact on air conditioner performance in humid climates', *Journal of Solar Energy Engineering*, vol 124, pp63–69

Onsite SYCOM Energy Corporation (1999) *Review of Combined Heat and Power Technologies*, US Department of Energy, Washington DC

Onsite SYCOM Energy Corporation (2000) *The Market and Technical Potential for Combined Heat and Power in the Industrial Sector*, prepared for Energy Information Association, Washington, DC

Orsato, R. (2006) 'Competitive environmental strategies: When does it pay to be green?', *California Management Review*, vol 48, no 2, Winter

The Pacific Institute (2007) *California Water – Success Stories*, The Pacific Institute, Seattle, WA

Paevere, P. and Brown, S. (2008) *Indoor Environment Quality and Occupant Productivity in the CH2 Building: Post-Occupancy Summary*, Report no USP2007/23, Commonwealth Scientific and Industrial Research Organisation, Australia

Pearce, F. (2002) 'Green foundations', *New Scientist*, vol 175, pp39–40

Pears, A. (1998) 'Energy-efficient, environmentally-preferable gas appliances for a sustainable world', presented at Australian Gas Association Annual Conference, Adelaide, November

Pears, A. (2004a) *Energy Efficiency – Its Potential: Some Perspectives and Experiences*, Background paper for International Energy Agency Energy Efficiency Workshop, Paris, April 2004

Pears, A. (2004b) *Greenhouse Challenge for Energy*, Report to Victorian Department of Infrastructure and Department of Sustainability and Environment, The Allen Consulting Group

Pears, A. (2005) *Potential for Replacing Hazelwood with Alternatives, Particularly Energy Efficiency*, RMIT University, Melbourne, Australia

Pears, A. (2008) Personal communication with Allan Pears, Sustainable Solutions, 15 November

Pears, A. (2009) Personal communication with Alan Pears, Director, Sustainable Solutions, 6–15 May

Penny, J. (2004) 'Commissioning controls for energy efficiency', *EcoLibruim*, July, pp21–24

Peon, R., Doluweera, G., Platonova, I., Irvine-Halliday, D. and Irvine-Halliday, G. (2005) 'Solid state lighting for the developing world – The only solution', Optics & Photonics, Fifth International Conference on Solid State Lighting, San Diego, *Proceedings of SPIE*, vol 5941, pp109–123,

PEP (2006) 'European embedding of Passive Houses, energy saving potential', Working Paper (partially supported by the European Commission under the Intelligent Energy Europe Programme), Promotion of European Passive Houses

Pereira, P. R. (1994) 'New technologies – Opportunities and Threats', ch 13 in Sagasti, F., Salomon, J. J. and Sachs-Jeantet, C. (eds) *The Uncertain Quest: Science, Technology, and Development*, UNU Press, New York

Petz, I. (2008) 'Wind power holds visionary solutions for shipping', *Credit Suisse*, 29 September

Pezzey, J. C. V. (2003) 'Emission taxes and tradeable permits: A comparison of views on long-run efficiency', *Environmental and Resource Economics*, vol 26, no 2, pp329–342

Phillips, G. (2008) 'Green Cement', *ABC Catalyst*, 22 May

Pianoforte, K. (2008) 'Marine coatings market: Increasing fuel efficiency through the use of innovative antifouling coatings is a key issue for ship owners and operators', *Coatings World*, May

Piebalgs, A. (2006) 'Energy efficiency: The best way towards a sustainable, competitive and secure energy system', speech delivered to the Round Table on Energy Efficiency in the Committee of Regions, Brussels, 7 December

Pigou, A. C. (1920) *The Economics of Welfare*, Macmillan, London

Pizer, W. A. (2002) 'Combining price and quantity controls to mitigate global climate change', *Journal of Public Economics*, vol 85, no 3, pp409–434

Plambeck, E. and Denend, L. (2007) *Wal-Mart's Sustainability Strategy*, Stanford University, Harvard Business Publishing

Postel, S. (2001) 'Growing more food with less water', *Scientific American*, vol 284, no 2, pp46–50

Postel, S., Polak, P., Gonzales, F. and Keller, J. (2001) 'Drip irrigation for small farmers: A new initiative to alleviate hunger and poverty', *Water International*, vol 26, no 1, p8

Prakash, A. and Potoski, M. (2006a) 'New dependencies: FDI and the cross-country diffusion of ISO14001 management systems', presentation at the First Annual Conference on Institutional Mechanisms for Industry Self-Regulation, Tuck School of Business, Dartmouth College, February 24–25

Prakash, A. and Potoski, M. (2006b) 'Racing to the bottom? Trade, environmental governance, and ISO 14001', *American Journal of Political Science*, vol 50, no 2, pp350–364, Midwest Political Science Association

Prather, M. and Hsu, J. (2008) 'NF3, the greenhouse gas missing from Kyoto', *Geophysical Research Letters*, vol 35

Price, L. (2006) 'Prospects for efficiency improvements in China's cement sector', Sector Cement Energy Efficiency Workshop organized by IEA in cooperation with WBCSD, Paris, 4–5 September

Price, L., Ernest Orlando Lawrence Berkeley National Laboratory, Worrell, E. and Ecofys (2006) 'Global energy use, CO_2 emissions and the potential for reduction in the cement industry', proceedings of IEA Conference, 'Energy Efficiency and CO_2 Emission Reduction Potentials and Policies in the Cement Industry', 4–5 September, Paris

Princen, T. and Finger, M. (1994) *Environmental NGOs in World Politics: Linking the Local and the Global*, Routledge, London

Provis, J. and van Deventer, J. (eds) (2009) *Geopolymers: Structures, Processing, Properties and Industrial Applications*, University of Melbourne, Australia, Woodhead Publishing Limited, Abington, Cambridge

Qun, Z. (2007) *Talk about the Chinese Iron and Steel Industry Development and Environment Protection*, Beijing University of Science and Technology, Beijing

Raina, S. (2002) *Energy Efficiency Improvements in Indian Cement Industry*, IIPEC, Report from the Director General of the National Council for Cement and Building Materials (NCB) to the IIPEC Programme, 22 September

Ramanathan, V. and Carmichael, G. (2008) 'Global and regional climate changes due to black carbon', *Nature Geoscience*, 23 March, pp221–222

Reich, D., Goodin, R. and Broner, I. (2009) 'Micro-sprinkler irrigation for orchards', Fact Sheet no. 4.703, Colorado State University, Fort Collins, CO

Reinhart, C. F. (2002) 'Effects of interior design on the daylight availability in open plan offices', ACEEE 2002 Summer Study on Energy Efficiency in Buildings, American Council for an Energy-Efficient Economy, Washington, DC, pp309–322

REN21 (2005) *Renewables: 2005 Global Status Report*, Renewable Energy Policy Network, Worldwatch Institute, Washington, DC

Reuters (2008) 'Factbox: Aviation in the EU Emissions Trading Scheme', Reuters, 24 October

Richardson, E. and Newman, P. (2008) *Transport for Sustainable Cities*, Sinclair Knight Merz and Curtin University

Richter, S. (2004) 'Buying biodiesel "off the rack": CHS investing in new injection technology to streamline biodiesel blending process', *Rural Cooperatives*, 1 July, Special Section: 'Co-ops and Biofuels'

Riedy, C., Milne, G. and Reardon, C. (2008) *Technical Manual: Design for Lifestyle and the Future*, Commonwealth of Australia

Rijsberman, F. (2004) *The Water Challenge: The Copenhagen Consensus Challenge Paper*, International Water Management Institute, Battaramulla, Sri Lanka

Robert Bosch GmbH (2004) *Automotive Handbook*, Robert Bosch GmbH, Warrendale, PA

Robins, N., Clover, R. and Singh, C. (2009) *A Climate for Recovery – The Colour of Stimulus Goes Green*, HSBC Global Research, London

Rocky Mountain Institute (2004) '#5 Water Heating', *RMI Home Energy Briefs*, Rocky Mountain Institute, Snowmass, CO

Rocky Mountain Institute (2007) 'Household Energy Efficiency', *RMI Home Energy Briefs*, Rocky Mountain Institute, Snowmass, CO

Rocky Mountain Institute (2008) *Smart Garage Charrette Report*, Rocky Mountain Institute, Snowmass, CO

Rocky Mountain Institute, Wilson, A., Seal, J., McManigal, L., Lovins, L. H., Cureton, M. and Browning, W. (1998) *Green Development: Integrating Ecology and Real Estate*, John Wiley & Sons Inc., Malden, MA

Roland-Holst, D. (2008) 'Energy efficiency, innovation, and job creation in California', Research Papers on Energy, Resources, and Economic Sustainability, University of California, Berkeley, CA

Romm, J. (1994) *Lean and Clean Management: How to Boost Profits and Productivity by Reducing Pollution*, Kodansha Amer Inc., New York

Romm, J. J. and Browning, W. D. (1998) *Greening the Building and the Bottom Line: Increasing Productivity Through Energy-Efficient Design*, Rocky Mountain Institute, Snowmass, CO

Roth, K., Goldstein, F. and Leinman, J. (2002) *Energy Consumption by Office and Telecommunications Equipment in Commercial Buildings, Volume 1: Energy Consumption Baseline*, Arthur D. Little, Cambridge, MA

Rubin, J. (2007) *The Efficiency Paradox*, CIBC World Markets, Toronto and New York

Rubin, R. and Tal, B. (2007) 'Does energy efficiency save energy?', in Rubin, J. (ed) *The Efficiency Paradox*, CIBC World Markets, Toronto and New York, pp4–7

Rubinstein, F. and Johnson, S. (1998) *Advanced Lighting Program Development*, Final Report, Lawrence Berkeley National Laboratory, Berkeley, CA

Safe Drinking Water Foundation (2004) *Water Consumption*, Safe Drinking Water Foundation, Saskatoon, Canada

Saunders, H. D. (1992) 'The Khazzoom-Brookes postulate and neoclassical growth', *The Energy Journal*, 1 October

Schaeffer, J., Pratt, D. and Real Good Staff (1996) *Real Goods Solar Living Source Book: The Complete Guide to Renewable Energy Technologies and Sustainable Living*, 9th edition, Chelsea Green Publishing Company, White River Junction, VT

Schlegelmilch, K. (ed) (1999) *Green Budget Reform in Europe*, Springer, Berlin

Schmidheiny, S. and the Business Council for Sustainable Development (1992) *Changing Course: A Global Business Perspective on Development and the Environment*, MIT Press, Cambridge MA

Schnepf, R. (2004) *CRS Report for Congress: Energy Use in Agriculture*, CRS, The Library of Congress, p2

Schnieders, J. (2003) 'CEPHEUS – Measurement results from more than 100 dwelling units in passive houses', Results of ECEEE 2003 Summer Study, Passive House Institute, Darmstadt

Schurr, S. (1985) 'Energy conservation and productivity growth – Can we have both', *Energy Policy*, vol 13, no 2, pp126–132

Schwartzapfel, S. (2008) 'Plug-in hybrids aren't coming – They're here', *Wired*, 5 October

Scialabba, N. H. and Hattam, C. (eds) (2002) *Organic Agriculture, Environment and Food Security*, Food and Agriculture Organization of the United Nations, Rome

Science Daily (2008) 'Cow power could generate electricity for millions', *Science Daily – Science News*, 25 July

Shaheen, S. and Cohen, A. (2006) *Worldwide Carsharing Growth: An International Comparison*, submitted to Transportation Research Board

Shaheen, S. and Meyn, M. (2002) 'Shared-use vehicle services: A survey of North American market developments', presented at the ITS World Congress, October 14–17, Chicago, IL

Sheppard, K. (2009) 'Obama lays down plans for high-speed rail', *Grist*, 16 April

Sherman, M. H. and Jump, D. A. (1997) 'Thermal energy conservation in buildings', in *CRC Handbook of Energy Efficiency*, CRC Press, Boca Raton, FL, pp269–303

Shi, C., Krivenko, P. V. and Roy, D. M. (2006) *Alkali-Activated Cements and Concretes*, Taylor and Francis, Abingdon

Shirley, W. (2006) *Decoupling Utility Profits from Sales*, prepared for Arizona Decoupling Stakeholder Meeting, Regulatory Assistance Project (RAP)

Shock, C. C. (2006) *Drip Irrigation: An Introduction*, Malheur Experimentation Station – Information for Sustainable Agriculture, Oregon State University, Corvallis, OR

Shrank, D. L. and Lomaz, T. J. (2007) *The 2007 Urban Mobility Report – What Does Congestion Cost Us?*, Texas Transportation Institute, Texas A & M University, College Station, TX

Sinden, G. (2005) *Variability of Wave and Tidal Stream Energy Resources*, Oxford University Environmental Change Institute

Sinha, R., Cross, A., Graubard, B., Leitzmann, M. and Schatzkin, A. (2009) 'Meat intake and mortality: A prospective study of over half a million people', *Archives of Internal Medicine*, vol 169, no 6, pp562–571

Sloman, L. (2006) *Car Sick – Solutions for Our Car Addicted Culture*, Green Books, Totnes, Devon

Smith, M. and Hargroves, K. (2009) 'Achieving both economic growth and reduced environmental pressures in the current financial climate', *CSIRO ECOS*, no 148, pp30–31

Smith, M. and Hargroves, K. (2010) *Cents and Sustainability: Decoupling Economic Growth from Environmental Pressures* (In Press) The Natural Edge Project, Earthscan, London, www.naturaledgeproject.net/centsandsustainability.aspx, accessed 10 June 2009

Smith, M., Hargroves, K., Stasinopoulos, P., Stephens, R., Desha, C. and Hargroves, S. (2007) *Energy Transformed: Sustainable Energy Solutions for Climate Change Mitigation*, The Natural Edge Project (TNEP), Australia

Smith, S. (1995) *'Green' Taxes and Charges: Policy and Practice in Britain and Germany*, The Institute for Fiscal Studies, London

Smith, S. (2008) *Environmentally Related Taxes and Tradable Permit Systems in Practice*, OECD paper COM/ENV/EPOC/CTPA/CFA (2007) 31/Final, 11 June

Spangenberg, J. H. (2009) 'The multi-bubble-trouble', *Global Responsibility*, vol 59, pp5–7

Srinivas, S. (undated) 'Green buildings: The opportunities and benefits', Confederation of Indian Industry, Sohrabji Godrej Green Business Centre

Stasinopoulos, P., Smith, M., Hargroves, K. and Desha, C. (2008) *Whole System Design: An Integrated Approach to Sustainable Engineering*, Earthscan, London, and The Natural Edge Project, Australia

State of California (2005) *Design Guide: Big Savings on Small HVAC Systems*, Public Interest Energy Research Program, State of California Energy Commission

Stavins, R. N. (1998) 'What can we learn from the grand policy experiment? Lessons from SO_2 allowance trading', *Journal of Economic Perspectives*, vol 12, no 3, pp69–88

Steinfield, H., de Haan, C. and Blackburn, H. (1998) 'Livestock and the environment: Issues and options', in Lutz, E. (ed) *Agriculture and the Environment: Perspectives on Sustainable Rural Development*, World Bank, Washington, DC, pp283–301

Stephens, R., Desha, C. and Hargroves, K. (2007) 'The philosophy and practice of water sensitive urban design – Is it consistent with a whole system approach?', *Environmental Design Guide*, August, vol 1, GEN 14

Stern, N. (2007) *The Stern Review: The Economics of Climate Change*, Cambridge University Press, Cambridge

Stiglitz, J. (2002) *Globalization and Its Discontents*, Norton & Norton, New York

Stiglitz, J. (2006) *Making Globalization Work*, Penguin Books, London

Stockholm STAD (2006) *Evaluation of the Effects of the Stockholm Trial on Road Traffic*, Stockholm STAD, Sweden

Stodolsky, F. (2002) *Analysis of Technology Options to Reduce Truck Idling*, Argonne National Laboratory, Argonne, IL

Stodolsky, F., Gaines, L. and Vyas, A. (2002) *Railroad and Locomotive Technology Roadmap*, Center for Transportation Research, Energy Systems Division, Argonne National Laboratory, Argonne, IL

Strieber, A. (2008) 'Volt price watch: Plug-in hybrid now said to cost $40k', *MotorTrend Magazine*, 19 June

Stubbles, J. (2000) *Energy Use in the U.S. Steel Industry*, US Department of Energy, Washington, DC

Subler, S. (2009) 'Does your farm have the operational capability to produce carbon credits?', *Ag Nutrient Management*, Progressive Dairy Publishing

Sumikura, I. (1998) 'A brief history of Japanese environmental administration: A qualified success story?', *Journal of Environmental Law*, vol 10, pp241–256

Summers, L. (2007) 'Practical steps to climate control', *Financial Times*, 29 May

Sustainability Victoria (2006) *HVAC Tips (Heating, Ventilation and Air Conditioning)*, Sustainability Victoria

Sustainability Victoria (2008) *Case Study 04: 40 Albert Road – Sustainability Meets Sophistication*, Commercial Office Building Energy Innovation Initiative (COBEII)

Suzuki, D. and Gordon, A. (1991) *It's a Matter of Survival*, Harvard University Press, Cambridge, MA

Suzuki, D., McConnell, A. and Mason, A. (2007) *The Sacred Balance*, Douglas McIntyre, Vancouver

Sydney Morning Herald (2007) 'Spending our way to climate change', *Sydney Morning Herald*, 18 August

Sydney Water (2007) *Water Conservation: Best Practice Guidelines for Cooling Towers in Commercial Buildings*, Sydney Water

Taylor, D., Sulaiman, M. and Sheahan, M. (2001) 'Auditing of environmental management systems: A legitimacy theory perspective', *Managerial Auditing Journal*, vol 16, no 7, Emerald Press

Taylor, M. (2008) 'City's two-wheel transformation', *The Guardian*, 9 February

Taylor, P. W. (2008) *Simply Green: A Few Steps in the Right Direction toward Integrating Sustainability into Public Sector IT*, Centre for Digital Government, eRepublic, Inc.

Terhark, C. (2005) 'The good ship', *Utne*, July–August, pp88–89

Tesco (2008) *Sustainability Report: More than the Weekly Shop: Corporate Responsibility Review*, Tesco Inc.

Thomson, E. (2006) 'Engineers forge greener path to iron production', *MIT News*, 25 August

Tickell, O. (2005) 'Wave, wind, sun and tide is a powerful mix', *The Guardian*, 12 May

Todesco, G. (2004) 'Integrated design and HVAC equipment sizing', *ASHRAE Journal*, vol 46, no 9, ppS42–S47

Transek (2006) *Cost-Benefit Analysis of the Stockholm Trial*, Transek AB, Sweden

Traum, M. (2007) 'China's Pearl River Tower may be world's first zero-energy skyscraper', *Design News China*, 17 September

Troy, P. (2008) *Troubled Waters: Confronting the Water Crisis in Australia's Cities*, Australian National University Epress

Trubka, R., Newman, P. and Bilsborough, D. (2008) *Assessing the Costs of Alternative Development Paths in Australian Cities*, Curtin University Sustainability Policy Institute and Parsons Brinkerhoff, Fremantle

UK Carbon Trust (2006) *Agriculture and Horticulture – Introducing Energy Saving Opportunities for Farmers and Growers*, UK Carbon Trust

UNDP/WEC/UNDESA (2000) *World Energy Assessment*, United Nations Development Programme, New York

UNEP (2002) 'Sustainable consumption and production', presentation to the 2002 World Summit in Sustainable Development, Johannesburg, 26 August to 4 September

UNEP/GRID-Arendal (2004) 'Recycling rates for selected OECD countries', *Vital Waste Graphics*

UNESCO (2000) *Water Use in the World: Present Situation/Future Needs*, United Nations Educational, Scientific and Cultural Organization

United Nations Food and Agriculture Organization (2006) *Livestock's Long Shadow*, FAO, Rome

United Nations World Water Development Report (UNWWDR) (2003) *Water for People, Water for Life*, United Nations Educational, Scientific and Cultural Organization, Paris

University of California (2008) 'Black carbon pollution emerges as major player in global warming', *PHYSORG.com*, 23 March

US Department of Commerce (2000) *Global Steel Trade: Structural Problems and Future Solutions*, Report to the President, US Department of Commerce, International Trade Administration

US Department of Energy (USDOE/OSTI) (2000) *Technology Roadmap for the 21st Century Truck Program*, US Department of Energy, 21CT-01

US Environmental Protection Agency (2007) *Energy Trends in Selected Manufacturing Sectors: Opportunities and Challenges for Environmentally Preferable Energy Outcomes*, Final Report, Prepared for the US Environmental Protection Agency

US Environmental Protection Agency (2009a) *Draft Inventory of US Greenhouse Gas Emissions and Sinks: 1990–2007*, US EPA

US Environmental Protection Agency (2009b) *Guide to Anaerobic Digesters*, US EPA

US General Services Administration (GSA) (1999) *The Integrated Workplace: A Comprehensive Approach to Developing Workspace*, US General Service Administration, Office of Government-wide Policy and Office for Real Property

USDA (2007) *International Agricultural Baseline Projections to 2007*, United States Department of Agriculture

USGS (2005) *Minerals Yearbook 2004*, US Geological Survey, Reston, VA

USGS (2006) *Minerals Yearbook*, US Geological Survey, Reston, VA

Van Hofwegen, P. and Svendsen, M. (2000) *A Vision of Water for Food and Rural Development*, The Netherlands: The World Water Forum, The Hague

Vandenbergh, M. (2007) *The New Wal-Mart Effect: The Role of Private Contracting in Global Governance*, Vanderbilt University Law School, Nashville, TN

Vattenfall AB (2007) *Global Mapping of Greenhouse Gas Abatement Opportunities up to 2030: Industry Sector Deep-Dive*, Vattenfall AB, Stockholm, Sweden

Virginia Tech (2007) 'Hardy rice: Less water, more food', *ScienceDaily*, 11 September

von Weizsäcker, E. and Jesinghaus, J. (1992) *Ecological Tax Reform: A Policy Proposal for Sustainable Development*, Zed Books, London

von Weizsäcker, E., Lovins, A. B. and Lovins, L. H. (1997) *Factor 4: Doubling Wealth, Halving Resource Use*, Earthscan, London

von Weizsäcker, E. U., Young, O. and Finger, M. (2005) *Limits to Privatization: How to Avoid Too Much of a Good Thing?*, Earthscan, London

von Weizsäcker, J. (2009) 'Greening the debt', Op-Ed Contributer, *International Herald Tribune*, 15 April

Waide, P., Lebot, B. and Harrington, P. (2004) 'The historic and potential impact of residential electrical equipment energy efficiency policies in the OECD', in proceedings of the EEDAL'03 conference, Softech, Turin, Italy, 1–3 October

Walton, T. (2008) 'Jaguar XJ-X350', *Jaguar XJ News*, 28 July

Wang, I. (2008) 'The energy management and emission control with Chinese cement industry', China Building Materials Academy, presentation to the 'Cleaning up China's Cement Sector' session in the China Environment Forum, Washington, DC, 15 May

Wara, M. (2007) 'Is the global carbon market working?', *Nature*, vol 445, pp595–596

Watson, R. T., Noble, I. R., Bolin, B., Ravindranath, N. H., Verardo, D. J. and Dokken, D. J. (2000) *Special Report on Land Use, Land-Use Change, and Forestry*, Intergovernmental Panel on Climate Change, Cambridge University Press, Cambridge, p204

Watts, J. (2009) 'China to plough extra 20% into agricultural production amid fears that climate change will spark food crisis', *Guardian.co.uk*, 5 March

Webber, M. and Cuellar, A. (2008) 'Cow power: The energy and emissions benefits of converting manure to biogas', *Environmental Research Letters*, vol 3

Went, A., Newman, P. and James, W. (2008) 'Renewable transport: How renewable energy and electric vehicles using vehicle to grid technology can make carbon free urban development', Discussion Paper, Curtin University Sustainability Policy Institute, Fremantle, Australia

Whole Building Design Guide Productive Committee (2007) *Productive*, National Institute of Building Sciences, Washington, DC

Whole Foods Market (2008) *Whole Foods Market 2008 Annual Report*, Whole Foods Market, US

Whyte, B. (2007) 'HARDY rice: Less water, more food', *Bio-Medicine*, 9 October

Wigginton, M. and Harris, J. (2002) *Intelligent Skins*, Butterworth-Heinemann, Oxford, pp143–148

Wilentz, S. (2008) *The Age of Reagan: A History, 1974–2008*, HarperCollins, London

Williams, C. A. and Aguilera, R. V. (2008) 'Corporate social responsibility in a comparative perspective', in Crane, A., McWilliams, A., Matten, D., Moon, L. and Siegel, D. S. (eds) *The Oxford Handbook of Corporate Social Responsibility*, Oxford University Press, Oxford

Wong, A. (1999) *Sustainable Use of Water California Success Stories: Executive Summary/Introduction*, The Pacific Institute, Seattle, WA

Wood, R. M. and Bauer, S. X. S. (2003) *Simple and Low-Cost Aerodynamic Drag Reduction Devices for Tractor-Trailer Trucks*, SOLUS – Solutions and Technologies International, Virginia Beach, VA

Woolsey, R. (2005) *High Cost of Crude: The New Currency of Foreign Policy*, Testimony of R. James Woolsey, US Senate Committee on Foreign Relations

Workman, D. (2007) 'Top soybean countries', *Suite 101.com*, 17 September

World Bank (1997) *At China's Table: Food Security Options*, China 2020 Series, World Bank, Washington, DC

World Business Council for Sustainable Development (2004) *Mobility 2030 Report: Meeting the Challenges to Sustainability*, WBCSD, Geneva, Switzerland

World Business Council for Sustainable Development (2009) *Energy Efficiency in Buildings: Business Realities and Opportunities – Facts and Trends*, Summary Report, WBCSD, Geneva, Switzerland

World Future Council (2008) *Feed-in Tariffs: Boosting Energy for Our Future*, World Energy Council, Hamburg

World Health Organization (2004) *Global Burden of Disease, Update 2004*, WHO, Geneva, Switzerland

World Steel Association (2008) *2008 Sustainability Report of the World Steel Industry*, World Steel Association, Brussels

World Wild Fund for Nature (2009) *Virtual Meetings and Climate Innovation in the 21st Century*, World Wild Fund for Nature

Worldwatch Institute (2008) *Vital Signs 2007–2008*, Worldwatch Institute, W.W. Norton & Company, New York

Worldwatch Institute (2009) *Worldwatch Report: Mitigating Climate Change Through Food and Land Use*, Worldwatch Institute, Washington, DC

Worrell, E. (2004) 'Industrial energy use – Past developments and future potential', presentation at EEWP Expert Workshop International Energy Agency, 26–27 April, Paris

Worrell, E., Martin, N. and Price, L. (1999) *Energy Efficiency and Carbon Dioxide Emissions Reduction Opportunities in the US Iron and Steel Sector*, Environmental Energy technologies Division, Ernest Orlando Lawrence Berkeley National Laboratory, Berkeley, CO

Worrell, E., Price, L. and Galitsky, C. (2004) *Emerging Energy-efficient Technologies in Industry: Case Studies of Selected Technologies*, Ernest Orlando Lawrence Berkely National Laboratory, Berkeley, CA

Worrell, E., Price, L., Martin, N., Hendriks, C. and Meida, L. (2001) 'Carbon dioxide emissions from the global cement industry', *Annual Review of Energy and the Environment*, vol 26, pp303–329

Xia, J., Wang, J., Wang, Y. and Xing, R. (2008) 'Stakeholder pressures and the global diffusion of the ISO 14001 initiative: A resource dependence perspective', *International Journal of Sustainable Society*, vol 1, no 1, pp4–28

Xinhua News Agency (2008) 'China announces huge rail investment', *Xinhua News Agency*, 27 October

Xu, H., Provis, J. L., van Deventer, J. and Krivenko, P. V. (2008) 'Characterization of aged slag concretes', *ACI Materials Journal*, March/April

Yamaguchi (2005) 'Factors that affect innovation, deployment and diffusion of energy-efficient technologies – Case studies of Japan and iron/steel industry', in-session workshop on Mitigation at SBSTA22 (Subsidiary Body for Scientific and Technological Advice, 22nd session), 23 May

Yong, S. L., Feng, D. W., Lukey, G. C. and van Deventer, J. S. J. (2007) 'Chemical characterisation of the steel-geopolymeric gel interface', *Colloids and Surfaces A – Physicochemical and Engineering Aspects*, vol 302, nos 1–3, pp411–423

Yoong, Y. (2008) 'Pusat Tenaga Malaysia's zero energy office', Malaysia Building Integrated Photovoltaic (MBIPV) Technology Application Project

Zhou, N. (2007) *Energy Use in China: Sectoral Trends and Future Outlook*, Energy Analysis Division, Lawrence Berkeley National Laboratory, Berkeley, CA

Zhou, N., McNeil, M.A., Fridley, D., Jiang, L., Price, L., de la Rue du Can, S., Sathaye, J. and Levine, M. (2008) 'Energy use in China: Sectoral trends and future outlook', Paper LBNL-61904, Lawrence Berkeley National Laboratory, Berkeley, CA

Zhu, Y. (2008) *Sectoral Study on the Iron and Steel Industry*, Interdependencies on Energy and Climate Security Environment Energy and Development Programme, Chatham House, London

Ziebek, A. and Stanek, W. (2001) 'Forecasting of the energy effects of injecting plastic wastes into the blast furnace in comparison with other auxiliary fuels', *Energy*, vol 26, pp1159–1173

Zimmer, D. and Renault, D. (2006) *Virtual Water in Food Production and Global Trade – Review of Methodological Issues and Preliminary Results*, FAO Water, Food and Agricultural Organization of the United Nations, Rome

Zongrin, Li., Ding, Z. and Shang, Y. (2004) 'Development of sustainable cementitious materials', proceedings of the International Workshop on Sustainable Development and Concrete Technologies, 20–21 May, Beijing, China, pp55–76

Index